TRADE AND PUBLIC HEALTH

Noncommunicable diseases, associated with risk factors such as tobacco consumption, poor diet, and alcohol use, represent a growing health burden around the world. The seriousness of noncommunicable diseases is reflected in the adoption of international instruments such as the WHO Framework Convention on Tobacco Control; the WHO Global Strategy on Diet, Physical Activity, and Health; and the WHO Global Strategy to Reduce the Harmful Use of Alcohol. In line with these instruments, states are beginning to use measures such as taxes, restrictions on marketing, product regulation, and labeling measures for public health purposes. This book examines the extent to which the law of the World Trade Organization restricts domestic implementation of these types of measures. The relationship between international health instruments and the WTO Agreement is examined, as are the WTO-covered agreements themselves.

Benn McGrady is an Australian lawyer based at the O'Neill Institute for National and Global Health Law at Georgetown University. He is an Adjunct Professor at the Georgetown University Law Center and a Research Assistant Professor in the Department of International Health, School of Nursing and Health Studies. He has provided legal advice to public health bodies, foreign governments, and intergovernmental organizations concerning the impact of international trade and investment law on measures to protect public health and has published work in journals such as the *Journal of International Economic Law, World Trade Review,* and *Journal of World Trade.*

TRADE AND PUBLIC HEALTH

THE WTO, TOBACCO, ALCOHOL, AND DIET

BENN MCGRADY
O'Neill Institute for National and Global Health Law,
Georgetown University

CAMBRIDGE
UNIVERSITY PRESS

CAMBRIDGE UNIVERSITY PRESS
Cambridge, New York, Melbourne, Madrid, Cape Town,
Singapore, São Paulo, Delhi, Mexico City

Cambridge University Press
32 Avenue of the Americas, New York NY 10013-2473, USA

Published in the United States of America by Cambridge University Press, New York

www.cambridge.org
Information on this title: www.cambridge.org/9781107657564

First published 2011
First paperback edition 2013

A catalogue record for this publication is available from the British Library

Library of Congress Cataloguing in Publication Data
McGrady, Benn.
Trade and public health: the WTO, tobacco, alcohol, and diet / Benn McGrady.
p. cm.
ISBN 978-1-107-00841-0 (hardback)
1. World Trade Organization. 2. Foreign trade regulation. 3. Public health laws.
I. Title.
K4610.M39 2011
362.1′042–dc22 2010045991

ISBN 978-1-107-00841-0 Hardback
ISBN 978-1-107-65756-4 Paperback

For my parents

Contents

Preface

This study sketches out the implications of trade law for domestic attempts to address noncommunicable disease. Much remains to be written about this subject. Nonetheless, I hope that this work fills some gaps in the literature and raises questions for further research.

Although this study lies at the intersection of trade law and public health, it is a legal study. The difficulty associated with differing research methodologies meant that a choice had to be made in favor of one discipline or another. The choice to cast this work as a legal study has the advantage of permitting a deeper legal analysis of some issues, but the disadvantage of being less accessible to members of the public health community who do not have legal training. There is some inevitable trade-off in this approach, and my hope is that this study will help public health lawyers and trade lawyers bridge gaps between their fields.

This study also straddles the fields of international trade law, global/international health law, and public international law. There is a very real chance that the study will leave trade lawyers wanting a more detailed analysis of trade law and public health lawyers wanting more detailed analysis of international law in a health context. Unfortunately, this is an inevitable consequence of a monograph that does not seek to cover the field. The intention of this study is not to end all debates about application of trade law to noncommunicable disease. My more modest hope is that this work will clarify key legal issues and give some shape to debates about the issues discussed herein.

This book has roots in a number of institutions and countries. I began research on the implications of WTO law for tobacco control while I was a Research Assistant at the VicHealth Centre for Tobacco Control, The Cancer Council Victoria in Melbourne. With support provided by an Australian Postgraduate Award, I later undertook a PhD on the same subject at Monash University, also in Melbourne. I spent a significant part of my candidature conducting research and living in Bangkok. I was later offered the opportunity to expand my doctoral thesis into this study through a Postdoctoral Fellowship at the O'Neill Institute for National and Global Health Law at Georgetown University in Washington, DC. In association with this role, I was privileged to have appointments as a Research Assistant Professor in the Department of International Health, School of Nursing and Health Studies, and as an Adjunct Professor at the Georgetown University Law Center.

Over the past few years, I have also been privileged to provide legal and policy advice to organizations working on public health issues at the international level. The analytical focus of this book reflects that experience. Whereas trade lawyers may take different views concerning which legal issues are significant, this book is focused on the types of issues that arise for discussion in the context of public health lawmaking at the domestic and international levels.

I am particularly indebted to three people. Jeff Waincymer supervized my doctoral studies. Jonathan Liberman introduced me to the issues and provided support and comments throughout the process. Jeff Collman then showed enough faith in me to facilitate completion of this book at Georgetown.

A number of other people have read or commented on parts of this work at various stages, including Jane Bradley, Tomer Broude, Darren Lim, Tania Voon, Sanjula Weerasinghe, and anonymous reviewers. Tania Voon was also kind enough to read and comment on a late draft of this book in May 2010. I am also grateful to participants at conferences hosted by the Asian Centre for WTO & International Health Law and Policy, National Taiwan University, and the international economic law interest group of the American Society of International Law, as well as to participants at workshops hosted by the Institute for International Economic Law and the O'Neill Institute for National and Global Health Law, both at Georgetown University Law Center. As always, all errors remain my own.

A number of other people at Georgetown also deserve acknowledgment. Bernhard Liese and Larry Gostin have been very supportive during my time here. Lindsay Wiley was also particularly supportive and provided the initial push for me to teach a course on International Trade and Health, which has shaped some of the views in this book.

On a personal note, I would like to thank my partner, Sanjula Weerasinghe, for her invaluable support throughout the process.

Washington, DC
September 2010

Abbreviations

CAP	European Common Agricultural Policy
CEDAW	Convention on the Elimination of all Forms of Discrimination Against Women
CPI	Consumer Price Index
CRC	Convention on the Rights of the Child
DSB	Dispute Settlement Body
DSU	Understanding on Rules and Procedures Governing the Settlement of Disputes
EC	European Commission
EU	European Union
FCTC	World Health Organization Framework Convention on Tobacco Control
FDI	Foreign Direct Investment
GATS	General Agreement on Trade in Services
GATT	General Agreement on Tariffs and Trade (1994)
Global Strategy Alcohol	WHO Global Strategy to Reduce the Harmful Use of Alcohol, 2010
Global Strategy Diet	WHO Global Strategy on Diet, Physical Activity and Health, 2004
GMO	Genetically modified organism
HFCS	High fructose corn syrup
HIV/AIDS	Human immunodeficiency virus/acquired immune deficiency syndrome
ICESCR	International Covenant on Economic, Social and Cultural Rights
ICJ	International Court of Justice
IHR (2005)	International Health Regulations (2005)
ILC	International Law Commission

ISO	International Organization for Standardization
MERCOSUR	Southern Common Market
MFN	Most-favored-nation
NAFTA	North American Free Trade Agreement
PICTA	Pacific Island Countries Trade Agreement, done at Nauru 18 August 2001
SARS	Sudden acute respiratory syndrome
SCM Agreement	Agreement on Subsidies and Countervailing Measures
SPS	Sanitary and phytosanitary
SPS Agreement	Agreement on the Application of Sanitary and Phytosanitary Measures
TBT Agreement	Agreement on Technical Barriers to Trade
TRIPS	Agreement on Trade Related Aspects of Intellectual Property Rights
UN	United Nations
UNCLOS	United Nations Convention on the Law of the Sea
UNTOC	United Nations Convention on Transnational Organized Crime
U.S.	United States of America
Vienna Convention	Vienna Convention on the Law of Treaties
WHA	World Health Assembly
WHO	World Health Organization
WTO	World Trade Organization
WTO Agreement	Marrakesh Agreement Establishing the World Trade Organization

1

Intersections between Trade and Noncommunicable Disease

1. INTRODUCTION

The impact of the Marrakesh Agreement Establishing the World Trade Organization (WTO) (hereafter WTO Agreement)[1] – and its linkage to other social issues has long been a subject of debate.[2] One aspect of this debate is the linkage of trade and public health. In 2006 the World Health Assembly (WHA) passed a resolution stressing the need for greater coordination in the development of trade and health policies and recognizing the "demand for information on the possible implications of international trade and trade agreements for health and health policy at national, regional and global levels."[3] Following this, in 2007, the foreign ministers of Brazil, France, Indonesia, Norway, Senegal, South Africa, and Thailand issued the Oslo Ministerial Declaration. The declaration affirmed the interconnectedness of trade and health policies "in the formulation of all bilateral, regional and multilateral trade agreements."[4]

More recently, in early 2009, *The Lancet*, a leading public health journal, published a series of papers on trade and health. A number of commentators called for greater interaction between the public health and trade policy communities and for the public health community to play a greater role

[1] Marrakesh Agreement Establishing the World Trade Organization, April 15, 1994, The Legal Texts: The Results of the Uruguay Round of Multilateral Trade Negotiations 4 (1999), 33 I.L.M. 1144 (1994) [hereinafter WTO Agreement].

[2] See, for example, the "Symposium on the Boundaries of the WTO" in 96(1) *American Journal of International Law*,(January 2002).

[3] Fifty-Ninth World Health Assembly, International Trade and Health – 59/15 available at http://www.who.int/gb/ebwha/pdf_files/WHA59/A59_R26-en.pdf (visited 12/12/07).

[4] "Oslo Ministerial Declaration – Global Health: A Pressing Foreign Policy Issue of Our Time," 369 *The Lancet*, London, (2007), pp. 1371–1378.

in trade policy making.[5] This series of papers was reflective of the trade and health issues that have garnered attention since the conclusion of the Uruguay Round, such as those relating to intellectual property rights and access to medicines[6] as well as trade in health services.[7] These issues have largely arisen by virtue of the post-1994 trade architecture and the conclusion of new agreements like the Agreement on Trade-Related Aspects of Intellectual Property Rights (TRIPS) and the General Agreement on Trade in Services (GATS).

Although this focus on new agreements and their impact on health has merit, little attention has been given to the way that changes in public health practice have affected the relationship between trade and health. When the General Agreement on Tariffs and Trade (GATT) 1947 was agreed, the primary focus of public health practice was to address infectious disease. This was also the case in 1994 when the GATT was incorporated into the WTO Agreement. However, over recent years new conceptualizations of public health have expanded the field to encompass efforts to address noncommunicable diseases associated with risk factors such as tobacco consumption, alcohol consumption, and unhealthy diet.

There are at least two obvious points of tension between this new public health and the trade regime. The first is a theoretical tension between trade liberalization and measures to reduce the consumption of certain goods at the population level. The general benefits of liberal trade policies, such as greater competition and lower prices, can translate into negative health consequences. In particular, where increased competition and lower prices stimulate consumption of harmful products, there is likely to be a correlative increase in associated morbidity and mortality. This also has flow-on effects for health systems. Tariffs and subsidies affect the cost of goods, meaning that the use of these instruments can form an important part of the environment in which choices are made about consumption.

For example, a number of studies have offered empirical confirmation of the conclusion that trade liberalization may stimulate demand for tobacco

5 See, for example, David Fidler, Nick Drager, and Kelley Lee, "Managing the Pursuit of Health and Wealth: The Key Challenges," 373(9660) *The Lancet*, London, (Jan 24–30, 2009), pp. 325–331; Richard D. Smith, Kelley Lee, and Nick Drager, "Trade and Health 6: Trade and Health: An Agenda for Action," 373(9665) *The Lancet*, London, (Feb 28–Mar 6, 2009), pp. 768–773; Rhona MacDonald and Richard Horton, "Trade and Health: Time for the Health Sector to Get Involved," 373(9660) *The Lancet*, London, (Jan 24–30, 2009), pp. 273–274.

6 Richard Smith, Carlos Correa, and Cecilia Oh, "Trade and Health 5: Trade, TRIPS, and Pharmaceuticals," 363(9664) *The Lancet*, London, (Feb 21–27, 2009), pp. 684–691.

7 Richard Smith, Rupa Chanda, and Viroj Tangcharoensathien, "Trade and Health 4: Trade in Health-Related Services," 363(9663) *The Lancet*, London, (Feb 14–20, 2009), pp. 593–601.

products. Frank Chaloupka and Adit Laixuthai[8] were the first to address the issue in an examination of the opening of tobacco markets in Japan, Taiwan, South Korea, and Thailand. Chaloupka and Laixuthai concluded that "cigarette consumption was nearly ten percent higher, on average, in 1991 in the four countries whose markets were opened to US cigarettes than it would have been if the markets had remained closed."[9] Similarly, Chee-Ruey Hsieh, Teh Wei Hu, and Chien Fu Jeff Lin[10] examined the impact of the opening of the Taiwanese market to U.S. cigarettes and concluded that "opening the market to cigarette imports led to a 20% increase in per capita cigarette consumption in 1987."[11]

A number of studies have also examined the relationship between general trade openness (using a share of trade in gross domestic product as a measure) and tobacco consumption.[12] In this respect, Craig Depken concluded that the "openness of a country to international trade ... causes a decrease in the price of cigarettes."[13] Similarly, Allyn Taylor and others concluded that trade liberalization leads to increased smoking, particularly in low- and middle-income countries that have traditionally been less open.[14] Douglas Bettcher and others drew substantially the same conclusion.[15]

In addition, Bettcher and others found that "increased levels of [foreign direct investment] should lead to higher levels of cigarette consumption."[16]

8 Frank Chaloupka and Adit Laixuthai, "U.S. Trade Policy and Cigarette Smoking in Asia," NBER Working Paper Series, Working Paper 5543, (April 1996) [hereinafter Chaloupka and Laixuthai, "U.S. Trade Policy"].

9 Ibid., p. 15.

10 Chee-Ruey Hsieh, Teh Wei Hu, and Chien Fu Jeff Lin, "The Demand for Cigarettes in Taiwan: Domestic Versus Imported Cigarettes," 17(2) *Contemporary Economic Policy*, (April 1999), pp. 223–234 [hereinafter Hseih, Hu, and Lin, "The Demand for Cigarettes in Taiwan"].

11 Ibid., p. 231.

12 Craig Depken, "The Effects of Advertising Restrictions on Cigarette Prices: Evidence from OECD Countries," 6 *Applied Economics Letters*, (1999), pp. 307–309 [hereinafter Depken, "Advertising Restrictions"]; Allyn Taylor, Frank Chaloupka, Emmanuel Guindon et al., "The Impact of Trade Liberalization on Tobacco Consumption" in Prabhat Jha and Frank Chaloupka (eds), *Tobacco Control in Developing Countries*, World Bank and World Health Organization, Oxford University Press, (2000), pp. 343–364 [hereinafter Jha and Chaloupka, *Tobacco Control in Developing Countries*]; Douglas Bettcher, Chitra Subramaniam, Emmanuel Guindon et al., "Confronting the Tobacco Epidemic in an era of Trade Liberalization," WHO Commission on Macroeconomics and Health, World Health Organization, (2001), CMH Working Paper Series, WG 4: 8 [hereinafter Bettcher et al., "Confronting the Tobacco Epidemic"].

13 Depken, "Advertising Restrictions," p. 308.

14 Taylor et al., "The Impact of Trade Liberalization on Tobacco Consumption," p. 360.

15 Bettcher et al., "Confronting the Tobacco Epidemic," p. 51.

16 Ibid., p. 52.

This conclusion is consistent with the observations of Anna Gilmore and Martin McKee, who charted investment levels and tobacco production and consumption levels in former Soviet countries between 1991 and 2000.[17] Gilmore and McKee concluded that cigarette consumption increased almost exponentially in line with rapid increases in cigarette production, and that such increases in consumption were concentrated in countries receiving tobacco industry investment.[18] Increases in consumption of approximately 56 percent were recorded for countries that received major tobacco industry investment, whereas a 1 percent drop in consumption was recorded in those countries that did not receive any such investment.[19]

The authors of these studies offer theories of why tobacco consumption increased. Chaloupka and Laixuthai offered two "possible explanations."[20] One explanation was that increased competition led to price reductions that stimulated demand. Another explanation was that increases in advertising and promotion of U.S. cigarettes stimulated demand.[21] In addition to these factors, Bettcher and others considered potential explanations that include brand proliferation and the targeting of untapped market segments.[22] Both Taylor and others and Bettcher and others also make reference to differences in the quality of domestic and imported tobacco products as a potential motivator for trade,[23] the implication being that newly imported products may satisfy latent demand for higher-quality products. Gilmore and McKee drew similar conclusions, arguing that women and young people were targeted by the introduction of new brands in the former Soviet Union, and that consumption levels prior to 1990 may have been artificially low due to lack of supply.[24]

Although there is less empirical evidence of the relationship between trade liberalization and harmful use of alcohol,[25] it stands to reason that trade

17 Anna Gilmore and Martin McKee, "Exploring the Impact of Foreign Direct Investment on Tobacco Consumption in the Former Soviet Union," 14 *Tobacco Control*, (2005), pp. 13–21 [hereinafter Gilmore and McKee, "Exploring the Impact"].

18 Ibid., p. 18.

19 Ibid., p. 19.

20 Chaloupka and Laixuthai, "U.S. Trade Policy," p. 14.

21 In this regard, Chaloupka and Laixuthai recognized that this conclusion was supported to some degree by anecdotal evidence and also by the Japanese study on advertising. A. Hagihara and Y. J. Takeshita, "Impact of American Cigarette Advertising on Imported Cigarette Consumption in Osaka, Japan," 4 *Tobacco Control*, (1995), pp. 239–244.

22 Bettcher et al., "Confronting the Tobacco Epidemic," p. 49.

23 Ibid.; Taylor et al., "The Impact of Trade Liberalization on Tobacco Consumption," p. 344.

24 Gilmore and McKee, "Exploring the Impact," pp. 19–20.

25 One example can be found in Meichum Kup, Jean-Luc Heeb, Gerhard Gmel et al., "Does Price Matter? The Effect of Decreased Price on Spirits Consumption in Switzerland," 27(4) *Alcoholism: Clinical and Experimental Research*, (2006), pp. 720–725.

liberalization may have similar effects in the alcohol sector as in the tobacco sector. Lower prices may stimulate consumption,[26] and increases in marketing may have a similar effect.[27] Thus, to the extent that increases in consumption increase morbidity and mortality, liberalization in the alcohol sector may have negative effects on public health.[28]

It is also possible to observe a relationship between trade liberalization and increasing levels of obesity.[29] As Corinna Hawkes has argued, trade liberalization "affects the whole food supply chain by influencing the incentives farmers and agribusinesses have to produce different foods, food imports and exports (very directly), and food processing retailing and advertising, which have all been profoundly affected by the growth of global food companies."[30] More specifically, trade liberalization has facilitated a trend toward increased consumption of vegetable oils, meats, and highly processed foods, all of which are associated with a nutrition transition.[31] Some commentators attribute this to the role that freer trade has played in reducing the relative cost of dietary energy in a context in which energy-dense foods and diets cost relatively less than nutrient-dense foods and diets and in which consumption of energy-dense foods increases as income declines.[32]

[26] Alexander Wagenaar, Matthew Salois, and Kelli Komro, "Effects of Beverage Alcohol Price and Tax Levels on Drinking: A Meta-Analysis of 1003 Estimates from 112 Studies," 104 *Addiction*, (2009), pp. 179–190; see contra Jon Nelson, "Alcohol Advertising Bans, Consumptions and Control Policies in Seventeen OECD Countries, 1975–2000," *Applied Economics*, (2008), pp. 1–21.

[27] Peter Anderson, Avalon de Bruijn, Kathryn Angus et al., "Impact of Alcohol Advertising and Media Exposure on Adolescent Alcohol Use: A Systematic Review of Longitudinal Studies," 44(3) *Alcohol & Alcoholism*, (2009), pp. 229–343.

[28] Some support for this proposition can be found in a resolution of the WHO Regional Committee for South-East Asia SEA/RC59/R8 Alcohol Consumption Control – Policy Options, in which the committee notes that "certain trade agreements … facilitate the free flow of and investment in alcohol, which boosts the consumption and negative impact of alcohol in the region."

[29] See generally Chantal Blouin, Mickey Chopra, and Rolph van der Hoeven, "Trade and Health 3: Trade and Social Determinants of Health," 373(9662) *The Lancet*, London, (Feb 7–13, 2009), pp. 504–505; Corinna Hawkes, Chantal Blouin, Spencer Hensen et al., *Trade, Food, Diet and Health: Perspectives and Policy Options*, Oxford, Wiley Blackwell, (2010) [hereinafter Hawkes et al., *Trade, Food, Diet and Health*].

[30] Corinna Hawkes, "The Influence of Trade Liberalisation and Global Dietary Change: The Case of Vegetable Oils, Meat and Highly Processed Foods," in Hawkes et al., *Trade, Food, Diet and Health*, pp. 35–59, p. 36.

[31] Hawkes, "The Influence of Trade Liberalisation and Global Dietary Change," pp. 55–56.

[32] Adam Drewnowski, Andrew Hanks, and Trenton Smith, "International Trade, Food and Diet Costs, and the Global Obesity Epidemic," in Hawkes et al., *Trade, Food, Diet and Health*, pp. 77–90.

As in the tobacco context, some commentators also draw a connection between trade liberalization and increased marketing. This is sometimes associated with the term "coca-colonization," which refers to the spread of Western cultural and dietary influences through increased investment in marketing and other processes.[33] Not surprisingly, there is also a concern that food marketing is targeted toward children. One salient example can be found in the promotional toys offered with the sale of meals by fast food outlets.[34]

Any impact that liberalization may have on health will differ from place to place and from one risk factor to another. The necessarily harmful character of tobacco products means that liberalization is unlikely to be beneficial to health in any meaningful way. However, although liberalization of trade in alcoholic beverages may stimulate alcohol consumption, it may also offer some consumers access to beverages that are safer to consume than locally produced beverages. This may be the case, for example, where beverages are produced illegally or informally and contain methanol or other contaminants.

In the case of food, liberalization could increase food security and improve access to foods of high nutritional value, such as fruits and vegetables, on a year-round basis.[35] Other trade-related agricultural policies may also have a disparate impact on consumers. For example, it has been argued that the European Common Agricultural Policy (CAP) has kept prices in the European Union (EU) higher than international prices and that international prices have been suppressed by policies such as export subsidization.[36] Assuming a relationship between consumption and price, this would suggest that EU policy is likely to have suppressed consumption in the EU while stimulating consumption in food-importing countries. The relative costs and benefits of trade-related policies of this type will depend on a wide variety of factors. For example, export subsidies of this type may improve the nutritional status of a region facing undernutrition but may also stimulate overconsumption in regions not facing this problem.[37] Similarly, export subsidies on fresh fruits and vegetables may

33 Tim Lobstein, "Tackling Childhood Obesity in an Era of Trade Liberalisation," in Hawkes et al., *Trade, Food, Diet and Health*, pp. 195–218.

34 For a discussion of marketing targeting children in this context, see Lobstein, "Tackling Childhood Obesity in an Era of Trade Liberalisation," in Hawkes et al., *Trade, Food, Diet and Health*, pp. 198–203.

35 Sophia Huang, "Global Trade of Fruits and Vegetables and the Role of Consumer Demand," in Hawkes et al., *Trade, Food, Diet and Health*, pp. 60–76.

36 Josef Schidhuber and Prakash Shetty, "The European Union's Common Agricultural Policy and the European Diet: Is there a Link?" in Hawkes et al., *Trade, Food, Diet and Health*, pp. 131–147.

37 Ibid., p. 145

be expected to result in better nutritional outcomes outside of the EU than export subsidies on sweeteners such as sugar.

The impact of liberalization on health will also depend on the regulatory strategies adopted by domestic governments. An obvious response to the risk that liberalization will alter consumer preferences in a manner harmful to human health is the imposition of regulatory measures that counter these impacts. The GATT panel report in *Thailand – Cigarettes* reflects this idea.[38] Thailand had argued that a licensing system that effectively resulted in a closed tobacco market was necessary to protect human health from dangers such as the effects that market opening would have on consumption. The licensing system was not considered to be necessary for the protection of human health or life under Article XX(b) of the GATT.[39] Rather, the GATT panel held that Thailand could implement taxation measures and nondiscriminatory bans on tobacco advertising, and that these measures were reasonably available alternatives to the maintenance of the licensing system.

Equally, *Thailand – Cigarettes*, which was decided under the old GATT system, did not settle conclusively the extent to which the GATT or other WTO-covered agreements preserve domestic regulatory autonomy. In fact, some public health advocates have argued that the GATS limits the ability of WTO Members to restrict product advertising, because to do so may contravene market-access commitments for advertising service suppliers.[40] This reflects concerns about regulatory autonomy, which is the second point of tension between the trade regime and the new public health. For example, tobacco-control advocates have argued that trade agreements governing the implementation of nontariff barriers to trade limit domestic regulatory freedom to such an extent that comprehensive and effective tobacco control is not permitted.[41] Similar concerns are

[38] GATT Panel Report, *Thailand – Restrictions on Importation of and Internal Taxes on Cigarettes*, DS10/R, adopted 7 November 1990, BISD 37S/200 [hereinafter *Thailand – Cigarettes*].

[39] Ibid., paras 78–81.

[40] See, for example, Jim Grieshaber-Otto, Scott Sinclair, Noel Schacter, "Impacts of International Trade, Services and Investment Treaties on Alcohol Regulation," 95(Supplement 4) *Addiction*, (2000), pp. S491–S504; Ellen Gould, "Trade Treaties and Alcohol Advertising Policy," 26(3) *Journal of Public Health Policy*, (2005), pp. 359–376.

[41] See, for example, John Bloom, "Public Health, International Trade and the Framework Convention on Tobacco Control," Campaign for Tobacco-Free Kids, (March 2001) available at http://tobaccofreekids.org/campaign/global/framework/docs/Policy.pdf (visited 12/12/07); Cynthia Callard, Hatai Chitanondh, and Robert Weissman, "Why Trade and Investment Liberalisation may Threaten Effective Tobacco Control Efforts," 10 *Tobacco Control*, (2001), pp. 68–70 [hereinafter Callard, Chitanondh, and Weissman, "Why Trade"]; Cynthia Callard, Neil Collishaw, and Michele Swenarchuk, "An Introduction to International Trade Agreements

held by some advocating increased government intervention to reduce harmful alcohol use and obesity.[42]

Differences in the regulatory contexts between infectious and noncommunicable diseases also raise questions about the adequacy of trade rules. For example, it is not clear how the overriding principle that trade-restrictive measures must be necessary to protect human health will be applied in the context of noncommunicable disease. In this respect, one important distinction between infectious and noncommunicable disease is the question of cause and effect. There is a clear causal relationship between the transmission of infectious diseases and harm to human health. For this reason, exposure to infectious diseases is often a proximal cause of disease, meaning that a risk factor acts either directly or almost directly to cause disease. In this context, it can be expected that there will be a close relationship between measures used to reduce transmission of infectious disease, such as import restrictions, and the protection of human health.

In contrast, the risk factors for noncommunicable disease are often more remote. Distal causes of disease are further down in the chain of causation. A compelling example of this can be found in the context of diet. Whereas consuming food-borne pathogens might directly result in disease, consumption of foods high in fat or sugar is likely to have a less direct impact on a person's health. Threats posed by high-fat food may not be as direct as threats posed by a food containing harmful pathogens. In the case of high-fat food, there is a longer chain of causation between consumption and the onset of disease, and there are likely to be a greater number of ways in which a WTO Member may address the risks.

Notwithstanding the differences in context between infectious diseases and the new public health, measures falling within each field are examined under the same legal framework of the WTO-covered agreements. The underlying requirement of this framework is that measures must be "necessary" for the protection of human life or health. The fact that this framework applies in both contexts raises a broader question concerning how that framework may or may not be suited to addressing the questions of concern.

and their Impact on Public Measures to Reduce Tobacco Use," Physicians for a Smoke Free Canada, (2001), available at http://www.smoke-free.ca/pdf_1/Trade&Tobacco-April%202000.pdf (visited 10/01/08) [hereinafter Callard, Collishaw, and Swenarchuk, "An Introduction"]; Robert Weissman, "International trade agreements and tobacco control: threats to public health and the case for excluding tobacco from trade agreements," (November 2003), v 2.0 available at http://www.fctc.org/x/cd/documents/EA_trade_backgrd.pdf (visited 26/11/07).

42 See for example, Donald Zeigler, "International Trade Agreements Challenge Tobacco and Alcohol Control Policies," 25 *Drug and Alcohol Review*, (November 2006), pp. 567–579.

Another issue that merits consideration is whether the WTO Agreement leaves sufficient policy space for WTO Members to address the link between economic specialization and poor diet. In this respect, the Global Strategy on Diet, Physical Activity, and Health emphasizes the need for local production of fresh produce.[43] At first glance, it is difficult to see how promoting local production, as opposed to importation, might benefit public health. However, some small island states have found that the lowering of trade barriers abroad has encouraged local farmers to produce single crops destined for export markets. This increased economic specialization has affected the availability of fresh fruits and vegetables, having a flow-on effect for traditional diets in places such as the Pacific Islands.[44] The relatively small markets in these states and the difficulties associated with shipping fresh produce to them may also be reasons for the failure of the market to ensure an adequate and affordable supply of fresh foods. Because food choices are made in the context of one's environment, issues such as price and availability are important and suggest that there may in fact be a compelling case for government intervention to ensure local production of certain foods. In this context, the lawfulness of subsidies for domestic production is worth considering. In addition, the limited budgets of many small island states suggest that other approaches, such as taxes and tariffs, may be the policy tools of choice.

At a more practical level, public health authorities continue to grapple with these questions of regulatory autonomy in their work. In 2007 the World Health Organization (WHO), in its role as chair of the United Nations Ad Hoc Interagency Task Force on Tobacco Control (of which the WTO is a member), called for further examination of the relationship between the international trade regime and global efforts aimed at tobacco control.[45] In the context of negotiations concerning illicit trade in tobacco products, World Health Organization Framework Convention on Tobacco Control (FCTC) parties have also been struggling to understand the implications of the WTO-covered agreements for measures to prevent illicit trade.[46]

43 Global Strategy on Diet, Physical Activity and Health, World Health Assembly, WHA57.17, (May 2004), para. 41(3).

44 Anne Marie Thow and Wendy Snowdon, "The Effect of Trade and Trade Policy on Diet and Health in the Pacific Islands," in Hawkes et al., *Trade, Food, Diet and Health: Perspectives and Policy Options*, Oxford, Wiley Blackwell, (2010), pp. 147–168, pp. 161–162.

45 Report of the United Nations Ad Hoc Interagency Task Force on Tobacco Control, Conference of the Parties to the WHO Framework Convention on Tobacco Control, Second Session, A/FCTC/COP/2/4, 26 April 2007 available at http://www.who.int/gb/fctc/PDF/cop2/FCTC_COP2_4-en.pdf (visited 12/12/07).

46 See, for example, Revised Chairperson's Text on a Protocol on Illicit Trade in Tobacco Products, and General Debate, Expert Review on a Possible Ban on Internet sales of

There are two explanations for the gap in knowledge faced by public health officials. First, existing scholarship concerning application of WTO law to measures to prevent noncommunicable disease is very general in character and focused largely on the tobacco context. For example, a joint WTO and WHO study merely concluded that "[d]epending on how governments choose to manage trade in tobacco and tobacco products, a number of WTO rules could come into play."[47] Although general analysis of this type may be useful, as John Jackson has argued with respect to issues of linkage between the WTO and other regimes, the "devil is in the detail."[48] That is, there is a need for a more detailed analysis of the relationship between trade and public health.

The need for a fresh analysis of the issues is also highlighted by a number of contemporary controversies. At the time of writing, disputes concerning tobacco and alcohol are afoot: The panel in *Thailand – Customs and Fiscal Measures on Cigarettes from the Philippines*[49] is soon to hand down its report, the European Communities (EC) (now European Union) has requested consultations with India concerning taxes and other measures on imported wine and spirits,[50] and the United States has sought the establishment of a panel concerning taxes on distilled spirits in the Philippines.[51] Although these disputes appear peripheral to questions of domestic regulatory autonomy to protect health, other controversies appear to be more central to those concerns. For example, Indonesia has requested consultations with the United States concerning measures banning flavored cigarettes, including clove cigarettes produced in Indonesia.[52] The measure in question is said to relate to

Tobacco Products, WHO Framework Convention on Tobacco Control, Intergovernmental Negotiating Body on a Protocol on Illicit Trade in Tobacco Products, Third Session, Geneva, Switzerland, 28 June–5 July, 2009, FCTC/COP/INB-IT/3/INF.DOC./4, 7 May 2009.

47 WTO Agreements and Public Health: A Joint Study by the WHO and the WTO Secretariat, World Health Organization and World Trade Organization, (2002), available at http://www.wto.org/english/res_e/booksp_e/who_wto_e.pdf (visited 12/12/07).

48 John Jackson, "Fragmentation or Unification Among International Institutions: The World Trade Organization," 31 *New York University Journal of International Law and Politics*, (1998–1999), pp. 823–831, p. 823.

49 See *Thailand – Customs and Fiscal Measures on Cigarettes from the Philippines*, Request for the Establishment of a Panel by the Philippines, World Trade Organization, WT/DS371/3, 6 October 2008.

50 *India – Certain Taxes and Other Measures on Imported Wines and Spirits*, Request for Consultations by the European Communities, World Trade Organization, WT/DS380/1, G/L/855, G/SCM/D79/1, 25 September 2008.

51 *Philippines – Taxes on Distilled Spirits*, Request for Consultations by the United States, World Trade Organization, WT/DS403/1, G/L/914, 18 January 2010.

52 *United States – Measures Affecting the Production and Sale of Clove Cigarettes*, Request for Consultations by Indonesia, World Trade Organization, WT/DS406/1, G/L/917, G/SPS/GEN/1015, G/TBT/D/38, 14 April 2010.

the attractiveness of flavored tobacco products to children. Equally, the fact that the measure exempts menthol-flavored cigarettes is likely to be a point of controversy.

Canada has implemented similar measures by prohibiting the sale of flavored cigarettes, little cigars, and blunt wraps.[53] Like the U.S. measures, menthol is excluded from the restrictions. Health Canada has sought to justify this on the basis that menthol-flavored cigarettes are established in the market and the measure is targeted at new products designed to entice children to tobacco use.[54] Although the menthol exemption may also be controversial for the Canadian measures, they go further by restricting flavors that are used in production of blended-style cigarettes that include burley (a type of tobacco). At present, the Canadian market is composed primarily of tobacco products that use Virginia tobacco, which does not require flavoring. A number of WTO Members have objected to the measures and indicated their intention to address the issue through WTO dispute settlement.

WTO Members have also raised concerns about alcohol labeling measures that Thailand intends to implement. The warnings appear to be modeled on those used in the tobacco context and would include both text and pictures.[55] A number of WTO Members have expressed concern in the Committee on Technical Barriers to Trade (TBT). Some members have argued that the measures create unnecessary barriers to trade and that public information campaigns would be less restrictive means of protecting health. Concerns have also been expressed about the potential for the warnings to suggest that any level of drinking may be harmful to health.[56] At the same meeting, concerns were also expressed about a Brazilian labeling requirement as applied to alcoholic beverages.[57] A number of WTO Members expressed concerns about the requirement that alcoholic content be indicated on the front of a label.[58]

53 Cracking Down on Tobacco Marketing Aimed at Youth Act, Bill C 32.

54 See http://www.hc-sc.gc.ca/hc-ps/tobac-tabac/legislation/federal/amend_faq-modif-eng.php (visited 26/09/10).

55 Notification, Committee on Technical Barriers to Trade, World Trade Organization, Thailand, G/TBT/N/THA/332, 21 January 2010.

56 WTO: 2010 News Items, 24 and 25 March 2010 Technical Barriers To Trade, Tobacco and alcohol technical barriers among members' trade concerns available at http://www.wto.org/english/news_e/news10_e/tbt_24mar10_e.htm (visited 18/04/10).

57 Notification, Committee on Technical Barriers to Trade, World Trade Organization, Brazil, G/TBT/N/BRA/362, 12 February 2010.

58 WTO: 2010 News Items, 24 and 25 March 2010, Technical Barriers To Trade, Tobacco and alcohol technical barriers among members' trade concerns available at http://www.wto.org/english/news_e/news10_e/tbt_24mar10_e.htm (visited 18/04/10).

The need for a fresh analysis of the issues can also be illustrated by reference to some of the arguments that have been made in the past. One such argument is that public health measures will be lawful so long as they do not discriminate in favor of domestic goods.[59] Another argument is that specific trade interventions are rarely going to be an effective way of protecting public health in the context of noncommunicable diseases.[60] For example, David Fidler has argued that measures regulating trade in goods or services are unlikely to be effective means of combating obesity.[61] However, such conclusions fail to acknowledge the distinction between measures that are overtly trade related and measures that appear to be legitimate internal regulation that may also have the effect of protecting domestic production. For example, a broad conclusion concerning compliance with principles of nondiscrimination fails to take full account of the fact that origin-neutral measures that are nondiscriminatory on their face may lead to violations of national treatment provisions through their indirect impact on imported products.

Another argument made on a routine basis is that Article XX(b) of the GATT, which creates an exception for measures necessary to protect human health, will preserve sound public health measures.[62] This conclusion should not be accepted at face value. Rather, it is arguable that the current approach to the application of Article XX gives rise to a high degree of uncertainty. In particular, uncertainty surrounds application of the requirement that measures be necessary to protect human health, to sets of complementary measures designed to achieve the same ends,[63] to consideration by a WTO panel of the importance

59 See, for example, with respect to taxation, Kristyn Noeth, "Taxation to Control Tobacco in Developing States," in Edith Brown Weiss and John Jackson (eds), *Reconciling Environment and Trade*, Ardsley, NY, Transnational Publishers, (2001), pp. 101–132, p. 132; Joseph Eckhardt, "Balancing the Interests in Free Trade and Health: How the WHO's Framework Convention on Tobacco Control can Withstand WTO Scrutiny," 12 *Duke Journal of Comparative and International Law*, (Winter 2002), pp. 197–230, p. 223; Elisabeth Bürgi, "The Regulatory Aspects of International Trade in Tobacco," in "WTI Study," p. 21.

60 See, for example, Tim Josling, David Orden, and Donna Roberts, "National Food Regulations and the WTO Agreement on Sanitary and Phytosanitary Measures: Implications for Trade-Related Measures to Promote Healthy Diets," in Hawkes et al., *Trade, Food, Diet and Health*, pp. 219–237, p. 236.

61 David Fidler, "The Impact of International Trade and Investment Rules on the Ability of Governments to Implement Interventions to Address Obesity: A Case Study on the European Charter on Counteracting Obesity," in Hawkes et al., *Trade, Food, Diet and Health*, pp. 279–297, p. 279.

62 Alyssa Woo, "Health Versus Trade: The Future of the WHO's Framework Convention on Tobacco Control," 35 *Vanderbilt Journal of Transnational Law*, (2002), pp. 1731–1768, p. 1731.

63 Benn McGrady, "Necessity Exceptions in WTO Law: Retreaded Tyres, Regulatory Purpose and Cumulative Regulatory Measures," 12 *Journal of International Economic Law*, (2009), pp. 153–173.

of a member's regulatory goal[64] and problems associated with the implementation and enforcement of so-called reasonably available alternatives.[65]

There is also an inherent gap in knowledge between different epistemic communities, such as the public health community and the trade policy community. This gap in knowledge may also be widened by the differing perspectives of the relevant actors. One perspective on the WTO Agreement is that it is as much a diplomatic instrument as it is a legal instrument. This view follows partly from the WTO's prior incarnation as the GATT 1947. As Robert Hudec described it, the GATT legal system was a "diplomat's jurisprudence," and the GATT 1947 was not intended to be enforced "to the letter."[66] On the contrary, the focus of dispute settlement was the preservation of tariff commitments.[67] As Jackson put it, the diplomacy of the GATT 1947 was power oriented rather than rule oriented.[68] An alternative perspective on the WTO is that its creation largely remedied this power orientation and replaced it with a rule-oriented system in which rights and obligations are expected to be enforced to the letter.

Of course, neither of these perspectives is completely accurate in the sense that the WTO Agreement falls somewhere between the two. Nonetheless, these perspectives highlight the fact that the relationship between trade and public health is not strictly a legal relationship. As such, members of the trade policy community might be more inclined to accept the view that the GATT Article XX exceptions will protect legitimate public health measures, albeit in a somewhat unpredictable and ad hoc manner. Similarly, those familiar with the system might conclude that WTO Members are unlikely to bring claims relating to the lawfulness of public health measures unless those measures possess some specific discriminatory element.

On the other hand, those who are less familiar with WTO diplomacy might be more likely to view the WTO-covered agreements at face value as

64 Robert Howse and Elisabeth Türk, "The WTO Impact Upon Internal Regulations: A Case Study of the Canada – EC Asbestos Dispute," in George Bermann and Petros Mavroidis (eds), *Trade and Human Health and Safety*, New York, Cambridge University Press, (2006), pp. 77–117, p. 116.

65 On this issue, in the context of the Thai Cigarettes Case, see Robert Howse, "The Legitimacy of the World Trade Organization," in Jean-Marc Coicaud and Viejo Heiskanen (eds), *The Legitimacy of International Organizations*, Tokyo, New York, United Nations University Press, (2001), pp. 355–407, p. 392.

66 See generally Robert Hudec, "The GATT Legal System: A Diplomat's Jurisprudence," 4 *Journal of World Trade Law*, (1970), pp. 615–665.

67 Ibid.

68 See John Jackson, "The Crumbling Institutions of the Liberal Trade System," 12 *Journal of World Trade Law*, (1978), pp. 93–106; John Jackson, "Governmental Disputes in International Trade Relations: A Proposal in the Context of GATT," 13 *Journal of World Trade Law*, (1979), pp. 1–21.

the binding legal instruments that they are. Those who fall into this camp might not view the likelihood of a claim being brought as relevant to the normative issues at hand. This group might also argue that the bringing of claims turns on the domestic politics of a situation, including the extent to which different WTO Members are either risk tolerant or risk averse. Public health advocates are more likely to be concerned with whether legal guarantees preserving domestic regulatory autonomy are adequate and sufficiently certain so as to negate "regulatory-chill."

1.1. *The Importance of Examining the Issues in Greater Detail*

From an intellectual perspective, the aforementioned gaps in knowledge are sufficient reason to examine the issues in further detail. At a more practical level, tobacco, alcohol, and poor diet stand out among determinants of health as major risk factors for noncommunicable disease. Although there are important differences between these risk factors, they each have significant public health, economic, and social implications that highlight the practical importance of further discussion.

A. Tobacco

Tobacco consumption causes the premature death of approximately 50 percent of regular smokers in middle age.[69] Consumption of and exposure to tobacco products are believed to have caused approximately 5 million premature deaths in the year 2000[70] and 5.4 million deaths in the year 2006.[71] It is also predicted that by the year 2030, approximately 10 million deaths will be caused annually by tobacco consumption.[72]

Developing countries are also gradually increasing their share of the disease burden associated with tobacco consumption. In the year 2000 approximately half of the global deaths were in developing countries, and approximately 70 percent of the expected global deaths in the year 2030 are predicted to be in developing countries. This is problematic from a developmental perspective in that

[69] R. Doll, R. Peto, K. Wheatley, et al., "Mortality in Relation to Smoking: 50 Years' Observation on Male British Doctors," 309 *British Medical Journal*, (Oct. 8, 1994) 901–911.

[70] Majid Ezzati and Alan Lopez, "Estimates of Global Mortality Attributable to Smoking in 2000," 362(9387) *The Lancet*, London, (2003), pp. 847–852.

[71] Tobacco Free Initiative, World Health Organization, Facts and Figures about tobacco, June 2007, available at http://www.who.int/tobacco/framework/cop/facts_and_figures_about_tobacco.pdf (visited 01/02/08).

[72] C. K. Gajalakshmi, Prabhat Jha, Kent Ranson, et al., "Global Patterns of Smoking and Smoking Attributable Mortality," in Jha and Chaloupka (eds), *Tobacco Control in Developing Countries*, pp. 11–39, p. 35.

tobacco consumption can contribute to poverty by diverting household income away from basic necessities such as food, health care, and education.[73] Similarly, the allocation of health-care resources to preventable tobacco-related illness results in the diversion of limited health-care resources from other areas.

In response to the risks associated with tobacco consumption, the international community concluded the FCTC. The FCTC was adopted by the World Health Assembly (WHA) in 2003 and came into force in 2005. At the time of writing, the FCTC has 171 parties.

As its name suggests, the FCTC is a framework convention that establishes a broad framework for tobacco control. This framework compels and encourages the use of measures to protect health through five means. Those means are (1) demand reduction, (2) provision of information to consumers, (3) supply reduction, (4) reduction of exposure to tobacco smoke, and (5) minimization of the harm caused by individual tobacco products. As discussed in further detail later, many FCTC provisions have a discretionary character, leaving a measure to be implemented in line with domestic circumstances. Other instruments also supplement the provisions of the FCTC. At the time of writing, the Conference of the Parties to the FCTC has adopted guidelines on Article 8 (protection from exposure to tobacco smoke), Article 5.3 (industry involvement in the setting and implementation of public health policies), Article 11 (packaging and labeling of tobacco products), and Article 13 (tobacco advertising, promotion, and sponsorship).[74]

B. Alcohol

Like tobacco consumption, harmful alcohol use is a significant public health issue. In 2008, the World Health Organization (WHO) reported to the WHA on strategies to reduce the harmful use of alcohol. In that report, the concept of harmful alcohol use was defined as referring to a variety of different circumstances including drinking an excessive amount over time (a risk factor for disease), a pattern of drinking that leads to intoxication, drinking in an environment that may increase the risk of injuries or the transmission of disease, and drinking beverages that are contaminated with toxic substances.[75]

73 On the relationship between tobacco and poverty, see Katharine Esson and Stephen Leeder, "The Millennium Development Goals and Tobacco Control: An Opportunity for Global Partnership," World Health Organization, 2004, available at http://www.who.int/tobacco/publications/mdg_final_for_web.pdf (visited 12/12/07).

74 See WHO Framework Convention on Tobacco Control, Guidelines for Implementation: Article 5.3, Article 8, Article 11, Article 13, World Health Organization, Geneva 2009.

75 Strategies to Reduce Harmful Use of Alcohol, World Health Organization, 61st World Health Assembly, A61/13, 20 March 2008, para. 2.

A 2007 report prepared by an expert committee for the WHO concluded that in 2002 harmful alcohol use caused approximately 3.7 percent of global mortality (2.3 million deaths) and 4.4 percent of the global disease burden (taking into account the protective effects of low and moderate alcohol consumption).[76] The report also concluded that alcohol-related deaths increased for both men and women between the years 2000 and 2002,[77] suggesting a trend of increasing morbidity and mortality. These estimates are also supported by a more recent study, which estimates that alcohol consumption causes 3.8 percent of global deaths, 4.6 percent of the global disease burden, and that costs associated with alcohol consumption amount to more than 1 percent of gross national product in high- and middle-income countries.[78]

Harmful alcohol use is a "risk factor for neuropsychiatric disorders and other non-communicable diseases such as cardiovascular diseases, cirrhosis of the liver and various cancers."[79] Other disorders relating to alcohol include mouth and oropharynx cancers, esophageal cancer, colon, and rectal cancers, liver cancer, breast cancer, diabetes mellitus, and alcohol-use disorders. Drinking alcohol during pregnancy is of particular concern, because of the possibility of numerous forms of prenatal damage.[80] Less directly, harmful alcohol use is associated with road traffic accidents, other unintentional injuries, and violent crimes. In addition, the majority of alcohol-attributable burden of disease occurs within the age group fifteen to twenty-nine years (33.6 percent), followed by the age group thirty to forty-four (31.3 percent).[81] As in the tobacco context, the burden of disease associated with alcohol use is greatest in developing countries.[82]

In May 2010, the WHA adopted the Global Strategy to Reduce the Harmful Use of Alcohol (Global Strategy Alcohol).[83] This nonbinding instrument recommends that WHO Members adopt a range of different policies to address harmful alcohol use. These policies include improving the response of health services,

76 WHO Expert Committee on Problems Related to Alcohol Consumption, WHO Technical Reports Series, Second Report, World Health Organization, Geneva 2007, p.19.

77 Ibid.

78 Jürgen Rehm, Colin Mathers, Svetlana Popova et al., "Global Burden of Disease and Injury and Economic Cost Attributable to Alcohol Use and Alcohol-Use Disorders," 373 *The Lancet*, London, (June 27, 2009), pp. 2223–2233.

79 Strategies to reduce the Harmful Use of Alcohol, World Health Organization, Executive Board, 126th Session, 22 January 2010, EB126.R11, para. 3.

80 Ibid., para. 5.

81 Rehm, "Global Burden of Disease," pp. 2229–2230.

82 Ibid., p. 2231.

83 Global Strategy to Reduce the Harmful Use of Alcohol, World Health Assembly, WHA 63.13, 21 May 2010.

strengthening drinking-and-driving laws, and minimizing harm such as through the use of measures to prevent violence in pubs and bars. Other approaches of more relevance in the context of WTO law include measures to restrict the availability of alcohol, restrict the marketing of alcoholic beverages, and increase the retail cost of alcoholic beverages through higher taxes and prices.

C. Diet

In the dietary context, a "nutrition transition" that is characterized by a shift from the consumption of fresh fruits and vegetables to "energy dense, nutrient poor foods that are high in fat, sugar and salt"[84] is under way. This transition is associated with a number of risk factors for noncommunicable disease, such as high blood pressure, high concentrations of cholesterol in the blood, and overweight or obesity (which is itself associated with these other risk factors).[85] Inadequate fruit and vegetable intake alone, causes approximately 2.7 million deaths annually from conditions such as gastrointestinal cancer, ischemic heart disease, and stroke.[86]

The nutrition transition constitutes one explanation for increases in noncommunicable diseases and for obesity prevalence rates that now exceed 25 percent of the population in some states.[87] As a response, in May 2004, the WHA adopted the Global Strategy on Diet, Physical Activity and Health (Global Strategy Diet). The Global Strategy Diet is a nonbinding instrument that sets out a number of principles and "responsibilities" for action that are directed at WHO member-states, the WHO itself, other international organizations, civil society, nongovernmental organizations, and the private sector.

The multicausal nature of dietary-related disease means that the Global Strategy Diet focuses on the reduction of risk factors. Risk factors include issues such as how conducive one's environment is to exercise and one's socioeconomic status. In addition, the accessibility of healthy foods and beverages and the incentives that exist for the consumption of healthy foods play a role. Despite the increased complexity of the policy environment in the context of dietary-related disease, some of the regulatory approaches contemplated in the Global Strategy Diet resemble those used in the tobacco

84 Global Strategy Diet, para. 10; On the nutrition transition generally, see Barry M. Popkin, "The Implications of the Nutrition Transition for Obesity in the Developing World," in David Crawford and Robert W. Jeffery, *Obesity Prevention and Public Health*, Oxford University Press, (2005), pp. 75–100.

85 Global Strategy Diet, para. 4

86 For discussion, see The World Health Report 2002: Reducing Risks, Promoting Healthy Life, Geneva, World Health Organization, 2002, pp. 60–61.

87 See the World Health Organization Global Database on Body Mass Index, available at http://www.who.int/bmi/index.jsp

and alcohol contexts. For example, the Global Strategy Diet contemplates the use of tax measures in order to create incentives for the consumption of healthful foods as well as restrictions on marketing to children of relatively unhealthy foods. The Global Strategy Diet also contemplates the use of other measures relevant to WTO law, such as subsidization of fruit and vegetable farming.

D. Justifications for government intervention in each area

Regulatory interventions to address the implications of tobacco, alcohol, and poor diet are often contested at the domestic level as a consequence of concerns relating to individual liberty and paternalism. Consequently, it is worthwhile to touch on some of the justifications for government intervention in these specific contexts.[88] Justifications include that it is the basic obligation of government to protect health (as reflected in various human rights instruments), that paternalism is justified in the case of children or addicts, that intervention is necessary to remedy market failures, and that intervention addresses questions of distributive justice.

The basic responsibility of government to protect human health is reflected in the codification of a human right to the highest attainable standard of health. Article 25 of the Universal Declaration of Human Rights provides that everyone has "the right to a standard of living adequate for the health and well-being of himself and of his family." Similarly, the Constitution of the WHO recognizes that "[t]he enjoyment of the highest attainable standard of health is one of the fundamental rights of every human being without distinction of race, religion, political belief, economic or social condition."

Article 12 of the International Covenant on Economic, Social and Cultural Rights (ICESCR)[89] is the most detailed elaboration of the right. The provision obliges states parties to take steps to ensure the realization of this right to the fullest extent possible and includes an obligation to prevent, treat, and control epidemic diseases.[90] Article 12 states:

> 1. The States Parties to the present Covenant recognize the right of everyone to the enjoyment of the highest attainable standard of physical and mental health.

[88] For a more detailed summary of the rationales for government intervention to protect health, see Tracey Epps, *International Trade and Health Protection: A Critical Assessment of the WTO's SPS Agreement*, Cheltenham, Edward Elgar, (2008), pp. 58–91.

[89] International Covenant on Economic, Social and Cultural Rights, GA Res. 2200A (XXI), 21 UN GAOR Supp. (No. 16) at 49, UN Doc. A/6316 (1966); 993 UNTS 3; 6 ILM 368 (1967).

[90] Article 12(2)(c).

2. The steps to be taken by the States Parties to the present Covenant to achieve the full realization of this right shall include those necessary for:
   (a) The provision for the reduction of the stillbirth-rate and of infant mortality and for the healthy development of the child;
   (b) The improvement of all aspects of environmental and industrial hygiene;
   (c) The prevention, treatment and control of epidemic, endemic, occupational and other diseases;
   (d) The creation of conditions which would assure to all medical service and medical attention in the event of sickness.

The preamble to the FCTC recalls Article 12 of ICESCR. In addition, in its General Comment 14, the Committee on Economic, Cultural and Social Rights referred to "the failure to discourage production, marketing and consumption of tobacco" as a violation of the obligation to protect individuals within their jurisdiction from the infringement of their rights by third parties.[91] In addition, the preamble to the FCTC recalls the Convention on the Elimination of All Forms of Discrimination against Women (CEDAW)[92] and, in particular, the obligation on parties to take appropriate measures to eliminate discrimination against women in the field of health care. Similarly, the preamble to the FCTC recalls the Convention on the Rights of the Child (CRC)[93] and, in particular, the right of children to the highest attainable standard of health. A growing body of academic commentary[94] also highlights the existence of a number of specific human rights obligations relating to issues

[91] The Right to the Highest Attainable Standard of Health, General Comment 14, Committee on Economic, Social and Cultural Rights, Twenty-second session, E/C.12/2000/4, 11 August 2000, para. 51.

[92] Convention on the Elimination of All Forms of Discrimination Against Women, GA res. 34/180, 34 UN GAOR Supp. (No. 46) at 193, UN Doc. A/34/46; 1249 UNTS 13; 19 ILM 33 (1980).

[93] Convention on the Rights of the Child, GA res. 44/25, annex, 44 UN GAOR Supp. (No. 49) at 167, U.N. Doc. A/44/49 (1989); 1577 UNTS 3; 28 ILM 1456 (1989).

[94] See, for example, Jonathan Wike, "The Marlboro Man in Asia: U.S. Tobacco and Human Rights," 29 *Vanderbilt Journal of Transnational Law*, (1996), pp. 329–361; Lucien Dhooge, "Smoke Across the Waters: Tobacco Production and Exportation as International Human Rights Violations," 22 *Fordham International Law Journal*, (1998), pp. 355–456; Melissa Crow, "Smokescreens and State Responsibility: Using Human Rights Strategies to Promote Global Tobacco Control," 29 *Yale Journal of International Law*, (2004), pp. 209–250; Benjamin Mason Meier, "Breathing Life in the Framework Convention on Tobacco Control: Smoking Cessation and the Right to Health," 5 *Yale Journal of Health Policy, Law and Ethics*, (2005), pp. 137–192; Carolyn Dresler and Stephen Marks, "The Emerging Right to Tobacco Control," 28 *Human Rights Quarterly*, (2006), pp. 599–651 [hereinafter "The Emerging Right"].

such as the treatment of women[95] and children and the liability of transnational corporations for human rights violations in the tobacco context.[96]

Leaving aside the general duty incumbent upon governments that flows from the aforementioned rights, the necessity of government intervention at the domestic level lies in the public health, social, and economic harms caused by noncommunicable disease.

Developing countries bear the greatest share of the global burden of mortality, morbidity, and disability associated with noncommunicable disease.[97] This occurs in a context in which undernutrition can be a serious problem and where the dominant disease burden in many developing countries comes from infectious diseases such as HIV/AIDS and malaria. These and other infectious diseases also constitute cross-border threats to health and human security. Because the cross-border spread of such diseases turns partly on the strength of a state's health system, noncommunicable diseases must be viewed in the broader context of infectious diseases and in light of the concept of "global health," which suggests that the health of all states is linked.

The fact that noncommunicable diseases have a disproportionate impact on developing countries also means that established development goals are threatened. Good health is itself regarded as a goal of development. Millennium Development Goals concerning child health, maternal health, and HIV/AIDS attest to the importance of promoting health as a (noneconomic) development objective.

There are also economic justifications for government intervention. There is a positive correlation between good population health and economic growth. Good health can drive economic growth by reducing the costs associated with morbidity and mortality, ensuring the productivity of a workforce, encouraging investment, and ensuring that children learn more in school.[98] The reverse is also true: Economic growth can improve population health.

95 Robin Appleberry, "It's a Woman Thing: Sex, Status, and Human Rights in the Tobacco Epidemic," 15 *Berkeley Women's Law Journal*, (2000), pp. 312–326; Robin Appleberry, "Breaking the Camel's Back: Bringing Women's Human Rights to Bear on Tobacco Control," 13 *Yale Journal of Law and Feminism*, (2001), pp. 71–96.

96 For discussion of transnational corporations, see Dresler and Marks, "The Emerging Right," pp. 634–637.

97 Global Strategy Diet, para. 6.

98 See Dean Jamison, Joel Breman, Anthony Measham, et al., "Investing in Health," in Dean Jamison et al., *Disease Control Priorities in Developing Countries* (2nd ed), Oxford University Press, The World Bank, (2006), New York, pp. 3–34.

Intervention may also be justified as a means of correcting market failures. Market failures include the inadequacy of information available to consumers about the health risks posed, inadequate information about addiction (in the case of tobacco and alcohol), the inability of some children to make rational decisions in their own best interests, and the imposition of costs on other members of society. These costs include physical costs such as exposure to tobacco smoke and financial costs such as public expenditure on health care.[99] Costs associated with health care are also particularly problematic for the health systems of developing countries. The fiscal constraints faced by many developing countries mean that national health systems are often underfunded and, therefore, underequipped to address disease of any type. In 2005, average total spending per capita on health in low-income countries (as designated by the World Bank) was $19, with only $6 being from government sources. This compares to average per-capita spending in high-income countries of $3,835, with $2,346 of that amount being from government sources.[100]

2. THE APPROACH OF THIS STUDY

As discussed, trade processes may pose at least two risks to public health in the context noncommunicable diseases. First, trade processes may stimulate consumption of goods in a way that has negative consequences for public health. Second, trade agreements might restrict regulatory freedom to such a point that comprehensive and effective attempts to protect public health are not lawful.[101] The occurrence of so-called regulatory chill is also associated with the latter risk.

In light of these possible risks, this study examines whether the domestic regulatory autonomy available to WTO Members reflects an appropriate balance between the protection of public health and the interests underlying trade agreements. Before going further, it is worthwhile to explain what is meant by the concept of balance.

[99] In the tobacco context, see Prabat Jha, Philip Musgrove, Frank Chaloupka, et al., "The Economic Rationale for Intervention in the Tobacco Market," in Jha and Chaloupka (eds), *Tobacco Control in Developing Countries*, pp. 153–174.

[100] For further information see National Health Accounts http://www.who.int/nha/country/en/index.html (visited 24/04/09).

[101] See, for example, Carlos Correa, "Implementing National Public Health Policies in the Framework of WTO Agreements," 34(5) *Journal of World Trade*, (2000), pp. 89–121, [hereinafter "Correa, Implementing National Public Health Policies"], p. 89.

2.1. *Determinacy*

It is assumed that WTO law must be reasonably determinate in order for balance to exist. That is, health authorities must be in a position from which it is reasonably possible to determine the effect of their WTO obligations on measures to protect health. The basis of this assumption lies in the potential for regulatory chill to prevent health authorities from acting in the interests of public health. Although it is beyond the scope of this study to chart the extent to which regulatory chill exists, it is assumed for purposes of this study that such a chill may occur.

Examples from the tobacco-control context support this common sense assumption. One well-documented example is of a Philip Morris submission to the Canadian Standing Committee on Health, which considered the introduction of plain packaging in 1994.[102] The opinion, offered by former U.S. trade representative Carla Hills, argued that plain packaging would violate Canada's future obligations under the TRIPS agreement. Similarly, when Canada moved to ban the use of misleading descriptors, such as "light" and "mild," Philip Morris argued that such a ban would violate Canada's obligations under chapter 11 of the North American Free Trade Agreement (NAFTA) as well as the Agreement on Technical Barriers to Trade (TBT Agreement).

Although the relationship between the Philip Morris submissions and the decision not to implement plain packaging but rather to ban misleading descriptors is unknown, the tobacco lobby has traditionally been quite successful in its attempts to pervert or water down tobacco-control measures.[103] This success is so notorious that a provision was included in the FCTC to address it. Article 5.3 states that "[i]n setting and implementing their public health policies with respect to tobacco control, Parties shall act to protect these policies from commercial and other vested interests of the tobacco industry in accordance with national law." The second session of the Conference of the Parties to the FCTC recognized the continuing importance of this issue by adopting a detailed set of guidelines to Article 5.3.[104]

[102] Carla Hills, "Legal Opinion with Regard to Plain Packaging of Tobacco Products Requirement under International Agreements," 3 May 1994, presented to the Canadian Standing Committee on Health.

[103] For an example and references to some of the literature, see E.M. Sebrié, J. Barnoya, E.J. Pérez-Stable, et al., "Tobacco Industry Successfully Prevented Tobacco Control Legislation in Argentina," 14 *Tobacco Control*, (2005), e2.

[104] Guidelines for implementation of Article 5.3 of the WHO Framework Convention on Tobacco Control on the protection of public health policies with respect to tobacco control from commercial and other vested interests of the tobacco industry, WHO Framework Convention on Tobacco Control, Conference of the Parties to the Framework Convention on Tobacco Control, Third Session, Durban, South Africa, FCTC/COP/3/5, 21 August 2008.

If it is assumed that indeterminacy may contribute to regulatory chill, it is also reasonable to assume that this will have its greatest impact in states that have relatively weak capacity in the field of trade law. This appears most relevant in some developing countries.

2.2. *Balancing Trade and Health*

The theory of comparative advantage underpins the trade regime. This theory provides that two or more countries gain from international trade where they have divergent opportunity costs. Such gains come in the form of surpluses to either producers or consumers and may encourage increased production and consumption.[105]

The theory of comparative advantage is subject to a significant number of qualifications, including one that is particularly important in the present context. Jagdish Bhagwati's theory of immiserizing growth suggests that trade in goods with negative externalities may result in negative growth or economic losses.[106] For example, where a state imports tobacco products to be consumed in that state's territory, the negative externalities associated with harmful products may more than offset the consumer surpluses (price reductions) associated with trade in that good. For this reason, it has been suggested that the theory of comparative advantage has no application in the context of tobacco trade.[107] However, trade in tobacco products may still result in economic gains despite the fact that consumption of the traded product causes negative externalities. In theory, external costs can be offset by their internalization in the cost of goods through taxation. In such a circumstance there remains scope for economic gain from trade in goods associated with negative externalities, although this is dependent on the implementation and enforcement of tax measures.

Leaving the theory of immiserizing growth aside, the WTO Agreement has only a weak claim to being the embodiment of the theory of comparative advantage despite the fact that it underpins the regime. Although the WTO Agreement is a force for trade liberalization, the WTO-covered agreements have any number of features that suggest the trade regime is far from a pure implementation of the theory. For example, provisions governing most-favored-nation

[105] For a useful summary in a trade law context, see Raj Bhala, International Trade Law: Interdisciplinary Theory and Practice, 3rd edition, LexisNexis, 2008, pp. 201–216.

[106] See Jagdish Bhagwati and T.N. Srinivasan, *Lectures on International Trade, Cambridge Mass*, MIT Press, (1983), pp. 245–251.

[107] Bloom, "Public Health, International Trade," p. 6; see also Ira Shapiro, "Treating Cigarettes as an Exception to the Trade Rules," XXII no. 1 *SAIS Review* (Winter-Spring 2002), pp. 87–96, p. 89.

treatment are subject to exemptions such as for free trade agreements (FTAs) that result in the diversion of trade from its most efficient path.[108] Similarly, the GATT actually permits WTO Members to maintain tariffs at or below the bound levels set out in their respective schedules of commitments.

Given this qualified claim to the theory of comparative advantage, it is worthwhile to note the preamble to the WTO Agreement. The preamble recognizes that the WTO Agreement seeks to balance both economic and social goals. In particular, the first paragraph states:

> Recognizing that their relations in the field of trade and economic endeavour should be conducted with a view to raising standards of living, ensuring full employment and a large and steadily growing volume of real income and effective demand, and expanding the production of and trade in goods and services, while allowing for the optimal use of the world's resources in accordance with the objective of sustainable development, seeking both to protect and preserve the environment and to enhance the means for doing so in a manner consistent with their respective needs and concerns at different levels of economic development …

Equally, these overarching goals only provide general guidance on the purposes of the WTO Agreement. The more pressing issue in the context of this study concerns what purposes are pursued by rules governing nontariff barriers to trade such as the aforementioned regulatory approaches. In this respect, the third paragraph of the preamble states:

> Being desirous of contributing to these objectives by entering into reciprocal and mutually advantageous arrangements directed to the substantial reduction of tariffs and other barriers to trade and to the elimination of discriminatory treatment in international trade relations …

Invocation of the concepts of reciprocity and mutually advantageous arrangements reflect the fact that the focus of legal analysis under the WTO-covered agreements concerns whether members have complied with market-access commitments.[109] Provisions such as Articles III and XI of the GATT are intended to ensure that market-access commitments in the form of tariff commitments are not circumvented through nontariff barriers to trade.[110] Even provisions

[108] See Jagdish Bhagwati, *Termites in the Trading System: How Preferential Agreements Undermine Free Trade*, New York, Oxford University Press, (2008).

[109] Kyle Bagwell, Petros Mavroidis, and Robert Staiger, "It's a Question of Market Access," 96 *American Journal of International Law*, (2002), pp. 56–76.

[110] John Jackson, *World Trade and the Law of GATT*, Charlottesville, VA, The Michie Company, (1969), p. 277.

encouraging harmonization in the Agreement on the Application of Sanitary and Phytosanitary Measures (SPS Agreement) and the TBT Agreement are linked to concerns about market access, because these provisions seek to minimize the market-access implications of regulatory diversity. These provisions have also been linked to concepts of economic efficiency. However, the history of WTO dispute resolution suggests that disputes are motivated by a member's need to secure reliable and predictable market access for its domestic constituents. This is the central rationale for states to participate in trade agreements and the central concern that must be balanced with regulatory autonomy in determining the proper shape of the law.

Various means of balancing the market-access interests of exporters with the public health interests of importers have been identified, and reference to them can help define what balance means in this study.[111] In this study, balance does not require cost-benefit analysis. There are a number of problems with using full cost-benefit analysis as a mechanism to balance the interests of trade and health under WTO law. One controversy surrounds the question of how health is to be valued. Another difficulty lies in the fact that, for the most part, the WTO is not intended to be a system of positive integration. WTO law does not envisage a panel weighing potential health costs to one state against potential economic costs to another state in order to optimize overall welfare. For these and other reasons, WTO case law has rightfully adopted a more qualitative approach that revolves around the level of health protection chosen by a member.[112]

Other commentators have viewed reconciling different interests as a balancing act requiring a WTO panel to weed out measures that are excuses for protectionism.[113] For example, in the context of Article XX of the GATT, Aaditya Mattoo and Arvind Subramanian have described the issue in the following terms:

> The difficulty lies in distinguishing between two types of situations. In one situation, a non-protectionist government cannot prevent certain domestic policies from incidentally discriminating against foreign competitors; in the

[111] For discussion, see Joel Trachtman, "Trade and ... Problems: Cost-Benefit Analysis and Subsidiarity," 9 *European Journal of International Law*, (1998), pp. 32–85.

[112] Although for an early view contradicting this conclusion, see Alan Sykes, "The Least Restrictive Means," 70(1) *The University of Chicago Law Review*, (2003), pp. 403–419, where it is argued that least restrictive means analysis is a crude form of cost-benefit analysis.

[113] For this idea in a broader context, see Pascal Lamy, "The Emergence of Collective Preferences in International Trade: Implications in Regulating Globalisation," Conference on "Collective Preferences and Global Governance: What Future for the Multilateral Trading System," Brussels, 15 September 2004.

> other, a protectionist government uses a legitimate objective as an excuse to design domestic policies which inhibit foreign competition. The challenge is to devise rules which are sensitive to the difference between these two situations, exonerating the former while preventing the latter.[114]

Similarly, Pascal Lamy has argued that "trade restrictions imposed to implement non-trade considerations will be able to prevail over WTO market access obligations so long as they are not protectionist."[115] However, seeking to draw a distinction between health protection and health protectionism in this way is too narrow an approach. A range of factors are usually taken into account in health policy making. These include the effectiveness and benefits of a measure, its cost, and any potential disparate impacts on different population groups.[116] When governments implement measures there may also be any number of underlying motives, and the motives of one actor engaged in policy making may differ from those of another.[117] In this sense, a measure can have a protectionist effect while also playing a legitimate role in health protection.

It is also quite clear that the WTO-covered agreements seek to do more than merely distinguish between health protection and bad-faith health protectionism. For example, under Article XX (general exceptions) of the GATT, absence of bona fides only comes into formal consideration in evaluation of the manner in which a measure is applied under the *chapeau* of the provision. Similarly, it is clear that necessity requirements in the SPS and TBT Agreements are not focused solely on prohibiting health protectionism. Rather, the primary focus of the policy-balancing mechanisms found in the WTO-covered agreements is to determine the regulatory legitimacy of a measure by reference to how suited that measure is to achieving a recognized regulatory goal. This determination of regulatory legitimacy, coupled with an examination of the application of a measure, serves to distinguish lawful health measures from unlawful health measures.

This raises the question of whether the WTO is a proper forum to judge the legitimacy of a health measure at all. Although there is a rich body of literature concerning the legitimacy of WTO Dispute Settlement Body (DSB)

[114] Aaditya Mattoo and Arvind Subramanian, "Regulatory Autonomy and Multilateral Disciplines: The Dilemma and a Possible Resolution," 1 *Journal of International Economic Law*, (1998), pp. 303–322, p. 303.

[115] Pascal Lamy, "The Place of the WTO and its Law in the International Legal Order," 17(5) *European Journal of International Law*, (2006), pp. 969–984, p. 980.

[116] Lawrence Gostin, *Public Health Law: Power, Duty Restraint*, (2nd ed.) University of California Press Berkeley and Los Angeles, (2008), pp. 54–70.

[117] Tania Voon, *Cultural Products and the World Trade Organization*, Cambridge, Cambridge University Press, (2007), p. 61.

as an arbiter of environmental and health problems,[118] it seems likely that such issues will remain a constant part of WTO dispute settlement. The question that this raises concerns how the DSB should draw a line between the lawful and unlawful. In the context of provisions like Article XX(b) of the GATT, this task is achieved by examining the necessity of a measure. This involves both an examination of the suitability of the measure to protect health and whether the health goal in question could be achieved by less trade-restrictive means.

It is important to stress that this test defies wholesale redefinition[119] other than incrementally. There is nothing fundamentally wrong with the type of balancing exercise contemplated in the necessity test. Rather, the question is one of how it is applied in different circumstances and what implications this has for regulatory autonomy. The adequacy of policy space found in the relevant balancing tests turns ultimately on a case-by-case analysis of what is and is not permitted and how this may affect public health as a value in and of itself.

Equally, this is not to suggest that exceptions such as Article XX(b) of the GATT are the only sources through which the interests underlying the trade regime can be balanced with those underlying public health. On the contrary, a balanced relationship depends also on the interpretation of prohibitive and obligatory provisions. In addition, the question of balance may also be viewed through the lens of institutional choice. In this respect, the relationship between the trade regime and extraneous regimes (including the decision-making bodies of those regimes) is important.

A. Prohibitions and obligations

A balance between trade and health would require that the prohibitions and obligations of the covered agreements are not interpreted in an overly broad manner. This can only be judged on a case-by-case basis by identifying those measures that are not sufficiently protectionist to merit the strict scrutiny associated with a necessity exception and those that are. Similarly, where necessity serves as a positive obligation rather than an exception, the scrutiny (as under the SPS and TBT Agreements) should not be so strict so as to shift the focus from upholding market-access commitments to some form of positive integration between states that is premised on goals relating to pursuit of economic freedom.

118 Correa, "Implementing National Public Health Policies," p. 110.

119 See discussion in Robert Howse, "From Politics to Technocracy-and Back Again: The Fate of the Multilateral Trading Regime," 96(1) *American Journal of International Law*, (January, 2002), pp. 94–117, pp. 95 – 96.

B. The interaction of different international instruments and regimes

The focus of this study is domestic regulatory autonomy and not the interaction between different regimes under international law or the so-called fragmentation of international law.[120] Nonetheless, a balanced relationship between trade and health under WTO law should also be reflected in the relationship between different instruments under international law. A balanced relationship would maximize normative interaction between trade and health instruments. That is, a balanced relationship would maximize the extent to which the relevant instruments provide normative guidance to one another and should, therefore, maximize coherence.

The extent of normative interaction also makes a statement about how the relationship between trade and health is balanced. Although such a statement may only be symbolic, it has the potential to flow down into the establishment of policy priorities at the domestic level. Accordingly, the openness of WTO law to different health instruments is also relevant to regulatory chill.

The extent of normative interaction between treaties, such as the FCTC and the WTO Agreement, also affects the question of when conflicts may arise under the law of treaties. Conflicts are assumed to be undesirable for two reasons. First, the existence of a conflict between treaties signals that the two instruments cannot be reconciled. In the present context, this would suggest that mechanisms governing policy space, such as the necessity test in Article XX(b) of the GATT, have failed to deliver a balanced outcome.

Second, substantive legal conflicts are also associated with the potential for procedural disorder. One concern is that the proliferation of different courts and tribunals will lead to more than one court having jurisdiction over the same subject matter. This possibility may cause a number of problems, including differential treatment for like cases in different fora. As Jonathan Charney puts it: "[I]f like cases are not treated alike, the very essence of a normative system of law will be lost. Should this develop, the legitimacy of international law as a whole will be placed at risk."[121] As Charney argues, it is possible for the proliferation of different tribunals to undermine the coherence of

[120] On this issue, see generally Fragmentation of International Law: Difficulties Arising from the Diversification and Expansion of International Law, Report of the Study Group of the International Law Commission, Finalized by Martii Koskenniemi, International Law Commission, Fifty-eighth Session, Geneva, 1 May–9 June and 3 July–11 August 2006, A/CN.4/L.682, 13 April 2006 [hereinafter Koskenniemi, Fragmentation of International Law].

[121] Jonathan Charney, "The Impact of the International Legal System of the Growth of International Courts and Tribunals," 31 *New York Journal of International Law and Politics*, (1998–1999), pp. 697–708, p. 699.

international law as a whole.[122] This point is echoed by Gerhard Hafner, who has argued that the "disintegration of the legal order jeopardises the credibility, reliability, and, consequently, the authority of international law."[123] In this respect, Hafner points to the risk of forum shopping, whereby states would seek the forum that corresponds best to their interests. Hafner also points to the risk of "divergent solutions," where "a settlement reached by one organ will only resolve a dispute within that system and not necessarily for the purpose of another or the universal system."[124] Put another way, there is a "risk of contradiction or conflict of findings and interpretations undermining the substantive unity of the legal order and increasing rather than decreasing the indetermination of law through the exercise of the judicial function."[125]

The emergence of a conflict between treaties can also reflect competing views on questions of institutional choice and the proper allocation of authority. For example, WTO law might allocate authority to the DSB, whereas an extraneous treaty might seek to minimize the authority of the DSB by theorizing permissible health intervention in a more complete manner. In this sense, the delegation of authority, international legalization, and harmonization are all important to the balance between trade and health.

3. OUTLINE

Analysis of the issues is divided into seven chapters.

Chapter 2 examines normative integration at the international level between international health instruments and the WTO-covered agreements. More specifically, the different ways in which the FCTC, the global strategies, and the right to the highest attainable standard of health may be taken into account in WTO law are considered. This discussion forms a backdrop to the legal analysis in Chapters 3–5 and to discussion in Chapter 6 of how international health instruments might be shaped so as to maximize normative integration with WTO law.

Chapter 3 examines the extent to which prohibitions in the WTO-covered agreements limit regulatory autonomy. Public health measures are analyzed in the context of the most relevant WTO prohibitions. Among the measures

[122] Ibid., p. 707.

[123] Gerhard Hafner, "Pros and Cons Ensuing from Fragmentation of International Law," 25 Michigan Journal of International Law, (2004), pp. 849–863 [hereinafter Hafner, "Pros and Cons"], p. 856.

[124] Ibid., pp 857–858.

[125] Georges Abi-Saab, "Fragmentation or Unification: Some Concluding Remarks," 31 *New York Journal of International Law and Politics*, (1998–1999), pp. 919–933, p. 922.

discussed are taxation measures, subsidies, and restrictions on marketing. These measures are analyzed in the context of agreements such as the GATT, the GATS, the Agreement on Subsidies and Countervailing Measures (SCM) Agreement, and the Agreement on Agriculture.

Chapter 4 examines application of health exceptions such as GATT Article XX(b). WTO case law is examined in light of the concerns about regulatory autonomy expressed earlier. Particular focus is afforded to the requirement that measures be necessary to protect human health or life as well as to the strictness with which this requirement is interpreted. The suitability of this test in the context of multicausal medical conditions is also examined.

Chapter 5 examines regulatory autonomy under the SPS and TBT Agreements by reference to case studies concerning product-regulation measures, including labeling measures. Chapter 5 addresses the implications of necessity being a positive requirement under these agreements and potential differences to the concept of necessity under GATT Article XX(b). This chapter also addresses the difficulty associated with basing some dietary measures on risk assessments under Article 5 of the SPS Agreement, and the difficulty in maintaining consistent approaches to risk where risk is a function not only of the qualities of a product, but also of consumer behavior. Finally, the uncertain application of the TBT Agreement is examined.

Chapter 6 examines questions of delegation, legalization, and harmonization by reference to various proposals to rebalance the relationship between trade and health. The chapter considers the allocation of authority through delegation to judicial bodies, such as the DSB. The chapter considers the merits of further international legalization as a response to the trade regime. More specifically, the conclusion of treaties with respect to alcohol and diet is considered. Lastly, the chapter considers the merits of further harmonization as a means of balancing trade and health and filling out the open-textured character of WTO law.

Finally, Chapter 7 draws together the conclusions of this study.

4. LIMITATIONS

The scope of this study is limited in a number of ways. This study does not address every public health measure that might be used in the contexts of tobacco, alcohol, or diet. Rather, a handful of measures from each context are used to illustrate aspects of the relationship between these fields and WTO law. This approach is adopted because there is a need to place some reasonable limitations on the scope of the study. There are any number of different measures that a WTO Member might introduce in each of the contexts of tobacco, alcohol, and diet. These measures could also be implemented in any number of different ways, making it impossible to carry out a comprehensive legal analysis that anticipates all possible considerations. Consequently, taxes, restrictions on marketing, and product regulation including labeling measures are examined in a way that casts light both on domestic regulatory autonomy and on WTO law more broadly. These measures are chosen partly for their commonality and partly because they are central to the relevant international approaches, suggesting that there is likely to be significant domestic regulatory activity in these areas. It is hoped that this analysis might constitute one modest step in the direction of better understanding the issues.

Perhaps the most significant omission resulting from this approach is discussion of the implications of labeling measures for trademark rights under TRIPS. At the time of writing, Australia has announced its intention to require plain packaging of tobacco products, and questions have been raised about the consistency of this measure with TRIPS. This issue has not been discussed in this study for two reasons. First, attention has been focused on those provisions of WTO law thought most likely to affect a wide range of public health measures. Second, the issue has been addressed by the author in earlier work.[126]

This study also does not examine the use of tariffs for health-promotion purposes. Under Article II of the GATT, each WTO Member has undertaken to comply with the bound tariff rates found in its schedule of concessions. Although a member might distinguish between goods on the basis of the health consequences of consumption, there is no clear public health rationale for using a tariff as compared to a facially nondiscriminatory tax that is applied to both domestic and imported goods.[127] One possible exception to this is where there is no local production of the type of good in question and no prospect of it being produced locally. In such a circumstance, a tariff may have the same effect as nondiscriminatory taxation. This may occur, for example, in some small island states.

Some clarification of definitions is worthwhile in light of the narrow focus on taxes, product regulation, and marketing restrictions. The first clarification is that food can pose a variety of different threats to health, and food safety has

[126] Benn McGrady, "TRIPS and Trademarks: The Case of Tobacco," 3(1) *World Trade Review*, (2004), pp. 53–82 [hereinafter McGrady, "TRIPS and Trademarks"].

[127] David Fidler, "The Impact of International Trade and Investment Rules on the Ability of Governments to Implement Interventions to Address Obesity: A Case Study on the European Charter on Counteracting Obesity," in Hawkes et al., *Trade, Food, Diet and Health*, pp. 279–297, pp. 283–284.

been the subject of study in the context of WTO law.[128] This study is focused, however, on poor diet as a risk factor for noncommunicable disease, and not on other risks associated with traded food. The second clarification is that for purposes of this study, the phrase "tobacco control" does not contemplate an outright prohibition on the sale or consumption of tobacco. Although it may be true that WTO Members possess the regulatory freedom to impose such a prohibition, the approach set out in the FCTC reflects the fact that the benefits of prohibition are questionable. It should not be assumed that prohibition is an effective approach to the protection of public health. Rather, the ability of different states to enforce prohibition is likely to differ significantly depending on their circumstances.

The focus of this study is also on substantive law rather than institutional interaction or procedural law. Issues such as the role that public health experts might play in dispute settlement are not addressed in this study. Although institutional arrangements and procedural rules may have a significant bearing on regulatory autonomy, this is not specific to the context of tobacco, alcohol, or diet.[129]

Another implication of the focus on substantive law is that the study does not include any original empirical data or analysis. This study draws on existing empirical studies without offering critical analysis of the conclusions contained therein. Another implication is that the purpose of the study is not to make policy prescriptions at the national level. For example, this study does not address the merits of structuring tariffs and subsidies to achieve particular outcomes. Rather, the purpose is to examine the adequacy of domestic regulatory autonomy under the international legal framework that is in place. This also means that this study does not make policy prescriptions at the international level. For example, this study does not argue that the Doha Round negotiations concerning agriculture should be tailored to addressing concerns relating to obesity and poor diet.[130]

The focus of this study is the application of WTO law to measures implemented by WTO Members, and not specifically the interaction of WTO law with international instruments in the field of public health. The primary reason

[128] See, for example, Alberto, Alemanno, *Trade in Food: Regulatory and Judicial Approaches in the EC and WTO*, London, Cameron May, (2007).

[129] For a recent study addressing procedural issues, see Jonathan Liberman and Andrew Mitchell, "In Search of Coherence Between Trade and Health: Inter-Institutional Opportunities," 25 *Maryland Journal of International Law*, (2010), pp. 143–186.

[130] For this suggestion see Brent Pickett, "From Rhetoric of Nostalgia to Health-Based Policy: Tobacco, Obesity and the WTO," 19(1) *Cambridge Review of International Affairs*, (2006), pp. 139–154, p. 141.

for this approach is that states often go well beyond the minimum requirements of these international instruments. One reason for this is that instruments such as the FCTC and the global strategies are negotiated international instruments and do not always go so far as to reflect best practice in the field of public health. The FCTC has a high degree of flexibility and generality, with much being left to the discretion of domestic authorities, and the global strategies are nonbinding instruments. Thus, instruments such as the FCTC and the global strategies are cited because they are indicative of the types of strategies states are taking or may take, and because interaction between these instruments and WTO law affects domestic regulatory autonomy. However, these instruments are not themselves the central focus of this study.

Another implication of the focus on WTO law is that regulatory autonomy under other trade agreements is not the concern of this study. Although the proliferation of free trade agreements (FTAs) and regional agreements may have important implications for regulatory autonomy, it is not feasible for this book to cover the breadth of materials associated with such agreements. The WTO Agreement is the focus of this study because it is central to the trade regime. Many of the conclusions drawn with respect to WTO law will also be applicable in the context of other trade agreements.

2

Normative Integration: Using Health Instruments in Interpretation of the WTO-Covered Agreements

Normative integration refers to a process whereby disparate norms, such as health norms and trade norms, are integrated or merged through judicial interpretation.[1] In the context of the law of treaties, the process arguably finds its roots in the presumption against conflict. The presumption against conflict provides that treaties shall be read alongside one another unless a subsequent treaty evinces a different legislative intention to a previous treaty.[2] In accordance with this presumption, a treaty interpreter should consider whether two treaties can be read together before considering whether one treaty should be limited in its application as a result of conflict.

The extent to which health norms are integrated into WTO law in the context of dispute settlement is a natural starting point for analysis of how WTO law applies to the new public health. Examination of the issue is a precursor to examining application of the covered agreements. The extent to which WTO law integrates international health norms is also of importance to the question of how international health instruments should be shaped so as to best interact with WTO law. For example, Tomer Broude has argued that the integration of norms in international law tends to lead to the integration of international authority, and that as a consequence, softer or less binding means of integration are less threatening influences on the allocation of authority.[3] In accordance with this argument, nonbinding instruments may enhance the integration of health norms into WTO law to a greater degree than binding

1 See generally, Tomer Broude, "Principles of Normative Integration and the Allocation of International Authority: The WTO, the Vienna Convention on the Law of Treaties, and the Rio Declaration," Hebrew University of Jerusalem, Faculty of Law, Research Paper No. 07–08, August 2008.

2 Wilfred Jenks, "Conflict of Law-Making Treaties," 30 *British Year Book of International Law*, (1953), pp. 401–453 [hereinafter "Jenks, Conflict of Law-Making Treaties"], pp. 427–428.

3 See generally Broude, "Principles of Normative Integration."

norms. The ways in which nonbinding and binding norms are integrated into WTO law therefore affects the analysis in Chapter 6, where arguments for new health treaties are examined.

The extent of normative integration could also give an indication of regulatory autonomy under the covered agreements, because international health norms are an expression of what WTO Members are doing at the domestic level. The extent to which extraneous norms are integrated into WTO law also reflects how open WTO law is to nontrade interests. In this sense, the extent to which health norms are integrated into WTO law can be viewed as an expression of the relationship between public health and trade and as a lens through which the question of whether that relationship is balanced can be analyzed. As Pascal Lamy has noted, "[t]he effectiveness and legitimacy of the WTO depend on how it relates to norms of other legal systems."[4]

This chapter examines how relevant international health norms might be integrated into WTO law through judicial interpretation of the WTO-covered agreements. Part 1 of this chapter gives a brief outline of the relevant health instruments and their potential role in WTO law. Part 2 examines the different methods by which the instruments might be used in WTO dispute settlement. International health instruments might be used as evidence of facts, in interpretation of norms, as international standards, or by virtue of Article 31(3)(c) of the Vienna Convention on the Law of Treaties (Vienna Convention).[5]

The general question of how WTO law relates to other aspects of international law is an issue that has been addressed in significant detail elsewhere and need not be revisited here.[6] Equally, it is necessary to examine normative integration in the distinct contexts of tobacco, alcohol, and diet. This analysis guides examination of the question of how international health instruments might be shaped so as to maximize normative integration with WTO law. This issue is discussed in further detail in Chapter 6.

1. OVERVIEW OF RELEVANT HEALTH INSTRUMENTS

There are a number of international instruments relevant to public health, and their legal status and content differ. In Chapter 1, the right to the highest

4 Pascal Lamy, "The Place of the WTO and its Law in the International Legal Order," 17(5) *European Journal of International Law*, (2007), pp. 969–984, p. 977.

5 Vienna Convention on the Law of Treaties, May 23, 1969, 1155 U.N.T.S. 331; 8 I.L.M. 679 (1969).

6 For an excellent study, see generally Joost Pauwelyn, *Conflict of Norms in Public International Law: How WTO Law Relates to Other Rules of International Law*, New York, Cambridge University Press, (2003) [hereinafter Pauwelyn, *Conflict of Norms*].

attainable standard of health was outlined. This right has a basis in treaties, such as ICESCR and the constitution of the WHO. Some might also argue that the right has a basis in customary international law.[7] However, the right to the highest attainable standard of health is very general in character. Article 12 of ICESCR, which is the most specific elaboration of the right to health, prescribes only a few specific steps that a state must take. Accordingly, Article 12 must be read in light of Article 2(1), which provides that each party "undertakes to take steps, individually and through international assistance and co-operation, especially economic and technical, to the maximum of its available resources, with a view to achieving progressively the full realization of the rights recognized in the present Covenant by all appropriate means, including particularly the adoption of legislative measures."

The generality of the right is partly attributable to the fact that, with the few exceptions listed in Article 12 of ICESCR, the right is progressively realizable. This concept envisions that states work to achieve the highest standard of health over time. Consequently, there is great difficulty in identifying specific acts or omissions that constitute violations of the right in question. It is perhaps for this reason that WTO Members do not often seek recourse to the right in defending health measures during dispute settlement. More particularly, the uncertain content of the right makes it difficult to see how it could be integrated into WTO law in a meaningful way. Accordingly, the right is likely to serve only as a general backdrop to public health measures.

In contrast, the FCTC is a binding treaty with a higher degree of specificity. The FCTC obliges parties to implement a range of regulatory measures, including tax or price measures (Article 6), packaging and labeling measures (Article 11), and restrictions on advertising promotion and sponsorship (Article 13). Equally, the terms of the FCTC reflect the fact that it is a framework convention in the sense that the obligations are quite general in their character. The basic obligations set out in a number of provisions have been supplemented by guidelines that are an expression of best practice.[8] Although these guidelines are not binding instruments in themselves, in some cases they may have the status of a subsequent agreement between the parties under Article 31(3)(a) of the Vienna Convention on the Law of Treaties. Assuming this to be the case, these guidelines arguably fill out the content of basic FCTC

7 See Restatement (Third) of the Foreign Relations Law of the United States, St Paul Minnesota, 1987, §702.

8 WHO Framework Convention on Tobacco Control, Guidelines for Implementation: Article 5.3, Article 8, Article 11, Article 13, World Health Organization, Geneva 2009.

obligations and would be relevant in interpretation of WTO law in much the same way as the provisions of the FCTC itself.

The Global Strategy Diet is also more specific than the right to the highest attainable standard of health; it directs a number of recommendations at member states of the WHO. The Global Strategy Diet recommends that states: devise national strategies, policies, and action plans on diet and physical activity; ensure that consumers have access to balanced information that enables them easily to make healthy choices; ensure that sponsorship, promotion, and advertising directed at children are appropriate; and ensure that national food and agricultural policies are consistent with the protection and promotion of public health. Unlike the FCTC, however, the Global Strategy Diet is not intended to be a legally binding instrument, and therefore does not have the status of a treaty under international law.

Similarly, the Global Strategy Alcohol is not a treaty under international law. The instrument merely recommends the use of different measures to address the harmful use of alcohol. These measures include price and tax measures to suppress demand, the use of labeling measures to convey information to consumers, and the use of restrictions on marketing.

Notwithstanding the fact that treaties addressing alcohol and diet do not exist under international law, both global strategies were adopted by resolution of the WHA. The WHA has also adopted numerous other resolutions over the years on the same subject matter.[9] Some commentators would refer to these instruments as "soft-law" because they are nonbinding.[10]

In terms of normative integration, the status of different instruments affects the ways in which they may be used in interpretation of the WTO-covered agreements. Three categories of norms must be considered. The first is the right to the highest attainable standard of health, which, although a treaty right, is difficult to define, particularly in a context of noncommunicable diseases. This lack of definition makes integration of the norm into other treaty regimes difficult. The second category of norm is that of an obligation to regulate, a treaty obligation found in the FCTC. The third category is a nonbinding expression of best practice, found in resolutions such as those passed by the WHA. This final category may also include aspects of FCTC guidelines that do not go to interpretation of an FCTC provision and cannot, therefore, be considered a subsequent agreement of FCTC parties.

9 See, for example, Fifty-Seventh World Health Assembly, Health Promotion and Healthy Lifestyles, WHA 57.16; Fifty-Eight World Health Assembly, Public Health Problems Caused by Harmful Use of Alcohol, WHA 58.26.

10 For a discussion of hard and soft law, see Kal Raustiala, "Form and Substance in International Agreements," 99 *American Journal of International Law*, (2005), pp. 581–614.

2. USING HEALTH NORMS IN INTERPRETATION OF THE WTO-COVERED AGREEMENTS

Joost Pauwelyn identifies at least four methods of normative integration that may be relevant in the present context. Each of the methods has a distinct basis, and this affects the way in which an extraneous instrument may be used as well as which types of instruments may be used. In the case of the first two methods, there is no distinction between treaties and other instruments.

2.1. *The Use of Extraneous Rules and Resolutions as Evidence of Facts*

Extraneous treaty rules and nonbinding resolutions have been used in treaty interpretation as evidence in respect of questions of fact.[11] A nonbinding instrument, such as a global strategy, may include statements of fact, as are often found in the preamble to such instruments. Similarly, an extraneous legal rule found in a treaty may constitute proof or evidence in support of an argument relating to the violation of a treaty (as distinct from the use of an extraneous rule in determining the general content or scope of a norm).[12] Although use of a treaty in this manner is not restricted by the fact that some WTO Members are not parties to the treaty, it seems more likely that significant weight may be attached to an extraneous treaty as evidence of a fact where it has a high number of parties.[13]

Instruments such as the FCTC and the global strategies could be used as evidence of facts in a number of different ways under a necessity test such as that in Article XX(b) of the GATT. Article XX(b) states:

> Subject to the requirement that such measures are not applied in a manner which would constitute a means of arbitrary or unjustifiable discrimination between countries where the same conditions prevail, or a disguised restriction on international trade, nothing in this Agreement shall be construed to prevent the adoption or enforcement by any contracting party of measures:
>
> (b) necessary to protect human, animal or plant life or health

The FCTC and the global strategies might provide evidence of the existence of a risk to health, evidence of the regulatory goal underlying a measure,

[11] Although this method is like the second method in that it is carried out without recourse to an enabling provision, it is treated differently here because it can be utilized in different circumstances to the second method discussed later.

[12] Pauwelyn, *Conflict of Norms*, p. 463.

[13] Ibid.

evidence of the contribution of the measure to achievement of a given regulatory goal, or evidence of the importance of the goal. The case for attaching evidentiary weight to these instruments might also be bolstered by preparatory documents that set out the evidence base for the interventions in question.

By way of illustration, the inclusion of a measure within the FCTC or either global strategy may be sufficient to suggest that the measure is one for the protection of health under Article XX(b) of the GATT. Similarly, in determining the regulatory goal held by a member, a panel will consider objective factors such as texts of statutes, legislative history, and the pronouncements of government agencies and officials.[14] Instruments such as the FCTC or the global strategies may also be taken into account in this way.

Some provisions of the FCTC also recognize the contribution that a specific measure can make to the protection of health. For example, Article 13.1 states that "[p]arties recognize that a comprehensive ban on advertising, promotion and sponsorship would reduce the consumption of tobacco products." Similarly, in Article 6.1 the parties recognize that "price and tax measures are an effective and important means of reducing tobacco consumption by various segments of the population, in particular young persons."

2.2. *The Use of Extraneous Instruments without Recourse to an Enabling Rule*

The use of an extraneous instrument as evidence of a fact falls within the overarching category of instruments used without recourse to any rule of interpretation enabling their use. On at least two occasions the Appellate Body has used extraneous treaties in the interpretation of WTO-covered agreements in this fashion. In *US – Shrimp* the Appellate Body relied on the United Nations Convention on the Law of the Sea (UNCLOS)[15] and the Convention on Biological Diversity[16] in determining whether the Article XX(g) phrase "exhaustible natural resources" applies to living things.[17] Similarly, in *US – FSC (Article 21.5 – EC)* the Appellate Body interpreted the phrase "foreign

[14] Appellate Body Report, *United States – Measures Affecting the Cross-Border Supply of Gambling and Betting Services*, WT/DS285/AB/R, adopted 20 April 2005, para. 304.

[15] Done at Montego Bay, 10 December 1982, UN Doc. A/CONF.62/122; 21 ILM 1261.

[16] Done at Rio de Janeiro, 5 June 1992, UNEP/Bio.Div./N7-INC5/4; 31 ILM 818.

[17] Appellate Body Report, *United States – Import Prohibition of Certain Shrimp and Shrimp Products*, WT/DS58/AB/R, adopted 6 November 1998, DSR 1998:VII, 2755 [hereinafter *US – Shrimp*], para. 130.

source income" by reference to the use of the phrase in a number of regional and bilateral agreements.[18]

The basis for the use of extraneous rules in this fashion is open to question. The panel in *EC – Approval and Marketing of Biotech Products* considered that the Appellate Body in *US – Shrimp* "drew on other rules of international law because it considered that they were informative and aided it in establishing the meaning and scope of the term 'exhaustible natural resources.'"[19] In characterizing the use of extraneous treaties in this manner the panel also stated:

> We think that, in addition to dictionaries, other relevant rules of international law may in some cases aid a treaty interpreter in establishing, or confirming, the ordinary meaning of treaty terms in the specific context in which they are used. [footnote omitted] Such rules would not be considered because they are legal rules, but rather because they may provide evidence of the ordinary meaning of terms in the same way that dictionaries do.[20] [footnote omitted]

Because the "ordinary meaning" of a term should be apparent without reference to extraneous materials, the panel's conclusion is open to question. Pauwelyn has argued that the references can be justified on the basis that it is the common intentions of the parties that a treaty interpreter must seek to identify, and that the approach in *US – Shrimp* reflected the "common intentions" of the parties to the WTO Agreement.[21] Put differently, the agreement of the parties to the treaty under interpretation can be established through use of an extraneous treaty.

One notable feature of *US – Shrimp* is that extraneous treaties were drawn on without reference to their membership. The Appellate Body was not concerned with the fact that neither all WTO Members nor all parties to the dispute were also parties to the extraneous treaties. Although it may appear from this that extraneous treaties are tools that are readily available in treaty interpretation, this is not necessarily the case. There are a number of limitations on the use of extraneous treaties. The most obvious of these limitations is that

[18] Appellate Body Report, *United States – Tax Treatment for "Foreign Sales Corporations" –* Recourse to Article 21.5 of the DSU by the European Communities, WT/DS108/AB/RW, adopted 29 January 2002, DSR 2002:I, 55, paras 141–145.

[19] Panel Report, EC – *Measures Affecting the Approval and Marketing of Biotech Products,* (7 February 2006), WT/DS291–293, [hereinafter EC – *Approval and Marketing of Biotech Products*], para. 7.94.

[20] Panel Report, EC – *Approval and Marketing of Biotech Products*, para. 7.92.

[21] See Pauwelyn, *Conflict of Norms*, pp. 257– 260.

use of extraneous treaties in this manner depends on the need for extraneous materials in discerning the meaning of the terms of a treaty.

The dominant view is also that extraneous treaties cannot themselves be applied by WTO panels, meaning that the covered agreements constitute the applicable law for purposes of a dispute. The view finds support in Article 3.2 of the DSU, where it is stated that the "[r]ecommendations and rulings of the DSB cannot add to or diminish the rights and obligations provided in the covered agreements." Although Pauwelyn has argued otherwise, no panel has used an extraneous treaty as the applicable law of a dispute, and it seems unlikely that this approach would be adopted. Most recently, in *Mexico – Soft Drinks* the Appellate Body expressed the view that WTO panels and the Appellate Body should not become adjudicators of non-WTO disputes.[22] Although this statement was made in the context of a questionable assumption that Mexico's submission would require the Appellate Body to assess whether the NAFTA had been violated,[23] the Appellate Body's views on applicable law seem clear.

With this in mind, there arises a question as to how instruments like the FCTC could be used in norm interpretation within the context of the covered agreements. In *Dominican Republic – Import and Sale of Cigarettes* the panel was confronted with just this issue in examining whether a tax-stamp measure was necessary to secure compliance with tax laws and regulations. Although the FCTC was yet to come into force, the panel considered the treaty in assessing the usefulness of tax stamps as a means of preventing tax evasion. The panel then acknowledged the general usefulness of tax stamps before considering the necessity of the specific measure in place.[24]

This suggests that treaties such as the FCTC might be used in interpretation of exceptions, such as that found in Article XX(b) of the GATT. Whether this approach accords with the meaning of Article XX persists. Given that some WTO Members are not FCTC parties and that the FCTC was concluded after the WTO Agreement, the appropriateness of using the FCTC in this manner is an issue that a panel would have to examine. How this issue would be decided remains to be seen. This question notwithstanding, it is argued later in this chapter that not all WTO Members need to be FCTC parties in order for the FCTC to be taken into account in applying a WTO-covered agreement. It is also argued later in this chapter that the evolving

22 Appellate Body Report, *Mexico – Tax Measures on Soft Drinks and Other Beverages*, WT/DS308/AB/R, adopted 24 March 2006, para. 78.

23 On this assumption, see William Davey and André Sapir, "The Soft Drinks Case: The WTO and Regional Agreements," 8(1) *World Trade Review*, (2009), pp. 5–23, pp. 17–18.

24 Panel Report, *Dominican Republic – Measures Affecting the Importation and Internal Sale of Cigarettes*, WT/DS302/R, adopted 19 May 2005, paras 7.216–7.217.

nature of necessity as a concept requires an evolutionary interpretation of Article XX(b), and that the fact that the FCTC was concluded after the WTO Agreement is not important.

2.3. *The Use of Standards under the SPS and TBT Agreements*

The Agreement on the Application of Sanitary and Phytosanitary Measures (SPS Agreement) and the Agreement on Technical Barriers to Trade (TBT Agreement) each embed the use of external international standards in determining compliance with WTO law. Each agreement obliges WTO Members to base measures on international standards (international standards, guidelines, or recommendations in the case of the SPS Agreement) unless a limited range of circumstances applies. Each agreement also creates a presumption of compliance. In the case of the SPS Agreement, Article 2.4 creates a presumption that SPS measures conforming to international standards, guidelines, or recommendations are consistent with the relevant parts of the SPS Agreement and also with the GATT. These measures are also deemed necessary to protect human health. Similarly, Article 2.5 of the TBT Agreement provides that "[w]henever a technical regulation is prepared, adopted or applied for one of the legitimate objectives explicitly mentioned in paragraph 2, and is in accordance with relevant international standards, it shall be rebuttably presumed not to create an unnecessary obstacle to international trade."

These presumptions suggest that international health instruments could play a significant role in the interpretation of the SPS and TBT Agreements. The scope and application of these agreements is discussed in further detail in Chapter 5. For present purposes, it is sufficient to note that there are a number of limitations on the potential use of instruments such as the FCTC and the global strategies in the way described.

First, each of the SPS and TBT Agreements has a limited scope and is unlikely to apply to the full range of measures that a WTO Member might use in addressing tobacco, alcohol, and diet. In Chapter 5 it is argued that the SPS Agreement is likely to apply to product regulation measures, including labeling measures, in the contexts of food and alcohol, but not tobacco. The TBT Agreement is likely to apply to tobacco-control measures of this type, as well as to some alcohol-control measures. However, neither agreement is likely to apply to other measures, such as tax measures or restrictions on advertising. Accordingly, the limited scope of the SPS and TBT Agreements is a notable limitation on the incorporation of international standards into the decision making of a panel under WTO law.

Secondly, both the SPS and TBT Agreements limit the types of instruments that might be used in this way. Paragraph 3 of Annex A of the SPS Agreement defines "international standards, guidelines and recommendations" in the following terms:

(a) for food safety, the standards, guidelines and recommendations established by the Codex Alimentarius Commission relating to food additives, veterinary drug and pesticide residues, contaminants, methods of analysis and sampling, and codes and guidelines of hygienic practice;
(b) for animal health and zoonoses, the standards, guidelines and recommendations developed under the auspices of the International Office of Epizootics;
(c) for plant health, the international standards, guidelines and recommendations developed under the auspices of the Secretariat of the International Plant Protection Convention in cooperation with regional organizations operating within the framework of the International Plant Protection Convention; and
(d) for matters not covered by the above organizations, appropriate standards, guidelines and recommendations promulgated by other relevant international organizations open for membership to all Members, as identified by the Committee.

In the context of the TBT Agreement, Annex 1 defines the term standard as a:

> Document approved by a recognised body, that provides, for common and repeated use, rules, guidelines or characteristics for products or related processes and production methods, with which compliance is not mandatory. It may also include or deal exclusively with terminology, symbols, packaging, marking or labelling requirements as they apply to a product, process or production method.

Each of these definitions is a significant limitation on the role that instruments such as the FCTC and the global strategies might play. As is discussed in further detail in Chapter 6, only those standards approved by the Codex Alimentarius Commission are relevant (for purposes of this study) under the SPS Agreement. Whereas the TBT Agreement establishes a more open definition of what may constitute a standard, where compliance with a document is mandatory, as is the case for states parties to the FCTC, it will not qualify. In effect, this means that nonbinding private standards might be of presumptive value under the TBT Agreement, whereas binding public standards, such as those set out in the FCTC, would not carry this weight. Although the definition of the term "standard" may grant presumptive force to nonbinding FCTC guidelines, it is problematic that private standards might play a greater role than a mandatory treaty commitment.

In the SPS context, the Codex Alimentarius Commission was established jointly by the WHO and the Food and Agriculture Organization of the United Nations (FAO). This suggests that the policy goals underlying the Global Strategy Diet may be translated into standards, guidelines, or recommendations for purposes of the SPS Agreement. In fact, the Global Strategy Diet contemplates the use of Codex standards:

> Public health efforts may be strengthened by the use of international norms and standards, particularly those drawn up by the Codex Alimentarius Commission. [footnote omitted] Areas for further development could include: labelling to allow consumers to be better informed about the benefits and content of foods; measures to minimize the impact of marketing on unhealthy dietary patterns; fuller information about healthy consumption patterns, including steps to increase the consumption of fruit and vegetables; and production and processing standards regarding the nutritional quality and safety of products. Involvement of governments and nongovernmental organizations as provided for in the Codex should be encouraged.[25]

This passage suggests that the Codex Alimentarius Commission provides an avenue for the assertion of public health goals in the interpretation of the SPS Agreement. However, the final sentence of this passage reflects some of the persistent criticisms of the commission. These criticisms include that Codex is a forum dominated by a handful of developed countries and associated corporate interests, in which civil society and some developing countries find participation difficult.[26] These criticisms call the legitimacy of Codex standards into question and suggest that the use of international standards, guidelines, or recommendations in interpretation of the WTO-covered agreements may sometimes undermine regulatory autonomy.

On the one hand, standards, guidelines, and recommendations may reinforce and assert public health goals by virtue of the presumptions present in the SPS and TBT Agreements. On the other hand, the purpose underlying provisions addressing international standards in the TBT Agreement and standards, guidelines, or recommendations under the SPS Agreement is

[25] Global Strategy Diet, para. 59.

[26] See generally Steven Bernstein and Erin Hannah, "Non-State Global Standard Setting and the WTO: Legitimacy and the Need for Regulatory Space," 11(3) *Journal of International Economic Law*, (2008), pp. 575–608.

regulatory harmonization. The presumptions of lawfulness sit alongside more fundamental obligations that require members to base SPS measures and technical regulations on relevant international standards. Thus, the use of an instrument in interpretation of the WTO-covered agreements cannot always be associated with increased regulatory autonomy. On the contrary, the adoption of standards, guidelines, or recommendations that are overly rigid or that fall below best practice may be viewed as constraining regulatory autonomy if WTO Members have to justify departure from those instruments.

Accordingly, the potential for standardization to ensure a balanced relationship between trade and health under international law depends largely on the substance of the instruments concerned. Existing standards are, therefore, discussed in further detail in Chapter 5 as part of a discussion concerning application of the SPS and TBT Agreements to various measures. The potential use of standardization as a tool for law reform is then discussed in Chapter 6.

2.4. *Treaty Rules and Article 31(3)(c) of the Vienna Convention on the Law of Treaties*[27]

Article 31(3)(c) of the Vienna Convention on the Law of Treaties (Vienna Convention) provides that in treaty interpretation "[t]here shall be taken into account, together with the context … any relevant rules of international law applicable in the relations between the parties." When the International Law Commission (ILC) reported the conclusions of a study group addressing the fragmentation of international law,[28] this provision was a prominent aspect of discussion. Martii Koskenniemi, in his role as chairman of the study group, concluded that the provision gives expression to a principle of "systemic integration"[29] that is an important mechanism in ensuring that the outcome of individual disputes are resolved in light of the broader international legal environment.[30]

27 Reproduced with permission of Kluwer Law International from Benn McGrady, "Fragmentation of International Law or Systemic Integration of Treaty Regimes: EC – Biotech Products and the Proper Interpretation of Article 31(3)(c) of the Vienna Convention on the Law of Treaties," 42(4) *Journal of World Trade*, (2008), pp. 589–618

28 See *Fragmentation of International Law: Difficulties Arising from the Diversification and Expansion of International Law*, Report of the Study Group of the International Law Commission, Finalized by Martii Koskenniemi, International Law Commission, Fifty-eighth Session, Geneva, 1 May–9 June and 3 July–11 August 2006, A/CN.4/L.682, 13 April 2006 [hereinafter Koskenniemi, *Fragmentation of International Law*].

29 In respect of this phrase see Campbell McLachlan, "The Principle of Systemic Integration and Article 31(3)(c) of the Vienna Convention," 54 *International & Comparative Law Quarterly*, (2005), pp. 279–319 [hereinafter McLachlan, "The Principle of Systemic Integration"].

30 Koskenniemi, *Fragmentation of International Law*, pp. 243–244, paras 479–80.

Koskenniemi also concluded that a discussion of the actual and potential uses of Article 31(3)(c) "would constitute a useful contribution to the study of the alleged fragmentation (or diversification) of international law."[31]

Article 31(3)(c) is of importance because its terms suggest the presence of a legal compulsion on WTO panels to take account of health norms set out in treaties. The importance of this compulsion, and the importance of giving the terms of Article 31(3)(c) a broad interpretation, cannot be overstated. Given that mandatory FCTC obligations may not constitute standards for purposes of the TBT Agreement, FCTC rules must be considered in interpretation of the TBT Agreement through other means. If this were not the case, a panel would have to give presumptive value to private-industry-led standards under the TBT Agreement without being subject to any compulsion to take account of public rules negotiated between states. This would be an extraordinary allocation of authority to private industry in a context where compulsory dispute settlement may bind the conduct of states. It will be argued in Chapters 5 and 6 that such an outcome is not sustainable. More specifically, it will be argued that the presumption against conflict in the law of treaties means that treaties extraneous to the WTO can have presumptive effect in WTO law. It will be argued that where a measure is implemented pursuant to an international treaty, that measure should be presumed to be compliant with the WTO-covered agreements. In the case of the TBT Agreement, this would at least give international treaties similar status to that held by private-industry-led standards. By the same token, the presumption against conflict is not likely to be applied in this way unless Article 31(3)(c) is also applied in a broad manner.[32]

This central question of how Article 31(3)(c) should be interpreted can be examined by reference to the question of whether the phrase "applicable in relations between the parties" means that Article 31(3)(c) is only triggered when all parties to a treaty under interpretation are also parties to the extraneous treaty in question. The WTO panel in *EC – Approval and Marketing of Biotech Products* took this view of the provision, notwithstanding the potential of this restrictive view to isolate WTO law from the broader body of international law.

There are strong arguments to suggest that the view adopted by the panel in *EC – Approval and Marketing of Biotech Products* is not the correct interpretation of Article 31(3)(c). The wording of the Vienna Convention does not support

[31] Ibid., p. 213, para. 423.

[32] The same might also be said for the UDHR if it does constitute a rule of customary international law. However, as noted earlier, the generality of the right makes it difficult to see how this right may be used in a meaningful way in interpretation of the covered agreements.

the panel's conclusion, and the potential consequences of the panel's view are such that it is untenable. On closer examination of the meaning of Article 31(3)(c) in the broader context of the Vienna Convention, it appears that the restrictive view of the provision is the only untenable view of the provision.

A. The Article 31(3)(C) debate

In its entirety Article 31 of the Vienna Convention states:

> Article 31
> General rule of interpretation
>
> 1. A treaty shall be interpreted in good faith in accordance with the ordinary meaning to be given to the terms of the treaty in their context and in the light of its object and purpose.
> 2. The context for the purpose of the interpretation of a treaty shall comprise, in addition to the text, including its preamble and annexes:
>   (a) any agreement relating to the treaty which was made between all the parties in connection with the conclusion of the treaty;
>   (b) any instrument which was made by one or more parties in connection with the conclusion of the treaty and accepted by the other parties as an instrument related to the treaty.
> 3. There shall be taken into account, together with the context:
>   (a) any subsequent agreement between the parties regarding the interpretation of the treaty or the application of its provisions;
>   (b) any subsequent practice in the application of the treaty which establishes the agreement of the parties regarding its interpretation;
>   (c) any relevant rules of international law applicable in the relations between the parties.
> 4. A special meaning shall be given to a term if it is established that the parties so intended.

As is evident from its wording, Article 31(3)(c) has three elements. The first element concerns whether the extraneous treaty or its content constitutes a "rule of international law." For purposes of discussion it is assumed that this requirement will generally be fulfilled in the context of treaty law. That treaties may constitute or include "rules of international law" for the specific purposes of Article 31(3)(c) finds support in case law external to the WTO,[33] in Ian Sinclair's commentary on the Vienna Convention,[34] and

33 See, for example, Dispute Concerning Access to Information Under Article 9 of the OSPAR Convention, Final Award (*Ireland v. the United Kingdom*) (2 July 2003) Permanent Court of Arbitration, 42 I.L.M. (2003), 1138, paras 101–105.

34 Ian Sinclair, *The Vienna Convention on the Law of Treaties*, Manchester, Manchester University Press, 2nd edn, 1984, p. 119 (citing official records of the Vienna Conference).

in the inclusion of conventions (treaties) as a source of law applied by the International Court of Justice (ICJ) under Article 38 of its statute.[35] Similarly, in the context of the WTO, the panel in *EC – Approval and Marketing of Biotech Products* held that conventions (treaties) fall within the scope of Article 31(3)(c).[36]

The second element concerns whether the extraneous treaty is relevant for the purposes at hand. Again, for the sake of discussion, it is assumed that this requirement will be established. In the context of the WTO-covered agreements an extraneous rule will be relevant where it "sheds light on the meaning of a WTO term," and will not be relevant where it "has no bearing upon it."[37] Duncan French argues that the provision is imprecise, but that there should be a presumption that it is "much looser" than the phrase "same subject matter" under Article 30 of the Vienna Convention.[38] Although it is clear that the question of relevance will depend largely on the circumstances of a dispute, the issue should be treated as a threshold test, and the term given a broad application. The need for such an approach is reflected in the fact that any extraneous rule that is capable of influencing interpretation is necessarily relevant. As such, the relevance requirement is a rule stating that decision makers are not compelled to take account of extraneous rules that are in no way capable of influencing interpretation of the treaty under consideration.

Thus, the issue for discussion concerns the meaning of the phrase "applicable in the relations between the parties." This question is the most controversial and uncertain aspect of Article 31(3)(c). In *EC – Approval and Marketing of Biotech Products* the panel viewed the issue as being whether the phrase "the parties" refers to all of the parties to a treaty or merely the parties to a dispute. The panel adopted the former, or "restrictive," approach.[39] This conclusion also finds support in a body of commentary that tends to give weight to concerns regarding

35 Statute of the International Court of Justice, 3 Bevans 1179; 59 Stat. 1031; T.S. 993; 39 AJIL Supp. 215 (1945); Although the ICJ is not the relevant forum for the resolution of disputes under the WTO Agreement, Article 38 is generally recognized as setting out the sources of international law. For this reason, Article 38 is of guidance in determining what constitutes a "relevant rule of international law" under the Vienna Convention.

36 Panel Report, *European Communities – Measures Affecting the Approval and Marketing of Biotech Products*, WT/DS291/R, WT/DS292/R, WT/DS293/R, Corr.1 and Add.1, 2, 3, 4, 5, 6, 7, 8 and 9, adopted 21 November 2006 [hereinafter Panel Report, *EC – Approval and Marketing of Biotech Products*], para. 7.67.

37 Pauwelyn, *Conflict of Norms*, p. 264.

38 Duncan French, "Treaty Interpretation and the Incorporation of Extraneous Legal Rules," 2006, 55(2) *International & Comparative Law Quarterly*, (2006), pp. 281–314, p. 304 [hereinafter French, "Incorporation of Extraneous Legal Rules"].

39 Panel Report, *EC –Approval and Marketing of Biotech Products*, para. 7.68.

consent and consistency in decision making.[40] However, a body of commentary also supports the latter view that the phrase refers to the parties to a dispute.[41] This commentary tends to emphasize that the restrictive view imposes significant limitations with respect to the interpretation of large multilateral treaties.

There is, however, also a third possible approach that was not identified by the panel. The phrase "the parties" could refer to the parties to the treaty under interpretation (here the WTO Agreement), but the phrase "applicable in relations between" might be interpreted so as to refer to relations between the parties to the treaty (WTO membership) generally. Under this interpretation, the provision does not refer to the extraneous treaty having binding force over all the parties to the treaty under interpretation or over all disputants.[42] Rather, the phrase simply concerns whether the extraneous treaty is applicable (an issue discussed later, where it is argued that the applicability of an extraneous treaty for purposes of Article 31(3)(c) relates to its scope).

Thus, there are three possible interpretations. The first is the restrictive approach favored by the panel in *EC – Approval and Marketing of Biotech Products* . The second is a broad approach that might see divergences in the interpretation of a treaty between some of its parties. The third is also a broad approach that is similar to the use of extraneous treaties without reference to an enabling rule. For purposes of discussion, these will be referred to as the restrictive, divergent, and broad approaches respectively.

How then did the panel in *EC – Approval and Marketing of Biotech Products* reach its conclusion? In that dispute, the EC argued that the panel was *bound* to take an extraneous treaty[43] into account in interpretation of the WTO Agreement, notwithstanding the fact that neither all WTO Members nor all parties to the dispute were also parties to that protocol.[44] The EC based its submission on the decision of the Appellate Body in *US – Shrimp*.

40 See David Leebron, "Linkages," 96 *American Journal of International Law* (January 2002), pp. 5–27, p. 17 [hereinafter Leebron, "Linkages"]; Pauwelyn, *Conflict of Norms*, pp. 257–263; McLachlan, "The Principle of Systemic Integration," p. 315.

41 See David Palmeter and Petros Mavroidis, "The WTO Legal System: Sources of Law," 92(3) *American Journal of International Law*, (1998), pp. 398–413, p. 411; French, "Incorporation of Extraneous Legal Rules," p. 307; Koskenniemi, *Fragmentation of International Law*, p. 238, para. 472.

42 For a similar argument, see Robert Howse, "The Use and Abuse of Other 'Relevant Rules of International Law' in Treaty Interpretation: Insights from WTO Trade/Environment Litigation," ILJ Working Paper 2007/1, Institute for International Law and Justice, New York University School of Law, available at http://www.iilj.org/publications/documents/2007–1.Howse.web.pdf (visited 12/01/08) [hereinafter Howse, "Use and Abuse"].

43 In that instance, the Cartagena Protocol on Biosafety to the Convention on Biological Diversity 39 ILM 1027 (2000); UN Doc. UNEP/CBD/ExCOP/1/3, at 42 (2000).

44 Panel Report, *EC – Approval and Marketing of Biotech Products*, para. 7.52.

In particular, the EC relied on the fact that the Appellate Body had taken an extraneous treaty into account when neither all WTO Members nor all parties to that dispute were parties to the extraneous treaty.[45] In relying on *US – Shrimp* in this manner, the EC appears to have argued in favor of the broad approach.

In response, the panel expressly noted that in *US – Shrimp* the Appellate Body did not refer to Article 31(3)(c) of the Vienna Convention or indicate that it felt compelled to take an extraneous treaty into account.[46] Rather, on the panel's construction of *US – Shrimp*, the Appellate Body had voluntarily drawn on extraneous rules in order to establish the meaning of the phrase "exhaustible natural resources."[47]

The question of when a decision maker may take an extraneous treaty into account in treaty interpretation is distinct from the question of when Article 31(3)(c) binds a decision maker to do so. That is, contrary to Margaret Young's conclusion that a panel cannot take account of an extraneous treaty unless Article 31(3)(c) is triggered,[48] a panel may in fact do so in the absence of a prohibition. In this sense, the EC appeared to be arguing that Article 31(3)(c) compels a decision maker to take an extraneous treaty into account wherever it is relevant and applicable to the circumstances.

There is little doubt that the panel's approach merits further analysis. The Appellate Body has not reviewed the report, commentators are divided, and there is little case law to offer guidance. Against this backdrop, the three possible interpretations are considered below.

B. Wording and context

In accordance with Article 31(1) of the Vienna Convention, the starting point in interpretation is the ordinary meaning of the terms of a treaty in their context. The panel in *EC – Approval and Marketing of Biotech Products* recognized that interpretation of Article 31(3)(c) turns partly on how the phrase "the parties" is interpreted. If the phrase refers to the parties to a dispute, the divergent approach could be correct. On the other hand, if the phrase refers

45 Ibid., para. 7.52.
46 Ibid., para. 7.94 and fn 271.
47 Ibid., para. 7.94.
48 Margaret Young, "The WTO's Use of Relevant Rules of International Law: An Analysis of the Biotech Case," 56 *International & Comparative Law Quarterly*, (October 2007), pp. 907–930, [hereinafter Young, "Relevant Rules of International Law"], p. 929 (see the second dot point where Young states "the Panel could not take account of 'relevant rules of law applicable in the relations between the parties' in its interpretation of the relevant WTO agreements unless they had identical membership to the WTO."

to the parties to a treaty under interpretation, either of the restrictive or broad approaches could be correct. In respect to this question, however, the text of Article 31(3)(c) appears entirely ambiguous. As a result, emphasis must be placed on the context of the provision.

Article 31 has application in two contexts.[49] The first context is that of general treaty interpretation, such as where a foreign office interprets a treaty in order to determine its content. In this context, it is natural to conclude that the phrase "the parties" refers to the parties to the treaty under interpretation. On the other hand, Article 31 also has application in the resolution of disputes and is intended to govern the actions of a decision maker overseeing a dispute. In this context, it is natural to conclude that the phrase "the parties" refers to the parties to a dispute.

As such, the general context of the provision is in fact two contexts that do not give an indication as to which interpretation of Article 31(3)(c) is correct. Rather, the general context of the provision suggests at least three plausible meanings. Accordingly, reliance might be placed on definitions clauses, the use of similar terms, and the structure of Article 31.

(a) DEFINITION CLAUSES AND THE USE OF SIMILAR TERMS

The panel in *EC – Approval and Marketing of Biotech Products* drew on the definition of the term "party" in Article 2(1)(g) of the Vienna Convention and other usage of the phrase "the parties" throughout the convention.

(i) *The Definition of the Term "Party" in Article 2(g).* Article 2 of the Vienna Convention defines the term "party" as "a State which has consented to be bound by the treaty and for which the treaty is in force." In separate commentary, Pauwelyn, Campbell McLachlan, and Young have all relied on the definition in Article 2(1)(g) in arguing that the restrictive interpretation of Article 31(3)(c) is correct.[50] Similarly, the panel in *EC – Approval and Marketing of Biotech Products* drew on this definition, concluding that

> It may be inferred from these elements that the rules of international law applicable in the relations between "the parties" are the rules of international law applicable in the relations between the States which have consented to be bound by the treaty which is being interpreted, and for which that treaty is in force.[51]

49 French, "Incorporation of Extraneous Legal Rules," p. 287; Panel Report, *EC – Approval and Marketing of Biotech Products*, fn 241.

50 See Pauwelyn, *Conflict of Norms*, p. 257; McLachlan, "The Principle of Systemic Integration," p. 315; Young, "Relevant Rules of International Law," p. 915.

51 Panel Report, *EC – Approval and Marketing of Biotech Products*, para. 7.68 (footnote omitted).

Upon a more detailed examination of Article 2(1)(g), it is clear that the definition of the term "party" in Article 2(g) does not necessarily apply to the term "parties" in Article 31(3)(c). Although it might be assumed that a definition applies to the plural form of a defined term, there is no provision in the Vienna Convention to this effect. In this context, it is significant that there are twelve uses of the phrase "all the parties" in the Vienna Convention.[52] Were it the case that the definition in Article 2 applied to the term "parties," the twelve usages of the phrase "all of the parties" would be superfluous, because the term "parties" itself would encompass all states bound by a treaty. The manner in which the term "parties" is used in Article 3(c) also supports this conclusion. That provision refers to international agreements to which subjects of international law other than states are also "parties." The use of the term "parties" in this context is a clear departure from the conclusion of the panel because that definition only encompasses states.

It is worth noting that the conclusion that the Article 2(1)(g) definition does not necessarily apply to the term "parties" does not substantially undermine the utility of provision. To the contrary, Article 2(1)(g) defines when a state becomes a party to a treaty. In this sense, the conclusion that the definition of the term "party" does not necessarily apply to the term "parties" does not undermine the substance of the definition. This argument does, however, undermine the conclusion of the panel in *EC – Approval and Marketing of Biotech Products*, because that decision was (partly at least) based on application of the definition in Article 2(g) to Article 31(3)(c).

(ii) *Usage of the Phrase "the parties" in the Vienna Convention.* The conclusion that the definition in Article 2 does not necessarily apply to the phrase "the parties" is also supported by the usage of the phrase in other provisions of the Vienna Convention. As the panel noted, there are three relevant formulations of the phrase in the Vienna Convention. Article 31(2)(b) uses the phrase "one or more parties,"[53] Article 66 uses the phrase "the parties to a dispute,"[54] and Article 31(2)(a) uses the phrase "all the parties."

It is tempting to conclude that the presence of the phrases "one or more parties" and "the parties to a dispute" exclude the possibility that the reference to "the parties" in Article 31(3)(c) refers to the parties to a dispute.[55] That is, the drafters could have used these phrases in Article 31(3)(c) had they wished to adopt the divergent view. This conclusion, however, suffers from some obvious

52 See Articles 15(c), 20(2), 30(3), 30(4), 31(2)(b), 40(2), 54(b), 57, 59(1), 60(2)(ii).
53 Ibid., para. 7.68; fn 240.
54 Ibid., para. 7.68; fn 241.
55 An application of the maxim *expressio unis est exclusio alterius*.

flaws. First, the phrase "one or more parties" would not fit in the context of Article 31(3)(c) because it is not possible to have relevant rules of international law applicable in relations between "*one* or more parties." As such, no inference should be drawn from the presence of this phrase. Secondly, as the panel recognized, the fact that Article 31(3)(c) lays down general interpretive rules as well as rules for the resolution of disputes means that the phrase "the parties to a dispute" would not be appropriate in the context of the provision.[56]

On the other hand, it might be suggested that the absence of the phrase "all the parties" in Article 31(3)(c) indicates that the divergent view is correct. The panel acknowledged this argument (albeit only in a footnote) and concluded that the phrase was not useful because it had been used in Article 31(2)(a) by necessity, as a result of the fact that Article 31(2)(b) referred to "one or more parties."[57] Although this explanation is questionable at best, not much turns on it. Rather, in light of the dual contexts of Article 31(3)(c), even if the term "all" were used in Article 31(3)(c), it could refer to all of the parties to the treaty under interpretation or to all of the parties to the dispute.

The phrase "the parties" is used in at least three ways and has no fixed definition. In some instances the phrase is used to refer to the parties to a dispute. For example, both Article 66 of the Vienna Convention and its Annex govern the resolution of disputes, and in this context each uses the phrase "the parties" when referring to parties to a dispute.[58] In other instances the phrase is used to refer to all parties to a treaty. For example, Article 59 uses the phrases "all the parties" and "the parties" interchangeably. Similarly, Article 55 governs reductions in the numbers of parties to a treaty below the level necessary for its entry into force. In this context, the use of the phrase "the parties" obviously refers to the parties in their totality.[59]

To add further confusion, in some provisions the phrase refers to some but not all of the parties. For example, Article 72, which governs suspension of the operation of a treaty including between some but not all parties, uses the phrase "the parties."[60]

56 *Panel Report, EC – Approval and Marketing of Biotech Products*, fn 241.

57 Ibid., fn 242.

58 See Article 66(a) where the phrase "unless the parties by common consent agree ..." is used; See also paragraphs 3–6 of the Annex.

59 A range of other provisions use the phrase "the parties" in reference to all parties to a treaty. These provisions include Articles 26, 70, 71, 77(1)(b), 77(1)(e) and 79(2)(a).

60 Similarly, Article 39 sets out the general rule regarding the amendment of treaties and provides that "(a) treaty may be amended by agreement of the parties." When Article 39 is read in light of the specific rule set out in Article 41, which governs agreements to modify multilateral treaties between certain of the parties only, otherwise known as *inter se* agreements, it

These three usages of the phrase "the parties" suggest that each interpretation of Article 31(3)(c) can claim to be available upon a reading of the text. However, rather than indicating that one interpretation is correct, this usage serves to highlight the ambiguity of the phrase as used in the dual contexts of Article 31(3)(c).

(b) ARTICLE 31(3)(A) AND (B)

Pauwelyn has argued that Articles 31(3)(a) and 31(3)(b) support the restrictive approach. Pauwelyn argues that under these provisions, which immediately precede Article 31(3)(c), it is only subsequent agreements and subsequent practice that reflect the common intentions of all parties to a treaty that may be taken into account in interpretation.[61] In respect of Article 31(3)(a) Pauwelyn relies on a decision in the unadopted GATT panel report in *US – Restrictions on Imports of Tuna*.[62] With respect to Article 31(3)(b) Pauwelyn relies on the preparatory work of Sir Humphrey Waldock in which he stated:

> It is only subsequent practice which clearly establishes the understanding of all the parties regarding the meaning of the treaty which is recognised as equivalent to an interpretive agreement and the reason is, of course, that two parties or even a group of parties cannot, by their interpretation of the treaty, bind other parties as to its correct interpretation.[63]

If it is accepted for the sake of argument that Articles 31(3)(a) and (b) relate only to subsequent agreements and practice concerning all parties, the restrictive view of Article 31(3)(c) may find support. That is, if Article 31(3)(c) is situated in the context of two other paragraphs where the focus is on agreements and practice that relate to all parties, this may suggest that Article 31(3)(c) concerns other rules of international law in force between all parties to the treaty under interpretation.

Although this context may appear important at first glance, recourse to the records of the ILC indicate that nothing should be read into the location of the rule in Article 31(3)(c). As the ILC explained in 1966, the commission decided to move the provision to paragraph (3) simply because it did not belong anywhere else. The 1964 draft stated:

becomes apparent that the reference to "the parties" in Article 39 does not necessarily refer to all parties to a treaty.

61 Pauwelyn, *Conflict of Norms*, p. 258.

62 Unadopted GATT Panel Report, *United States – Restrictions on Imports of Tuna*, GATT Doc. DS29/R (June 16, 1994), 33 I.L.M. 839 (1994), para. 5.19.

63 Sixth Report on the Law of Treaties by Sir Humphrey Waldock, Special Rapporteur, Extract from the Yearbook of the International Law Commission: 1966, vol. II, A/CN.4/186 and Add.1, 2/Rev.1, 3–7, p. 90, para. 9.

Article 70. — General rules

1. The terms of a treaty shall be interpreted in good faith in accordance with the natural and ordinary meaning to be given to each term —
   (a) in its context in the treaty and in the context of the treaty as a whole; and
   (b) in the context of the rules of international law in force at the time of the conclusion of the treaty....[64]

In 1966 the commission explained that what is now Article 31(3)(c) was transferred to its place alongside subsequent agreements and practice because it was an element that was extrinsic both to the text and to the context.[65] That is, the commission placed paragraph (c) in Article 31(3) because it did not belong in either of what is now Articles 31(1) or 31(2).

C. The merits of the restrictive view

The primary advantage of the restrictive view is that it protects nonparties to an extraneous treaty from legal consequences flowing from that treaty. On the other hand, the restrictive view constitutes an inflexible rule in a context where extraneous treaties are used as evidence of facts or in norm interpretation without reference to an enabling rule. This inflexibility has prompted arguments relating to the fragmentation of international law and concerning treaties with nonsovereign entities as members. Those and two other arguments are worth considering in further detail.

(a) THE FRAGMENTATION OF INTERNATIONAL LAW

The existence of concern surrounding the so-called fragmentation of international law has been recognized by the work program of the ILC[66] and implicitly by the Appellate Body of the WTO in its calls to avoid reading the WTO Agreement in "clinical isolation" from international law.[67] At first glance, this goal weighs against the restrictive interpretation. Under this approach, Article 31(3)(c) will be triggered in the interpretation of multilateral treaties

[64] See Third Report on the Law of Treaties, by Sir Humphrey Waldock, Special Rapporteur, Extract from the Yearbook of the International Law Commission:-1964, vol. II, Document:-A/CN.4/167 and Add.1–3, [hereinafter Waldock, 1964], pp. 52–53.

[65] Draft Articles on the Law of Treaties with commentaries 1966, Reports of the Commission to the General Assembly, Yearbook of the International Law Commission, 1966, vol. II., [hereinafter, ILC Report to General Assembly, 1966], p. 222, para. 16.

[66] See generally, Koskenniemi, *Fragmentation of International Law.*

[67] Appellate Body Report, *United States – Standards for Reformulated and Conventional Gasoline,* WT/DS2/AB/R, adopted 20 May 1996, DSR 1996:I, 3 [hereinafter *U.S. – Gasoline*], p. 17.

in relatively rare circumstances. That is, the object and purpose of Article 31(3)(c) is to ensure that the terms of a treaty are not interpreted in isolation from other international law obligations. To some extent, the adoption of a restrictive interpretation of the provision undermines this purpose in that it will be extremely difficult for a cross-over in membership to occur in the context of large multilateral treaties. This interpretation also increases the fragmentation of international law and undermines efforts toward harmonization of substantive international law.[68] Indeed, as Gabrielle Marceau has noted, were the restrictive interpretation of Article 31(3)(c) adopted, it would have the ironic effect that as the membership of international organizations such as the WTO increases, that organization becomes more isolated from international law by virtue of the unlikelihood that different international treaties will share membership.[69]

On the other hand, the provision would retain significant utility even if the restrictive view were adopted. The provision continues to compel a decision maker to take rules of international law other than treaties into account. In this sense, the fact that the restrictive view of Article 31(3)(c) limits the utility of the provision should not be viewed as an argument that the purpose of the provision is undermined. Rather, it is simply an argument to the effect that the restrictive interpretation undermines the harmonization of multilateral treaty obligations.

Equally, however, the divergent interpretation of Article 31(3)(c) does not unify the international legal order. To the contrary, permitting divergences in the interpretation of a treaty emphasizes the existence of bilateral relationships within the multilateral context. In this sense, the divergent view seeks a unification of substantive international law but does nothing for (and arguably undermines) any attempt at creating a unified order. In this sense, the divergent view may enhance substantive unity for some parties but may also reinforce consent as the basis for treaty law, supporting an international order made up of divergent obligations. Similarly, the divergent view may increase the benefits of forum shopping. If this were to lead to decision makers in different fora interpreting treaties differently or inconsistently, it may ultimately increase fragmentation.

In summary, of the three possible interpretations it is only the broad view that is likely to limit the fragmentation of international law.

[68] McLachlan, "The Principle of Systemic Integration," p. 286.

[69] Gabrielle Marceau, "WTO Dispute Settlement and Human Rights," 14(4) *European Journal of International Law* (2002), pp. 753–814, p. 781.

(b) NONSOVEREIGN ENTITIES

Marceau has also argued that if the phrase "the parties" refers to all WTO Members, it will be impossible for the provision to have application to extraneous treaties, because the WTO admits nonsovereign members that are not capable of becoming parties to an extraneous treaty.[70] Leaving aside for a moment whether Marceau's conclusion is correct, the conclusion does not actually offer support for either the divergent or broad interpretations. Rather, it must be emphasized that Article 31(3)(c) is a rule of general application. As such, application of the rule in one treaty regime should not be determinative of the general application of the rule.

In any case, Marceau's conclusion is brought into doubt when Article 31(3)(c) is read in the context of Articles 1, 2, and 3 of the Vienna Convention. Article 1 governs the scope of the Vienna Convention and provides that it "applies to treaties between States." This is qualified by Article 3(c), which provides:

> The fact that the present Convention does not apply to international agreements concluded between States and other subjects of international law or between such other subjects of international law, or to international agreements not in written form, shall not affect:
>
> ...
>
> (c) the application of the Convention to the relations of States as between themselves under international agreements to which other subjects of international law are also parties.

Accordingly, Article 3(c) of the Vienna Convention effectively provides that in circumstances such as the WTO Agreement, the rules of treaty interpretation continue to apply in the relations between states that are parties to that agreement. In such circumstances, Article 31(3)(c) would continue to have application in respect of extraneous treaties under all three interpretations provided that "the parties" in question are states. Article 31(3)(c) cannot, however, have effect in relations between a nonsovereign entity and another WTO Member.

As such, contrary to Marceau's argument, the fact that the WTO includes nonsovereign entities within its membership does not mean that the restrictive interpretation of Article 31(3)(c) should be avoided for fear of rendering the provision inapplicable in the context of extraneous treaties. Importantly, however, this suggests that even the restrictive view may result in divergences in interpretation between states and nonstate entities.

[70] Ibid.

(c) UNEQUAL INTERPRETIVE RELATIONSHIPS BETWEEN TREATIES

The adoption of the restrictive approach could lead to one-way interpretive relationships between treaties. For example, where all WTO Members are parties to treaty A, a panel would be compelled to take treaty A into account in interpreting the WTO Agreement (as between states, at least). However, the reverse (that the WTO Agreement be taken into account in interpretation of treaty A) would not necessarily be the case. Were treaty A to have members that are not also parties to the WTO Agreement, the restrictive interpretation would not compel a decision maker to take the WTO Agreement into account in interpreting treaty A.

Whereas parties to the respective treaties could establish a one-way interpretive relationship of this type between two treaties through the use of express wording, it is undesirable that an interpretive rule of general application such as Article 31(3)(c) could have the effect of creating such a relationship. A one-way interpretive relationship ascribes an importance to one treaty that the other treaty lacks in the sense that only one of the treaties is capable of casting light on the other. Although such a circumstance does not establish a hierarchy between the treaties in question,[71] the establishment of an unequal interpretive relationship between two treaties is a significant consequence that ought to be left to the express intention of the parties as evinced from the terms of a treaty.

(d) ALTERATIONS TO TREATY MEMBERSHIP MAY SHIFT THE INTERPRETIVE GROUND BENEATH A DECISION MAKER

Another implication of the restrictive view is that the use or non-use of an extraneous treaty can change with changes to the membership of a multilateral treaty. For example, if every WTO Member (that is a state) were also a party to an extraneous treaty the restrictive interpretation of Article 31(3)(c) would require a panel to take that extraneous treaty into account in interpreting the WTO Agreement. However, this situation would be altered where a state that is not a party to the extraneous treaty accedes to the WTO Agreement. In accordance with the restrictive view, the consequence of this would be that a panel would no longer be compelled by Article 31(3)(c) to take the extraneous treaty into account in interpreting the WTO Agreement. This shifts the ground beneath a decision maker.

[71] It will be recalled that Article 30 governs the application of treaties relating to the same subject matter and that as such Article 31(3)(c) merely permits an extraneous treaty to cast light on the meaning of the treaty under interpretation.

One consequence of this is that one state has the power to influence what are effectively reciprocal relations of a bilateral type between two other states under a multilateral treaty. That is, under the restrictive interpretation, whether one WTO Member is a party to the extraneous treaty might alter how the WTO Agreement is interpreted between WTO Members that are also parties to the extraneous treaty.

(e) CONCLUSION ON THE RESTRICTIVE VIEW

Although none of the criticisms of the restrictive view indicates that it is completely unviable, they do demonstrate that it is potentially problematic and an undesirable approach to treaty interpretation. Most important, the restrictive view prejudges the use of one treaty in interpretation of another. This issue is addressed in further detail later in this chapter.

D. The merits of the divergent view

There is a body of commentary concerning the divergent interpretation that argues that this approach is neither appropriate nor available in a legal sense. This commentary primarily concerns the importance of the consent of parties to a treaty and consistency in decision making.

Prior to addressing these arguments it is worth noting that, as a matter of law, multilateral treaties may diverge between different parties. That is, for example, obligations owed under a multilateral treaty by party A to party B may be different to the obligations owed under that same treaty by party A to party C. This conclusion is reflected in a number of provisions of the Vienna Convention. Examples include Article 41,[72] which governs *inter se* agreements, Article 21, which contemplates the use of reservations with respect to certain of the parties only, and Article 30(4), which governs the application of treaties relating to the same subject matter.

This concept is, however, subject to limitations. For example, Article 19 imposes limitations on the circumstances in which reservations to treaties may be formulated. Similarly, in the context of *inter se* agreements these limitations are express. Article 41 states:

[72] See Joost Pauwelyn, "A Typology of Multilateral Treaty Obligations: Are WTO Obligations Bilateral or Collective in Nature?" 14(5) *European Journal of International Law* (2003), pp. 907–951 [hereinafter Pauwelyn, "Typology of Multilateral Treaty Obligations"], p. 912, where it is argued that traces of Fitzmaurice's categorization can be found in Articles 30, 41, 53, 58, 60, and 64 of the Vienna Convention.; See Young, "Relevant Rules of International Law", p. 916.

Article 41
Agreements to modify multilateral treaties between certain of the parties only

1. Two or more of the parties to a multilateral treaty may conclude an agreement to modify the treaty as between themselves alone if:
   (a) the possibility of such a modification is provided for by the treaty; or
   (b) the modification in question is not prohibited by the treaty and:
      (i) does not affect the enjoyment by the other parties of their rights under the treaty or the performance of their obligations;
      (ii) does not relate to a provision, derogation from which is incompatible with the effective execution of the object and purpose of the treaty as a whole.

The limitations in Article 41(1) stem from two concerns. Article 41(1)(b)(i) seeks to address concerns relating to consent, an issue addressed later in this chapter. Meanwhile, Article 41(1)(b)(ii) concerns the notion that not all treaties are merely reciprocal in nature. Rather, in the drafting of Article 30 of the Vienna Convention, Gerald Fitzmaurice recognized three classes of treaties. The ordinary class involves "a mutual interchange of benefits and performances on an individually reciprocating basis."[73] That is, ordinary treaties involve "a mutual exchange of benefits between the parties, or a reciprocal course of conduct by each towards each, of such a kind that a default by one party would be a *default in that party's relations with some other party*, and could be compensated for by a counter default by that party *towards the defaulting party*."[74]

Fitzmaurice contrasted "ordinary" treaties or treaties of the "reciprocal benefits and concessions type"[75] to treaties that "involved a more absolute type of obligation so that it was not really possible to speak of the treaty being applied by each party merely in its relations with each of the others."[76] These "collective-type"[77] treaties are divided into two classes. The first class encompasses "interdependent-type" treaties. Pursuant to these treaties, "the obligation of each party [is] dependent on a corresponding performance by *all* the

73 Third Report on the Law of Treaties by Mr. G.G. Fitzmaurice, Special Rapporteur, A/CN.4/115 and Corr.1, Yearbook of the International Law Commission, 1958, Vol. II, [hereinafter Fitzmaurice, 1958] p. 44.

74 Ibid. (emphasis in original).

75 Second Report on the Law of Treaties by Mr. G.G. Fitzmaurice, Special Rapporteur, A/CN.4/107, Yearbook of the International Law Commission, 1957, vol. II, [hereinafter Fitzmaurice, 1957] p. 54, para. 124.

76 Fitzmaurice, 1958, p. 44, para. 91.

77 For this characterization see Pauwelyn, "Typology of Multilateral Treaty Obligations," pp. 907–915.

parties."[78] Fitzmaurice gave the example of a disarmament treaty as constituting an interdependent-type treaty.[79]

The second class encompasses "integral-type" treaties. Integral-type treaties are such that the obligation to perform is independent of the performance by other parties.[80] Fitzmaurice described these obligations as obligations owed to all the world rather than particular parties and as "self-existent, as opposed to concessionary, reciprocal or interdependent."[81] Fitzmaurice gave the example of a humanitarian convention such as the Convention on the Prevention and Punishment of the Crime of Genocide[82] as an example of an integral-type treaty.[83]

This categorization has two implications for the interpretation of Article 31(3)(c). First, the categorization of treaties confirms that it is acceptable for multilateral treaty obligations of the ordinary/reciprocal type to apply unequally between different parties. In this light, there is also nothing inherently wrong with the suggestion that a treaty could be interpreted differently or "diverge" from a common meaning depending on the makeup of the parties to a dispute (at least in respect of ordinary/reciprocal-type treaty obligations). In this vein, McLachlan has relied on the distinctions between treaty types to argue that the divergent interpretation of Article 31(3)(c) is appropriate where the extraneous treaty is a bilateral treaty between the parties to a dispute.[84] However, why this rationale would apply only in respect of extraneous bilateral as opposed to multilateral treaties is unclear.

Secondly, in the case of interdependent- and integral-type treaty obligations, it is not strictly possible to speak solely of one party's obligations to another party in a reciprocal manner. The ILC Study Group on fragmentation of international law argued that the consequence of the distinction between types of treaty obligations is that there can be no divergence in interpretation between certain parties to a treaty with respect to interdependent- or integral-type obligations.[85] Although this may be the case, it does not follow that Article 31(3)(c) has no application in respect of particular treaties. To the contrary, many treaties contain both reciprocal- and interdependent- or integral-type obligations. In addition, the provision continues to apply to interdependent and integral

78 Fitzmaurice, 1958, p. 44 para. 91 (emphasis in original).
79 Ibid.
80 Ibid.
81 Fitzmaurice, 1957, p. 54, para. 126.
82 Convention on the Prevention and Punishment of the Crime of Genocide,78 UNTS 277.
83 Fitzmaurice, 1958, p. 44 para. 91.
84 McLachlan, "The Principle of Systemic Integration," p. 315.
85 Koskenniemi, *Fragmentation of International Law*, p. 238, para. 472.

obligations with limitations on the manner in which extraneous treaties may be taken into account (discussed later in this chapter).

In summary, although the potential for divergence in interpretation of a treaty may be unappealing, it is not necessarily a departure from the norm. Additionally, this potential has advantages in that it can facilitate agreement and permit states to organize and harmonize their relations at the bilateral level even where the source of those relations is multilateral in character. It is this aspect of the divergent view that makes it worthy of consideration.

(a) CONSENT AND THE COMMON INTENTIONS OF PARTIES TO A TREATY

Pauwelyn draws on the principle of "*pacta tertiis nee nocent necprosunt*"[86] to argue that all parties to any type of treaty must also be parties to an extraneous treaty in order for it to be used in interpretation under Article 31(3)(c). This principle is expressed in Article 34 of the Vienna Convention, which states that "a treaty does not impose either obligations or rights for a third State without its consent." Pauwelyn argues that the principle of *pacta tertiis* mandates that "a treaty can, in principle, only be interpreted with reference to elements that reflect the *common* intentions of all the parties to the treaty."[87]

There are two issues that Pauwelyn's argument raises. The first relates to whether the principle of *pacta tertiis* is upheld with respect to nonparties to an extraneous treaty when the divergent interpretation of Article 31(3)(c) is applied. In this respect, it is implicit in the recognition that ordinary treaties are reciprocal in nature that a dispute may affect the disputants without affecting other treaty parties. This conclusion is also reflected in the formulation of Article 41(1)(b)(i). As is explained earlier, it is only in the case of interdependent or integral-type obligations that a treaty party that is not also party to a dispute will *necessarily* have its rights or obligations affected by the interpretation of a treaty in dispute resolution.

There is of course, a risk that the use of an extraneous treaty may bind a nonparty in an informal manner. For example, the reasoning adopted in a particular dispute may be adopted in a subsequent dispute where the parties to that dispute are not also parties to the extraneous treaty. Two points must be stressed in this regard. First, this outcome is in no way compelled by the divergent application of Article 31(3)(c). Rather, it is a product of subsequent reasoning in the sense that it rests on a subsequent determination that prior reasoning is sound and applicable to a new dispute.

86 See ILC Report to General Assembly, 1966, p. 226.

87 Pauwelyn, *Conflict of Norms*, p. 257 (emphasis in original).

Secondly, the fact that the reasoning in question had as its root an extraneous treaty does not necessarily render that reasoning invalid or irrelevant in the context of a new dispute. To the contrary, as the WTO Appellate Body demonstrated in *US – Shrimp*, there are circumstances in which an extraneous treaty will be relevant to interpretation of another treaty generally, irrespective of whether both parties to a dispute are also parties to the extraneous treaty.

The limited nature of decisions as binding instruments in international law also protects consent. As French argues, it is not ordinarily possible for judicial-type decisions to bind states other than those that are parties to a dispute.[88] For example, Article 59 of the Statute of the ICJ provides that decisions of the ICJ only have binding force between the parties to a dispute.[89] In the context of the WTO, this concept finds root in the accepted principle that panel and Appellate Body reports only bind those members that are party to a dispute. As such, considerations of *pacta tertiis* as a rule, which ensures that parties are not bound by obligations they have not accepted, do not necessarily arise if the divergent interpretation of Article 31(3)(c) is accepted.

The second issue that Pauwelyn's argument raises is the relevance for Article 31(3)(c) of the interpretive method of seeking the common intentions of all treaty parties. That a treaty interpreter seeks the common intention or agreement of the parties is not questioned here.[90] Rather, the significance of this approach for interpretation of Article 31(3)(c) is at issue. Pauwelyn argues that an extraneous treaty "can only be referred to under Article 31(3)(c) if [it] reflects the common intentions of all parties to the treaty under interpretation."[91] This appears, however, to be not only an argument about interpretive method, but rather an argument that there should be only one authoritative interpretation of a treaty.

In evaluating this argument, the distinction that Pauwelyn draws between the *application* and *interpretation* of a treaty is important.[92] Whereas interpretation revolves around a determination of the content of a treaty, application concerns the extent to which that treaty applies to a given circumstance. In essence, Pauwelyn argues that *applying* a treaty differently depending on the

88 French, "Incorporation of Extraneous Legal Rules," p. 306.

89 In this respect, French refers to Article 63.2, which extends the binding force of decisions to third parties who intervene in a dispute before the ICJ.

90 The Appellate Body of the WTO has affirmed that panels ought to adopt this approach in Appellate Body Report, *United States – Measures Affecting the Cross-Border Supply of Gambling and Betting Services*, WT/DS285/AB/R, adopted 20 April 2005, paras 159–160.

91 Pauwelyn, *Conflict of Norms*, p. 258.

92 See ibid., Chapter 8.

disputing parties (say by virtue of Article 30 or 41 of the Vienna Convention) is acceptable, but that *interpreting* a treaty differently depending on the disputing parties is a threat to uniformity (in Pauwelyn's study, the uniformity of WTO law).[93]

French argues that the notion of a treaty having a uniform interpretation is an unrealistic ideal that is undermined in respect of many treaties by systems of consensual jurisdiction and the fact that nonparties to a dispute are not bound by the outcome.[94] Although French's argument may go more to the enforcement of treaty obligations than their interpretation, it is nonetheless correct that uniform interpretation may be nothing more than an ideal in many instances. In this respect, there is nothing to prevent an *inter se* agreement from governing the interpretation of a treaty and thus diverging from what may be a uniform or authoritative interpretation of that treaty. In this sense, the Vienna Convention does not support a distinction between treaty interpretation and application with respect to differing or diverging relationships within multilateral treaties.[95]

French also argues that "the extensive use of bilateral commitments, even within a multilateral context, ensures that, in most cases, such uniform interpretations are not actually required."[96] In support of this point, Pauwelyn's case for uniformity in treaty interpretation (as opposed to application) rests on the premise that the principle of *pacta tertiis* is necessarily offended where the broad interpretation of Article 31(3)(c) is adopted. In light of the argument that this is not necessarily the case with respect to ordinary/reciprocal-type treaties, the distinction between the need for uniformity in interpretation (but not application) of treaties appears to fall away.

(b) THE MEANING OF AND LIMITATIONS ON THE PHRASE "TAKEN INTO ACCOUNT"

In considering the merits of the divergent and broad approaches, the meaning of the phrase "taken into account" is of some consequence. As the panel in *EC – Approval and Marketing of Biotech Products* noted, no particular outcome is prescribed by the obligation to take an extraneous treaty into account.[97]

93 See ibid., pp. 474–476.
94 French, "Incorporation of Extraneous Legal Rules," pp. 306–307.
95 See Koskenniemi, *Fragmentation of International Law*, p. 237, para. 471 where it is argued that the restrictive view would prevent the use of *inter se* agreements. The ILC Study Group is presumably referring only to their use under Article 31(3)(c) and not their application under other provisions of the Vienna Convention such as Article 30.
96 French, "Incorporation of Extraneous Legal Rules," p. 307.
97 Panel Report, *EC – Approval and Marketing of Biotech Products*, para 7.69.

Similarly, Philippe Sands has noted that the phrase "take account" is not defined in international law, and that the phrase "taken into account" indicates a range of approaches and results.[98] He argues that "[o]rdinary usage suggests that the formulation is stronger than 'take into consideration' but weaker than 'apply.'"[99] The panel in *EC – Approval and Marketing of Biotech Products* considered that the obligation to interpret a treaty in good faith means that

> where consideration of all other interpretative elements set out in Article 31 results in more than one permissible interpretation, a treaty interpreter following the instructions of Article 31(3)(c) in good faith would in our view need to settle for that interpretation which is more in accord with other applicable rules of international law.[100]

The ILC Study Group has argued that all that is required by Article 31(3)(c) is the incorporation into legal reasoning of a sense of coherence and meaningfulness.[101] This approach appears correct in that the obligation to take an extraneous treaty into account is similar to the obligation to take the context of a treaty into account. That is, a decision maker should not ignore relevant rules of international law applicable in the relations between the parties, but rather should incorporate the existence of such rules into legal reasoning when appropriate.

At first glance, this approach still leaves a treaty interpreter a large degree of freedom with respect to how an extraneous treaty may be used. It is apparent, however, that a number of implications must be read into the phrase in order to give proper effect to other rules and principles set out in the Vienna Convention. These implied limitations undermine some of the arguments made against the divergent view.

(i) *Consent must be considered.* Perhaps the most important point to be made in respect of issues surrounding Pauwelyn's consent argument[102] is that it does not actually go to the question of whether the divergent interpretation of Article 31(3)(c) is correct. Rather, because the principle of *pacta tertiis* will not be offended in every situation where an extraneous treaty is taken into account under the divergent (or broad) interpretation of Article 31(3)(c), Pauwelyn's argument actually goes to the manner in which such treaties may

[98] Philippe Sands, "Treaty, Custom and the Cross-Fertilisation of International Law," 1 *Yale Human Rights and Development Law Journal*, (1998), pp. 85–105, p. 103, [hereinafter Sands, "Cross Fertilisation"].

[99] Ibid.

[100] Panel Report, *EC – Approval and Marketing of Biotech Products*, para. 7.69.

[101] Koskenniemi, *Fragmentation of International Law*, p. 211, para. 419.

[102] As opposed to the argument on uniform interpretation.

be taken into account.[103] That is, *pacta tertiis* is more properly viewed as a constraint on how extraneous treaties may be used in treaty interpretation, and not a limitation on the preliminary question of when they ought to be taken into account.

In this context, the limitation on the use of *inter se* agreements expressed in Article 41(1)(b)(i) ought to be implied in Article 31(3)(c). That is, the maxim of *pacta tertiis* provides that an extraneous treaty cannot be "taken into account" in a manner that affects the enjoyment by the other parties (nonparties to the extraneous treaty) of their rights under the treaty or the performance of their obligations in the absence of their consent thereto. In the case of ordinary/reciprocal obligations in the context of the divergent view, this limitation means that an extraneous treaty can only cast light on the legal relations between parties to the extraneous treaty. That is, unless all parties to the treaty under interpretation consent to the use of the extraneous treaty, or, to use Pauwelyn's phrase, unless it reflects their "common intentions," the extraneous treaty cannot cast light on the way that the terms of the treaty apply to all parties.

It is worth noting at this point that in this context Article 31(3)(c) merely acts as a procedural compulsion on a decision maker to take an extraneous treaty into account. In doing so, a decision maker could use such a treaty either in the interpretation of norms, as evidence of a fact in issue, or as a supplementary means of interpretation in accordance with Article 32 of the Vienna Convention.

In addition, under the divergent view, Article 31(3)(c) might be used, where appropriate, to cast light only on the legal relations between the parties to a dispute. To a large extent, the way in which this may occur would depend on the treaties and rights or obligations in question. In this respect, it is implicit in the ILC Study Group's call for further research into the actual and potential uses of Article 31(3)(c)[104] that the manner in which it might be utilized is somewhat unclear.

The implied consent-based limitation on use of an extraneous treaty is of additional significance in the context of interdependent and integral treaty obligations. It will be recalled that it is not permissible to have a divergence in treaty interpretation between some of the parties with respect to an obligation of this nature, because all parties are affected by the interpretation. As such, a decision maker may only take an extraneous treaty into account in

[103] French alludes to this point when he argues that judicial discretion should not be marginalized. See French, "Incorporation of Extraneous Legal Rules," p. 307; See also Howse, "Use and Abuse," p. 25.

[104] Koskenniemi, *Fragmentation of International Law*, p. 213, para. 423.

interpretation of an interdependent- or integral-type treaty where it accords with the consent or "common intentions" of all parties. That is, in the case of interdependent and integral obligations, Article 31(3)(c) continues to compel a decision maker to take relevant extraneous treaties applicable in the relations between parties to a dispute into account. However, the manner in which such treaties may be taken into account is limited by the consent of all parties to the treaty under interpretation. When interpreted in this manner, Article 31(3)(c) continues to serve as a procedural obligation, which compels a decision maker to consider the role of an extraneous treaty to which parties to a dispute are also party.

(ii) *Article 31 does not govern "Conflicts" between Treaties or, Therefore, the Applicability of Treaties.* Article 30 of the Vienna Convention governs the situation where successive treaties relate to the same subject matter, or so-called conflicts between treaties. The specific rules set out in Article 30 suggest that Article 31(3)(c) only applies (in respect of treaties, at least) to situations where two treaty obligations are capable of being read together. That is, Article 31(3)(c) applies where those obligations are not in "conflict" with one another. As such, an extraneous treaty cannot be *applied* by a decision maker[105] and cannot modify the applicability of the treaty under interpretation. Rather, the role of the extraneous treaty is to cast light on the question of how the obligations set out in the treaty under interpretation are to be applied.

Admittedly, the distinction between modifying the applicability of obligations and interpreting obligations may present some difficulty in practice. For example, Judge Higgins, in her separate opinion in the *Case Concerning Oil Platforms*,[106] criticized the majority for focusing on application of extraneous rules rather than on their use in interpretation.[107] Nonetheless, the distinction between application and interpretation remains meaningful.

(iii) *Other Rules of Treaty Interpretation Continue to Apply.* The fundamental rules of treaty interpretation continue to apply where an extraneous treaty is taken into account. Article 31(1) sets out the fundamental rule of treaty interpretation that "[a] treaty shall be interpreted in good faith in accordance with the ordinary meaning to be given to the terms of the treaty in their context and in the light of its object and purpose." The introductory passage of Article 31(3) provides that an extraneous treaty shall be taken into account "together

[105] Sands, "Cross Fertilisation," p. 103; Pauwelyn also draws this distinction, see Pauwelyn, *Conflict of Norms*, chapter 8.

[106] *Case Concerning Oil Platforms (Iran v. United States of America)* (Merits) ICJ Reports 2003; 42 ILM 1334 (2003).

[107] Ibid., Separate Opinion of Judge Higgins, para. 47.

with the context." As such, it is clear that the ordinary meaning of the terms of a treaty, in their context and in light of the object and purpose of the treaty, remain the focus of interpretation even where an extraneous treaty is taken into account.[108] Similarly, Judge Higgins in her separate opinion in the *Case Concerning Oil Platforms*, concluded that the context of the treaty under interpretation is pertinent to the question of which extraneous rules ought to be taken into account.[109]

The effect of the primacy afforded to the terms of a treaty in interpretation is a significant limitation on Article 31(3)(c). This primacy means that the parties to a treaty control how it is to be interpreted. One example of such control is the ability in Article 19(a) to prohibit reservations through the inclusion of express terms in a treaty. Similarly, in the context of Article 31(3)(c), the parties could prohibit a decision maker from taking extraneous treaties into account in interpretation. Such extraneous treaties could include a specific treaty, a group of treaties, or treaties of a specific class. Additionally, the parties could prohibit a decision maker from taking extraneous treaties into account unless all parties to the treaty are also parties to the extraneous treaties.

The ability to exclude the use of Article 31(3)(c) in respect of particular treaties also permits treaty parties to protect themselves from any risk that is said to arise in respect of their consent to be bound.

(c) ARGUMENTS RELATING TO THE CONSEQUENCES OF THE DIVERGENT AND RESTRICTIVE APPROACHES TO ARTICLE 31(3)(C)

Having considered whether divergence in interpretation is permissible under the law of treaties as well as the question of what limitations the divergent approach would be subjected to, its consequences are now considered.

(i) *Consistency in Decision Making.* The divergent interpretation increases the chance that differing approaches to interpretation will be adopted in different disputes depending on the makeup of the parties to the dispute and their treaty obligations. McLachlan goes so far as to argue that the divergent interpretation could lead to inconsistent interpretations of an agreement.[110]

On the other hand, as is the case with issues surrounding consent, differing or inconsistent decision making is not necessitated by the use of an extraneous treaty in interpretation. Rather, the issue also goes to the question of how such

108 See McLachlan, "The Principle of Systemic Integration," p. 311.
109 *Case Concerning Oil Platforms*, Separate Opinion of Judge Higgins, para. 46.
110 McLachlan, "The Principle of Systemic Integration," p. 315.

an extraneous treaty is "taken into account" and not the preliminary question of whether a decision maker ought to be compelled to consider the issues. Although this may be the case, the divergent view would appear to have no advantages when compared to the broad view if it doesn't actually result in divergences in interpretation. In this sense, consistency in decision making is an issue presented by the divergent view. The extent to which this issue may be problematic is unclear. In particular, there would appear to be a greater chance of consistency where an extraneous treaty is used in application of a rule to a factual scenario as compared to where it is used in general norm interpretation.

By the same token, consistency in decision making is also an issue facing the restrictive view. In particular, the presence of nonsovereign entities as WTO Members exposes the restrictive interpretation to some of the criticisms associated with its divergent counterpart. For example, to the extent that potentially inconsistent decision making raises a problem under the divergent interpretation, this problem also arises under the restrictive interpretation in respect of nonsovereign members. That is, where all states that are WTO Members are also parties to an extraneous treaty, two divergent approaches to interpretation may apply. Similarly, to the extent that use of an extraneous treaty may affect the interests of nonparties to the extraneous treaty, that risk also exists in respect of nonsovereign members where all states that are WTO Members are also parties to an extraneous treaty.

Of course, this conclusion may not necessarily mirror reality. It is difficult to envisage a handful of nonsovereign entities being treated differently from the remainder of the WTO membership. Although this may be the case, the point still stands. That is, some of the arguments against the divergent interpretation of Article 31(3)(c) of the Vienna Convention also apply in the context of the restrictive interpretation because it could itself produce divergences with respect to nonsovereign entities.

(ii) *MFN Treatment.* It has been suggested that applying an extraneous treaty only between those parties to a dispute would violate most-favored-nation (MFN) principles of the WTO-covered agreements.[111] Leaving the merits of this argument aside, this argument is specific to treaties with MFN provisions. It is not an argument relevant to the general interpretation of Article 31(3)(c). Rather, it is framed as an argument against the application of particular interpretations in the context of the WTO-covered agreements, an issue that is addressed later in this chapter.

[111] Leebron, "Linkages," p. 22.

(iii) *The Absence of Practice Confirming the Divergent Interpretation.* As French recognizes, the failure of judicial decision makers to apply the divergent view of Article 31(3)(c) weighs against the acceptance of that view.[112] Although this argument may appear compelling at first glance, it must also be recalled that the case law does not offer significant support for the restrictive view or the broad view. With the exception of the panel report in *EC – Approval and Marketing of Biotech Products* there is no other decision known to this author that actually offers express support for either view.

Of course, it could be argued that the absence of practice supporting the divergent view indicates that this view of Article 31(3)(c) does not reflect the customary international law of treaty interpretation. Such an argument raises some difficult conceptual issues with respect to the nature of customary rules of treaty interpretation. As Humphrey Waldock noted in 1964, some commentators, including James Brierly and Hersch Lauterpacht, expressed doubts as to the existence of customary rules of treaty interpretation.[113] Others, such as Fitzmaurice, expressed concern with respect to the obligatory nature of canons of interpretation, but recognized the existence of general rules applied in treaty interpretation.[114] Where customary international law is ordinarily created by acts of states that amount to a settled practice that is carried out in such a way as to evidence a belief that this practice is rendered obligatory by a rule of law requiring it,[115] the argument that rules of treaty interpretation are not customary international law appears to have some merit. Contrary to this view, however, Article 3.2 of the WTO Understanding on Rules and Procedures Governing the Settlement of Disputes (DSU) provides that WTO-covered agreements should be interpreted in accordance with "the customary rules of interpretation of public international law." This suggests that at least the 153 member states of the WTO understand there to be such customary rules, a view supported by the consistent application of the Vienna Convention as custom by the Appellate Body of the WTO[116] and other judicial bodies.[117]

[112] French, "Incorporation of Extraneous Legal Rules," p. 306.

[113] Waldock, 1964, p. 53 referring to J L Brierly, *Law of Nations* (6th edn), p. 325, H. Lauterpacht, Rapport å l'Institut de droit international, Annuaire de l'Institut, 1950, vol. 1, pp. 336–374.

[114] Ibid., referring to Gerald Fitzmaurice, "The Law and Procedure of the International Court of Justice 1951 – 4: Treaty Interpretation and Other Treaty Points," 33 *British Yearbook of International Law*, (1957), pp. 203–293

[115] *North Sea Continental Shelf Cases* (*Federal Republic of Germany v. Denmark*; *Federal Republic of Germany v. The Netherlands*) ICJ Reports 1969, 3, para. 77.

[116] Appellate Body Report, *US – Gasoline*, p. 17.

[117] See, for example, *Territorial Dispute Case* (*Libyan Arab Jamahiriya v. Chad*) ICJ Rep 1994, 6, para. 41.

This uncertain conceptual underpinning of the customary rules of treaty interpretation highlights the absence of a clear methodology for the determination of when an approach to treaty interpretation attains the status of a customary rule. Without doubt, judicial practice is relevant to the determination of customary rules of interpretation. In fact, such practice was drawn on heavily by the ILC in the drafting of the Vienna Convention. It must be stressed, however, that the ILC also drew on other sources including, importantly, the comments of states on drafts of the eventual Vienna Convention. In this sense, in determining the customary status of Article 31(3)(c), some significance must be attributed to the presence of the provision in the Vienna Convention in a form that leaves the divergent interpretation open.

In any case, the divergent view does not advocate the existence of a particular customary rule. To the contrary, the divergent view argues that the recognized rule (that a treaty must be interpreted in light of other relevant rules of international law) applies in a particular way with respect to extraneous treaty obligations. In this sense, the divergent view is an argument addressing the question of how a recognized customary rule ought to apply to a particular fact pattern and is merely one application of the general customary rule. When the argument is viewed in this light and in a context where practice does not support the customary application of either the restrictive or divergent approach, the suggestion that one or the other approach does not reflect custom due to an absence of judicial practice appears invalid.

(d) CONCLUSION ON THE DIVERGENT VIEW

When the limitations on application of Article 31(3)(c) are identified, many of the criticisms leveled at the divergent view fall away. This stems from the fact that Article 31(3)(c) is little more than a procedural obligation to consider the issues. Although the potential for differing approaches to decision making could be problematic, whether this would be the case remains to be seen (and addressed) in individual circumstances.

E. The merits of the broad view

Much of the analysis with respect to the divergent view is also applicable to the broad view. The most obvious difference is that the broad view does not recognize the possibility of divergences in interpretation of a treaty. With this difference, the question of consistency in decision making largely falls away. Similarly, the broad view has a different effect on the fragmentation of international law. Because the broad view seeks substantive unity and does not permit divergences, this view minimizes fragmentation to the greatest extent. In this light, the merits of the broad view are apparent.

One criticism of the broad view is that use of an extraneous treaty may not accord with the consent of all parties to a treaty. This argument has, however, already been answered. Article 31(3)(c) only compels a decision maker to take an extraneous treaty into account but does not compel a particular outcome.

The criticism most problematic for the broad view is that it is not available on an ordinary reading of Article 31(3)(c). In particular, some definition needs to be given to the notion that an extraneous treaty is applicable in relations between parties. There are a number of different approaches to be considered.

In the *Case Concerning Oil Platforms*, the majority of the ICJ referred to international law applicable to the question at hand.[118] This approach was criticized by the minority on the basis that the approach extended the court's jurisdiction in that dispute. Another criticism of this somewhat opaque formulation is that it does not clarify the distinction between rules that are relevant and rules that are applicable.

The ILC Study Group and Howse have advocated an approach whereby the question of whether a treaty is applicable concerns whether it is accepted widely enough that it reflects the common intentions of the parties to the treaty under interpretation.[119] The problem with this approach, however, is that it does not really reflect the language of Article 31(3)(c). That is, the approach seems somewhat divorced from the text of the provision. Additionally, focusing on how widespread acceptance is of a treaty may be problematic in the sense that even one nonconsenting state should not be bound by the terms of a treaty. In this light, the focus of a decision maker should be on the manner in which an extraneous treaty can influence decisions and whether that manner is a legitimate interpretation of the treaty in question.

An alternative approach would be to focus on the ordinary meaning of the term applicable. In the context of the Vienna Convention, the term does not refer to whether a state is a party to a treaty. Rather, in addressing this concept, the definition of the term "party" in Article 1(g) refers to whether a treaty is "in force." This suggests that applicability refers to questions of scope. That is, rules are often limited in their scope so as to apply to a particular set of circumstances. Where the applicability of an extraneous rule is limited in this fashion and does not apply to the circumstance under consideration, it is reasonable that a decision maker not be compelled to consider that rule, even

118 *Case Concerning Oil Platforms*, para. 42.

119 Koskenniemi, *Fragmentation of International Law*, p. 239, para. 472; Howse, "Use and Abuse," p. 39.

if it is of general relevance to a dispute. One reason to limit Article 31(3)(c) in this fashion is that limitations on the scope of a rule reflect the consent of the parties to the extraneous treaty. Where the parties to an extraneous treaty have not consented to the extension of a rule to particular circumstances and those circumstances are at issue, it seems natural that a decision maker would not be obliged to consider that rule in interpretation of another treaty, even if that rule is of general relevance.

In adopting this approach, the question of applicability is distinct from the question of relevance. Whereas relevance concerns whether an extraneous treaty can influence interpretation, applicability concerns whether the relevant rule extends to the circumstances at hand, despite not being the applicable law for purposes of resolving a dispute.

F. Which view should be preferred?

In assessing which view should be preferred, the first conclusion that may be drawn is that the restrictive view is undesirable. The restrictive interpretation is not only too restrictive in its scope, but also suffers from a lack of flexibility. In contrast, both the divergent and the broad interpretation permit application of Article 31(3)(c) to all treaties in a flexible manner. This flexibility permits a decision maker the scope to take account of concerns or problems with respect to the use of an extraneous treaty in interpretation. Importantly, this flexible approach gives maximum effect to a general rule of treaty interpretation.

The broad and divergent interpretations are significant in that they preserve the realistic possibility that Article 31(3)(c) will be used in the reconciliation of obligations under multilateral treaty regimes. Whereas the broad view may achieve this and preserve substantive unity, there is also merit to the suggestion that states should be able to organize their relations at a bilateral level even where the source of those relations is multilateral in character. This characteristic is ultimately what makes the divergent view worthy of the discussion it was afforded earlier. For example, under the broad view it is conceivable that an extraneous treaty will not be used in interpretation of some aspects of the WTO Agreement because of concerns relating to the consent of nonparties to the extraneous treaty. However, if both disputants were parties to the extraneous treaty there is a strong argument that it should be capable of being used in determining relations between them. Unless all such circumstances fell within the bounds of estoppel or similar doctrines, a somewhat absurd outcome could otherwise ensue.

In this context, it is arguable that each of the divergent and broad views is acceptable. That is, a decision maker should consider the appropriateness of using an extraneous treaty as a tool in the interpretation of a treaty as it applies to all parties. In the event, however, that such use is inappropriate, the decision maker should be able to fall back on the divergent interpretation.

The broad and divergent views are also significant in that they compel a decision maker to interpret one treaty in light of another in a greater range of circumstances than the restrictive view does. This, of course, also empowers courts and tribunals and in so doing may lead to increased judicial activism. It is perhaps this and the fear of entire treaty regimes being overrun by other interests that underlies the restrictive view of Article 31(3)(c). In this respect, French is correct to argue that dispute settlement and the exercise of judicial discretion is a key element of the interpretive process that should not be marginalized.[120] Moreover, it must be recalled that the parties to a treaty determine its terms and, therefore, retain control over how a treaty is to be interpreted.

G. Can either the divergent or broad interpretation apply in the context of the WTO?

There should be little doubt that the broad interpretation is capable of applying in the context of the WTO Agreement. That interpretation is little more than an obligation to consider use of extraneous treaties in a manner similar to that in *US – Shrimp*. However, the issue is not as clear in the context of an argument to the effect that the interpretation of the covered agreements can diverge between certain of the parties.

One possible objection to the divergent approach is the argument that *inter se* modifications are not permissible in the context of the WTO Agreement. Although this argument is debatable,[121] rules governing amendment of the WTO Agreement say nothing with respect to its interpretation. In this context, the argument might not be relevant.

It could also be argued that the effect of the MFN provisions in WTO-covered agreements means that an interpretation of Article 31(3)(c) that permits divergences cannot apply with respect to those agreements. Along these lines, Chios Carmody has argued that the effect of MFN provisions means that WTO obligations are collective in nature rather than reciprocal.[122]

Although the conclusion that WTO obligations are collective in nature is questionable,[123] an abstract categorization of obligations as collective in nature

[120] French, "Incorporation of Extraneous Legal Rules," p. 307.

[121] See, for example, Pauwelyn, *Conflict of Norms*, p. 475.

[122] See generally Chios Carmody, "WTO Obligations as Collective," 17(2) *European Journal of International Law*, (2006), pp. 419–443.

[123] See generally Pauwelyn, "A Typology of Multilateral Treaty Obligations."

does not mean that the broad approach to Article 31(3)(c) is inapplicable to such obligations. To the contrary, the test to be applied is whether application of the provision in a broad manner will affect the rights or obligations of other WTO Members that are not parties to the extraneous treaty. As such, the issue must be considered in the individual circumstances of a dispute and not in the abstract.

Without detracting from the conclusion that issues of this nature must be considered in light of their circumstances, some general comments can be made about this MFN argument. In effect, the argument relates to the general principle of MFN treatment and not to the specific way in which MFN provisions are used in the WTO-covered agreements. When considering the general principle of MFN treatment, it is natural to conclude that divergences in interpretation between some of the parties are impermissible. In contrast, it is not implicit in the WTO provisions themselves that divergences are impermissible. This conclusion can be illustrated by reference to Article I of the GATT. Article I:1 sets out the prohibitive content of the provision. It states:

> With respect to customs duties and charges of any kind imposed on or in connection with importation or exportation or imposed on the international transfer of payments for imports or exports, and with respect to the method of levying such duties and charges, and with respect to all rules and formalities in connection with importation and exportation, and with respect to all matters referred to in paragraphs 2 and 4 of Article III,* any advantage, favour, privilege or immunity granted by any contracting party to any product originating in or destined for any other country shall be accorded immediately and unconditionally to the like product originating in or destined for the territories of all other contracting parties.

This prohibitive provision is then followed by a number of exceptions in Articles I:2 and I:3. These exceptions relate to preferences in force prior to the formation of the GATT and to preferences in force between neighboring countries. Thus, it is clear that divergences in the application of obligations are permissible and that the general principle of MFN treatment has been modified in the GATT. The effect of this with respect to Article 31(3)(c) is that the divergent interpretation of the provision could conceivably apply in the same circumstances as the exceptions set out in Article I.

With respect to the prohibitive content of Article I, it is also not clear that the use of an extraneous treaty in interpretation of a WTO-covered agreement would result in an "advantage, favour, privilege or immunity" being granted. That is, every member is in the same position in that they can elect to become parties to the extraneous treaty.

Additionally, with respect to the possibility that a party to an extraneous treaty could itself receive treatment less favorable, it is likely that principles of estoppel or good faith would bar such an argument. Such principles have been discussed by both panels and the Appellate Body[124] and ought to prevent a party from denying the significance of their extraneous obligations.

Finally, the obligation under Article I is an obligation to extend any advantage, favor, privilege, or immunity to all WTO Members. A consequence of this is that, to the extent that an advantage does follow from the use of an extraneous treaty in interpretation, the obligation is on the party conferring that advantage to accord it to all other parties. To the extent that a party softens its rights with respect to another party to an extraneous treaty, it must also soften its rights in the same manner to all WTO Members. When viewed in this light, it is clear that the MFN obligation may have implications for parties to extraneous treaties, but that it is not prohibitive of the divergent application of Article 31(3)(c) to the WTO Agreement.

H. Do temporal requirements prevent the use of treaties such as the FCTC in interpretation of the WTO Agreement?

In some cases a rule of "inter-temporality" or "contemporaneity" prohibits reference to extraneous materials not in existence at the time a treaty is concluded. The rationale for this approach is that the intention and understanding of the parties to a treaty can only be determined at the time of its conclusion. Although the fact that this rule is not codified in the Vienna Convention creates a lack of clarity,[125] the rule finds support in decisions of the ICJ.[126] However, this rule is not rigidly applied, and an evolutionary approach to interpretation is applied where the terms of a treaty are not static in nature

[124] See Appellate Body Report, *United States – Tax Treatment for "Foreign Sales Corporations,"* WT/DS108/AB/R, adopted 20 March 2000, DSR 2000:III, 1619, paras 162–5; Panel Report, *Guatemala – Definitive Anti-Dumping Measures on Grey Portland Cement from Mexico*, WT/DS156/R, adopted 17 November 2000, DSR 2000:XI, 5295, para. 8.23; Panel Report, *Chile – Price Band System and Safeguard Measures Relating to Certain Agricultural Products*, WT/DS207/R, adopted 23 October 2002, modified by Appellate Body Report, WT/DS207AB/R, DSR 2002:VIII, 3127, para. 7.100; although see also discussion in Appellate Body Report, *European Communities – Export Subsidies on Sugar*, WT/DS265/AB/R, WT/DS266/AB/R, WT/DS283/AB/R, adopted 19 May 2005, para. 312, which relates to estoppels in the context of the initiation of disputes.

[125] On this issue, see the Separate Opinion of Judge Weeramantry in the *Case Concerning the Gabcikovo-Nagymaros Project (Hungary v. Slovakia)*, ICJ Reports 1997, 7, p. 114.

[126] See United States Nationals in Morocco (1951) ICJ Reports, 189; Guinea-Bissau / Senegal Maritime Boundary Arbitration (Award of 31 July 1989 (1990)) 83 ILR 1, 85; Separate Opinion of Judge Bedjaoui in the *Case Concerning the Gabcikovo-Nagymaros Project (Hungary v. Slovakia)*, (1997) ICJ Reports.

or of fixed content.[127] The rationale for this approach is that, in order to give full effect to a treaty, it is sometimes necessary to interpret terms in light of contemporary developments. This approach to interpretation finds support in decisions of the ICJ[128] and in the Appellate Body's interpretation of the phrase "exhaustible natural resources" in *US – Shrimp*.[129]

The extent to which an evolutionary approach may be applied will depend on the provisions under interpretation and what they show to be the intentions of the parties to the treaty under interpretation.[130] In respect of the general exceptions set out in Article XX of the GATT, McLachlan argues that they "must inherently adapt their application according to the situation as it develops over time."[131] McLachlan gives the example of the protection of shrimp, stating that "the measures necessary to protect shrimp will evolve depending upon the extent to which the survival of the shrimp population is threatened."[132] Indeed, in *US – Shrimp* the Appellate Body interpreted Article XX(g) "in light of contemporary concerns of the community of nations"[133] and concluded that the content of Article XX(g) was "by definition evolutionary."[134]

Although the context of preserving exhaustible natural resources is distinct from the concept of protecting human health, each must be interpreted in light of contemporary concerns. This suggests that Article XX(b) should also be interpreted in an evolutionary manner, meaning that instruments such as the FCTC may be used in interpretation of Article XX(b) of the GATT and similar provisions of other covered agreements.

I. Conclusion on Article 31(3)(c)

Article 31(3)(c) has not been used in the broad manner by WTO panels or the Appellate Body. Rather, panels and the Appellate Body have chosen to draw on extraneous treaties without reference to an enabling rule and without

[127] See generally, Pauwelyn, *Conflict of Norms*, pp. 266–268.

[128] See, for example, Gabcikovo-Nagymaros Project, para. 140; For discussion, see Pauwelyn, *Conflict of Norms*, p. 266, note 84.

[129] Appellate Body Report, *United States – Import Prohibition of Certain Shrimp and Shrimp Products*, WT/DS58/AB/R, adopted 6 November 1998 [hereinafter *US – Shrimp*], paras 128–132.

[130] Hugh Thirlway, "The Law and Procedure of the International Court of Justice 1960–1989 Part Three," 62 *British Year Book of International Law*, (1991), pp. 1–76, p. 57 (referring to the approach adopted in decisions of the ICJ).

[131] McLachlan, "The Principle of Systemic Integration," p. 318.

[132] Ibid.

[133] Appellate Body Report, *US – Shrimp*, para. 129.

[134] Ibid., para. 130.

reference to the consent of the WTO membership. The aforementioned interpretations of Article 31(3)(c) suggest that this practice should be formalized in the sense that decision makers should be bound to consider the impact of extraneous treaties where relevant and applicable. This would not only promote consistency in terms of the approach adopted, but would also encourage panels and the Appellate Body to justify the manner in which extraneous treaties are used in interpretation. Moreover, this is a far more tenable approach to Article 31(3)(c) than that offered by the panel in *EC – Approval and Marketing of Biotech Products*.

2.5. *Conclusion on Normative Integration*

The first issue examined in this chapter was the question of how instruments such as the FCTC and the global strategies might be used in the interpretation of the WTO-covered agreements. In practice, WTO panels have generally observed the Appellate Body's position that WTO law should not be interpreted in isolation from public international law. Both extraneous treaties and nonbinding international instruments have been used in the interpretation of the WTO-covered agreements.

In terms of rules-based guarantees, however, there are only two mechanisms to compel a panel to consider international health instruments. One of these mechanisms is Article 31(3)(c) of the Vienna Convention. This provision applies only to rules, meaning that nonbinding instruments such as the global strategies do not fall within its scope. In addition, Article 31(3)(c) has been interpreted in such a narrow fashion by the panel in *EC – Approval and Marketing of Biotech Products* that the use of treaties under this provision is also marginalized. Although there are strong arguments to suggest that Article 31(3)(c) should be given a broader application than it has been given, this has not occurred to date, and the Appellate Body has not shown an inclination to support a broader approach to Article 31(3)(c).

Mechanisms compelling WTO panels to consider international health instruments can also be found in the SPS and TBT Agreements. Provisions creating a presumption of compliance with those agreements (and of compliance with the GATT under Article 2.4 of the SPS Agreement) impose a binding framework of normative integration. Equally, the types of instruments that may be used in this manner are limited, and the presumptions of lawfulness are limited to a handful of covered agreements.

Nonetheless, the way in which Article 31(3)(c) has been interpreted suggests that nonbinding instruments are a useful source of norms for purposes of normative integration. The way in which the panel in *EC – Approval and Marketing of Biotech Products* interpreted Article 31(3)(c) also suggests that Broude's argument about normative integration and the allocation of international authority may have some merit. That is, more forceful obligations to integrate health norms into WTO law may be more likely to face resistance by WTO panels than less forceful means or means that are themselves built into WTO law, as is the case in the context of the SPS and TBT Agreements.

3

Freedom to Use Taxes, Subsidies, and Restrictions on Marketing

To some degree the regulatory strategies adopted in the contexts of tobacco, alcohol, and diet are premised on the assumption that small shifts in risk across a population can have a significant impact on population health as a whole. In each context the underlying strategy is to either eliminate or minimize exposure to risk factors for disease. The rationale underpinning the measures discussed in this study is to focus government intervention on the consumption patterns of the population. This legal and regulatory approach does not reflect the entirety of government attempts to reduce noncommunicable disease. Public health authorities also use medical approaches to assist high-risk individuals. Examples include smoking-cessation programs, medical approaches to weight loss, and counseling. Authorities also use education and community-awareness programs and other approaches that are not necessarily regulatory in character.

In the case of tobacco products, the threats posed to human health are direct, and action is usually aimed at reducing consumption of tobacco products to the greatest extent possible. As mentioned in Chapter 1, tobacco control relies on five complementary strategies: (1) demand reduction, (2) provision of information to consumers, (3) supply reduction, (4) reduction of exposure to tobacco smoke, and (5) minimization of the harm caused by individual tobacco products. These strategies are reflected in various provisions of the FCTC, including Article 6 (price and tax measures to reduce demand for tobacco), Article 8 (protection from exposure to tobacco smoke), Article 9 (regulation of the contents of tobacco products), Article 10 (regulation of tobacco-products disclosures), Article 11 (packaging and labeling of tobacco products), Article 12 (education, communication, training, and public awareness), Article 13 (tobacco advertising, promotion, and sponsorship), Article 14 (demand-reduction measures concerning tobacco dependence and cessation), and Article 15 (illicit trade in tobacco products). These approaches are used in a complementary manner, meaning that they each form part of a comprehensive tobacco-control strategy.

The regulatory approach in the tobacco context can in some ways be contrasted with the dietary context because foods and beverages are essential to nutrition, and even harmful foods may not necessarily be damaging to health, depending on how they are consumed. To put it in the terms of the food industry, "every food and beverage can contribute to a healthy diet."[1]

The difference in approach is reflected in the objectives of the Global Strategy Diet, which include "the reduction of risk factors from noncommunicable diseases that stem from unhealthy diets."[2] In this respect, the Global Strategy Diet sets out the following dietary recommendations:

- achieve energy balance and a healthy weight
- limit energy intake from total fats and shift fat consumption away from saturated fats to unsaturated fats and toward the elimination of trans-fatty acids
- increase consumption of fruits and vegetables, and legumes, whole grains, and nuts
- limit the intake of free sugars
- limit salt (sodium) consumption from all sources and ensure that salt is iodized[3]

Another distinction between the regulatory contexts of tobacco and diet is that physical activity is an important component of ensuring energy balance. Although not all dietary-related noncommunicable diseases are associated with energy imbalances, taking steps to encourage physical activity may alleviate some of the health concerns associated with overconsumption, such as obesity. An approach that emphasizes physical activity in the achievement of energy balance also minimizes concerns about liberty that may arise in the context of more interventionist measures.

National and cultural differences are also likely to be far more important in the context of dietary-related diseases than they are in the context of tobacco control. Although tobacco-control measures can be targeted at particular population groups, the effects of the basic FCTC measures are similar in most

[1] Global Strategy on Diet, Physical Activity and Health, World Health Organization Meeting with Industry Associations, Geneva 17 June 2003, Meeting Note available at http://www.who.int/dietphysicalactivity/media/en/gscon_cs_privatesector.pdf (visited 27/02/10).

[2] Ibid., para. 18.

[3] Ibid., para. 22.

countries.[4] On the other hand, it remains to be seen how regulatory initiatives relating to diet will be received in countries with different cultural norms, cuisines, and different access to foods. Similarly, the nutritional profile of a population may play an important role in the determination of risk tolerance. For example, where undernutrition is a widespread problem, authorities may be more willing to accept the risks associated with the consumption of energy-dense foods.

Although these differences may make the regulatory environment more complex in the dietary context, they do not detract from the underlying similarities between the Global Strategy Diet and the FCTC. Each instrument contemplates similar regulatory strategies to shape consumer behavior in order to minimize risk. Similar approaches are also adopted in the context of harmful alcohol use. In a 2008 report to the WHA, the WHO secretariat identified a number of strategies to reduce alcohol-related harm. The WHO suggested that strategies and policy options should be focused on preventing harmful drinking and should target the population at large as well as vulnerable groups such as young people, pregnant women, and individuals with particular problems.[5] The strategies mentioned include raising awareness and political commitment, preventive measures adopted within the health sector, community-based action, drinking-and-driving policies and countermeasures, measures to address the availability of alcohol (such as for minors and at-risk groups), measures to address the marketing of alcoholic beverages, pricing policies, measures to reduce alcohol-related harm in the night-life environment, and measures to reduce the health impact of informally and illegally produced alcohol.[6]

Although these strategies are similar in many respects to those adopted in the tobacco and dietary contexts, there are also some differences. Alcohol-control strategies are aimed not only at reducing risk factors across the population, but also at preventing harm that may occur as a consequence of overconsumption on any one occasion. It also seems unlikely that public health authorities will seek the complete eradication of alcohol consumption (short of prohibition) as they may in the tobacco context, where each product consumed is considered harmful. Rather, alcohol-control policies are more

4 For a meta-analysis of a number of the different measures, see Prabhat Jha and Frank Chaloupka (eds), *Tobacco Control in Developing Countries*, World Bank and World Health Organization, Oxford University Press (2000) [hereinafter Jha and Chaloupka, *Tobacco Control in Developing Countries*].

5 *Strategies to Reduce the Harmful Use of Alcohol*, Report by the Secretariat, Sixty-First World Health Assembly, World Health Organization, 20 March 2008, A61/13, [hereinafter *Strategies to Reduce the Harmful Use of Alcohol*], para. 8.

6 Ibid., paras 9–17.

likely to be aimed at reducing the frequency of intoxication and reducing the total volume of alcohol consumed.[7]

In all three regulatory contexts, policies to address the price of goods are either contemplated or in place depending on the location. These types of price measures raise questions about compliance with Article III:2 of the GATT as well as with the Agreement on Subsidies and Countervailing Measures (SCM Agreement) and the Agreement on Agriculture.

Some policies affecting the price of goods are intended to alter the conditions of competition between goods. For example, a graduated tax on alcoholic beverages that taxes beverages based on their alcoholic content may be intended to dissuade consumption of beverages with higher alcohol content. Depending on a range of factors, such as where beverages of differing alcohol content are produced, such a measure may favor domestic production. Ordinary excise taxes may also alter competitive conditions. For example, an excise tax on soft drinks may modify the conditions of competition in favor of other beverages, such as fresh juices.

Other price-based measures may also favor domestic production. Minimum prices (price floors) for goods may undermine the competitive advantages of cheaper goods depending where the floor is set. If a price floor is set above the cost of imported goods (raising the retail price of such goods) but below the cost of domestic goods, the measure may favor domestic production.

Health authorities may also wish to use subsidies to promote local production and consumption of foods. The Global Strategy Diet recognizes the benefits of ensuring that there is a local market for healthy foods[8] and encourages states to rely on local production.[9] This reflects the fact that as farmers specialize in the production of particular crops the diversity of agricultural commodities produced in an area may decrease. For example, some Pacific Island states have found that increased agricultural specialization has reduced the local production of traditional crops for the domestic market. These states also face difficulties that limit the flow of imported goods as a substitute for healthful goods previously farmed locally. These difficulties include the relative lack of market power due to the small size of some markets, geographic isolation, and problems of trade facilitation. In such a context, a state may wish to support domestic production, including through the use of subsidies.

7 Sally Casswell and Thaksaphon Thamarangsi, "Reducing Harm from Alcohol: Call to Action," 373(9682) *The Lancet*, (2009), pp. 2247–2257, p. 2253.

8 Global Strategy Diet, para. 43.

9 Ibid., para. 41.

Similarly, restrictions on marketing might be said to favor established brands. Where such brands are domestic brands, a question of compliance with Article III:4 of the GATT might arise. The outcome of *US – Gambling* also suggests that a variety of restrictions on marketing may violate market-access commitments under the GATS. For example, advertising bans may affect the provision of advertising services. Restrictions on the retail sale of goods via remote means such as the Internet or through restrictions on the number of liquor stores in a given area could also restrict market access in the context of distribution and retail services.

This chapter examines the extent to which WTO Members have autonomy to implement price policies and marketing restrictions under the prohibitions contained in the WTO-covered agreements. Of course, conceiving of all the different ways in which measures to address tobacco, alcohol, and diet might result in violation of a WTO-covered agreement is not possible. Accordingly, case studies are used to highlight how prohibitions in the GATT, GATS, SCM Agreement, and Agreement on Agriculture may restrict regulatory autonomy. Because the lawfulness of a particular measure can only be determined in light of circumstances at the time and place of its implementation, this chapter does not seek to draw definitive and abstract conclusions about the lawfulness of particular measures.

Unless otherwise stated, the analysis also proceeds on the assumption that WTO Members will implement measures in an origin-neutral manner. That is, it is assumed that WTO Members will implement measures in a form that does not discriminate openly between imported and domestic goods. The primary focus, therefore, is the question of when facially neutral measures might, through their effect, violate a prohibition in a covered agreement.

As mentioned in Chapter 1, this chapter addresses only prohibitions in the covered agreements; exceptions to the prohibitions are discussed in Chapter 4. Because it is application of the exceptions that ultimately determine the extent of regulatory autonomy, the primary focus of this chapter is to identify how the prohibitions apply to taxes, restrictions on marketing, and subsidies. Normative discussion of how the rules affect regulatory autonomy is undertaken in Chapter 4.

1. PRICE MEASURES

The use of taxes for health purposes is well established in the tobacco and alcohol contexts and is increasingly contemplated in the dietary context.[10]

[10] In the dietary context, see, for example, Australia: The Healthiest Country by 2020, National Preventative Health Strategy – The Roadmap for Action, 30 June 2009, pp. 104–105; "Taiwan

In the tobacco context, the widespread use of taxes is reflected in Article 6.1 of the FCTC, which recognizes the effectiveness of tax and price policies as means of reducing tobacco consumption. A large body of empirical evidence also suggests that tax measures can increase cessation of tobacco consumption, reduce the frequency of tobacco use by individuals, and reduce the initiation of smoking, particularly by young people.[11] For these reasons, tax measures are generally considered to be among the most important means of tobacco control.

The imposition of excise taxes on alcoholic beverages is also common. As is the case with tobacco, these taxes have not always been used with concerns exclusive to public health in mind. Rather, many taxes on alcoholic beverages and tobacco products are longstanding "sin taxes" used partly for the collection of government revenue and partly for public health purposes. These taxes are also often Pigovian taxes, meaning that they seek to internalize negative externalities associated with consumption of a product. The public health rationale for taxing alcoholic beverages is recognized in the Global Strategy Alcohol. Policy options and interventions listed in the document include "establishing a system for specific domestic taxation on alcohol accompanied by an effective enforcement system, which may take into account, as appropriate, the alcoholic content of the beverage."[12] This is consistent with the idea that taxes based on alcohol content have a greater impact on the consumption patterns of heavy drinkers and thereby are likely to reduce harm.[13]

The Global Strategy Diet also recognizes that product prices influence consumption choices in the dietary context and recognizes the role of fiscal policies in promoting healthy choices. The strategy states that "[p]ublic policies can influence prices through taxation, subsidies, or direct pricing in ways that encourage healthy eating."[14] This language contemplates the use of taxes that decrease the price of healthful foods and beverages relative to the price of less healthy foods and beverages.

Plans Junk Food Tax," AFP, December 22, 2009; Alison Mutler, "Romanians Move to Tax the Once Beloved Fast Food," AP, 17 February 2009.

11 See generally Frank Chaloupka, Teh-Wei Hu, Kenneth Warner et al., "The Taxation of Tobacco Products" in Prabhat Jha and Frank Chaloupka (eds), *Tobacco Control in Developing Countries, World Bank and World Health Organization* (2000), pp. 237–272, p. 267 [hereinafter Jha and Chaloupka, *Tobacco Control in Developing Countries*].

12 Draft Global Strategy to Reduce the Harmful Use of Alcohol, Revised version based on the outcomes of WHO Executive Board 126th Session, Geneva, 18–23 January 2010, 5 February 2010, para. 34.

13 *The Lancet*, "UK Alcohol Policy a Costly Decision for Public Health," 373(9672) *The Lancet*, (2009), 1312.

14 Global Strategy Diet, para. 41(2).

It is also worth noting that the domestic regulatory politics associated with differential taxation may result in the use of relatively crude measures. For example, a WTO Member might impose an excise tax on carbonated soft drinks rather than an excise that is based on the objective nutritional qualities of a beverage and applicable across the packaged beverage sector as a whole. The former measure would most likely be easier to implement, and in political terms is a visible response to problems such as obesity. Equally, the latter approach is more likely to be an even-handed regulatory approach and is more likely to create financial incentives to improve the nutritional content of packaged beverages, such as where lower sugar content results in less or no excise being levied.

Examples of the types of taxes used can be drawn from the tobacco context. The three types of taxes most commonly imposed on tobacco products are sales tax, value-added tax, and excise tax.[15] Sales taxes are levied at either one or a number of stages in the production or distribution chain of a product. Value-added taxes are general taxes levied on all or most goods and services in a manner that is proportionate to their price.[16] Excise taxes are particular to certain products and are found in the form of specific taxes (such as taxes based on quantity, i.e. a certain amount per pack of cigarettes) or *ad valorem* taxes, which are taxes based on a percentage of the value of the product.

As a general rule, specific taxes are used to discourage the consumption of a product because the tax burden is the same for each unit sold. However, each form of tax has advantages and disadvantages. A specific tax protects revenue where the price of a good declines,[17] and if the tax is sufficiently high, it can guard to some degree against the consumption-increasing effects of price reductions and discounting. In contrast, where *ad valorem* taxes are used, the tax received declines as the value of the product declines. The primary advantage, however, of an *ad valorem* tax is that it automatically keeps

[15] See generally Emil Sunley, Adya Yurekli, Frank Chaloupka, "The Design, Administration and Potential Revenue of Tobacco Excises in Curbing the Epidemic: Governments and the Economics of Tobacco Control," Washington D.C., World Bank, 1999 available at http://web.worldbank.org/WBSITE/EXTERNAL/TOPICS/EXTHEALTHNUTRITIONANDPOPULATION/EXTETC/0,,contentMDK:20361460~menuPK:376607~pagePK:148956~piPK:216618~theSitePK:376601,00.html, (visited 12/12/07) [hereinafter Sunley et al., "Tobacco Excises"]; Adya Yurekli, Joy De Beyer, Design and Administer Tobacco Taxes, World Bank Economics of Tobacco Toolkit available at http://web.worldbank.org/WBSITE/EXTERNAL/TOPICS/EXTHEALTHNUTRITIONANDPOPULATION/EXTETC/0,,contentMDK:20365047~menuPK:478898~pagePK:148956~piPK:216618~theSitePK:376601,00.html (visited 10/01/08) [hereinafter Yurekli and De Beyer, "Design and Administer Tobacco Taxes"].

[16] Yurekli and De Beyer, "Design and Administer Tobacco Taxes," p. 5.

[17] Sunley et al., "Tobacco Excises," p. 411.

pace with inflation,[18] whereas a specific tax must be pegged to the Consumer Price Index (CPI) and changed regularly to keep pace with inflation.[19] An advantage of a specific tax, at least in terms of WTO law, is that it levies the same amount of tax on different products irrespective of their value. Because taxes based on value result in higher tax burdens for higher value products, there is less chance that specific taxes will alter the conditions of competition between goods.

In addition to inflation, there are a range of other issues taken into account in the design of tobacco taxes. These issues relate to the effectiveness of a measure in reducing consumption, the capacity of a measure to internalize externalities (including potentially different externalities related to different types of products), the capacity of a state to enforce a measure, and the risk that a tax on products will be regressive, in the sense that it falls hardest on the poor.

1.1. *How the Covered Agreements Apply to Tax Measures*

Thailand – Cigarettes is the starting point in analyzing the use of tax measures in the contexts of tobacco, alcohol, and dietary-related disease.[20] It will be recalled from Chapter 1 that the GATT panel in *Thailand – Cigarettes* viewed the use of taxation measures as a reasonably available alternative to the maintenance of Thailand's import licensing system.[21] The GATT panel also suggested that Thailand could use tax measures as a means of addressing the lower prices that were likely to follow from increased competition in the Thai market.[22] This suggests that WTO Members have significant scope to implement tax measures in the interests of public health. For the most part, the use of origin-neutral excise taxes is not likely to result in a violation of the WTO-covered agreements.

Equally, a number of taxes on alcoholic beverages have been found to violate Article III:2.[23] Although health measures were not the focus of these

[18] Ibid., p. 414.

[19] Ibid.

[20] Although the SPS Agreement could, in theory, be an appropriate starting point, the absence of international standards in the context of tax measures means that analysis of tax measures under that agreement is unlikely to be fruitful.

[21] GATT Panel Report, *Thailand – Cigarettes*, para. 79.

[22] Ibid.

[23] See, for example, Appellate Body Report, *Japan – Taxes on Alcoholic Beverages*, WT/DS8/AB/R, WT/DS10/AB/R, WT/DS11/AB/R, adopted 1 November 1996, DSR 1996:I, 97 [hereinafter, *Japan – Alcoholic Beverages II*]; Appellate Body Report, *Korea – Taxes on Alcoholic Beverages*, WT/DS75/AB/R, WT/DS84/AB/R, adopted 17 February 1999, DSR 1999:I, 3.

disputes, they suggest that Article III:2 is most likely to be relevant where tax differentials are used to discourage the consumption of relatively unhealthy goods. For example, some of the case law has concerned measures that levy higher taxes on beverages with a relatively high alcohol content. This is not to suggest that merely favoring one type of good over another is likely to result in a violation of Article III:2. On the contrary, Article III concerns national treatment, meaning that differential taxes will only be problematic where the tax differential favors domestic goods. This will occur in a limited range of circumstances. For example, in *Chile – Alcoholic Beverages* excise tax rates were staggered depending on the alcoholic content of a beverage in such a way that the tax burden fell heavily on imported spirits but relatively lightly on pisco (a traditional Chilean liquor).[24] On the other hand, the tax structure in place meant that taxes also fell heavily on domestic alcoholic beverages, raising the question of where the line is to be drawn in terms of when a measure acts so as to afford protection to domestic production (an issue addressed in further detail later in this chapter).

This question is more likely to be relevant in the alcohol and dietary contexts than in the tobacco context. The concept of so-called reduced harm tobacco products is controversial, partly because public health bodies have previously been duped by so-called light and mild cigarettes, and partly because all tobacco products are harmful to health. This can be contrasted with the alcohol context, where graduated taxes may be used to reduce overall alcohol intake, and the dietary context, where selective taxation, such as a soft-drink tax, creates differences in the tax regime applicable to different goods.

Drawing the line between legitimate government regulation and protection of domestic production may also be an issue in the context of minimum prices (price floors). The Global Strategy Alcohol includes the establishment of minimum prices for alcohol as a policy option.[25] However, the point at which a price floor is set will affect the impact it has on domestic as compared to imported goods. A price floor might be set above the cost of imported goods but below the cost of domestic goods, thereby reducing the price competitiveness of imported goods. The opposite may also be true, in that a price floor could be set above the cost of domestic goods but below the cost of imported goods, thereby favoring imports. However, in most instances these scenarios are likely to present an oversimplification of the issue. Both imported and

[24] See Appellate Body Report, *Chile – Taxes on Alcoholic Beverages*, WT/DS87/AB/R, WT/DS110/AB/R, adopted 12 January 2000, DSR 2000:I, 281 [hereinafter *Chile –Alcoholic Beverages*].

[25] Draft Global Strategy to Reduce the Harmful Use of Alcohol, para. 34.

domestic goods of various types are likely to cost either more or less than a price floor, making the impact on competition more difficult to assess.

With these issues in mind, it is worthwhile to make some general observations about Article III:2 and its application to tax measures of the type under discussion. Paragraphs 1 and 2 of Article III state:

Article III*

National Treatment on Internal Taxation and Regulation

1. The contracting parties recognise that internal taxes and other internal charges, and laws, regulations and requirements affecting the internal sale, offering for sale, purchase, transportation, distribution or use of products, and internal quantitative regulations requiring the mixture, processing or use of products in specified amounts or proportions, should not be applied to imported or domestic products so as to afford protection to domestic production.*
2. The products of the territory of any contracting party imported into the territory of any other contracting party shall not be subject, directly or indirectly, to internal taxes or other internal charges of any kind in excess of those applied, directly or indirectly, to like domestic products. Moreover, no contracting party shall otherwise apply internal taxes or other internal charges to imported or domestic products in a manner contrary to the principles set forth in paragraph 1.*

Article III:1 is not a prohibition of an obligatory character, but is used in interpretation of Article III:2 and Article III in general.[26] As such, paragraphs 1 and 2 of Article III of the GATT create two obligations, which are found in the first and second sentences of Article III:2.

The first sentence of Article III:2 prohibits internal taxes or charges in excess of those applied to like domestic products. Under the first sentence there is no need to demonstrate the presence of a protective application beyond the specific requirements of the provision.[27] In contrast, the second sentence of Article III:2 is a broader prohibition relating to the protection of domestic production. As the additional note to paragraph III:2 indicates, the second sentence applies to directly competitive or substitutable products that are not similarly taxed. The note states:

> A tax conforming to the requirements of the first sentence of paragraph 2 would be considered to be inconsistent with the provisions of the second sentence only in cases where competition was involved between, on the one hand, the taxed product and, on the other hand, a directly competitive or substitutable product which was not similarly taxed.

[26] Appellate Body Report, *Japan – Alcoholic Beverages II*, pp. 17–18.

[27] Ibid., p. 18.

With these basic aspects of Article III:2 in mind, one question that arises is to what extent the regulatory character of a differential tax measure will be taken into account in interpretation of Article III:2. In this respect, Article III forms the first limb of what Robert Hudec has referred to as a two-step analysis.[28] If Article III prohibits a measure, its lawfulness may nonetheless be upheld under the exceptions in Article XX of the GATT, which include an exception for measures necessary for the protection of human health or life.[29] At face value, this suggests that the extent to which a measure protects domestic production is the sole focus of Article III, whereas issues of regulatory legitimacy are to be considered under Article XX. This argument finds some support in the purposes of Article III. The national treatment obligations in Article III have the dual purposes of protecting tariff concessions granted by WTO Members and of preventing the use of internal taxes and regulations as a means of protecting domestic production.[30]

In this context, it is also worth noting the role played by Article III:4 of the GATT. Whereas Article III:2 imposes a national treatment obligation with respect to internal taxes and charges, Article III:4 imposes an obligation that has application to a broader range of internal regulation. The text of the provision states:

> The products of the territory of any contracting party imported into the territory of any other contracting party shall be accorded treatment no less favourable than that accorded to like products of national origin in respect of all laws, regulations and requirements affecting their internal sale, offering for sale, purchase, transportation, distribution or use.

Like Article III:2, Article III:4 seeks to preserve the benefits of tariff commitments made by WTO ,members while also guarding against other forms of protectionism. The fundamental purpose of Article III:4 is to "ensure equality of competitive conditions between imported and like domestic products."[31]

On the other hand, Article XX sets out a limited range of exceptions that do not encompass all of the legitimate regulatory objectives that a WTO Member

28 Robert Hudec, "GATT/WTO Constraints on National Regulation: Requiem for an 'Aim and Effects' Test," in Robert Hudec, *Essays on the Nature of International Trade Law*, London, Cameron May, (2000), pp. 359–395, [hereinafter Hudec, "Requiem"], p. 360.

29 Article XX(b).

30 John Jackson, *World Trade and the Law of GATT*, Charlottesville, VA, The Michie Company, (1969), p. 277.

31 Appellate Body Report, *Canada – Certain Measures Concerning Periodicals*, WT/DS31/AB/R, adopted 30 July 1997, DSR 1997:I, 449, [hereinafter *Canada – Periodicals*], p. 18.

might pursue through a tax measure.[32] Thus, an alternative view of Article III is that the provision should balance the need to prevent protectionism and the need for regulatory autonomy. As Robert Howse and Elisabeth Türk have put it:

> [C]asting the net too broadly might transform the WTO dispute settlement organs into a routine reviewing court for ordinary domestic regulations, placing undue limits on non-protectionist regulatory purposes. [footnote omitted] On the other hand, a failure to consider seriously the possibility of *de facto* discrimination could undermine the integrity of disciplines of discrimination generally, providing a ready means of cheating with impunity on those specific commitments.[33]

Nicholas Di Mascio and Joost Pauwelyn have argued that the case law on this question can be divided into different periods. They argue that earlier case law minimized the role of regulatory legitimacy, whereas there has been a recent shift toward emphasizing regulatory legitimacy in the analysis.[34] This possibility can be explored through the two avenues through which regulatory purposes such as the protection of health might be accommodated within Article III:2. One avenue is in a determination of whether products that are taxed differently are "like" or "directly competitive or substitutable." The other avenue, applicable only to the second sentence, is in a determination of whether a measure acts "so as to afford protection to domestic production."

A. The first sentence of Article III:2

In the context of Article III:2, the like products standard is interpreted narrowly.[35] This narrow construction stems from the relationship with the second sentence of Article III:2, which applies to products that are "directly competitive or substitutable." Like products are a subset of this broader grouping. As the Appellate Body explained in *Korea – Alcoholic Beverages*:

> [A]ll like products are, by definition, directly competitive or substitutable products, whereas not all "directly competitive or substitutable products" are

[32] Although this concern suggests that Article III ought to accommodate legitimate regulation, this concern is to some extent irrelevant to this study because the measures ordinarily fall within the ambit of exceptions such as paragraphs (b) and (d) of Article XX.

[33] Robert Howse and Elisabeth Türk, "The WTO Impact Upon Internal Regulations: A Case Study of the Canada – EC Asbestos Dispute," in George Bermann and Petros Mavroidis (eds), *Trade and Human Health and Safety*, New York, Cambridge University Press, (2006), pp. 77–117, p. 79.

[34] Nicholas Di Mascio and Joost Pauwelyn, "Nondiscrimination in Trade and Investment Treaties: Worlds Apart or Two Sides of the Same Coin?" 102 *American Journal of International Law*, (2008), pp. 48–89.

[35] Appellate Body Report, *Japan – Alcoholic Beverages II*, p. 19.

> "like" [footnote omitted]. The notion of "like products" must be construed narrowly [footnote omitted] but the category of directly competitive or substitutable products is broader [footnote omitted]. While perfectly substitutable products fall within Article III:2, first sentence, imperfectly substitutable products can be assessed under Article III:2, second sentence.[36]

There is no precise definition of the meaning of the phrase "like products."[37] Rather, a range of factors, such as those set out in the report of the Working Party on Border Tax Adjustments,[38] are regularly referred to by panels and the Appellate Body[39] in making case-by-case determinations of likeness. The report on border tax adjustments refers to the end uses of a product in a given market, consumers' tastes and habits (which may vary from country to country), and the product's properties, nature, and quality as criteria that may assist in the determination of likeness on a case-by-case basis.[40] In addition, the tariff classification of the products in question is also often considered.

In *EC – Asbestos* (which addressed application of Article III:4) the Appellate Body indicated that these factors are considered in order to identify the extent to which the products in question are in a competitive relationship. The Appellate Body stated, "[i]f there is – or could be – no competitive relationship between products, a Member cannot intervene, through internal taxation or regulation, to protect domestic production."[41] As the Appellate Body stressed, however, this does not mean that questions of likeness are dictated solely by market-based considerations. All evidence pertinent to the question of likeness must be taken into account, including the physical characteristics of the relevant products and the health risks associated with their use.[42]

The health risk posed by products can influence consumers' tastes and habits and is, therefore, relevant to an examination of likeness.[43] In *EC – Asbestos* the Appellate Body had to consider the likeness of chrysotile asbestos fibers (a known carcinogen) and PCG fibers (an asbestos substitute that is not known

36 Appellate Body Report, *Korea – Alcoholic Beverages*, para. 118.

37 Panel Report, *Japan – Alcoholic Beverages II*, para 6.21.

38 Report of the Working Party on Border Tax Adjustments, adopted 2 December 1970, (L/3464) [hereinafter Working Party on Border Tax Adjustments].

39 See discussion in Panel Report, *Japan – Alcoholic Beverages II*, para 6.21.

40 Working Party on Border Tax Adjustments, para. 18.

41 See discussion in Appellate Body Report, *European Communities – Measures Affecting Asbestos and Asbestos-Containing Products*, WT/DS135/AB/R, adopted 5 April 2001, DSR 2001:VII, 3243, [hereinafter *EC – Asbestos*], para. 117.

42 Ibid., para. 113.

43 Ibid., paras 115–116.

to be carcinogenic). Whereas the Appellate Body emphasized that the issue of consumers' tastes and habits can only be judged in light of the evidence presented,[44] it also stated that, given one of the products was a known carcinogen, there was a very heavy burden placed on Canada (the complainant) to show under the second and third criteria that the products were in a competitive relationship.[45] That is, where products taxed differently pose divergent risks to health, the risks may constitute evidence suggesting that the products in question are not in a competitive relationship.

Although this suggests that the health implications of consuming different products may indicate that such products are not like, this conclusion is qualified. As the Appellate Body noted in *EC – Asbestos*:

> [C]onsumers' reactions to products posing a risk to human health vary considerably depending on the product, and on the consumer. Some dangerous products, such as tobacco, are widely used, despite the known health risks. The influence known dangers have on consumers' tastes and habits is, therefore, unlikely to be uniform or entirely predictable.[46]

In addition to being relevant to consumer preferences, the health consequences of consumption are relevant to how like the properties, nature, and quality of different products are.[47]

Although the circumstances in which likeness will be made out cannot be determined in the abstract, the greater the difference between products in terms of health consequences, the less chance there is that those products will be considered like. Therefore, to some degree at least, likeness may turn on the risks associated with consuming different products. By the same token, giving consideration to the health consequences of different goods may not open the door entirely to a general determination of whether a differential tax measure is a legitimate regulatory measure. This approach was rejected by the Appellate Body with the "aim and effects" test in *Japan – Alcoholic Beverages II*.[48] This test was developed by GATT panels in order to determine which distinctions between products might form the basis for the maintenance of lawful regulatory distinctions between products.[49] By rejecting the "aim and effects" test and focusing on the competitive relationship between

44 Ibid., para. 145.
45 Ibid., para. 118.
46 Ibid, para. 122 in fn 103.
47 Appellate Body Report, *EC – Asbestos*, para. 113.
48 Appellate Body Report, *Japan – Alcoholic Beverages II*, p. 29.
49 GATT Panel Report, *United States – Taxes on Automobiles*, DS31/R, 11 October 1994, unadopted [hereinafter *US – Taxes on Automobiles*], para. 5.6.

goods, the case law has minimized the extent to which a legitimate regulatory purpose might be considered in the context of this element of Article III:2.

Finally, it is worth noting that, as the Appellate Body itself has recognized, a determination of likeness involves an "unavoidable element of individual, discretionary judgement."[50] This is especially so where the "like" products standard involves identifying a different degree of competitiveness to the "directly competitive or substitutable" standard. As Hudec argued, "[t]he normal response of most tribunals ... is to decide the case as best they can by making a seat-of-the-pants judgement about whether the defendant government is behaving correctly or incorrectly – a process of judgement known in some circles as the 'smell-test.'"[51]

In the context of the types of taxes identified earlier, this suggests two things. First, there is some inherent unpredictability about whether goods will be treated as like under provisions such as Article III:2 and III:4 of the GATT. Much will depend on the evidence brought by the parties to a dispute. Secondly, the focus of the test is whether the relevant goods are in competition with one another, because protection is not an issue in the absence of competition between goods. This suggests that the regulatory distinctions underlying differential taxation of goods will not always be significant in application of Article III:2, first sentence.

B. The second sentence of Article III:2

The second sentence of Article III:2 is the more general of the two requirements. It has already been noted that the directly competitive or substitutable standard is broader than the like products standard and that the directly competitive or substitutable standard applies to imperfectly substitutable products. Wherever goods are considered like, they will also be directly competitive and substitutable. Where goods are not considered like, this test will have to be considered.

(a) DIRECTLY COMPETITIVE OR SUBSTITUTABLE PRODUCTS

In *Korea – Alcoholic Beverages* the panel discussed the distinction between "directly" competitive or substitutable products and products that are "indirectly" competitive or substitutable. It stated:

> At some level all products are at least indirectly competitive. Because consumers have limited amounts of disposable income, they may have to arbitrate between various needs such as giving up going on a vacation to buy a

50 Ibid., pp. 20–21.

51 Hudec, "Requiem," p. 376.

> car or abstaining from eating in restaurants to buy new shoes or a television set. However, an assessment of whether there is a direct competitive relationship between two products or groups of products requires evidence that consumers consider or could consider the two products or groups of products as alternative ways of satisfying a particular need or taste.[52]

On the one hand, the very nature of differential taxation is to encourage the consumption of one product and to discourage consumption of another. In this sense, the cross-price elasticity of the goods should indicate that they are in a competitive relationship.[53] If the cross-price elasticity does not indicate this, then it suggests the measure to be ineffective. On the other hand, in *Korea – Alcoholic Beverages* the Appellate Body stressed that cross-price elasticity is not the decisive criterion in determining whether products are directly competitive or substitutable. Rather, analysis should focus on "the nature of competition" between the products in question.[54] What exactly this refers to is unclear.

The decision of the Appellate Body in *EC – Asbestos* could be read to suggest that questions of likeness under Article III:4 (a standard that is not broader than the two standards of Article III:2 combined[55]) may not be determined solely by reference to the extent to which goods compete. In particular, one member of the Appellate Body felt compelled to express a separate but concurring opinion within the text of the report to the effect that the health risk posed by the asbestos fibers and asbestos products was such that evidence relating to economic competitive relationships could not outweigh those risks in an analysis of likeness. The member stated that "the necessity or appropriateness of adopting a 'fundamentally' economic interpretation of the 'likeness' of products under Article III:4 of the GATT 1994 does not appear to me to be free from substantial debate."[56]

However, this statement is in effect a minority opinion that differs from the majority approach, which was to focus on the health risks only as an indicator of the extent to which the goods in question were in a competitive relationship. In summary, therefore, the present application of the "like" products test in Article III:2 is such that there appears to be little scope for regulatory purpose to be considered. This suggests that differential tax measures of the type

[52] Panel Report, *Korea – Alcoholic Beverages*, paras 10.37–10.40.

[53] On the issue of price elasticity see Appellate Body Report, *Japan – Alcoholic Beverages II*, p. 25.

[54] Appellate Body Report, *Korea – Taxes on Alcoholic Beverages*, WT/DS75/AB/R, WT/DS84/AB/R, adopted 17 February 1999, DSR 1999:I, 3, para. 134.

[55] Appellate Body Report, *EC – Asbestos*, para. 99.

[56] Ibid., para. 154.

described will often fulfill the like products requirement because the types of goods in question will often be in a competitive relationship. For example, beverages with differing alcohol or sugar content will often compete with one another, as will foods with differing fat, sugar, or sodium levels.

(b) SO AS TO AFFORD PROTECTION TO DOMESTIC PRODUCTION

Another aspect of the second sentence of Article III:2 that may leave policy space is the requirement that measures be applied so as to afford protection to domestic production. This question is examined separately to whether goods are similarly taxed. The issue is also said not to be one of regulatory intent, but rather to be examined objectively. As the Appellate Body stated in *Japan – Alcoholic Beverages II*, "it is possible to examine objectively the underlying criteria used in a particular tax measure, its structure and its overall application to ascertain whether it is applied in a way that affords protection to domestic products."[57] There are a number of relevant factors that may be taken into account, including the size of a tax differential, whether it isolates domestic products from foreign competition,[58] whether the beneficiaries of the measures are almost exclusively domestic producers,[59] and whether the measure is connected with its stated aims.[60]

In *Japan – Alcoholic Beverages II* the Appellate Body concluded that a determination of whether a measure acts "so as to afford protection" is not a question of legislative or regulatory intent. Rather, for this element of Article III to be made out, it is sufficient if the measure is "*applied* to imported or domestic products so as to afford protection to domestic production."[61] Thus, a legitimate regulatory purpose will not excuse a measure from the application of Article III under this element of the provision. Notwithstanding this, in *Chile – Alcoholic Beverages* the Appellate Body suggested that a regulatory purpose could be discerned from the objective features of a measure, and that a stated regulatory purpose might be used to suggest that a measure is applied so as to afford protection. For example, the fact that a measure is not connected with a stated purpose might suggest that it is protectionist (although whether a measure is necessary to achieve a stated purpose is not judged[62]).

57 Appellate Body Report, *Japan – Alcoholic Beverages II*, p. 29.

58 Ibid., p. 31 quoting the Report of the Panel at para. 6.35.

59 Panel Report, *Korea –Alcoholic Beverages*, para. 10.102.

60 Panel Report, *Chile – Taxes on Alcoholic Beverages*, WT/DS87/R, WT/DS110/R, adopted 12 January 2000, modified by Appellate Body Report, WT/DS87/AB/R, WT/DS110/AB/R, DSR 2000:I, 303, para. 71.

61 Appellate Body Report, *Japan – Alcoholic Beverages II*, p. 28 (emphasis in original).

62 Appellate Body Report, *Chile –Alcoholic Beverages*, para. 72.

Thus, it seems clear that a regulatory purpose may be relevant to the manner in which a measure is *applied*. However, this suggests that the "so as to afford protection" requirement is neither entirely about the intent of a party implementing a measure nor entirely about the effects of a measure on conditions of competition.

In the context of differential taxes it is possible to conceive of a range of different circumstances in which domestic goods will be favored and the requirements of this provision made out. In particular, there may be circumstances where the beneficiaries of the measure are almost exclusively domestic producers. For example, this was considered to be the case in the aforementioned *Chile – Alcoholic Beverages*.

This raises the question of to what degree the measure must protect domestic production. Lothar Ehring has characterized this issue as one of whether "national rules discriminating on a facially neutral basis violate the non-discrimination rule only if they impose a greater overall disadvantage on imports than on comparable domestic goods, or whether it is sufficient that they disfavour some imports."[63] If it is the case that an overall disadvantage to imports is required, facially origin-neutral measures are less likely to violate the provision inadvertently. In this sense, the overall disadvantage approach could play an important role in preserving the lawfulness of regulatory measures under Articles III:2 and III:4 of the GATT[64] and in ensuring that the limited range of general exceptions set out in Article XX of the GATT is not definitive of the classes of regulatory measures that might be lawful under the GATT.[65]

Although the case law on this question is somewhat ambiguous,[66] the Appellate Body arguably took a position in *EC – Asbestos*. In that instance, the Appellate Body considered the broad interpretation given to the phrase "like products" in the context of Article III:4:

> [W]e observe that there is a second element that must be established before a measure can be held to be inconsistent with Article III:4. Thus, even if

63 Lothar Ehring, "De Facto Discrimination in World Trade Law National and Most-Favoured-Nation Treatment – or Equal Treatment?" 36(5) *Journal of World Trade*, (2002), pp. 921–977, p. 922 [hereinafter Ehring, "De Facto Discrimination in World Trade Law"].

64 See generally Howse and Türk, "The WTO Impact Upon Internal Regulations."

65 See also William Davey and Joost Pauwelyn, "MFN Unconditionality: A Legal Analysis of the Concept in View of its Evolution in the GATT/WTO Jurisprudence with Particular Reference to the Issue of 'Like Product,'" in Thomas Cottier and Petros Mavroidis (eds), *Regulatory Barriers and the Principle of Non-Discrimination in World Trade Law*, Ann Arbor, University of Michigan Press, (2000), pp. 13–50, pp. 38–41; Horn and Mavroidis, "Still Hazy after All These Years," p. 59.

66 For a summary and analysis of the case law see Ehring, "De Facto Discrimination in World Trade Law," pp. 931–948.

> two products are "like," that does not mean that a measure is inconsistent with Article III:4. A complaining Member must still establish that the measure accords to the group of like imported products "less favourable treatment" than it accords to the group of "like" domestic products. The term "less favourable treatment" expresses the general principle, in Article III:1, that internal regulations "should not be applied … so as to afford protection to domestic production." If there is "less favourable treatment" of the group of "like" imported products, there is, conversely, "protection" of the group of "like" domestic products. However, a Member may draw distinctions between products which have been found to be "like," without, for this reason alone, according to the group of "like" imported products, "less favourable treatment" than that accorded to the group of "like" domestic products.[67]

This passage affirms the proposition that simply because like products are treated differently does not mean that imported products are treated less favorably under Article III:4.[68] The Appellate Body further explained this point in *Dominican Republic – Importation and Internal Sale of Cigarettes*, in which it emphasized that a measure must modify the conditions of competition in the relevant market *to the detriment of imported products*.[69] The Appellate Body went on to state that "the existence of a detrimental effect on a given imported product resulting from a measure does not necessarily imply that this measure accords less favourable treatment to imports if the detrimental effect is explained by factors or circumstances unrelated to the foreign origin of the product, such as the market share of the importer."[70]

This analysis is perfectly understandable in the context of *Dominican Republic – Importation and Internal Sale of Cigarettes*. In that dispute, Honduras argued that an import-bonding requirement (designed to secure payment of taxes) was less favorable to imported products because the market share of imported goods meant that higher bonds had to be paid by importers. In this context, the fact that an importer held the majority market share of an adversely affected good did not mean that a measure was necessarily less favorable to imported goods.

The panel in *EC – Approval and Marketing of Biotech Products* drew on this passage in considering the less favorable treatment requirement of

67 Appellate Body Report, *EC – Asbestos*, para. 100.

68 See Appellate Body Report, *Korea – Measures Affecting Imports of Fresh, Chilled and Frozen Beef*, WT/DS161/AB/R, WT/DS169/AB/R, adopted 10 January 2001, DSR 2001:I, 5 [hereinafter *Korea – Various Measures on Beef*], paras 135–137.

69 Appellate Body Report, *Dominican Republic – Measures Affecting the Importation and Internal Sale of Cigarettes*, WT/DS302/AB/R, adopted 19 May 2005, para. 96.

70 Ibid.

Article III:4. In that dispute, Argentina claimed that the failure of the EC to consider an application for approval of a biotech product resulted in less favorable treatment for imported biotech products as compared to like domestic products that were not biotech products. The panel held that Argentina's claim did not allege that products were treated differently depending on their origin and stated, "[i]n these circumstances, it is not self-evident that the alleged less favourable treatment of imported biotech products is explained by the foreign origin of these products rather than, for instance, a perceived difference between biotech products and non-biotech products in terms of their safety, etc."[71]

Robert Howse and Henrik Horn have argued that the panel report in *EC – Approval and Marketing of Biotech Products* is a large jurisprudential step that has been made in the absence of any engagement with the larger issues underlying the rejection of the aims and effects test.[72] Whether this is such a large step remains to be seen. It might be that the case law is responding to highly specific factual scenarios rather than evolving in a way that can be said to constitute a trend. Nonetheless, the panel's approach suggests that the relative quantities of domestic and imported goods favored and disfavored are not definitive and that there are no set requirements. Rather, the analysis should focus on how a measure affects the conditions of competition between imported and domestic goods more generally. For facially nondiscriminatory measures, this approach inevitably leads back to what Hudec described as a smell-test, but one that may take some account of legitimate regulatory purposes.

There are a few observations that can be made concerning the implications of these conclusions for measures in the contexts of tobacco, alcohol, and diet. One observation is that a great deal will depend on the circumstances at the time and place a measure is implemented. Measures intended to foster a local market in particular goods appear more likely to afford protection than measures that are based solely on a criterion of harmfulness. Take, for example, a member with trade facilitation problems that limit the ability of importers to import fresh foods. If such a member were to tax energy-dense processed foods at a higher rate than fresh fruits and vegetables, a claim under Article III:2 may be more likely to succeed than in the territory of a member where imported and domestic fresh fruits and vegetables compete under more level conditions of competition.

[71] Panel Report, *EC – Approval and Marketing of Biotech Products*, para. 7.2514.

[72] Robert Howse and Henrik Horn, "European Communities – Measures Affecting the Approval and Marketing of Biotech Products," 8(1) *World Trade Review*, pp. 49–83, p. 60.

By the same token, a measure based on a criterion of harmfulness will not always be lawful. Much will depend on the extent to which domestic and imported goods fall into product categories associated with tax differentials. The difficulty associated with classifying goods should also not be underestimated. For example, in the dietary context there exist a number of different systems for nutrient profiling. The technical approaches adopted by those systems on issues such as which nutrients should be examined and whether specific food categories should be examined influence the outcome of the profiling exercise. In this respect, it has been concluded that "when comparing how different systems rank the same foods, consistency is often relatively weak."[73]

A further difficulty is that classifications may not always be based solely on the objective characteristics of a good, such as its alcohol or fat content. Rather, tax differentials might be tailored to local circumstances, such as local dietary recommendations, which depend on the nutritional profile of a population. Similarly, taxes on alcoholic beverages might be higher on beverages associated with problem drinking in a local context, such as drinks popular with underage drinkers.

Finally, the fact that Article XX(b) of the GATT constitutes an exception to Article III means that the regulatory legitimacy of measures may ultimately be judged under Article XX(b). In difficult cases, this may also incline a panel to find that a measure violates Article III. Although on its face this may seem reasonable, it is possible to identify circumstances in which it may be problematic. For example, in Chapter 1 mention was made of the Request for Consultations that Indonesia made concerning U.S. bans on flavored cigarettes, including clove cigarettes made in Indonesia. The fact that the ban in question exempts menthol cigarettes may make the measure difficult to defend under the *chapeau* of Article XX. In this context, application of rules governing national treatment might take on added significance, and an attitude that shifts all questions of regulatory legitimacy to analysis under Article XX is arguably not appropriate.

C. Article III:4 and price floors

Much of the previous analysis is also relevant in the context of price floors. More specifically, the regulatory purpose underlying a price floor will not be determinative of whether such a measure complies with Article III:4. This conclusion is reflected in the report of the GATT panel in *Canada – Provincial*

73 Marketing of Food and Non-Alcoholic Beverages to Children, Report of a WHO Technical Forum and Technical Meeting Oslo, Norway, 2–5 May 2006, p. 13.

Liquor Boards (US).[74] In that dispute the United States challenged a number of measures implemented by Canadian provinces, including price floors for beer. Canada argued that the measures were implemented in pursuit of policy objectives to ensure the responsible use of alcohol and that the measures limited the ability of suppliers to engage in deep price discounting that encourages the consumption of alcohol.[75]

The United States framed its complaint under Article XI:1 rather than Article III:4, and the panel found that the measure fell within the scope of Article III rather than Article XI (an issue discussed in further detail later). Notwithstanding the fact that the United States did not argue the claim under Article III, the panel noted that whenever minimum prices "prevented imported beer from being supplied at a price below that of domestic beer, they accorded in fact treatment to imported beer less favourable than that accorded to domestic beer."[76]

Although the analysis of less favorable treatment suggests that this comment may be too categorical, it reinforces the point that price floors may give rise to violation of Article III:4 depending on the level at which they are set. The panel also considered that price floors may frustrate the effect of tariff concessions made under Article II. In this respect, the panel drew on the earlier decision of the GATT panel in *EEC – Oilseeds I* where it was stated that "the main value of the tariff concession is that it provides an assurance of better market access through improved price competition."[77] This suggests that a combination of specific taxes, restrictions on price promotions, and the use of antidumping duties (where appropriate) may have to be used instead of price floors in some situations in order to comply with Article III:4.

D. The use of tariffs to encourage healthy consumption habits

At first glance, taxes that apply on a facially neutral basis would appear to be a far more appropriate tool for purposes of shaping consumer preferences than tariffs. David Fidler has argued that using tariffs is questionable in terms of a public health strategy, because most countries are likely to have domestic

74 GATT Panel Report, *Canada – Import, Distribution and Sale of Certain Alcoholic Drinks by Provincial Marketing Agencies*, DS17/R, adopted 18 February 1992, BISD 39S/27 [hereinafter *Canada – Provincial Liquor Boards (U.S.)*].

75 Ibid., paras 5.31 and 4.60.

76 Ibid., para. 5.30.

77 GATT Panel Report, *European Economic Community – Payments and Subsidies Paid to Processors and Producers of Oilseeds and Related Animal-Feed Proteins*, L/6627, adopted on 25 January 1990, C/M/238, para. 148.

production of the goods subjected to the tariffs in question.[78] However, there are a number of contexts in which tariffs may prove to be a useful policy tool.

Where the type of good subjected to a tariff is not produced domestically, a tariff will have a similar effect to an excise applied to all goods of the category in question. Whereas trade theory suggests that a tariff of this type is likely to protect (and incentivize) domestic production, domestic production will not always occur in the context of such a tariff. For example, in small island states with relatively small markets and limited access to capital, domestic production may not be stimulated by a tariff. Of course, the merits of using a tariff as opposed to an excise tax remain questionable.

As trade theory suggests, a tariff is more likely to be a useful policy tool where a state is actually seeking to protect or encourage domestic production. This may be the case in the agricultural sector if existing domestic production and importation does not ensure an accessible supply of healthful foods. In the introduction to this chapter an example of this type was identified. Some small island states in the Pacific have seen a shift away from traditional diets as their agricultural sectors have specialized in order to serve export markets. These states have limited budgetary resources, meaning that taxes and tariffs are more likely to be used than subsidies that require a direct transfer from government to producers or consumers. Accordingly, tariffs may have a role as a measure to ensure the existence of a local market for certain agricultural commodities.

Of course, under Article II of the GATT, a WTO Member may not maintain tariffs in excess of the bound rates set forth in its schedule of concessions. It is also not clear that a violation of this fundamental commitment would ever be considered necessary to protect human health under Article XX(b) of the GATT. Accordingly, the level at which a member's bound rates are set is likely to be determinative of the policy space available where tariffs are considered a means of ensuring that healthful foods are accessible.

As Fidler has also noted, the fact that WTO Members may apply tariff rates lower than their bound rate is also significant in terms of policy space. The difference between a bound rate and an applied rate is often referred to as the "water" in a tariff, and is seen as permitting members flexibility to implement domestic policy goals. For example, Fidler argues that tariffs might be reduced on healthful goods in order to reduce their cost to consumers

[78] David Fidler, "The Impact of International Trade and Investment Rules on the Ability of Governments to Implement Interventions to Address Obesity: A Case Study on the European Charter on Counteracting Obesity," in Hawkes et al., *Trade, Food, Diet and Health*, pp. 279–297, p. 284 [hereinafter Fidler, "The Impact of International Trade"].

and encourage consumption.[79] There is no doubt about the autonomy of each WTO Member to adopt this approach. Equally, this approach will not always be desirable, such as in the example where promoting domestic production is a policy goal. Accordingly, the presence of "water" in a tariff does not alter the conclusion that policy space in terms of the use of tariffs is ultimately dependent on the bound rates set out in each member's schedule of concessions.

1.2. *Subsidies to Encourage Production and Consumption of Healthful Goods*

In the tobacco and alcohol contexts where public health authorities seek to reduce total consumption of tobacco products and alcoholic beverages, subsidies are not ordinarily a part of public health policy.[80] In the dietary context, however, the goal of authorities is not to reduce consumption, but to encourage energy balance and an adequate intake of nutrients. In this context, subsidies may play a role in shaping consumer preferences by reducing the relative price of goods such as fresh fruits and vegetables.

There are various types of subsidies that are used in this context. One type of subsidy involves a welfare transfer directly to the consumer. For example, the U.S. government has a large "food stamp" scheme in the form of the Supplemental Nutrition Assistance Program. The program extends a government benefit to low-income earners for the purchase of food. These types of programs, like school lunch programs, can be tailored to ensure the subsidization of healthful foods.[81]

Agricultural production subsidies are also used as a means of ensuring food security (and hence adequate nutrition). In theory, these types of schemes can be tailored to promote the production and consumption of healthful foods. However, there are a range of limitations on this possibility. First, the Agreement on Agriculture limits the types of agricultural subsidies that WTO Members may use. Second, the impact of production subsidies depends partly on the industrial uses of a food. For example, subsidization of corn in the United States is associated with the production of high fructose corn syrup, which is a high-calorie sweetener used in foods and beverages.

79 Ibid., p. 284.

80 One exception to this may be production-limiting subsidies that have the effect of reducing the total out of tobacco leaf.

81 At the time of writing the U.S. government is undertaking a pilot program known as the Healthy Incentives Pilot, which is intended to explore different ways of using the scheme to promote health and nutrition.

Third, the limited budgets of many developing countries make the payment of production subsidies difficult or impossible.

The impact of production subsidies on the incentives associated with production is obviously an important factor in setting policy. Flooding a market with a particular good is likely to push prices down and may ultimately undermine production. Accordingly, measures such as limits on total production and export subsidies are sometimes used in conjunction with production subsidies in order to ensure adequate production levels. This has a number of flow-on effects. For example, in the context of the European Common Agricultural Policy (CAP), export subsidies have ensured high food prices within Europe but have suppressed prices on the global market.[82] When coupled with other trade barriers such as tariffs, export subsidies have undermined the ability of some developing country farmers to compete with European goods. This has a flow-on effect for food security and the nutritional profile of those countries. Hence, there are a variety of policy goals for a member to factor into decision making about agricultural subsidization.

With this in mind, this part addresses subsidization in two contexts. First, this part addresses the circumstances in which differential taxes will give rise to questions of subsidization under the SCM Agreement and the potential implications for regulatory autonomy. Second, this part addresses the scope for subsidization under the Agreement on Agriculture.

A. Differential taxes and the SCM Agreement

The SCM Agreement may have implications for differential tax measures that are applied to manufactured goods such as alcoholic beverages, processed foods, and tobacco products. If the effect of a measure is to favor domestic goods, the measure might constitute an actionable subsidy. This could result in a member having to remove the subsidy or face countermeasures under Article 7 of the SCM Agreement.

It seems most likely that the SCM Agreement may be relevant where tax differentials are used at the point of manufacture rather than at the point of sale. For example, a member might not tax inputs in the production of healthful foods in order to create an incentive for the production of such foods. Equally, it is also conceivable that differential sales or excise taxes applied at the point of consumption could constitute subsidies under the SPS Agreement.

[82] Josef Schidhuber and Prakash Shetty, "The European Union's Common Agricultural Policy and the European Diet: Is there a Link?" in Hawkes et al., *Trade, Food, Diet and Health*, pp. 131–147, pp. 144–145.

At first glance, where a violation is already established under the GATT, a further violation of the SCM Agreement may not appear significant. However, the text of the SCM Agreement does not include an exception for measures necessary to protect human life or health. Rather, if a member wished to rely on a health exception, such as to justify a prohibited subsidy, it would have to argue that Article XX(b) of the GATT can justify measures that violate the SCM Agreement. In the case of actionable subsidies, countermeasures could also be authorized.

(a) WHEN MIGHT DIFFERENTIAL TAXATION CONSTITUTE A SUBSIDY?

Article 1 of the SCM Agreement defines the term "subsidy" for the purposes of that agreement. The relevant parts of the provision state:

> 1.1 For the purpose of this Agreement, a subsidy shall be deemed to exist if:
> (a)(1) there is a financial contribution by a government or any public body within the territory of a Member (referred to in this Agreement as "government"), i.e. where:
>
> …
>
> (ii) government revenue that is otherwise due is foregone or not collected (e.g. fiscal incentives such as tax credits);
>
> …
>
> and
>
> (b) a benefit is thereby conferred.

It is clear that where differential taxes are implemented through the grant of tax credits or by an omission to collect some or all due taxes, a subsidy within the terms of Article 1.1 would exist. However, the existence of a subsidy is less clear in the event that a measure is structured, for example, so that different tax rates apply to different types of goods. In *US – FSC (Article 21.5 – EC)* the Appellate Body gave some indication of how the provision is applied:

> Under Article 1.1(a)(1)(ii), a "financial contribution" does not arise simply because a government does not raise revenue which it could have raised. It is true that, from a *fiscal* perspective, where a government chooses not to tax certain income, no revenue is "due" on that income. However, although a government might, in a sense, be said to "forego" revenue in this situation, this alone gives no indication as to whether the revenue foregone was "otherwise due." In other words, the mere fact that revenues are not "due" from a fiscal perspective does not determine that the revenues are or are not "otherwise due" within the meaning of Article 1.1(a)(1)(ii) of the *SCM Agreement*.[83]

[83] Appellate Body Report, *United States – Tax Treatment for "Foreign Sales Corporations" –* Recourse to Article 21.5 of the DSU by the European Communities, WT/DS108/AB/RW,

In drawing this conclusion the Appellate Body was reiterating comments that it had made previously in *US – FSC*. There the Appellate Body stated:

> [T]he "foregoing" of revenue "otherwise due" implies that less revenue has been raised by the government than would have been raised in a different situation, or, that is, "otherwise." Moreover, the word "foregone" suggests that the government has given up an entitlement to raise revenue that it could "otherwise" have raised. This cannot, however, be an entitlement in the abstract, because governments, in theory, could tax *all* revenues. There must, therefore, be some defined, normative benchmark against which a comparison can be made between the revenue actually raised and the revenue that would have been raised "otherwise."[84]

Accordingly, a "normative benchmark" constituted by other rules of taxation in place in the territory of the WTO Member in question is used "to distinguish between situations where revenue foregone is 'otherwise due' and situations where such revenue is not "otherwise due.'"[85] Most important, the Appellate Body has clarified that Article 1.1(a)(1)(ii) does not simply concern whether a tax would have been due "but for" an exception. Rather, as the Appellate Body has stated, a panel should compare the fiscal treatment of legitimately comparable income to determine whether the contested measure involves the foregoing of revenue that is otherwise due.[86]

A consequence of this is that a large degree of unpredictability exists in the decision-making process. Although an ordinary reading of Article 1.1(a)(1)(ii) suggests that differential taxation for health purposes would not constitute a financial contribution, the Appellate Body's interpretation of the provision leaves this question open.

Article 1.1(b) also requires that any financial contribution must confer a benefit in order for a subsidy to exist. The notion of a benefit requires a market-based comparison with what might have been but for the financial contribution. That is, the recipient of the benefit must "be 'better off' than it would otherwise have been absent the contribution."[87] It can be assumed for purposes of this study that a benefit may be conferred in a wide range of circumstances.

adopted 29 January 2002, DSR 2002:I, 55, [hereinafter *US – FSC*(Article 21.5 – EC)], para. 88 (italics in original).

84 Appellate Body Report, *United States – Tax Treatment for "Foreign Sales Corporations,"* WT/DS108/AB/R, adopted 20 March 2000, DSR 2000:III, 1619, para. 90 (italics in original).

85 Appellate Body Report, *US – FSC* (Article 21.5 – EC), para. 89.

86 Ibid., para. 91.

87 Appellate Body Report, *Canada – Measures Affecting the Export of Civilian Aircraft*, WT/DS70/AB/R, adopted 20 August 1999, para. 157.

(b) WHEN IS A SUBSIDY SPECIFIC?

Article 1.2 provides that a subsidy "shall be subject to the provisions of Part II or shall be subject to the provisions of Part III or V ... only if such a subsidy is specific in accordance with the provisions of Article 2." The purpose of Article 2 is to identify whether a subsidy distorts the allocation of resources within an economy. Among other requirements, Article 1.2(b) provides that a subsidy is not specific if the legislation in question establishes objective criteria or conditions governing eligibility for the subsidy. This may suggest that the type of tax contemplated would not be a specific subsidy. However, a footnote to the provision defines objective criteria or conditions as meaning "criteria or conditions which are neutral, which do not favour certain enterprises over others, and which are economic in nature and horizontal in application, such as number of employees or size of enterprise." Because differential taxes may favor certain enterprises over others depending on what they produce, this footnote supports the idea that differential taxes of the type contemplated may be specific subsidies.

In any case, the effect of Article 2.1(c) is that a subsidy may be considered specific to an industry or enterprise if a limited number of certain enterprises use it. The nature of a tax differential is such that a limited number of enterprises (those that produce the goods falling into the lower tax bracket) are likely to enjoy the benefits of it. For example, brewers of beer might benefit from a tax differential whereas distillers might not. Although determinations about specificity are not made at the product level,[88] it is reasonable to expect that the alcohol industry is divisible into segments such that a tax differential could favor certain enterprises such as brewers, vintners, or distillers. Thus, Article 2.1(c) suggests that a differential tax of the type contemplated may sometimes result in a specific subsidy.

Equally, Article 2.2 provides that "the setting or change of generally applicable tax rates by all levels of government entitled to do so shall not be deemed to be a specific subsidy for the purposes of this Agreement." Although this might suggest differential taxes may not be specific subsidies, it remains to be seen how the phrase "generally applicable" is to be interpreted, and it is questionable whether a tax of the type contemplated would fall within this phrase. Accordingly, it can be assumed for purposes of analysis that the requirement of specificity may be made out for some differential tax measures.

[88] Panel Report, *United States – Final Countervailing Duty Determination with Respect to Certain Softwood Lumber from Canada*, WT/DS257/R and Corr.1, adopted 17 February 2004, modified by Appellate Body Report, WT/DS257/AB/R, DSR 2004:II, 641, para. 7.121.

(c) PROHIBITED AND ACTIONABLE SUBSIDIES

Article 3 of the SCM Agreement identifies those subsidies that WTO Members are prohibited from imposing. Article 3 states:

Article 3
Prohibition

3.1 Except as provided in the Agreement on Agriculture, the following subsidies, within the meaning of Article 1, shall be prohibited:
(a) subsidies contingent, in law or in fact, whether solely or as one of several other conditions, upon export performance, including those illustrated in Annex I;
(b) subsidies contingent, whether solely or as one of several other conditions, upon the use of domestic over imported goods.

3.2 A Member shall neither grant nor maintain subsidies referred to in paragraph 1.

So long as any differential tax scheme is not contingent either on export performance or on the use of domestic as compared to imported goods, Article 3 would not apply. However, if such a measure were contingent on the use of domestic goods, the measure would be prohibited. In the contexts of tobacco, alcohol, and diet, it is difficult to foresee how this would be problematic in terms of policy space. That is, it is difficult to see why it would be necessary to make a differential tax measure contingent on the use of domestic goods.[89]

Where a subsidy is not prohibited, the question for consideration is whether it is actionable. Pursuant to Article 5, a subsidy will be actionable when it causes adverse effects to the interests of other members. Differential taxes could cause adverse effects in a number of ways. For example, differential taxes could nullify or impair the benefits accruing to a member under the GATT 1994 by impairing the legitimate expectations of benefits from tariff negotiations.[90] Alternatively, a differential tax could cause serious prejudice to the interests of another member by displacing or impeding imports (although this outcome would most likely be covered by Article III:2 of the GATT).

If a subsidy is actionable, a member could be ordered to remove the adverse effects or the subsidy itself. Failing this, countermeasures would be available to the complaining party under Article 7. In some circumstances, the

89 One exception to this conclusion might lie in the case of a government that seeks to promote local production though a differential tax scheme

90 For an example of this, see Panel Report, *Japan – Measures Affecting Consumer Photographic Film and Paper*, WT/DS44/R, adopted 22 April 1998, DSR 1998:IV, 1179, para. 10.50.

complaining member might be permitted to impose a counter-subsidy (as a form of countermeasure) that undermines the effect of the tax differential.[91]

(d) CONCLUSION

Although it stretches the bounds of the SCM Agreement, it is conceivable that a differential tax scheme of the type discussed here could constitute an actionable subsidy, but unlikely that a tax measure of the type contemplated would inadvertently constitute a prohibited subsidy. It remains to be seen whether an argument of this type would be made out, but if it were, countermeasures could be authorized under the SCM Agreement.

B. Agricultural subsidies

The use of tariffs and subsidies to ensure an accessible supply of healthful foods occurs in a complex policy environment where the specific needs of different WTO Members influence the approaches chosen. If WTO Members were to gear their agricultural policies toward the promotion of healthful foods and beverages, there are a number of policy options that might be taken. One option is to reduce tariffs on healthful goods in order to reduce their cost to consumers while maintaining relatively high tariffs on relatively unhealthy goods.[92] Equally, some members, such as some small island states, face various barriers to importation that create a need to encourage local production of healthful goods. These members might use production subsidies or export subsidies for this purpose. Similarly, these measures might be used to ensure food security or as a part of a broader agricultural policy framework such as the CAP. In short, a wide variety of reasons exist for different policy approaches, and this translates into a wide variety of different possible approaches depending on the individual circumstances of a member. This diversity is reflected in the latitude WTO Members are given to implement agricultural trade policy measures under the Agreement on Agriculture.

There are a number of different measures that WTO Members may take in the context of domestic support. The widest latitude is given in the context of so-called green box measures, which are defined in Annex 2 to the Agreement on Agriculture. These measures are considered not to be distortive of trade or to be minimally distortive. Measures falling within the "green box" do not

[91] For discussion see Sherzod Shadikhodjaev, *Retaliation in the WTO Dispute Settlement System*, The Netherlands, Kluwer Law International, (2009), p. 99.

[92] Vincent Atkins, "Agricultural Trade Policy Instruments to Promote Healthy Diets in Developing Countries: An Assessment of the Opportunities within the Framework of the WTO Agreement and the Doha Development Agenda," in Hawkes et al., *Trade, Food, Diet and Health*, pp. 264–278, p. 272.

involve direct payments to producers or processors and include government provided services such as research, pest and disease control, training services, inspection services, and infrastructure services. Under the Agreement on Agriculture, members are under no obligation to limit the extent to which they implement "green box" measures of this type. Although WTO Members enjoy significant flexibility with respect to the implementation of these types of measures, they are unlikely to be particularly useful in a context where a member seeks to encourage the consumption of particular types of agricultural goods. That is, the minimally trade distortive character of these measures also reflects their limited usefulness for purposes of shaping consumer demand.

In contrast, to "green box" measures, "amber box" measures are considered to be means of domestic support that are distortive of trade. In each WTO Member's schedule, a commitment is made to reduce domestic support of this type. The extent to which an individual member may use domestic support is contingent on the extent of domestic support in place at the time the Agreement on Agriculture was negotiated. There are also *de minimis* exceptions to these bound levels of domestic support. Under Article 6(4)(a)(i) of the Agreement on Agriculture, developed countries are not required to reduce product-specific domestic support where such support does not exceed 5 percent of the member's total value of production of a basic agricultural commodity during the year. The *de minimis* allowance for developing countries is 10 percent. In addition, under Article 6(5)(a), direct payments of various types under production-limiting programs are not required to be subject to commitments to reduce support. Under Article 6.2, developing countries are exempt from reduction of domestic support commitments in the context of some investment subsidies and input subsidies.

The impact of these obligations on domestic regulatory autonomy is comparable to the impact of tariff commitments on autonomy. In each case, autonomy is dependent primarily on the bound levels in each member's schedule of commitments. Policy space can be maintained by granting levels of domestic support below the bound commitment, similar to the way in which a member may maintain "water" between a bound tariff rate and the applied tariff rate. Commitments to reduce tariffs on agricultural products also preserve some flexibility for WTO Members to choose which products will be the subject of tariff reductions in meeting an overall commitment to cut tariffs by a given percentage. For example, the Agreement on Agriculture required developing country members to make a minimum cut per tariff line of 10 percent, but to reduce tariffs by an average of 24 percent. Another flexibility that may be built into the Agreement on Agriculture as a part of the Doha Round is the possibility to designate special products as either exempt from the requirement of tariff reductions or as subject to lower deductions.[93]

Export subsidies are governed in much the same way as domestic support in the sense that Article 7 of the Agreement on Agriculture makes export subsidies the subject of reduction commitments. These reduction commitments are again based on the level of export subsidization in place in the territory of each member at the time the Agreement on Agriculture was negotiated. Thus, the extent to which a WTO Member enjoys autonomy to implement these measures is dependent on that member's bound commitments. Equally, it is worth noting that export subsidization is one area where the actions of a member are likely to have spill-over effects for other members. By suppressing the global price of a commodity, an export subsidy will not only undermine the competitiveness of farmers in foreign countries (often developing countries), but can also influence consumption patterns in a negative way. For example, export subsidization of sugar by the EU is likely to make sugar more expensive within the EU but cheaper on the global market. Depending on the nutritional profile of a country, this outcome may be undesirable from a public health perspective.

Leaving aside the policy space preserved by applying tariffs lower than the bound rate and use of subsidies below the level of a member's commitments, all WTO Members have some flexibility in the context of export restrictions. Export restrictions are governed by Articles XI:2(a) of the GATT and Article 12 of the Agreement on Agriculture. Article XI:2(a) of the GATT is an exception to the basic prohibition on quantitative restrictions in Article XI:1 of the GATT, which is discussed in further detail later in this chapter. Article XI:2(a) provides that Article XI:1 does not apply to "[e]xport prohibitions or restrictions temporarily applied to prevent or relieve critical shortages of foodstuffs or other products essential to the exporting contracting party." Article 12 of the Agreement on Agriculture complements this provision by creating a procedural regime governing when notice must be given to other WTO Members of a measure of this type.

Whereas export restrictions are unlikely to be used in the territory of most WTO Members as a means of promoting consumption of healthful foods, they might be useful in some contexts. For example, where a small island state finds that its agricultural sector no longer produces an adequate supply

93 See generally Bernabe, Riza (2008). Treatment of special products: Implications of the Chair's May 2008 draft modalities text, ICTSD Project on Special Products and a Special Safeguard Mechanism, Issue Paper No.14, International Centre for Trade and Sustainable Development, Geneva, Switzerland.

of healthful foods because it has specialized in a few commodities for export, that state might wish to limit food exports. This might be a particularly attractive option where lack of public funds makes subsidization too costly and where food imports have not responded to the reorientation of the domestic agricultural sector toward the export market.

Were a member to implement a measure of this type, a question might arise as to whether the measure relates to "critical shortages of foodstuffs" or "products essential to" the member in question. How such a question would be answered remains to be seen. The exception in Article XI:2(a) has been viewed traditionally as a measure to ensure food security, and was invoked in this context during the global food crisis by a number of WTO Members that restricted exportation of rice. Nonetheless, the growing significance of non-communicable diseases associated with diet may be such that certain foods would be viewed as essential to the member in question, depending on the circumstances.

With the exception of this one flexibility that is only likely to be useful in a very narrow range of circumstances, autonomy in the agricultural sector differs for each WTO Member, depending on the commitments made. As in the SCM Agreement, there is no exception equivalent to Article XX(b) of the GATT. In any case, it is difficult to imagine a WTO panel finding a violation of a scheduled commitment to be necessary under such an exception. Accordingly, in this context, regulatory autonomy is subject to the power politics associated with trade negotiations rather than to a legal regime governing the regulatory legitimacy of a measure serving a public health purpose.

2. RESTRICTIONS ON MARKETING

Given the role of marketing in shaping consumer preferences, it is not surprising that restrictions on marketing are relevant to each of the contexts of tobacco, alcohol, and diet.

Measures prohibiting tobacco advertising, promotion, and sponsorship are among the most common means of tobacco control. Such measures are a means of preventing the stimulation of tobacco consumption and, as the parties to the FCTC recognize in Article 13.1, have been shown to reduce the prevalence of tobacco consumption.[94] Article 13 of the FCTC obliges parties to implement a comprehensive ban on tobacco advertising, promotion,

[94] Henry Saffer, "Tobacco Advertising and Promotion," in Prabhat Jha and Frank Chaloupka (eds), *Tobacco Control in Developing Countries*, World Bank and World Health Organization, (2000), pp. 215–236 [hereinafter Saffer, "Tobacco Advertising and Promotion"].

and sponsorship, including cross-border advertising entering their territories. Although the term "comprehensive" is not defined in the FCTC, the Conference of the Parties to the FCTC has concluded guidelines to Article 13. These guidelines are indicative of trends at the national level with respect to restrictions on marketing.

The stated purpose of these guidelines is to "assist Parties in meeting their obligations" under Article 13.[95] The guidelines elaborate the responsibility of parties to prohibit cross-border advertising, promotion, and sponsorship and recognize that sales of tobacco products via the Internet inherently involve advertising and promotion. In order to prevent this, the guidelines recommend banning all sales of tobacco products via the Internet.

In the dietary context, the Global Strategy Diet recognizes that food and beverage advertising affects consumer choices and influences dietary habits. However, restrictions on marketing are less commonplace and less comprehensive than in the tobacco context. There is a growing argument that certain forms of advertising to children should be restricted. For example, it has been argued that states should prohibit the advertising of energy-dense, nutrient-poor foods directed at children.[96] This might occur either through restrictions on the types of advertising permitted during television programming directed at children, or through other means such as prohibiting the use of cartoon characters in promoting the sale of fast food. The Global Strategy Diet makes the following recommendations to WHO member states:

> Food and beverage advertisements should not exploit children's inexperience or credulity. Messages that encourage unhealthy dietary practices or physical inactivity should be discouraged, and positive, healthy messages encouraged. Governments should work with consumer groups and the private sector (including advertising) to develop appropriate multisectoral approaches to deal with the marketing of food to children, and to deal with such issues as sponsorship, promotion and advertising.[97]

Similar issues also arise in the alcohol context. In its report to the WHA concerning strategies to reduce harmful alcohol use, the WHO highlighted the role that advertising and promotion plays, particularly in attracting underage consumers. The WHO noted the difficulty in targeting advertising at young

[95] WHO Framework Convention on Tobacco Control, Guidelines for Implementation: Article 5.3, Article 8, Article 11, Article 13, World Health Organization, Geneva 2009, p. 51.

[96] Australia: The Healthiest Country by 2020, National Preventative Health Strategy – The Roadmap for Action, 30 June 2009, p. 16.

[97] Global Strategy Diet, para. 40(3).

adults without it also exposing young adults under the legal age of consumption. The WHO stated that "[c]ontrols or partial bans on volume, placement and content of alcohol advertising are important parts of a strategy ... in particular to protect adolescents and young people from pressure to start drinking."[98]

Given how well established marketing restrictions are around the world, it might be thought that concerns are unlikely to arise under WTO law. This first impression is given some support by the decision of the GATT panel in *Thailand – Cigarettes*, as that panel appeared to endorse the lawfulness under the GATT of nondiscriminatory bans on tobacco advertising.[99] This position notwithstanding, some tobacco-control advocates have expressed concern that advertising bans may not be lawful under WTO-covered agreements,[100] and participants in the alcohol industry have also argued that such bans are unlawful.[101]

There are a number of specific concerns that are worth exploring. One concern is that *Thailand – Cigarettes* did not actually address the potential for advertising bans to restrict trade under the GATT in any detail. Another concern is that the GATS has changed the legal framework applicable to advertising by bringing advertising services into consideration.

A further concern relates to the fact that regulators are now focused on prohibiting cross-border advertising, particularly in the tobacco context. In that context, domestic advertising bans are widespread, and there is significant concern about cross-border advertising, such as via the Internet, cable television, and in some periodicals.[102] WTO Members are, therefore, taking measures to prevent domestic-source and imported advertising and the exportation of advertising from their territories. Because measures restricting domestic-source and imported advertising may give rise to WTO disputes, they merit further attention.

98 Strategies to Reduce Harmful use of Alcohol, para. 14.

99 GATT Panel Report, *Thailand – Cigarettes*, para. 78.

100 See, for example, Cynthia Callard, Niel Collishaw, and Michele Swenarchuk, "An Introduction to International Trade Agreements and their Impact on Public Measures to Reduce Tobacco Use," Physicians for a Smoke Free Canada, 2001, pp. 29–30 available at http://www.smoke-free.ca/pdf_1/Trade&Tobacco-April%202000.pdf, (visited 13/12/07) [hereinafter Callard, Collishaw, and Swenarchuk, "An Introduction"].

101 See, for example, "Council of State 'Set to Oppose Ban' on Drink Ads,"*The Nation*, Friday, November 24, 2006; "Alcohol Consumption Bill Reaction, Boon Rawd: Law May Breach WTO Rules," Bangkok Post, Friday March 16, 2007.

102 This is reflected in WHO Framework Convention on Tobacco Control, Guidelines for Implementation: Article 5.3, Article 8, Article 11, Article 13, World Health Organization, Geneva 2009, (guidelines to Article 13).

Leaving aside questions relating to advertising, alcohol-control advocates have also expressed concern about the implications of the GATS for measures restricting the sale of alcoholic beverages.[103] For example, authorities often limit the times during which alcoholic beverages may be sold or use liquor licensing to limit the number of venues in a given area that may sell alcoholic beverages. Similarly, authorities may limit the types of retail outlets permitted to sell alcoholic beverages. For example, in some jurisdictions it is not permissible for supermarkets or convenience stores to sell alcoholic beverages. There is a concern that these types of measures may limit market access under the GATS in the context of retail and distribution services.

These issues are examined in two parts. First, the impact of the GATT on restrictions on advertising is examined. Secondly, the impact of the GATS on marketing restrictions is examined.

2.1. *The GATT and the Impact of Advertising Bans on Tobacco Products*

Advertising may constitute a good where it is a physical product or combines to constitute a physical product.[104] As such, posters, leaflets, advertisements in print publications, and the like may constitute goods. It is less clear whether advertisements in the form of television broadcasts, radio broadcasts, and Internet content may also constitute goods (whether digital products in purely electronic form should be classified as goods or services remains unresolved[105]). Nonetheless, if the determinative criterion of whether advertising is a good is whether it constitutes a physical product or part thereof, these forms of advertising may also constitute goods in certain circumstances. For example, if Internet content is printed, the printed paper including the content might constitute a good. Similarly, if radio or television broadcasts are recorded, the advertisements might combine with other products such as recording devices to constitute goods.

For the purpose of analysis, it will be presumed that advertising constitutes a good solely when it is a physical product or combines to form part of a physical product.

[103] Jim Grieshaber-Otto, Scott Sinclair and Noel Schacter, "Impacts of International Trade, Services and Investment Treaties on Alcohol Regulation," 95(Supplement 4) *Addiction*, (2000), S491–S504; Ellen Gould, "Trade Treaties and Alcohol Advertising Policy," 26(3) *Journal of Public Health Policy*, (2005), pp. 359–376.

[104] Appellate Body Report, *Canada – Periodicals*, pp. 17–19.

[105] See generally Sacha Wunsch-Vincent, *The WTO, the Internet and Trade in Digital Products: EC – US Perspectives*, Portland Or., Hart Publishing, (2006); see also Tania Voon, *Cultural Products and the World Trade Organization*, Cambridge, Cambridge University Press, (2007), p. 73.

A. Advertising bans and national treatment under Article III:4

At first glance, facially origin-neutral advertising restrictions appear unlikely to be impeded by the application of national treatment obligations under the GATT, provided that they apply equally to all types of tobacco products. However, it is arguable that advertising bans impede the entry of new products into a market, and that this may result in less favorable treatment for imported goods under Article III:4. This issue was touched upon by the GATT panel in *Thailand – Cigarettes*, in which it was stated that "it might be said that such a general ban on all cigarette advertising would create unequal competitive opportunities between the existing Thai supplier of cigarettes and new, foreign suppliers ... contrary to Article III:4."[106]

The factual context in which these comments were made is quite specific in the sense that the Thai market was in effect closed to brands other than local brands. In addition, claims of this type have not been made in respect of advertising bans in WTO dispute settlement. Nonetheless, it is worthwhile to give some brief treatment of whether bans of this type might lead to less favorable treatment.[107]

Whether advertising restrictions constitute a barrier to market entry has been the subject of debate.[108] As Kyle Bagwell has noted, one group of empirical studies suggests that advertising deters the entry of new products into a market, whereas another group suggests that advertising may facilitate entry.[109]

[106] GATT Panel Report, *Thailand – Cigarettes*, para. 78.

[107] The other elements of Article III:4 are not addressed here as there is a high probability that they will be made out in the event of a claim.

[108] For a summary of the empirical literature see Kyle Bagwell, "The Economic Analysis of Advertising," in M. Armstrong and R. Porter, (eds), *Handbook of Industrial Organization*, Vol. 3, Elsevier, (2007), p. 1701 [hereinafter Bagwell, "Economic Analysis of Advertising"],.

[109] Ibid., p. 45 referring to L Duetsch, "Structure, Performance, and the Net Rate of Entry into Manufacturing Industries," 41 *Southern Economic Journal*, (1975), pp. 450–456; P. Gorecki, "The Determinants of Entry by Domestic and Foreign Enterprises in Canadian Manufacturing," 58 *The Review of Economics and Statistics*, (1976), pp. 485–488; M. Harris, "Entry and Long-term Trends in Industry Performance," 21 *Antitrust Bulletin*, (1976), pp. 295–314; R. Masson and J. Shaanan, "Stochastic-Dynamic Limit Pricing: An Empirical Test," 64 *The Review of Economics and Statistics*, (1984), pp. 413–422; J. Schwalbach, "'Entry by Diversified Firms into German Industries,"' 5 *International Journal of Industrial Organization*, (1987), pp. 43–49; D. Shapiro and R. Khemani, "The Determinants of Entry and Exit Reconsidered," 5 *International Journal of Industrial Organization*, (1987), pp. 15–26; J. Rizzo and R. Zeckhauser "Advertising and Entry: The Case of Physician Services," 98 *Journal of Political Economy*, (1990), pp. 476–500; as compared to L. Telser (1962), 'Advertising and Cigarettes," 70 *Journal of Political Economy*, (1962), pp. 471–499; J. Ferguson, "Advertising and Liquor," 40 *Journal of Business*, (1967), pp. 414–34; M. Alemson, "Advertising and the Nature of Competition in Oligopoly Over Time: A Case Study," 80 *The Economic Journal*, (1970), pp. 282–306; M. Hirschey, "The Effect of Advertising on Industrial Mobility, 1947–72," 54 *Journal of Business*, (1981), pp. 329–339; J. MacDonald, "Entry and Exit on the Competitive Fringe," 52 *Southern Economic Journal*, (1986), pp. 640–652.

Upon a review of the empirical evidence supporting the two theories, Bagwell concluded:

> In total, the direct evidence of the association between advertising and entry is somewhat mixed. Advertising may be used to raise the cost of entry, but it also may be the means of effective entry. The appropriate interpretation of the advertising-entry relationship is subtle and seems to vary across industries.[110]

The evidence is also mixed in the case of the tobacco industry, where the issues have been studied. On the one hand, advertising is used as a market-entry strategy for new products,[111] and in the absence of advertising, consumers may be less likely to change consumption patterns by switching to new products.[112] On the other hand, established brands often possess goodwill that declines in value over time and that can be preserved through advertising.[113] In addition, established brands can receive a competitive benefit from the ability to advertise in the form of economies of scale (depending on where those brands sit in the product cycle).[114]

This evidence suggests that it is conceivable that tobacco-advertising restrictions may in some instances constitute a barrier to market entry. It must be noted, however, that whether a specific advertising ban constitutes such a barrier would have to be determined in light of the specific circumstances at work at the time and place of implementation.

The studies considered also have limitations. Each study relates to specific data sets stemming from the U.S. market. Furthermore, the studies are of particular relevance to the short-term effects of advertising restrictions but do not chart the long-term effects of such measures.

In legal terms, whether treatment "no less favorable" is afforded to imported products turns on whether "a measure modifies the conditions of competition in the relevant market to the detriment of imported products."[115] Although both established and new products may be disadvantaged by a ban, GATT and early WTO case law suggest that more favorable treatment of some imported

[110] Bagwell, "Economic Analysis of Advertising," p. 1743.

[111] Telser, "Advertising and Cigarettes," p. 474.

[112] S. Holak and S. Reddy, "Effects of a Television and Radio Advertising Ban: A Study of the Cigarette Industry," 50 *Journal of Marketing*, (October 1986), pp. 219–227, p. 226.

[113] Telser, "Advertising and Cigarettes," p. 498.

[114] Y. Peles, "Rates of Amortization of Advertising Expenditures,'" 79 *Journal of Political Economy*, (1971), pp. 1032–1058, p. 1036.

[115] Appellate Body Report, *Korea – Measures Affecting Imports of Fresh, Chilled and Frozen Beef*, WT/DS161/AB/R, WT/DS169/AB/R, adopted 10 January 2001, DSR 2001:I, 5 [hereinafter *Korea – Various Measures on Beef*], para. 137.

products cannot be balanced against less favorable treatment of other imported products.[116] That is, new imported products may still be treated less favorably even where established domestic products also suffer detriment.

Whether less favorable treatment will be made out turns on the way in which the test is to be applied, something that was discussed earlier in the context of Article III:2 of the GATT. This discussion suggests that a panel might examine whether imported goods are at an overall competitive disadvantage by virtue of a measure, but that an overall disadvantage is not an established requirement in order for less favorable treatment to be made out. For reasons discussed previously, this type of assessment is specific to the circumstances of any claim and the outcome would be difficult to predict.

B. Advertising bans as quantitative restrictions under Article XI:1

It could also be argued that advertising restrictions constitute a quantitative restriction on the importation of advertising goods under Article XI of the GATT. Article XI of the GATT governs quantitative restrictions. Paragraph 1 of the provision states:

> No prohibitions or restrictions other than duties, taxes or other charges, whether made effective through quotas, import or export licences or other measures, shall be instituted or maintained by any contracting party on the importation of any product of the territory of any other contracting party or on the exportation or sale for export of any product destined for the territory of any other contracting party.

Article XI sits alongside Article III as a rule fundamental to ensuring that WTO Members do not evade their tariff commitments. The provision expresses the preference of the GATT for the use of tariffs over quantitative restrictions as a means of protectionism.[117] Perhaps it was with this notion in mind that the GATT panel in *Japan – Semi-Conductors*[118] stated that the wording in paragraph 1 "was comprehensive: it applied to all measures instituted or maintained by a contracting party prohibiting or restricting the importation, exportation or sale for export of products other than measures that take the form of duties,

[116] GATT Panel Report, *United States Section 337 of the Tariff Act of 1930*, L/6439, adopted 7 November 1989, BISD 36S/345, para. 5.14; Appellate Body Report, *Canada – Certain Measures Concerning Periodicals*, WT/DS31/AB/R, adopted 30 July 1997, DSR 1997:I, 449, [hereinafter *Canada – Periodicals*], p. 29.

[117] Panel Report, *Turkey – Restrictions on Imports of Textile and Clothing Products*, WT/DS34/R, adopted 19 November 1999, modified by Appellate Body Report, WT/DS34/AB/R, DSR 1999:VI, 2363.

[118] GATT Panel Report, *Japan – Trade in Semi-Conductors*, para. 104.

taxes or other charges."[119] Article XI also applies to measures that constitute quantitative restrictions in effect as well as in form.[120] This approach suggests that the regulatory purpose of a measure is unlikely to be relevant to the question of whether it constitutes a quantitative restriction.

Equally, it is arguable that restrictions on the importation of advertising are qualitative in character rather than quantitative. On this basis, it is arguable that the measure would not fall within the ambit of Article XI. The additional note to Article III states:

> Any internal tax or other internal charge, or any law, regulation or requirement of the kind referred to in paragraph 1 which applies to an imported product and to the like domestic product and is collected or enforced in the case of the imported product at the time or point of importation, is nevertheless to be regarded as an internal tax or other internal charge, or a law, regulation or requirement of the kind referred to in paragraph 1, and is accordingly subject to the provisions of Article III.

The additional note recognizes that the GATT treats border measures separately from behind the border measures or domestic regulations.[121] This proposition finds support in the ordinary wording of the note and in reports of WTO and GATT panels. For example, in *EC – Asbestos* the panel upheld arguments made by the EC that the additional note clarifies that only Article III and not Article XI applies to measures that are enforced throughout a domestic economy and also enforced at the time or point of importation. In that case, the EC was referring to a French ban on the manufacture, import, export, domestic sale, and transfer of asbestos and products that contained asbestos.[122] The panel drew on the conclusion of the GATT panel in *United States – Section 337 of the Tariff Act of 1930*, in which it was concluded that Article III:4 as opposed to Article XI should be applied in relation to laws that establish special procedures for imported products suspected of violating a U.S. patent right.[123]

Similarly, in *Canada – Foreign Investment Review Act* the GATT panel stated:

> The General Agreement distinguishes between measures affecting the "importation" of products, which are regulated in Article XI:1, and those affecting

[119] Ibid., para. 104.

[120] Ibid., para. 106

[121] See generally Petros Mavroidis, *The General Agreement on Tariffs and Trade: A Commentary*, Oxford, Oxford University Press, (2005), pp. 46–48; See also Joost Pauwelyn, "Rien ne Va Plus? Distinguishing Domestic Regulation from Market Access in GATT and GATS," 4(2) *World Trade Review*, (2005), pp. 131–170.

[122] Panel Report, *EC – Asbestos*, para 8.89.

[123] See GATT Panel Report, *United States Section 337 of the Tariff Act of 1930*, L/6439, adopted 7 November 1989, BISD 36S/345, para. 5.10.

> "imported products," which are dealt with in Article III. If Article XI:1 were interpreted broadly to cover also internal requirements, Article III would be partly superfluous. Moreover, the exceptions to Article XI:1, in particular those contained in XI:2, would also apply to internal requirements restricting imports, which would be contrary to the basic aim of Article III.[124]

More recently, the panel in *India – Measures Affecting the Automotive Sector* concluded that the inclusion of issues within the scope of Article III does not necessarily lead to their exclusion from Article XI. Rather, the panel contemplated the possibility that different aspects of one measure may fall within the scope of Article XI and Article III respectively.[125] Although some uncertainty is created by this conclusion and by virtue of the fact that the Appellate Body has not commented on the existence of a distinction between regulations governing importation as compared to those affecting imported products, such a distinction ought to be upheld. As the GATT panel in *Canada – Foreign Investment Review Act* recognized, this distinction means that Article III retains its full effect as a provision governing internal regulations. In addition, this distinction functions as an important limitation on the scope of Article XI, which would otherwise prohibit an extremely broad array of regulatory activity.

Thus, the question at hand is whether a restriction on advertising would constitute a behind-the-border measure, a border measure, or both. In this respect, advertising restrictions will ordinarily be enforced throughout a domestic economy. A part of enforcing this restriction would include the seizure of any offending material at the point of importation. Although it is conceivable that this type of measure could be considered to fall under both Articles III:4 and XI:1 of the GATT, the systemic implications of this approach weigh in favor of the conclusion that the measure would fall under Article III to the exclusion of Article XI.

In summary, it appears unlikely that a restriction on advertising as a good in itself would result in violation of the GATT.

2.2. *The GATS*

As was noted, the GATS might be relevant to advertising bans and associated measures like bans on the sale of tobacco products via remote means (such as over the Internet) and restrictions on the retail sale of alcoholic beverages.

[124] GATT Panel Report, *Canada – Administration of the Foreign Investment Review Act*, L/5504, adopted 7 February 1984, BISD 30S/140, [hereinafter *Canada – FIRA*], para. 5.14.

[125] Panel Report, *India – Measures Affecting the Automotive Sector*, WT/DS146/R, WT/DS175/R and Corr.1, adopted 5 April 2002, DSR 2002:V, 1827, paras 7.217–7.224.

It appears clear that these measures could affect trade in services, which, according to Article I:2 is defined as the supply of a service:

> (a) from the territory of one Member into the territory of any other Member;
> (b) in the territory of one Member to the service consumer of any other Member;
> (c) by a service supplier of one Member, through commercial presence in the territory of any other Member;
> (d) by a service supplier of one Member, through presence of natural persons of a Member in the territory of any other Member.

In determining whether GATS is applicable a panel will asses "first, whether there is 'trade in services' in the sense of Article I:2; and, second, whether the measure in issue 'affects' such trade in services within the meaning of Article I:1."[126]

The phrase "'trade in services' is defined in Article I:2 as the 'supply of a service' in any one of the four listed modes of supply."[127] The phrase "supply of a service" is defined in Article XXVIII(b) as including "the production, distribution, marketing, sale and delivery of a service."[128]

The Services Sectoral Classification List confirms the existence of "advertising services." Within this list "advertising services" constitute a subcategory of "other business services" and are defined[129] as including the following:

> (i) sale or leasing services of advertising space or time (services provided in soliciting advertising space or time for newspapers, other periodicals, and television stations);
> (ii) planning, creating and placement of services of advertising (planning, creating and placement services of advertisements to be displayed through advertising media); and
> (iii) other advertising services (other advertising services not elsewhere classified, including outdoor and aerial advertising services and delivery services of sample and other advertising material.[130]

[126] Appellate Body Report, *Canada – Certain Measures Affecting the Automotive Industry*, WT/DS139/AB/R, WT/DS142/AB/R, adopted 19 June 2000, DSR 2000:VI, 2985, [hereinafter *Canada – Autos*], para. 155.

[127] Ibid., para 156.

[128] Article XXVIII(b) of the GATS.

[129] These services are defined by reference to group 871 of the UN provisional Central Product Classification.

[130] See Council for Trade in Services, Advertising Services, S/C/W/47, 9 July 1998 (98–2748).

In addition, the provision of retail services falls under the general category of distribution services. Within the group of retail services, there is also a further subcategory specifically devoted to retail sales of food, beverages, and tobacco.[131]

It is also possible that at least some of the different types of advertising and retail services may be supplied through the different modes of service supply. For example, it is conceivable that planning, creative services, and placement services or retail services could be supplied from the territory of one member to another under mode 1 of Article I:2. As such, there may be "trade in advertising services" and "trade in retail services" relating to tobacco products.[132]

It also appears likely that the measures in question would affect trade in advertising services.[133] The term "affecting" has been interpreted as implying that a measure must "have an effect on" trade in services,[134] and a measure need not govern supply of services directly in order for this to be the case.[135]

The direct effects of a restriction on advertising would include prohibition of the placement of advertisements by a service supplier based in a foreign territory. In addition, an advertising ban would indirectly affect the cross-border supply of other advertising services such as planning and creative services. Bans on remote sales of tobacco products, such as via the Internet, would have similar effects on the provision of retail services.

A. The prohibitive content of the GATS

In terms of regulatory autonomy, the first point to note about the GATS is that some elements of the GATS bind all WTO Members and service sectors. One such obligation (although it is subject to exemptions) concerns MFN treatment under Article II:1. That provision states:

> With respect to any measure covered by this Agreement, each Member shall accord immediately and unconditionally to services and service suppliers of any other Member treatment no less favourable than that it accords to like services and service suppliers of any other country.

[131] Group 631 of the UN provisional Central Product Classification.

[132] Although, see contra, Tsai-Yu Lin, "Addressing the Issue of Trade in Services and Public Health in the Case of Tobacco: Are the FCTC Restrictions on Tobacco Advertising Inconsistent with the GATS?," 7(4) *The Journal of World Investment & Trade*, (August 2006), pp. 545–561 [hereinafter Lin, "Trade in Services"]. Lin's argument conflates the question of whether advertising bans violate Article XVI with the threshold question of whether a "trade in services" exists. Such an approach was rejected in Appellate Body Report, *Canada – Autos*, paras 151–152.

[133] See contra Lin, "Trade in Services," p. 558.

[134] Appellate Body Report, *Canada – Autos*, para 158.

[135] Panel Report, *EC – Bananas III*, para. 7.285.

It has been suggested that bans on some forms of advertising but not others could result in discrimination in effect where a foreign service supplier holds a dominant share of the banned advertising services market.[136] This rationale is also applicable in the context of MFN treatment. In theory, it is conceivable (although perhaps far-fetched) that a violation of this nature could occur. For example, if a WTO Member banned the use of Web-based computer games in food promotion but permitted advertising in television programming for children, the advertising services sector of one WTO Member could conceivably be favored over that of another.

B. Specific commitments

Obligations with respect to national treatment (Article XVII) and market access (Article XVI) are specific commitments that only apply to sectors and modes of supply that each individual WTO Member has listed in its schedule to the agreement. The preservation of a large degree of regulatory autonomy is inherent in this approach.

Leaving aside the policy space left by the partly voluntary nature of the GATS, the question of to what degree provisions governing national treatment and market access preserve policy space is also worth examining. For purposes of this examination it will be assumed that a state implementing advertising bans has a full range of commitments in the advertising services sector without any qualifications written into its schedule.

(a) NATIONAL TREATMENT

The analysis of MFN treatment set out previously in this chapter suggests that it is conceivable that violations of the national treatment principle might occur where partial bans on marketing are in place. Article XVII states:

> 1. In the sectors inscribed in its Schedule, and subject to any conditions and qualifications set out therein, each Member shall accord to services and service suppliers of any other Member, in respect of all measures affecting the supply of services, treatment no less favourable than that it accords to its own like services and service suppliers.
> 2. A Member may meet the requirement of paragraph 1 by according to services and service suppliers of any other Member, either formally identical treatment or formally different treatment to that it accords to its own like services and service suppliers.

[136] Robert Weissman, International Trade Agreements and Tobacco Control: Threats to Public Health and the Case for Excluding Tobacco from Trade Agreements, v 2.0, November 2003, available at http://www.fctc.org/x/cd/documents/EA_trade_backgrd.pdf (visited 26/11/07), p. 16

3. Formally identical or formally different treatment shall be considered to be less favourable if it modifies the conditions of competition in favour of services or service suppliers of the Member compared to like services or service suppliers of any other Member.

The example given in the discussion of MFN treatment was of a ban on Web-based computer games targeted at children in the absence of a ban on comparable television advertising directed at children. Assuming that the services in question are like, it is conceivable that a ban could be less favorable to foreign service providers that produce Web-based games as compared to local service providers that produce advertising content for television. Without examining this example in great detail, it is possible to observe that restrictions other than complete bans on all forms of promotion run the risk of favoring one service supplier over another. Because different members may have different strengths in the advertising services sector, it is conceivable that violations could be established.

It is also worth noting that measures restricting the sale of goods in a remote manner, such as via the Internet, may result in violation of Article XVII. For example, a measure banning the sale of tobacco products by remote means could favor domestic retailers if tobacco products could only be sold in face to face transactions. Therefore, where a WTO Member has made specific commitments with respect to the cross-border supply of distribution services, a national treatment violation might occur.

(b) MARKET ACCESS

It has been suggested that tobacco advertising bans constitute a limit on the provision of advertising services and may violate market-access commitments under Article XVI of the GATS.[137] The same might be suggested in the context of retail services. In particular, it could be argued that through their effect, measures such as advertising bans and bans on remote sales constitute limits on the number of service suppliers under Article XVI:2(a) or limits on the total number of service operations or the total quantity of service output under Article XVI:2(c). The relevant portion of Article XVI states:

1. With respect to market access through the modes of supply identified in Article I, each Member shall accord services and service suppliers of any other Member treatment no less favourable than that provided for under the terms, limitations and conditions agreed and specified in its Schedule.
2. In sectors where market-access commitments are undertaken, the measures which a Member shall not maintain or adopt either on the basis of a

[137] See, for example, Callard, Collishaw, and Swenarchuk, "An Introduction," pp. 29–30.

regional subdivision or on the basis of its entire territory, unless otherwise specified in its Schedule, are defined as:

(a) limitations on the number of service suppliers whether in the form of numerical quotas, monopolies, exclusive service suppliers or the requirements of an economic needs test;

...

(c) limitations on the total number of service operations or on the total quantity of service output expressed in terms of designated numerical units in the form of quotas or the requirement of an economic needs test;[138]

...

This "market access" commitment is similar to the prohibition on quantitative restrictions found in Article XI of the GATT. The provision is intended to ensure quotas, and similar mechanisms are not used to erode the commitments made in GATS schedules. However, the distinction between border measures and behind-the-border internal regulations is less clear in the context of the GATS. This was illustrated in *US – Gambling* where the Appellate Body considered the application of paragraphs (a) and (c) in relation to a ban on the cross-border supply of gambling and betting services imposed by the United States. The United States had included such services in its schedule of specific commitments, and that schedule expressed no limitations on the modes by which such services may be supplied. The Appellate Body upheld the panel's finding that "a prohibition on one, several or all means of delivery cross-border is a limitation on the number of service suppliers in the form of numerical quotas within the meaning of Article XVI:2(a) because it totally prevents the use by service suppliers of one, several or all means that are included in mode 1."[139] The Appellate Body upheld the finding of the panel in relation to paragraph (c) that the ban constituted a zero quota because it "totally prevents the services operations and/or service output through one or more or all means of delivery that are included in mode 1."[140]

In *US – Gambling* the Appellate Body stated that Article XVI is intended to apply to quantitative or "quantitative-type" measures, and that the difficulty lies in drawing the line between quantitative and qualitative measures.[141]

[138] Subparagraph 2(c) does not cover measures of a Member, which limit inputs for the supply of services.

[139] Appellate Body Report, *United States – Measures Affecting the Cross-Border Supply of Gambling and Betting Services*, WT/DS285/AB/R, adopted 20 April 2005, [hereinafter *US – Gambling*], para. 239.

[140] Ibid., para. 252.

[141] See discussion in Appellate Body Report, *US – Gambling*, paras 248–250.

In this respect, the Appellate Body made reference to the 1993 Scheduling Guidelines, which form part of the preparatory work for GATS.[142] The guidelines set out an example of a quantitative-type measure covered by paragraph (c). The example was of "restrictions on broadcasting time available for foreign films." Although such a measure may not provide a numerical or unit-based limitation on the total quantity of service output, in effect, it places a ceiling on the amount of output, and in this sense is a quantitative-type measure. Such a measure might be contrasted with a measure banning films with particular content. A content-based restriction would relate to the qualities of the film and would therefore be qualitative rather then quantitative in nature and would not fall within the ambit of paragraph (c).

In the present context, advertising bans relate to the qualities of advertising, that is, the question of what advertising promotes. As such, the lawfulness of advertising bans should be preserved by the distinction between qualitative and quantitative measures so long as those measures do not have a numerical ceiling of some type.[143] Similarly, a restriction on the types of retail outlets that may sell alcoholic beverages would appear to be akin to a qualitative-type internal regulation rather than a quantitative-type border measure. On the other hand, a ban on the provision of remote retail services with respect to tobacco products is more analogous to the U.S. ban on the provision of cross-border gambling services. Although it remains arguable that the measure would be qualitative in character, *US – Gambling* suggests that the measure would violate Article XVI.[144]

C. Conclusion on application of the GATS

The fact that obligations relating to market access and national treatment only apply to the extent that a WTO Member has made specific commitments means that members have a high degree of regulatory autonomy in the context of the GATS. More specifically, where a WTO Member has not yet made a specific commitment in a particular services sector, that member may decline to do so in the future. Alternatively, if such a member chooses to make specific commitments in that sector, it may qualify those commitments so as to preserve the right to restrict advertising with respect to tobacco, alcohol,

[142] Appellate Body Report, *US – Gambling*, para. 249.

[143] In respect of quantitative ceilings, see Lin, "Trade in Services," p. 550.

[144] Revised Chairperson's Text on a Protocol on Illicit Trade in Tobacco Products, and General Debate, Expert Review on a Possible Ban on Internet Sales of Tobacco Products, WHO Framework Convention on Tobacco Control, Conference of the Parties, Intergovernmental Negotiating Body on a Protocol on Illicit Trade in Tobacco Products, Geneva, Switzerland, 28 June–5 July 2009, FCTC/COP/INB-IT/3/INF.DOC./4, 7 May 2009.

and foods and beverages. The latter approach is preferable in the sense that it would have a lesser impact on trade than a wholesale refusal to make a commitment in the sector as a whole.

WTO Members may also wish to consider this approach in the context of retail services, delivery services, and distribution services. Although this measure has not been discussed in detail in the context of this study, a number of states maintain restrictions on the sale of tobacco products via remote means, such as over the Internet. These restrictions are used to prevent sales to children and to enforce tax and other laws that may be evaded through remote sales. Because restrictions of this type might violate market-access commitments under Article XVI of the GATS, WTO Members may wish to qualify future commitments made as a part of ongoing negotiations in order to preserve policy space.

For those members that have already made unqualified commitments in these service sectors, it would be possible to modify their schedules of commitments under Article XXI of the GATS. However, under Article XXI:2, any other WTO Member whose benefits under the GATS are affected by the modification may seek compensation for the modification so as to ensure that the balance of benefits under the agreement is at a mutually advantageous level not less favorable to trade. Thus, each WTO Member could alter its specific commitments but would have to offer some form of compensation where another member is able to establish that its benefits under the GATS have been affected.

The possibility that compensation would be required means that WTO Members may be better off relying on the health exception in Article XIV(b) of the GATS in the event of a dispute. If a measure is found to be unlawful, a member could then choose to withdraw its commitments and offer compensation.

3. CONCLUSION

This chapter set out to examine the way in which the prohibitions of the WTO-covered agreements govern price-based measures and restrictions on marketing in the contexts of tobacco, alcohol, and diet. This issue was examined through an analysis of how the relevant provisions account for regulatory purpose, rather than by an attempt to compare hypothetical situations with prior case law. For the most part, the analysis suggests that regulatory purpose plays a very limited role in determining whether a measure violates a prohibition in the GATT, GATS, and SCM Agreements or the Agreement on Agriculture.

The focus of Article III of the GATT is squarely on the way in which a measure alters the conditions of competition between domestic and imported goods. The consequences of this focus for the types of public health measures contemplated could be significant. Measures that seek to shape consumer preferences alter the conditions of competition between goods. Thus, the lawfulness of these types of measures is very much dependent on the circumstances in which they are implemented. Whether the beneficiaries of a measure are primarily domestic producers is likely to play a significant part in a determination of lawfulness. For differential taxes, this highlights a risk that good-faith measures may result in violation of Article III:2. In some circumstances differential tax measures may also constitute actionable subsidies under the SCM Agreement, giving rise to a violation where it is not clear an exception such as that in Article XX(b) of the GATT applies.

The use of price floors may also be problematic under Article III:4 where such floors are set above the price of imported goods. Such a measure would undermine the competitiveness of imports on the basis of price, and in many situations would constitute a violation of Article III:4 of the GATT. By the same token, to the extent that price floors are used to prevent discounting, WTO Members should be able to use laws that limit this practice directly and in some instances may use antidumping duties.

More broadly, the approach to interpretation of Article III could affect a range of tobacco-control measures. For example, Canadian restrictions on flavored cigarettes were mentioned in Chapter 1. The analysis of differential taxation suggests that restrictions having the effect of prohibiting blended cigarettes could violate Article III:4 of the GATT. These products might be considered to be like Virginia-style cigarettes and, depending on the makeup of the Canadian tobacco market, the measure might be less favorable to imported products. Thus, conclusions drawn about Article III with respect to the case study of differential taxes have broader application.

In the contexts of tariffs and agricultural subsidies, each WTO Member enjoys a degree of regulatory autonomy that is specific to its scheduled commitments. Those states with high bound tariff rates and large scope for subsidization enjoy some policy space that allows them to adjust their measures without exceeding bound commitments. In this context regulatory autonomy is more a function of the power politics of trade negotiations than it is a function of the application of uniform rules governing the legitimacy of a particular regulatory approach.

Similarly, the extent of a member's regulatory autonomy to implement marketing restrictions is dependent on the extent of its specific commitments scheduled under the GATS. The decision of the Appellate Body in

US – Gambling suggests that the line between internal behind-the-border regulation and border measures may not be as clear in the context of the GATS as it is in the context of the GATT. This suggests that where unlimited specific commitments have been made in the context of market access, various restrictions on marketing will violate Article XVI of the GATS. These measures may include restrictions on tobacco sales via remote means such as the Internet and restrictions on the sale of alcoholic beverages in certain types of retail stores.

When viewed together, the analysis suggests two broad conclusions. First, the negotiation of specific scheduled commitments in the contexts of tariffs, services, and subsidies can have a significant impact on regulatory autonomy. This impact is not limited to the question of how states can protect domestic industry. On the contrary, commitments made prior to the emergence of noncommunicable diseases as a serious public health concern may limit the flexibility of WTO Members to address that concern in good faith.

Second, exceptions such as that in Article XX(b) of the GATT remain central to questions of regulatory autonomy. The prohibitive provisions of the GATT and GATS are not geared toward identifying the regulatory legitimacy of a measure. As a consequence, domestic regulatory autonomy can only be defined by reference to the exceptions.

4

Necessity and Regulatory Autonomy under the GATT

It was concluded in Chapter 3 that facially neutral measures to address the public health implications of tobacco-, alcohol-, and dietary-related diseases may violate a number of prohibitions in the covered agreements. Depending on the circumstances, differential taxation may lead to violations of Article III:2 of the GATT, the Agreement on Agriculture, as well as give rise to countermeasures under the SCM Agreement. In addition, prohibitions on product promotion and advertising could conceivably violate Article III:4 of the GATT and Article XVI of the GATS if a WTO Member has scheduled commitments with respect to advertising or retail services.

When the circumstances are such that a violation may be made out, lawfulness of the measures in question will turn on application exceptions such as Article XX(b) of the GATT and Article XIV(b) of the GATS. At first glance, it appears that the permissive content of the WTO-covered agreements, as reflected in these provisions, provides sufficient protection to enable effective and comprehensive public health protection. This conclusion finds support with respect to origin-neutral advertising bans and taxation measures in *Thailand – Cigarettes*.[1] In addition, the outcome of recent disputes suggests that, in practice, WTO panels and the Appellate Body show a high degree of deference to the regulatory choices of WTO Members. This deferential practice arguably began with the weighing and balancing approach set out by the Appellate Body

Parts of this chapter are reprinted with permission from Oxford University Press from Benn McGrady, "Necessity Exceptions in WTO Law: Retreaded Tyres, Regulatory Purpose and Cumulative Regulatory Measures," 12 *Journal of International Economic Law*, (2009), pp.153–173.

[1] GATT Panel Report, *Thailand – Restrictions on Importation of and Internal Taxes on Cigarettes*, DS10/R, adopted 7 November 1990, BISD 37S/200 [hereinafter *Thailand – Cigarettes*].

in *Korea – Various Measures on Beef*[2] and can be traced through disputes such as *EC – Asbestos*[3] to more recent decisions such as *Brazil – Retreaded Tyres*.[4]

By the same token, concerns remain about how provisions such as Article XX(b) are implemented. One of these concerns relates to the certainty of outcomes, which can be an important factor in regulatory decision making at the domestic level. Robert Hudec described the GATT as a "diplomat's jurisprudence,"[5] but the creation of the WTO was supposed to reflect a shift from a diplomatic order to a more legalistic one.[6] This shift should have increased certainty and minimized the possibility that disputes would be decided on the basis of what Hudec described as a "seat of the pants" judgment. Nonetheless, the terms of Article XX(b) have not changed since the GATT era, and there appear to be a number of points in Article XX analysis where a panel can shape its analysis to suit a predetermined outcome.

The suitability of the necessity test in the context of measures to address noncommunicable diseases is also of concern. The drafting of Article XX was influenced by the constitutional law of the United States, which among other issues addressed questions of regulatory legitimacy in a public health context. Public health cases decided in the context of U.S. constitutional law were concerned primarily with impositions on liberty, such as compulsory vaccination, isolation, and quarantine, which were used to address the spread of infectious diseases. In the case of restrictions on liberty of this type, U.S. case law developed so as to require a "strict scrutiny" standard of review. This standard requires authorities to show a compelling state interest in and the necessity of a measure, including that the state interest could not be achieved by less restrictive or discriminatory means.[7] Lower standards of review are applied where lesser restrictions on liberty are concerned.

2 Appellate Body Report, *Korea – Measures Affecting Imports of Fresh, Chilled and Frozen Beef*, WT/DS161/AB/R, WT/DS169/AB/R, adopted 10 January 2001, DSR 2001:I, 5 [hereinafter *Korea – Various Measures on Beef*].

3 Appellate Body Report, *European Communities – Measures Affecting Asbestos and Asbestos-Containing Products*, WT/DS135/AB/R, adopted 5 April 2001, DSR 2001:VII, 3243 [hereinafter *EC – Asbestos*].

4 Appellate Body Report, Brazil – *Measures Affecting Imports of Retreaded Tyres*, WT/DS332/AB/R, 3 December 2007 [hereinafter *Brazil – Retreaded Tyres*].

5 Robert Hudec, "The GATT Legal System: A Diplomat's Jurisprudence," 4 *Journal of World Trade Law*, (1970), pp. 615–665.

6 See John Jackson, "The Crumbling Institutions of the Liberal Trade System," 12 *Journal of World Trade Law*, (1978), pp. 93–106; John Jackson, "Governmental Disputes in International Trade Relations: A Proposal in the Context of GATT," 13 *Journal of World Trade Law*, (1979), pp. 1–21.

7 For a summary of how U.S. constitutional law applies in the context of public health, see Lawrence Gostin, *Public Health Law: Power, Duty Restraint*, (2nd ed.) Berkeley and Los Angeles, University of California Press, (2008), pp. 113–144.

The approach adopted under U.S. law could also be traced through the case law of the GATT 1947. GATT panels applied the necessity test in a strict fashion, requiring that parties use the least trade-restrictive or least GATT-inconsistent means of protecting human health where the Article XX(b) exception was invoked. However, the GATT 1947 was negotiated at a time when the primary focus of public health practice was to address infectious disease. This was also the case in 1994 when the GATT was incorporated into the WTO Agreement. This raises the question of whether provisions such as Article XX(b) will adapt to the changing character of public health. More specifically, there are two questions of importance.

The first question concerns how causation may affect application of the necessity test. Adverse health outcomes can be caused by risk factors that act directly or almost directly to cause disease (proximal causes) or factors that are further back in the chain of causation (distal causes). The position of a risk factor in the chain of causation is likely to affect whether a measure addressing that risk is considered necessary to protect human health. A measure is more likely to be considered necessary if it addresses a proximal cause of disease rather than a distal cause. In the case of distal causes, there is a looser relationship between a measure and a health impact, and it is also more likely that alternative measures capable of breaking the chain of causation will be reasonably available to policy makers.

The second question that arises is how a test that seeks out the least trade-restrictive means of achieving a given health goal applies in the context of comprehensive regulatory strategies that rely on the use of a number of different measures. For example, could a taxation measure be a reasonably available alternative to a restriction on advertising?

This chapter examines application of Articles XX(b) of the GATT and XVI(b) of the GATS to the measures discussed in Chapter 3. Part 1 addresses the question of when these exceptions might apply to a violation of the SCM Agreement or the Agreement on Agriculture. Part 2 examines the necessity test. Part 3 examines application of the *chapeau* of Articles XX(b) and XVI(b).

The necessity requirements set out in the SPS and TBT Agreements are not examined in this chapter. Rather, these requirements, which are obligatory rather than exceptional in character, are examined separately in Chapter 5. Nonetheless, the discussion in this chapter forms an important backdrop to Chapter 5. These measures also fall within the scope of the GATT, and the overlap between the SPS and TBT Agreements and the GATT respectively are discussed in Chapter 5.

It is argued in this chapter that the necessity test was not conceived with the types of risks to health discussed in this study in mind, and that the strict scrutiny that the necessity test has traditionally demanded is not amenable to the types of regulatory interventions in question. By the same token, the deference shown to domestic regulatory autonomy in recent disputes, particularly in *Brazil – Retreaded Tyres*, suggests that the necessity test is evolving with public health practice. The outcome of this dispute is perhaps the single most important factor in determining the extent to which WTO Members enjoy regulatory autonomy with respect to tobacco, alcohol, and diet.

1. OVERLAPS BETWEEN THE COVERED AGREEMENTS

There are two types of overlaps between the covered agreements that are worth touching upon. The first concerns the circumstances in which the GATT, the SCM Agreement and the Agreement on Agriculture may overlap in the contexts of differential taxes and subsidies. The second concerns the potential for overlap between the GATT and GATS in the context of restrictions on marketing.

1.1. *Differential Taxation: Overlaps between the GATT, the Agreement on Agriculture, and the SCM Agreement*

A differential-taxation measure might be examined under either the Agreement on Agriculture or the SCM Agreement, as well as the GATT. Neither the Agreement on Agriculture nor the SCM Agreement includes an exception for measures necessary to protect human health. Accordingly, if a measure were to violate the Agreement on Agriculture or the SCM Agreement, there might arise a question as to whether the GATT Article XX(b) exception applies. Obviously, Article XX(b) would apply to a contravention of the GATT, such as if the measure were to contravene Article III:2. However, whether Article XX(b) could be used as an exception protecting a member from violation of other covered agreements is another question.

In recent disputes, the Dispute Settlement Body (DSB) has shied away from whether Article XX of the GATT applies to violations of agreements other than the GATT. For example in *China – Publications and Audiovisual Products*, the panel assumed for the sake of argument that Article XX applied to a breach of China's obligations under its Accession Protocol.[8] The panel went on to

[8] Panel Report, *China – Measures Affecting Trading Rights and Distribution Services for Certain Publications and Audiovisual Entertainment Products*, WT/DS363/R and Corr.1, circulated to WTO Members 12 August 2009, [hereinafter *China – Publications and Audiovisual Products*], para. 7.743.

conclude that the terms of Article XX were not satisfied, thus avoiding the need to determine whether Article XX did in fact apply to obligations other than those found in the GATT. The Appellate Body addressed the availability of a defense under Article XX with respect to China's obligations under its Accession Protocol. However, the Appellate Body concluded that where a measure complies with the conditions of an exception, it represents an exercise of China's power to regulate trade under the terms of China's Accession Protocol.[9] Accordingly, the Appellate Body's decision does not answer the broader question of whether Article XX of the GATT applies to other covered agreements.

Nonetheless, the panel in *China – Publications and Audiovisual Products* stated that "we observe in this respect that Article XX contains the phrase 'nothing in this Agreement,' with the term 'Agreement' referring to the GATT 1994, not other agreements like the Accession Protocol."[10] This conclusion is reflected in the general interpretive note to Annex 1A of the Agreement Establishing the World Trade Organization:

> In the event of conflict between a provision of the General Agreement on Tariffs and Trade 1994 and a provision of another agreement in Annex 1A to the Agreement Establishing the World Trade Organization (referred to in the agreements in Annex 1A as the "WTO Agreement"), the provision of the other agreement shall prevail to the extent of the conflict.

Since Article XX of the GATT uses the phrase "this Agreement," rather than the "WTO Agreement," the ordinary wording of the provision suggests that Article XX can only be invoked as a defense to a violation of the GATT. Although this conclusion may seem simple enough, it is brought into question where GATT provisions are incorporated by reference into other Annex 1A agreements, and where a violation of the GATT is in addition to a violation of another provision. This was the case in *US – Customs Bond Directive*, where questions of law arose under Article VI (Anti-Dumping and Countervailing Duties) of the GATT as well as under the Anti-Dumping Agreement. In that dispute, the panel concluded that there was nothing in the language of Article XX to prevent the invocation of a defense under Article XX(d) where a violation of a provision of the GATT was made out.[11] On appeal, the Appellate

9 Appellate Body Report, *China – Measures Affecting Trading Rights and Distribution Services for Certain Publications and Audiovisual Entertainment Products*, WT/DS363/AB/R, adopted 19 January 2010, para. 230.

10 Panel Report, *China – Publications and Audiovisual Products*, para. 7.743.

11 Panel Report, *United States – Customs Bond Directive for Merchandise Subject to Anti-Dumping/Countervailing Duties*, WT/DS345/R, adopted 1 August 2008, as modified by Appellate Body Report WT/DS343/AB/R, WT/DS345/AB/R, para. 6.11.

Body assumed for the sake of argument that the defense was available, before concluding that Article XX(d) was not satisfied.[12]

Of course, it is one thing to say that an analysis of Article XX of the GATT is not precluded where a violation of the GATT occurs, but another thing to say that Article XX can be invoked as a defense to a violation other than the GATT violation in question. In this respect, it could be argued that the general interpretive note to Annex 1A suggests that any conflict between a GATT Article XX exception and a prohibition in another Annex 1A agreement should be resolved in favor of the Annex 1A agreement.

However, as described in Chapter 2, there exists a presumption against conflict under the law of treaties, to the effect that a treaty interpreter should seek to interpret the GATT and other Annex 1A agreements as consistent with one another wherever possible. Accordingly, it is arguable that the Article XX exceptions apply where conduct prohibited by a GATT provision is also prohibited by an Annex 1A agreement that incorporates the GATT provision in question. Under this interpretation, if conduct is not prohibited by the GATT, but is prohibited by the more specific terms of an Annex 1A agreement, the latter violation will stand. To the extent, however, that the conduct in question violates both a GATT provision and an Annex 1A agreement incorporating that GATT provision, Article XX should be available as a defense.

Equally, it is easier to articulate this approach in the abstract than it is to predict how it might apply to a case study. For example, Article 5(b) of the SCM Agreement provides that a subsidy is only actionable when it adversely affects the interests of other members and the provision invokes the concept of nullification or impairment of benefits found in Article XXIII of the GATT.[13] By the same token, Article 5(b) of the SCM Agreement concerns actionable subsidies and not prohibited subsidies, which are governed by Article 3. The distinction between actionable and prohibited subsidies could suggest that WTO Members intended to create a specific discipline to govern actionable subsidies irrespective of the types of policy concerns reflected in Article XX(b) of the GATT. This view is reinforced by the presence of Part IV of the SCM Agreement, which governs nonactionable subsidies.

In the context of the Agreement on Agriculture, Article 21.1 of that agreement states that "[t]he provisions of GATT 1994 and of other Multilateral

[12] Appellate Body Report, *United States – Customs Bond Directive for Merchandise Subject to Anti-Dumping/Countervailing Duties*, WT/DS343/AB/R, WT/DS345/AB/R adopted 1 August 2008, paras 304–319.

[13] This conclusion also assumes that the exceptions in Article XX of the GATT apply in the event of a nonviolation claim under Article XXIII (a likely outcome given the phrase "nothing in this Agreement" in Article XX).

Trade Agreements in Annex 1A to the WTO Agreement shall apply subject to the provisions of this Agreement." Like the interpretive note to Annex 1A of the WTO Agreement, this clause provides that the terms of the Agreement on Agriculture prevail in the event of conflict. However, it appears that whether Article XX(b) of the GATT could extend protection to a violation of the Agreement on Agriculture is less relevant than whether the provision could extend to the SCM Agreement. The reason for this is that the relevant provisions of the Agreement on Agriculture do not incorporate GATT prohibitions in the same manner as the SCM Agreement does. Accordingly, there is little reason to believe that Article XX(b) of the GATT should apply.

1.2. *Advertising: The GATT and the GATS*

In the case of restrictions on advertising and promotion, there is unlikely to be overlap between the covered agreements.[14] To the extent that measures of this type address trade in goods, they will fall under the GATT, and to the extent that the measures address trade in services, they will fall under the GATS. In addition, the necessity tests set out in the GATT and the GATS have been interpreted in much the same manner.[15] Concern about application of different tests is not a significant issue in this context.

2. APPLICATION OF THE GATT NECESSITY TEST

Article XX of the GATT establishes a range of general exceptions to the prohibitive content of the GATT. The relevant portion of Article XX reads:

> Subject to the requirement that such measures are not applied in a manner which would constitute a means of arbitrary or unjustifiable discrimination between countries where the same conditions prevail, or a disguised restriction on international trade, nothing in this Agreement shall be construed to prevent the adoption or enforcement by any contracting party of measures:
>
> ...
>
> (b) necessary to protect human, animal or plant life or health

[14] One possible exception to this is where measures prohibiting product promotion are also labeling measures falling within the context of the TBT Agreement or the SPS Agreement. Because this scenario is already addressed in the context of production regulation, it is not also addressed here.

[15] Panel Report, *United States – Measures Affecting the Cross-Border Supply of Gambling and Betting Services*, WT/DS285/R, adopted 20 April 2005, modified by Appellate Body Report, WT/DS285/AB/R, [hereinafter *US – Gambling*] para. 6.448.

Application of Article XX(b) requires a two-step analysis. In the first step a panel will consider whether a measure is necessary to protect human health. If so, the measure in question will be appraised under the introductory clauses of Article XX (the *chapeau*).[16]

2.1. *Measures Necessary to Protect Health*

The first issue addressed under Article XX(b) is whether a measure falls within the range of policies considered to protect human health or life.[17] A panel will first determine whether a risk to health exists, and where such a risk does exist, the objective of the measure will be assessed to determine whether the policy underlying the measure is to reduce that risk.[18] There is little doubt that the measures addressed in this study would fall within the general scope of Article XX(b). International instruments such as the FCTC and the global strategies are evidence of the general acceptance of the existence of threats to health. Because the measures in question are designed to reduce the threats to health in question, there is little doubt that they would fall within the scope of Article XX(b).

The more pressing question is under what circumstances the measures would be considered necessary. In this respect, it has been said that WTO Members have discretion to determine their own policy objectives and the level at which they wish to pursue them.[19] Put another way, "WTO Members have the right to determine the level of protection of health that they consider appropriate in a given situation."[20] Against this backdrop, the Appellate Body has approached the necessity test as requiring the weighing and balancing of a series of factors.[21] The factors to be weighed include, but are not limited to, the contribution of the measure to the regulatory goal and the restrictive impact of the measure on international trade. This process of weighing and balancing is carried out in light of the relative importance of the interests or values furthered by the challenged measure.[22]

16 Appellate Body Report, *United States – Standards for Reformulated and Conventional Gasoline*, WT/DS2/AB/R, adopted 20 May 1996, DSR 1996:I, 3 [hereinafter *US –Gasoline*], p. 20.

17 See, for example, Appellate Body Report, *EC – Asbestos*, paras 156 – 163.

18 Panel Report, *Brazil – Measures Affecting Imports of Retreaded Tyres*, WT/DS332/R, 12 June 2007, para. 7.42.

19 Appellate Body Report, *European Communities – Trade Description of Sardines*, WT/DS231/AB/R, adopted 23 October 2002, para. 7.120.

20 Report of the Appellate Body, *EC – Asbestos*, para. 168.

21 Appellate Body Report, *Korea – Various Measures on Beef*, para. 164.

22 Appellate Body Report, *United States – Measures Affecting the Cross-Border Supply of Gambling and Betting Services*, WT/DS285/AB/R, adopted 20 April 2005, para. 306; See also Appellate Body Report, *Korea – Various Measures on Beef*, para. 162; Appellate Body Report, *EC – Asbestos*, para. 172.

In *Korea – Various Measures on Beef* the Appellate Body suggested that these factors are weighed and balanced in order to determine whether "a WTO-consistent alternative measure which the Member concerned could 'reasonably be expected to employ' is available, or whether a less WTO-inconsistent measure is 'reasonably available.'"[23] However, the approach taken by the Appellate Body in *Brazil – Retreaded Tyres* suggests that an initial determination of whether a measure is justified as necessary should be made before an examination of reasonably available alternatives is undertaken.[24] Under this approach a measure may fail the necessity test either on the basis of the weighing and balancing of relevant factors, or on the basis that a less trade-restrictive, reasonably available alternative measure exists.

One question that this approach raises is whether the weighing and balancing test is in effect a proportionality test. Writing before *Brazil – Retreaded Tyres*, Jan Neumann and Elisabeth Türk argued that the weighing and balancing process is done in absolute rather than relative terms. That is, "if the value to be protected is important, if the measure is pretty effective and if the trade restriction is rather moderate on an absolute scale, the measure is very likely to be considered 'necessary,' while the alternative GATT-consistent or less inconsistent restriction will be seen as not 'reasonably available' although in relative terms the alternative would be less inconsistent or trade restrictive."[25]

Some panel reports support the conclusion that the test has been approached in this manner. For example, in *Brazil – Retreaded Tyres* the Appellate Body endorsed the panel's conclusion that the contribution of the measure outweighed its trade restrictiveness.[26] However, neither panels nor the Appellate Body refer to the test in terms of proportionality. In addition, the decision in *EC – Asbestos* suggests that there are clear limits on the weighing and balancing approach. There, the Appellate Body held that a WTO Member cannot be expected to employ an alternative measure if that measure would involve a continuation of the risk that the measure seeks to halt.[27]

[23] Ibid., para. 166.

[24] Appellate Body Report, *Brazil – Retreaded Tyres*, para. 178.

[25] Jan Neumann & Elisabeth Türk, "Necessity Revisited: Proportionality in World Trade Organization Law After Korea – Beef, EC – Asbestos and EC – Sardines," 37(1) *Journal of World Trade*, (2003), pp. 199–233 [hereinafter Neumann and Türk, "Necessity Revisited"], p. 211; see also Axel Desmedt, "Proportionality in WTO Law," 4 *Journal of International Economic Law*, (2001), pp. 441–480.

[26] Appellate Body Report, *Brazil – Retreaded Tyres*, para. 179.

[27] Appellate Body Report, *EC – Asbestos*, para.174; with respect to this see Robert Howse and Elisabeth Türk, "The WTO Impact Upon Internal Regulations: A Case Study of the Canada – EC Asbestos Dispute," in George Bermann and Petros Mavroidis (eds) *Trade and Human Health and Safety*, New York, Cambridge University Press, (2006), pp. 77–117, [hereinafter Howse and Türk, "The WTO Impact Upon Internal Regulations"] p. 113.

Under this approach, the necessity test does not appear to require a weighing of the health risk in question against the trade restrictiveness of a measure in order to find a regulatory compromise between the interests of trade and health. Rather, WTO Members retain the right to protect health to whatever degree they deem appropriate, so long as they do so in a manner that is necessary. Some have argued that in developing this weighing and balancing approach, the Appellate Body has attempted to formulate a more deferential approach.[28]

A. Characterizing a regulatory goal and the level of protection sought

The characterization of a member's regulatory goal and the extent to which that goal is pursued (often referred to as the "level of protection" sought) constitutes a backdrop against which the necessity of a measure must be determined, irrespective of the approach used in determining the necessity of a measure. A panel should not draw an abstract conclusion about whether a particular measure is necessary to protect human health in general. Rather, the existence of a particular risk to health and the extent to which a member seeks to alleviate that risk provide parameters for the analysis. If this was not the case, a panel would have an extremely wide discretion within which to make a judgment about a WTO Member's domestic health policy.

The factual characterization of a regulatory goal is, therefore, central to the application of the necessity test. It is apparent, however, that the importance of this aspect of necessity analysis has been neglected. Although this is an issue of general concern that is not specific to tobacco, alcohol, and diet, this question of judicial practice is likely to have important implications for the lawfulness of the measures discussed in Chapter 3.

At first glance, the characterization of a regulatory goal appears to be a simple process with a settled approach to guide a panel. The case law provides that a regulatory goal must be determined objectively, although a member's characterization of its goal as evidenced by texts of statutes, legislative history, and pronouncements of government agencies and officials may be taken into account.[29] A panel may also find guidance in the structure and operation of

[28] In support of this view, see Deborah Osiro, "GATT/WTO Necessity Analysis: Evolutionary Interpretation and its Impact on the Autonomy of Domestic Regulation," 29(2) *Legal Issues in Economic Integration*, (2002), pp. 123–41; Neumann and Türk, "Necessity Revisited," p. 210; Howse and Türk, "The WTO Impact Upon Internal Regulations," p. 111; See also discussion in Steve Charnovitz, "The WTO's Environmental Progress," 10(3) *Journal of International Economic Law*, (2007), pp. 685–706, p. 698, fn 67.

[29] Appellate Body Report, *US – Gambling*, para. 304.

the measure, in its effects,[30] and in any evidence offered by the complaining party to contradict the respondent's stated objective.[31]

Notwithstanding this settled approach, the factual characterization of a regulatory goal may be controversial. Because the necessity of a measure is determined in light of the regulatory goal, the characterization of that goal can affect how easy it is to justify a measure as necessary under Article XX.[32] This issue poses a particular problem for regulatory regimes, such as those in question, that rely on the adoption of a range of complementary measures to achieve the same or substantially similar objectives. The example of a tobacco advertising ban illustrates this point.

The regulatory goal underlying an advertising ban could be characterized in either a broad or narrow fashion. At its broadest, the goal could be "to protect health by reducing demand for tobacco products." A narrower construction could be "to reduce the stimulants of demand for tobacco products and thereby protect health by reducing consumption." Alternatively, the member in question might have a broader quantitative goal of reducing the prevalence of tobacco consumption by a particular amount, and an advertising ban might constitute one measure intended to contribute to this goal.

The significance of how the member's goal is characterized by a panel cannot be overstated, because the necessity of a measure always depends on what that measure is intended to achieve. Accordingly, the ease or difficulty of justifying a measure as necessary will ebb and flow depending on how the member's regulatory goal is characterized. For example, a narrow construction of the goal underlying an advertising ban is likely to ensure that the measure is protected by Article XX(b), because alternatives to the measure are not likely to be capable of achieving the regulatory goal. This result is not as likely if a broad construction of the regulatory goal is adopted. This conclusion is particularly compelling where the goal is characterized in a qualitative rather than quantitative manner, as was the case in *Brazil – Retreaded Tyres*.

In that dispute, Brazil sought to rely on Article XX(b) to justify a ban on the importation of retreaded tires. Brazil argued that retreaded tires have a shorter lifespan than new tires, and therefore the importation of retreaded tires increases the accumulation of waste tires to a greater degree than importation of new tires. Brazil further argued that waste tires pose threats to

[30] Appellate Body Report, *Australia – Measures Affecting Importation of Salmon*, WT/DS18/AB/R, adopted 6 November 1998, DSR 1998:VIII, 3327 [hereinafter *Australia – Salmon*], para. 207.

[31] Appellate Body Report, *US – Gambling*, para. 304.

[32] See in this regard Howse and Türk, "The WTO Impact Upon Internal Regulations," p. 113.

human health, such as by providing a breeding ground for disease carrying mosquitoes and by releasing harmful chemicals when burned.[33]

In its analysis of reasonably available alternatives the panel defined the regulatory goal in question as "preventing the generation of waste tyres to the maximum extent possible."[34] Shortly thereafter, as a part of the same analysis, the panel defined the level of protection sought by Brazil as the "non-generation of unnecessary tyre waste."[35] The panel could have characterized Brazil's regulatory goal in more general terms, for example, as being "to protect health by reducing the harmful impact of waste tyres." Had the panel taken this approach, any number of measures, including the cleanup of existing tires, could have been construed as reasonably available alternatives to the ban. In this respect, the EC argued that reasonably available alternatives existed and that they included "measures to improve the management of waste tyres in Brazil."[36] The panel, however, adopted a more specific regulatory goal that limited the possible alternatives to those that would prevent actual waste-tire generation.

It is not argued here that the outcome of *Brazil – Retreaded Tyres* was incorrect. The analysis even suggests that many aspects of the panel's decision show significant insight and are praiseworthy for this reason. Nonetheless, the panel's approach highlights the (perhaps obvious) fact that WTO panels have a high degree of discretion in application of the necessity test, and that application of the test can be unpredictable. In particular, the characterization of the level of protection sought by Brazil is difficult to explain in light of the regulatory goal. It will be recalled that the regulatory goal was characterized as "preventing the generation of waste tyres to the maximum extent possible," whereas the level of protection was characterized as the "non-generation of unnecessary tyre waste."[37] It is difficult to understand how "the non-generation of unnecessary tyre waste" says anything about the extent to which Brazil was pursuing its regulatory objective of preventing the generation of waste tires to the maximum extent possible. Rather, it appears that the regulatory objective identified by the panel actually encompasses the extent (or level) to which the policy is pursued, in the sense that it is pursued "to the maximum extent possible."

The conclusions of the panel could be attributed to the process of decision making. The phrase "non-generation of unnecessary tyre waste" is used only

[33] Panel Report, Brazil –*Retreaded Tyres*, para. 7.53.

[34] Ibid., paras 7.166 and 7.172.

[35] Ibid., para. 7.175.

[36] Ibid., para. 7.159.

[37] Ibid., para. 7.175.

in analysis of reasonably available alternatives. The phrase is not used earlier in passages that seek to characterize the regulatory goal for purposes of determining whether the measure fell within the ambit of Article XX(b). In this respect, the panel's approach is not unique. A cursory analysis of previous disputes highlights that the characterization of a regulatory goal is often afforded little analysis outside of a panel determining the threshold question of whether a measure falls under an exception.

In *EC – Asbestos* the Appellate Body merely stated that "the objective pursued by the measure is the preservation of human life and health through the elimination, or reduction, of the well-known, and life-threatening, health risks posed by asbestos fibres."[38] This conclusion was drawn in the absence of any analysis by the Appellate Body. In contrast, the panel in the same dispute had previously found that France's goal was "to protect the health of workers and consumers,"[39] and that this was a "general health objective."[40] The fact that the Appellate Body characterized the regulatory goal differently to the panel suggests either that the identification of a regulatory goal is a question of law or that the Appellate Body has improperly made findings of fact.

The same conclusion could also be drawn about *Korea – Various Measures on Beef*. In that dispute, Korea argued that its dual retail system for beef (whereby domestic and imported beef were required to have separate distribution channels) was aimed at the total elimination of fraud with respect to the origin of beef. However, the Appellate Body rejected Korea's characterization of the level of protection pursued on the basis that "[t]he total elimination of fraud would probably require a total ban of imports."[41] On this basis, the Appellate Body concluded that "Korea intended to *reduce considerably* the number of cases of fraud occurring with respect to the origin of beef sold by retailers."[42]

Because the chosen level of protection is a matter for a member, and characterization of a state's regulatory goal would seem to be a question of fact, it appears that the Appellate Body has improperly made findings of fact. One possible explanation for this, at least in the case of *Korea – Various Measures on Beef*, is that if the Appellate Body had to conduct its analysis in the context of Korea's statement concerning the level of protection sought, it would have been difficult for the necessity of Korea's measure to be questioned other than

[38] Appellate Body Report, *EC – Asbestos*, para. 172.
[39] Panel Report, *EC – Asbestos*, para. 8.173.
[40] Ibid., para. 8.174.
[41] Appellate Body Report, *Korea – Various Measures on Beef*, para. 178.
[42] Ibid.

on the basis of lack of effectiveness (an issue that will be discussed in further detail).

This conclusion reflects one of the central arguments of this chapter. That is, application of the necessity test often turns on the characterization of a regulatory goal and the extent to which that goal is pursued. Although this is an inevitable aspect of a necessity test that is truly deferential to a member's regulatory goal, the manner in which these issues have been approached makes application of the test unpredictable and open to judicial manipulation. This conclusion and its application to the measures discussed in Chapter 3 are further highlighted in the following analysis of necessity.

B. Applying the necessity test by reference to the various factors

Once the regulatory goal is established a panel will consider whether the measure is necessary to achieve that goal. The term "necessary" is interpreted in accordance with its ordinary meaning. In *Korea – Various Measures on Beef* the Appellate Body elaborated upon that meaning:

> We believe that, as used in the context of Article XX(d), the reach of the word "necessary" is not limited to that which is "indispensable" or "of absolute necessity" or "inevitable." Measures which are indispensable or of absolute necessity or inevitable to secure compliance certainly fulfill the requirements of Article XX(d). But other measures, too, may fall within the ambit of this exception. As used in Article XX(d), the term "necessary" refers, in our view, to a range of degrees of necessity. At one end of this continuum lies "necessary" understood as "indispensable"; at the other end, is "necessary" taken to mean as "making a contribution to." We consider that a "necessary" measure is, in this continuum, located significantly closer to the pole of "indispensable" than to the opposite pole of simply "making a contribution to." [43]

There is little doubt that this passage reflects a softening of the necessity requirement in deference to the regulatory choices of WTO Members.[44] This approach appears to be more permissive than the manner in which this test was applied in GATT disputes. Equally, the necessity test is applied hand-in-hand with the *chapeau*, and the relationship between the two can have important implications for regulatory autonomy. This will be discussed in further detail later in this chapter. For present purposes, it is worthwhile to examine how the weighing and balancing test casts light on the necessity of a measure.

43 Appellate Body Report, *Korea – Various Measures on Beef*, para. 161.

44 For this argument, see Howse and Türk, "The WTO Impact Upon Internal Regulations," pp. 114–115.

The burden rests on the state seeking to rely on the exception in Article XX(b) to make out a prima facie case that the measure is necessary.[45] Because a determination is made by weighing and balancing various factors, it is worthwhile to examine those factors individually.

(a) THE RELATIVE IMPORTANCE OF THE GOAL

In considering the application of Article XX(d) (which applies to measures necessary to secure compliance with laws or regulations that are not inconsistent with the GATT) in *Korea – Various Measures on Beef*, the Appellate Body stated:

> It seems to us that a treaty interpreter assessing a measure claimed to be necessary to secure compliance of a WTO-consistent law or regulation may, in appropriate cases, take into account the relative importance of the common interests or values that the law or regulation to be enforced is intended to protect. The more vital or important those common interests or values are, the easier it would be to accept as "necessary" a measure designed as an enforcement instrument. [46]

Given that this comment occurred in the distinct context of Article XX(d), and that Article XX(b) implicitly recognizes the importance of measures to protect health, it might be expected that this factor would not be considered in an Article XX(b) analysis. This argument finds support in the (albeit earlier) decision of the Appellate Body in *US – Gasoline* where it was stated that "Article XX contains provisions designed to permit important State interests – including the protection of human health as well as the conservation of exhaustible natural resources – to find expression."[47]

Contrary to this view, however, subsequent case law actually suggests that a panel is obliged to consider importance in the context of Article XX(b). In *Brazil –Retreaded Tyres* the Appellate Body stated that "a panel *must* assess all the relevant factors, particularly the extent of the contribution to the achievement of a measure's objective and its trade restrictiveness, in the light of the importance of the interests or values at stake" [my emphasis].[48] Although the Appellate Body also considered the importance of the measure in analysis of Article XX(b) in *EC – Asbestos*, it did not suggest that a panel was obliged to do so.

At this point, it is also worthwhile to note how this element of the weighing and balancing approach appears to have changed from *Korea – Various*

[45] Appellate Body Report, *US – Gambling*, para. 310.

[46] Appellate Body Report, *Korea – Various Measures on Beef*, para. 162.

[47] Appellate Body Report, *US – Gasoline*, pp 29–30.

[48] Appellate Body Report, *Brazil – Retreaded Tyres*, para. 156 (my emphasis).

Measures on Beef to *Brazil – Retreaded Tyres*. In the former dispute, the Appellate Body suggested that importance should be weighed with the trade restrictiveness and contribution of a measure. In the latter dispute, however, the Appellate Body suggested that these factors should be weighed in light of the importance of a goal rather than with it. The distinction is important, because the former concept suggests a proportionality type analysis, whereas the latter suggests a suitability analysis with a shifting standard of proof dependent on the importance of the goal in question.

Leaving this aside, given that the importance of a goal falling within Article XX(b) will be assessed, it is worthwhile to consider how previous cases have approached the issue. In *EC – Asbestos*, for example, the Appellate Body stated:

> [T]he objective pursued by the measure is the preservation of human life and health through the elimination, or reduction, of the well-known, and life-threatening, health risks posed by asbestos fibres. The value pursued is both vital and important in the highest degree.[49]

The panel in *Brazil – Measures Affecting Imports of Retreaded Tyres* drew on this statement and concluded that "to the extent that this same value is being protected here, the same reasoning would apply."[50] On this basis, the panel concluded that "the objective of protecting human health and life against life threatening diseases, such as dengue fever and malaria, is both vital and important in the highest degree."[51] The panel also had to consider the importance of the objective of protecting animal and plant life and health from exposure to toxic emissions from tire fires and the transmission of mosquito-borne diseases to animals as a result of mosquito breeding in tires. In considering this issue the panel drew on the report of the Appellate Body in *US – Shrimp* and the fact that the preamble to the WTO Agreement refers to the importance of environmental protection. On this basis the panel found "that the objective of protection of animal and plant life and health should also be considered important."[52]

This aspect of the panel's decision highlights the problematic nature of considering the importance of a goal in the context of the provision. That is, neither the panel nor the Appellate Body has a legitimate role in evaluating the importance of domestic policy goals that fall within the scope of

49 Appellate Body Report, *EC – Asbestos*, para. 172.

50 Panel Report, Brazil –*Retreaded Tyres*, para. 7.111.

51 Ibid.

52 Ibid., para. 7.112.

Article XX.[53] This process is a step in the direction of universal values, which is not appropriate in a multilateral regime that is largely about the negative integration of states that have vastly different interests and values. In this respect, the panel found the protection of human health to be important to the "*highest degree*," whereas the protection of animal and plant life was only "*also considered important*."[54] A similar approach was taken by the panel in *Canada – Wheat Exports and Grain Products*, where it was concluded that objectives such as ensuring the quality of Canadian grain and maintaining the integrity of the Canadian grading system for grain are not as important as other goals such as the protection of human life and health against a life-threatening health risk.[55]

The panel in *China – Publications and Audiovisual Products* took an even more notable approach. In considering the importance of China's stated goal of protecting public morals, the panel stated:

> In our view, it is undoubtedly the case that the protection of public morals ranks among the most important values or interests pursued by Members as a matter of public policy. We do not consider it simply accident that the exception relating to "public morals" is the first exception identified in the ten sub-paragraphs of Article XX.[56]

This comment appears to address the absence of any methodology by which a panel might determine the importance of a domestic policy goal. However, the approach proposed by the panel is deeply flawed. To the extent that the importance of a policy goal weighs in favor of the necessity of a measure, the panel's approach implies that regulatory goals to protect public morals are more important than goals to protect human life and health, which, in turn, are more important than goals to ensure compliance with laws. On this basis, the panel is in effect suggesting that it should be more difficult to justify as necessary a measure to protect human health than a measure to protect public morals, and that it should be more difficult to justify a measure to ensure compliance with laws as necessary than it is to justify the other two categories of measures. This seeks to create a hierarchy of universal values and ignores the fact that the same term "necessary" is used in each provision. Along these lines, the Panel in *Colombia – Indicative Prices and Restrictions on Ports of*

53 In this respect see Howse and Türk, "The WTO Impact Upon Internal Regulations," p. 116.

54 My emphasis.

55 Panel Report, *Canada – Measures Relating to Exports of Wheat and Treatment of Imported Grain*, WT/DS276/R, adopted 27 September 2004, upheld by Appellate Body Report, WT/DS276/AB/R, DSR 2004:VI, 2817, para. 6.303.

56 Panel Report, *China – Publications and Audiovisual Products*, para. 7.817.

Entry stated that "the relative importance of the common interests or value that may be addressed within the gamut of Article XX of the GATT 1994 (including all its subparagraphs) do not adhere to any hierarchical ranking or prioritisation of interests therein."[57]

The absence of a legitimate methodology to guide analysis of the importance of a policy goal heightens uncertainty. To date, neither a panel nor the Appellate Body has conducted an in-depth analysis of the importance of a particular regulatory goal. The only criterion evident in past disputes is that there should be some commonality in the interests pursued. However, this criterion is limited in its usefulness, because it reverts to universalism by suggesting the existence of a universally applicable set of policy priorities.

The concept of commonality also suggests that panels should consider regulatory goals with a degree of specificity. Although it is assumed that the broad goal of protecting human health is considered important because it is mentioned in the wording of Article XX(b), subgoals may be less so. For example, a panel might consider that addressing the spread of an infectious disease is an important policy, partly because infectious diseases transcend borders and pose a common threat to WTO Members. On the other hand, certain noncommunicable diseases may not pose a comparable threat, leading to the conclusion that the goal of addressing such diseases is relatively less important. Such an approach would be problematic for at least two reasons. First, different WTO Members will face different health problems to different degrees, undermining any appeal toward universalism. Second, the need for disputants to share common goals would appear far removed from the text of Article XX.[58]

The absence of any reasonable methodology by which to determine the importance of a regulatory objective has perhaps been overshadowed by the fact that considering the importance of a goal is intended to create a greater margin of appreciation and to give members greater regulatory freedom. In this vein, no panel has found a goal to be unimportant. Notwithstanding this, the current approach reflects an unfortunate and unpredictable midpoint between a proportionality test and a necessity test that is truly deferential to the regulatory goals of WTO Members. On one hand, the Appellate Body continues to assert that members have a discretion to determine their own policy objectives and the level at which they wish to pursue them. On the other

57 Panel Report, *Colombia – Indicative Prices and Restrictions on Ports of Entry*, WT/DS366/R and Corr.1, adopted 20 May 2009, para. 7.563.

58 Steve Charnovitz, "An Analysis of Pascal Lamy's Proposal on Collective Preferences," 8(2) *Journal of International Economic Law*, (2005), pp. 449–472, p. 468.

hand, however, the Appellate Body opens the importance of those objectives to review, and some panel reports suggest that policy objectives may be compromised in this weighing and balancing process.

To some extent, panels and the Appellate Body have to second-guess domestic policy choices in order to determine the necessity of a measure. That is, the outcome of a necessity analysis could result in a measure being unlawful. By the same token, there is no need for a decision maker to evaluate the importance of a member's regulatory objective in determining the necessity of a measure in pursuit of that objective. Rather, it would be sufficient for the law to recognize that all of the objectives listed in Article XX are important, and that every necessity analysis should be carried out against this backdrop. In effect, this is what panels have been doing in any case.

The practice of panels suggests that a panel is likely to ascribe importance to the regulatory goals underlying the measures discussed in this study irrespective of how those goals are characterized. In fact, previous disputes show panels to be reluctant to engage in any serious analysis of the importance of a policy goal. For the reasons already discussed, this approach might be intended to create greater deference to goals such as health protection, but there is also a risk that this process will undermine those goals.

(b) CONTRIBUTION TO THE REGULATORY GOAL

The second factor that may be taken into account in the weighing and balancing process is the extent to which a measure contributes to the realization of the ends pursued by it.[59] In *Brazil – Retreaded Tyres*, the Appellate Body stated that "a contribution exists where there is a genuine relationship of ends and means between the objective pursued and the measure at issue"[60] and that "a panel must be satisfied that [a measure] brings about a material contribution to the achievement of its objective."[61] It is clear, therefore, that a WTO Member invoking Article XX(b) need not demonstrate that a measure actually fulfills the objective pursued in order to establish the necessity of a measure.

By the same token, this low standard is only a threshold test in the sense that a measure making no contribution to the objective cannot be considered necessary. This low threshold should not be confused with the question of to what extent a particular measure contributes to the regulatory goal underlying it. The latter question is taken into account in the weighing and balancing

59 Appellate Body Report, *Korea – Various Measures on Beef*, para. 163; Appellate Body Report, *US – Gambling*, para. 306.

60 Appellate Body Report, *Brazil – Retreaded Tyres*, para. 145.

61 Ibid., para. 151.

process. The aspect of the Appellate Body's decision that arguably eases the test the most is the conclusion that it is permissible for a panel to assess the contribution of a measure in either quantitative or qualitative terms.[62] With respect to determining which approach should be used, the Appellate Body stated:

> The selection of a methodology to assess a measure's contribution is a function of the nature of the risk, the objective pursued, and the level of protection sought. It ultimately also depends on the nature, quantity, and quality of evidence existing at the time the analysis is made.[63]

For this reason, the Appellate Body concluded that a panel "should enjoy a certain latitude in designing the appropriate methodology to use and deciding how to structure or organize the analysis of the contribution of the measure at issue to the realization of the ends pursued by it."[64]

This aspect of the Appellate Body's decision is significant because it recognizes that a measure may be justified in either theoretical or empirical terms depending on the risk in question, the objective pursued (including the level of protection), and the availability of evidence. As already suggested, sometimes it is less likely that alternative measures will be able to achieve a qualitative regulatory goal. This is partly because alternative measures are less likely to make the same contribution to achievement of that goal. This idea is developed in further detail later in this chapter in discussion concerning complementary regulatory measures. For present purposes, however, it is sufficient to note two points. First, the characterization of a regulatory goal has a flow-on effect in examination of the contribution of a measure, thereby illustrating the pervasive impact of that process of factual characterization. Second, permitting members to pursue a qualitative goal is another mechanism that increases regulatory autonomy under the necessity test.

It is also worth noting that the concept of measuring the contribution of a measure in qualitative terms has been the subject of criticism. Bown and Trachtman have argued that the approach in *Brazil – Retreaded Tyres* is flawed because even a qualitative assessment of the contribution made by the import ban should assess magnitudes.[65] In referring to magnitudes Bown and

[62] Appellate Body Report, *Brazil – Retreaded Tyres*, para. 146.

[63] Ibid., para. 145.

[64] Ibid.

[65] Chad Bown and Joel Trachtman, "Brazil – Measures Affecting Imports of Retreaded Tyres: A Balancing Act," 8(1) *World Trade Review*, (2009), pp. 85–135; see also Joseph Weiler, "Comment, Brazil – Measures Affecting Imports of Retreaded Tyres (DS322)," 8(1) *World Trade Review*, (2009), pp. 137–144, p. 130.

Trachtman are referring to the extent to which a measure reduces the risk to health in question.

This approach could have significant implications for efforts to address noncommunicable disease. Because it is ordinarily easier to measure the effect of addressing a proximal cause of disease on morbidity and mortality, it will ordinarily be easier to measure the contribution of a measure addressing a proximal cause of disease in terms of morbidity and mortality. The argument advanced by Bown and Trachtman also neglects the point, made by the Appellate Body, that a result flowing from some regulatory actions can only be evaluated with the benefit of time.[66] This point is of particular importance in the context of noncommunicable diseases, because regulatory strategies often aim to improve population health over the long term through measures that minimize exposure to various risk factors.

The need for flexibility in an evidentiary sense is also reflected in the way in which Article XX(d) of the GATT has been applied. Because Article XX(d) protects measures necessary to secure compliance with other laws, there is an inherent uncertainty in application of the provision. The nature of the measures in question as law-enforcement measures means that their effectiveness cannot be guaranteed and will often be difficult to assess. As is the case with measures to address noncommunicable disease, there is also often a long chain of causation between a measure and enforcement of a law.[67] It is not surprising, therefore, that the Appellate Body has recognized that there is no requirement of certainty in the context of Article XX(d). In *Mexico – Soft Drinks* the Appellate Body stated:

> In our view, a measure can be said to be designed to "secure compliance" even if the measure cannot be guaranteed to achieve its result with absolute certainty [footnote omitted]. Nor do we consider that the "use of coercion" [footnote omitted] is a necessary component of a measure designed "to secure compliance." Rather, Article XX(d) requires that the design of the measure contribute "to securing compliance with laws or regulations which are not inconsistent with the provisions of" the GATT 1994.[68]

Equally, Bown and Trachtman argue that this approach is flawed because it establishes a different standard for the measure in dispute than for putative alternative measures. That is, where it is argued that a measure is a reasonably available alternative measure, the complaining member must establish that

66 Appellate Body Report, *Brazil –Retreaded Tyres*, para. 151

67 This might be the case, for example, in the context of a marking requirement such as a tax stamp or traceability requirement applied to tobacco or alcohol products.

68 Appellate Body Report, *Mexico – Soft Drinks*, para. 74.

the proposed measure will achieve a given regulatory goal despite the fact that the member invoking Article XX need not establish the effectiveness of the actual measure in dispute. Although this appears troubling at first glance, it is a function of the fact that the effects of a measure may be unknown at the time of a dispute or may need to be evaluated over time. Because Article XX ultimately gives (albeit conditional) preference to the interests listed in that provision, it makes sense for the necessity test to err in favor of upholding a measure where information is necessarily inadequate.

An approach that assesses the qualitative contribution of a measure is also consistent with a standard of proof that recognizes the limited role of courts in drawing empirical conclusions. The Appellate Body touched on this issue in *US – Continued Suspension*, a dispute under the SPS Agreement. The Appellate Body stated that the role of a panel is "not to determine whether the risk assessment undertaken by a WTO Member is correct, but rather to determine whether that risk assessment is supported by coherent reasoning and respectable scientific evidence and is, in this sense, objectively justifiable."[69]

Although the context is different, the same reasoning applies with respect to the GATT. Judicial-type bodies such as WTO panels have a limited fact-finding role and sit one step removed from questions of scientific or empirical controversy. The role of the court is to evaluate the adequacy of the evidence presented by the disputants in applying a burden of proof. It therefore seems inappropriate for a panel to require a quantitative analysis in every application of the necessity test, or to require an assessment of the contribution in terms of magnitudes. Whereas qualitative or theoretical arguments may be inadequate in some disputes, they may be valid in others.

(c) THE RESTRICTIVE IMPACT ON TRADE

The final factor to be weighed and balanced is the degree to which the measure in question restricts trade. In *Korea – Various Measures on Beef* the Appellate Body stated:

> Another aspect is the extent to which the compliance measure produces restrictive effects on international commerce [footnote omitted], that is, in respect of a measure inconsistent with Article III:4, restrictive effects *on imported goods*. A measure with a relatively slight impact upon imported products might more easily be considered as "necessary" than a measure with intense or broader restrictive effects.[70]

[69] Appellate Body Report, *United States – Continued Suspension of Obligations in the EC – Hormones Dispute*, WT/DS320/AB/R adopted 14 November 2008, para. 590

[70] Appellate Body Report, *Korea – Various Measures on Beef*, para. 163.

In a footnote following the phrase "international commerce," the Appellate Body stated:

> We recall that the last paragraph of the Preamble of the GATT of 1994 reads as follows:
>
> "Being desirous of contributing to these objectives by entering into reciprocal and mutually advantageous arrangements directed to the substantial reduction of tariffs and other barriers to trade *and to the elimination of discriminatory treatment in international commerce*."[71]

These passages raise the question of whether the concept of trade restrictiveness concerns only the manner in which a measure violates the GATT or some broader measure of the actual impact that the measure has on trade. Axel Desmedt has argued that this approach "puts the emphasis on a more quantifiable criterion based on the *trade restrictiveness* of a measure rather than on the degree of *consistency*."[72] On the other hand, Neumann and Türk take the view that the restrictiveness of a measure on international commerce is not an independent criterion to be taken into account.[73]

The language used by the Appellate Body suggests that trade restrictiveness must be determined by reference to the breach in question. In particular, the Appellate Body refers to the fact that in the case of a measure that is inconsistent with Article III:4 of the GATT, it is the impact on imported goods that must be taken into account. Similarly, the footnote to the phrase "international commerce" refers to "reciprocal and mutually advantageous arrangements," suggesting that the concept of "international commerce" is bound up in the provisions of the WTO-covered agreements themselves. This view also accords with the fact that the purpose of Article XX is to act as an exception to the terms of the prohibitions set out in the GATT. In this context the prohibited conduct must be the focus of any examination of trade restrictiveness, because it is that conduct that a WTO Member is seeking to justify as lawful under Article XX.

It is also noteworthy that in bringing a complaint under provisions such as Article III:4 of the GATT, a complaining party does not have to show that the impugned measure has had an actual impact on trade or commerce.[74] Rather, it is sufficient for the complaining party to demonstrate that the *conditions of*

[71] Ibid., fn 105 (emphasis in Appellate Body Report).

[72] Desmedt, "Proportionality in WTO Law," p. 468 (emphasis in original).

[73] Neumann and Türk, "Necessity Revisited," p. 214.

[74] Appellate Body Report, *European Communities – Regime for the Importation, Sale and Distribution of Bananas*, WT/DS27/AB/R, adopted 25 September 1997, DSR 1997:II, 591 [hereinafter EC – Bananas III, para. 216.

competition have been altered in a manner less favorable to imported goods. In this context evidence on the actual impact of a measure on trade or commerce is not necessarily available to a panel. This suggests that it is the noncompliance of a measure rather than its actual impact on trade that should be considered. Noncompliance will still be considered in terms of the impact on market access, but not necessarily using a quantitative approach.

What then, can be said about application of this factor to the measures discussed in Chapter 3? In one sense, the measures considered are far less trade restrictive than attempts to address noncommunicable disease might be. For example, a differential-taxation measure seeking to discourage the consumption of a particular class of product is less restrictive than a measure banning the sale of that product. The same could be said for other measures. In fact, the question of to what extent individual and economic liberty should be restricted in the interests of public health has been a central issue in discussion of the strategies to address tobacco, alcohol, and diet. On one side of the debate are commentators such as Lawrence Gostin, who view paternalism in health policy as justified where it is necessary to advance population health.[75] On the other side, paternalism is rejected as an inappropriate intrusion by government, except where an individual lacks competence. However, each side of the debate recognizes the importance of liberty, and this is reflected in the regulatory approaches described in Chapter 3.

This is not to suggest that every health measure to address tobacco, alcohol, or diet will be minimally trade restrictive. On the contrary, food products that cannot be reformulated have been banned outright in some locations. For example, Fiji has banned the importation of mutton flaps, a high-fat cut of meat from sheep.[76] Whereas measures such as this may be highly trade restrictive, many of the measures intended to reduce exposure to risk factors are likely to be minimally trade restrictive.

(d) WEIGHING THE NECESSITY OF A MEASURE

Prior to considering whether there are reasonably available alternatives to a measure, a panel must reach a preliminary conclusion on whether the measure is necessary.[77] This involves weighing and balancing the aforementioned factors in order to identify where on the sliding scale of necessity a measure falls. In practice, panels have taken different approaches to this process. As Neumann and Türk have argued, many panels have approached this task in

[75] Gostin, *Public Health Law*, p. 53.

[76] *Fiji Times Online*, "Nations in a Flap over Nothing," Thursday, January 7, 2010

[77] Appellate Body Report, *Brazil – Retreaded Tyres*, para. 156.

absolute terms along the lines of a proportionality test.[78] Equally, the suitability of a measure to achieve a given regulatory goal remains a part of this analysis. For example, a measure may fail the necessity test due to the fact that it does not make a contribution to the goal in question.

At different times the approach enunciated by the Appellate Body has been far from clear. A panel could be forgiven for thinking that a process of weighing and balancing is associated with a proportionality requirement, or, conversely, for thinking that the Appellate Body was merely trying to provide guidance to be used in examining the connection between the impugned measure and the member's regulatory goal. In addition, as laid out in *Korea – Various Measures on Beef*, the weighing and balancing approach was cast as a means of analyzing reasonably available alternatives, meaning that a panel could be forgiven for not treating this approach as a preliminary analysis of necessity.

In any case, it is at this point that the Appellate Body's softening of the necessity requirement is of importance to the measures discussed in Chapter 3. In particular, it will be recalled that a measure need not be indispensable – that a measure need only make a material contribution to the regulatory goal – and that the importance of a regulatory goal has only been used to bolster the conclusion that a measure is necessary. The impact of these points is most obvious in *Brazil – Retreaded Tyres*, in which the import ban was held to be necessary despite the remoteness of the ban from the onset of mosquito-borne diseases.

Although some such as Bown and Trachtman are critical of this gradual softening of the necessity test, it must be viewed in light of the broader context of Article XX. This step in the process is only the second of four requirements that a measure must satisfy in order to be defensible under Article XX(b). The first step is a threshold step requiring merely that the measure fall within the scope of the provision. The second step requires the consideration of a number of factors in order to determine necessity in a fairly abstract fashion. The third step then requires evaluation of whether alternative measures are reasonably available, and the final step requires application of the *chapeau*.

Each of these tests is linked in the sense that the softening of one requirement does not necessarily mean that the defense has become more accessible. By the same token, Bown and Trachtman have argued that the decision in *Brazil –Retreaded Tyres* also softens any requirement that a measure be the least trade-restrictive alternative that is reasonably available.

[78] Neumann and Türk, "Necessity Revisited," p. 211.

C. Reasonably available alternatives

If a complaining party argues that another measure is reasonably available to achieve the regulatory goal, the burden rests with the party relying on the exception to demonstrate that the purported alternative is not a reasonably available alternative measure.[79]

It is this variant of a "least-restrictive means" test that is perhaps most challenging for measures intended to address distal causes of disease and for measures that form one part of broader regulatory schemes. In the case of distal causes of disease, the longer chain of causation between a risk factor and the onset of disease means that there are more points in the chain at which a public health intervention can be made in order to prevent disease. In the case of measures falling within broader regulatory schemes, one measure might be considered an alternative to another.

In order to examine application of this aspect of the test in the context of noncommunicable disease, a tobacco advertising ban is used as a case study. In the context of tobacco advertising bans, it could be argued that a range of other measures are capable of reducing the prevalence of tobacco consumption. Along these lines, if the member defending the measure has a general goal, such as to protect health by reducing the prevalence of tobacco consumption, other measures might constitute reasonably available alternatives. It could also be argued that other interventions are available to break any causative relationship between advertising and tobacco consumption.

The FCTC sets out a range of different policies, including tax measures, health warnings, and educational measures such as counter-advertising and tobacco-dependence and cessation measures. As previously outlined, where a very general regulatory goal is pursued, it is possible to view measures such as tobacco taxes as alternatives to advertising bans. The primary reason for this is that differences between measures lose their relevance in light of the generality of the regulatory objective. By the same token, tobacco-control measures are intended to be complementary to one another. In Article 7 of the FCTC the parties recognize "that comprehensive non-price measures are an effective and important means of reducing tobacco consumption." These measures are set out in Articles 8 to 13. These measures are intended to be mutually supportive, and the use of one does not make another unnecessary in a regulatory sense. The same could also be said in other contexts. For example, public-information campaigns about the potential harm associated with alcohol consumption are not a genuine regulatory alternative to labeling measures.

79 Appellate Body Report, *US – Gambling*, para. 311.

These types of complementary regulatory measures pose a significant test for the WTO. On the one hand, the integrity of the trade regime is threatened by the erosion of obligations through the expansive interpretation of exceptions. On the other hand, if complementary measures are treated as reasonably available alternatives to one another, it may always be possible to imagine a less trade-restrictive alternative to any impugned measure.[80] This approach would narrow the necessity test to such a point that it would not only prevent legitimate regulatory measures, but would also threaten extraneous regulatory regimes such as the tobacco-control regime. This raises the question of how panels should approach measures that constitute one limb of a broader regulatory scheme.

The necessity test ought to make allowance for the maintenance of complementary regulatory measures such as tobacco taxes and tobacco advertising bans. Failure to make allowance for complementary regulatory measures would be a failure to recognize the proper balance between the trade regime and regulatory autonomy, and would ignore the fact that treaties such as the FCTC compel such approaches to regulation.

Brazil – Retreaded Tyres suggests that there are three different approaches that a panel might adopt in order to preserve the lawfulness of measures that form part of a broader complementary regime. These include relying on the regulatory goal and level of protection sought by a member, defining the distinction between complementary and alternative regulatory measures, and using extraneous instruments in interpretation.

(a) RELYING ON THE REGULATORY GOAL AND LEVEL OF PROTECTION SOUGHT IN ORDER TO EXCLUDE MEASURES AS ALTERNATIVES

It is well established that WTO Members have the freedom to choose the level of protection that they seek from a particular health risk[81] and that a member's chosen level of protection can be evaluated qualitatively.[82] Similarly, a measure is not a reasonably available alternative if it would involve the maintenance of the risk that a member is seeking to eliminate.[83] Accordingly, the way in which the regulatory goal and level of protection sought by a member are characterized can shield a measure from the conclusion that reasonably available alternatives exist.

[80] For a similar argument, see Daniel Farber and Robert Hudec, "GATT Legal Constraints on Domestic Environmental Regulations," in Jagdish Bhagwati and Robert Hudec (eds), *Fair Trade and Harmonization: Prerequisites for Free Trade?* Volume 2, Cambridge MA, MIT Press, (1996), pp. 59–94, p. 81.

[81] Appellate Body Report, *EC – Asbestos*, para. 168.

[82] Ibid., para. 167.

[83] Ibid., para. 174.

This was the case in *Brazil –Retreaded Tyres*, in which the regulatory goals and levels of protection sought played a large role in establishing necessity. It will be recalled from the discussion earlier that the panel defined Brazil's regulatory goal as "preventing the generation of waste tyres to the maximum extent possible"[84] and the level of protection sought by Brazil as the "non-generation of unnecessary tyre waste."[85]

As was argued earlier, it is difficult to understand how the "non-generation of unnecessary tyre waste" constitutes a level of protection. In this respect, Bown and Trachtman have taken a similar position, arguing that reducing the number of waste tires can only be understood as a means of protection from the health risks posed by waste tires.[86] They further argue:

> A *means* of protection is an alternative to be evaluated in determining the least-trade-restrictive-alternative under a traditional necessity test and is not itself a standard to which all other means can be held. If it were the latter, it would be circular, and no test at all.[87]

This criticism is addressed in further detail later. For present purposes, it is sufficient to note that the approach of the panel highlights the way in which characterization of a regulatory goal and the extent to which it is sought may be used to preserve the lawfulness of a measure. In the context of waste tires, the panel's approach recognized that WTO Members should have a range of complementary means at their disposal in order to address a health risk. That is, Brazil is permitted to address the generation of waste tires as well as their disposal, in the sense that measures adopting each of these means of health protection are not alternatives to one another.

In the context of a tobacco advertising ban, protection for the measure could also be provided if a panel were to characterize a regulatory goal narrowly. For example, if a panel were to characterize the goal as being "to reduce the stimulants of demand for tobacco products and thereby protect health by reducing consumption," it would limit the possible alternatives to those that act on demand stimulation.[88] A panel would then have the task of determining the extent to which a member is seeking to eliminate the stimulants of consumption. A panel could carry out this task by reference to the scope of the advertising ban, including the extent of any exemptions and by reference

84 Panel Report, *Brazil – Retreaded Tyres*, paras 7.166 and 7.172.

85 Ibid., para. 7.175.

86 Bown and Trachtman, "A balancing Act," p. 124.

87 Ibid., p. 125.

88 Notably, this approach avoids criticisms of circularity because the goal itself is not to eliminate the advertising, but rather the negative potential impact on health caused by advertising.

to the existence of other stimulants of demand. In contrast, a panel could, as the case law suggests it might, define the regulatory goal broadly as being "to protect health through the reduction of tobacco consumption." A panel would then have the task of evaluating the extent to which a member seeks to reduce tobacco consumption. This approach would invite an analysis of all methods capable of reducing tobacco consumption as possible alternatives.

The first (more specific) approach appears to be the better one. In particular, the second approach would require a panel to assess the extent to which a member seeks to reduce tobacco consumption in order to determine the level of protection sought. In the absence of specific policy statements, this task may be quite abstract in nature and difficult to carry out by reference to the impugned measure. By the same token, a panel might construe the level of protection sought in a qualitative fashion, thereby reducing the availability of alternatives. For example, a panel might characterize the level of protection sought as being the elimination of advertising as a stimulant of demand. Although this approach might preserve the lawfulness of advertising bans, it is less predictable, gives panels a high degree of discretion, and is open to manipulation.

The panel's decision in *Brazil – Retreaded Tyres* highlights some of the problems associated with this approach. Leaving aside the actual conclusions drawn by the panel, there were a number of problems with respect to the process by which those conclusions were drawn. The most obvious problem was that neither the regulatory goal nor the level of protection was subjected to detailed analysis. Although this is also the case in most disputes, the absence of analysis gives the impression either that important threshold questions were decided at the whim of a panel or that they were manipulated so as to achieve a desired outcome. The latter impression is reinforced by the fact that Brazil's objective and level of protection were characterized as a part of the panel's analysis of whether reasonably available alternatives to the measure exist. Clearly, the more judicious approach would be to identify the regulatory goal and the level of protection sought and to consider subsequently the availability of alternatives. Similarly, a conceptually clear approach would require a panel to do more than merely draw a distinction between a regulatory goal and the level of protection sought. That is, it should be clear why one is classified as a regulatory goal and why the other is a statement about the extent to which that goal is pursued.

With these comments in mind, two conclusions can be drawn. First, it is possible to use the process of characterizing a regulatory goal and the extent to which that goal is pursued in order to preserve the lawfulness of complementary regulatory measures. Secondly, the manner in which these issues are currently approached leaves the necessity test vulnerable to manipulation so as to support predetermined and possibly arbitrary decisions about the lawfulness of a measure.[89]

This conclusion raises the question of how this aspect of the necessity test could be applied by panels so as to increase predictability while preserving the lawfulness of complementary measures. The first answer to this question is that the regulatory goal and level of protection sought should be subjected to proper analysis by panels. Beyond this, one method of improving analysis would be for panels to define regulatory objectives with more specificity, and to give more weight to the means by which a measure affects health (as opposed to merely the means itself) in determining that objective.

The benefits of this approach can be illustrated by reference to the case study of a tobacco advertising ban. Such a ban reduces tobacco consumption by preventing demand stimulation. In this context, reference should be made to the prevention of demand stimulation in the regulatory goal. In such circumstances, only other measures that could also reduce (or eliminate, depending on the level of protection sought) demand stimulation would be considered as reasonably available alternatives. Similarly, as the panel in *Brazil – Retreaded Tyres* held, only measures capable of reducing the accumulation of waste tires could have been alternatives to Brazil's import ban.

Although this approach might appear far reaching, it does not mean that there will be no reasonably available alternatives to measures forming a part of a complementary regulatory scheme. On the contrary, there might still be less trade-restrictive means of implementing an advertising ban or a tax measure. However, under this approach a tax measure is less likely to be an alternative to an advertising ban. Nor does this approach fail to identify a protectionist purpose that is disguised by the pursuit of a legitimate objective. Rather, this question should be considered in the context of the *chapeau* to Article XX, which is discussed later.

In summary, the regulatory objective and level of protection sought by a member might protect measures discussed in Chapter 3 under a necessity analysis, particularly if members are careful in how they frame their objectives. However, the manner in which panels have approached these aspects of the necessity test suggests that it would be unwise to assume that these aspects of the test will necessarily offer protection to complementary regulatory measures of the type discussed.

89 For an analysis of this type of reasoning in the context of disputes under the GATT, see Steve Charnovitz, "GATT and the Environment: Examining the Issues," 4 *International Environmental Affairs*, (1992), pp. 203–233, p. 211.

(b) DEVELOPING THE CONCEPT OF COMPLEMENTARY MEASURES

The decisions of the panel and Appellate Body in *Brazil – Retreaded Tyres* suggest that necessity may turn on how the concept of an alternative measure is defined. Prior to that dispute, the concept of an alternative measure was understood by reference to the idea that a measure was not an alternative if it would not achieve the chosen level of protection sought by the member implementing a measure.[90] Put another way, a measure is not an alternative if it will not achieve the regulatory goal of the member in question. Aside from this requirement, there had been no serious attempt in the case law to define what an alternative is prior to *Brazil – Retreaded Tyres*. Earlier case law suggested the existence of other limitations, such as a requirement that the alternative is reasonably available, but these limitations did not actually seek to define the concept of an alternative itself. Rather, this latter requirement pertains to the circumstances in which a member can be expected to use an alternative.

In *Brazil – Retreaded Tyres* the panel took the case law a step further. The EC argued that measures to encourage domestic retreading of tires (among others) constituted a reasonably available alternative to the import ban on retreaded tires. In response, the panel stated:

> We also observe that Brazil has already implemented or is in the process of implementing such domestic measures. [footnote omitted] Indeed, the positive impact of both measures – i.e. the ban on imported short-lifespan retreaded tyres and domestic measures on domestic used tyres – could be cumulative rather than substitutable. We thus do not agree with the European Communities that the institution of domestic measures to encourage timely domestic retreading and to improve the retreadiblity of domestic used tyres would achieve the same outcome as the import ban on retreaded tyres.[91]

On appeal, the EC argued that the panel defined the concept of alternatives in an overly narrow fashion. However, the Appellate Body upheld the panel's conclusions, stating:

> Among the possible alternatives, the European Communities referred to measures to encourage domestic retreading or improve the retreadability of used tyres, as well as a better enforcement of the import ban on used tyres and of existing collection and disposal schemes. In fact, like the Import Ban, these measures already figure as elements of a comprehensive strategy designed by Brazil to deal with waste tyres. [footnote omitted] Substituting one element of this comprehensive policy for another would weaken the

[90] Appellate Body Report, *EC – Asbestos*, para. 174.

[91] Panel Report, *Brazil – Retreaded Tyres*, para. 7.169.

> policy by reducing the synergies between its components, as well as its total effect. We are therefore of the view that the Panel did not err in rejecting as alternatives to the Import Ban components of Brazil's policy regarding waste tyres that are complementary to the Import Ban.[92]

In these passages, the panel and Appellate Body indicated that there are some limits to the concept of alternative measures. Equally, neither the panel nor the Appellate Body defined the distinction between alternative and complementary measures.

(i) *The Legal Difference between Complementary and Alternative Measures.* The notion that measures may be complementary rather than alternative recognizes that two or more measures may each be necessary in order to achieve a particular regulatory goal. That is, the nature of the regulatory goal means that one particular measure cannot achieve that goal alone. In this sense, the necessity of one measure is not undermined by the availability of another to advance the regulatory goal. To use the terms associated with Article XX, a complementary measure is not an alternative.

In viewing the issue in this manner, it becomes apparent that recognizing particular measures as complementary is a means of preserving the lawfulness of a measure in the context of a regulatory goal that is broad in its character. Whereas characterizing a regulatory goal in a narrow fashion would narrow the list of measures that might achieve that goal, recognizing particular measures as complementary would remove them from consideration as alternatives.

By the same token, the individual measure in violation of the GATT must still pass the hurdle of the weighing and balancing test. In *Colombia – Indicative Prices and Restrictions on Ports of Entry*, Colombia sought to defend measures in violation of the GATT simply on the basis that they formed part of a comprehensive approach to enforcement.[93] Although the panel examined this comprehensive approach as a whole, the approach failed the necessity test without the need to consider the availability of alternatives. The primary reason for this was the lack of a contribution by the regulatory approach adopted to the enforcement problems in question.

(ii) *How to Define Complementary Measures.* In attempting to define the concept of complementary measures it is useful to consider first those issues or facts that might be dismissed as not definitive.

92 Appellate Body Report, *Brazil – Retreaded Tyres*, para. 172.

93 See discussion in Panel Report, *Colombia – Indicative Prices and Restrictions on Ports of Entry*, para. 7.503.

The first such issue concerns whether a purported alternative is already in place. In *Brazil – Retreaded Tyres* the panel relied on the fact that purported alternatives had already been implemented or were in the process of implementation in drawing the conclusion that those measures were in fact complementary measures rather than alternatives.[94] Although the fact that other measures have already been implemented indicates that a measure may be part of a broader regulatory scheme, this factor should not be determinative of whether a measure is an alternative. On the contrary, it may be the case that other measures already in place obviate the need for the impugned measure.

Obviously, it is easier to establish that the member implementing the measure intends to use a range of measures where other measures are in place. On the other hand, where such measures are not in place, the member in question may have no such intention. In such circumstances, the concept of complementary measures may act as a shield for the maintenance of a measure. Thus, although the fact that measures are in place or under implementation is not definitive of whether measures are complementary, it ought to be required before measures are categorized as complementary.

The second issue concerns whether, as a matter of practice, states implement the measures in question in a cumulative manner. Although it might be said that the practice of states is probative, that practice will not always be indicative of the necessity of all of the measures in question. Rather, the maintenance of a complementary set of measures could be for historical, political, or other reasons that do not relate to the effects of the measures. As such, state practice is not necessarily indicative that measures are complementary for purposes of the necessity test.

Additionally, whether a measure should be considered in the broader context of a range of measures or in an isolated fashion is not indicative that they are complementary. In *Brazil – Retreaded Tyres* the Appellate Body, without explanation, stated that Brazil's import ban "must be viewed in the context of the comprehensive strategy designed and implemented by Brazil to deal with waste tyres."[95] Accordingly, it might be said that where a measure ought to be viewed in the context of other measures, they ought to be considered complementary. There are, however, two problems with this conclusion. First, whether measures should be viewed together turns on what facts ought to be considered in order to appraise a measure. Accordingly, it is conceivable that some measures must be viewed in the context of exceptions to them or in the context of other measures with contrary purposes in order to be

94 Panel Report, *Brazil – Retreaded Tyres*, para. 7.169.

95 Appellate Body Report, *Brazil – Retreaded Tyres*, para. 154.

understood. In this sense, whether one measure should be viewed in the context of another has different conceptual foundations that weigh against this approach. Secondly, the question of when measures should be considered in a broader context is often difficult to resolve in the absence of specific rules. As a result, such an approach would increase the power and discretion of a panel, an outcome that the process of defining complementary measures should seek to avoid.[96] Thus, this issue should be separated from the question of whether measures are complementary.

This process of elimination suggests that in order for measures to be complementary, it is necessary that they either be in place or under implementation (this being a necessary but not sufficient requirement) and possess two other features. First, the measures in question must have different effects on the regulatory goal in order to be complementary. Put another way, two measures that have the same effect in terms of the achievement of a regulatory goal must be alternatives to one another. Second, one measure must "complement" the other in order for the two to be described as complementary. This means that the two measures must each work toward the same regulatory goal. Thus, when combined, these elements provide that complementary measures will exist where the measures in question work toward the same regulatory goal and have different effects on the achievement of that goal.

Of course, this approach means that particular measures cannot be identified categorically as complementary measures. Rather, whether measures have different effects on a goal will still turn partly on the characterization of a regulatory goal. For example, it is conceivable that an advertising ban and a tax measure could be alternatives to one another if a member's regulatory goal was to reduce tobacco consumption by a particular quantity and if each measure would have this effect independently of the other. Whether the tax measure would be reasonably available is another question. In this respect, issues such as enforceability and equity might arise depending on the size of the tax increase required.

Although this conclusion is also true in respect of measures to reduce the harm caused by waste tires and other complementary regulatory schemes, the impact of identifying complementary measures in this manner should not be overstated. On the contrary, this approach is not new or a departure from the current approach. Rather, this approach clarifies the conceptual

96 See Jeffrey Waincymer, "Reformulated Gasoline under Reformulated WTO Dispute Settlement Procedures: Pulling Pandora out of the Chapeau?" 18(1) *Michigan Journal of International Law*, (1996), pp. 141–181, pp. 158–164.

underpinnings of the treatment of complementary measures in the context of the necessity test.

(c) USING EXTRANEOUS TREATIES SUCH AS THE FCTC IN INTERPRETATION OF ARTICLE XX

The panel in *Brazil – Retreaded Tyres* twice referred to the Basel Convention Technical Guidelines on the Identification and Management of Used Tyres.[97] Those guidelines supplement the Basel Convention on the Control of Transboundary Movements of Hazardous Wastes and Their Disposal[98] and were used by the panel as evidence of facts relating to the storage and stockpiling of waste tires.[99] This raises the broader question of to what extent instruments such as the FCTC and the global strategies might be used in interpretation or application of the necessity test.

In the context of a case study on tobacco advertising bans, in Article 7 of the FCTC the parties recognize "that comprehensive non-price measures are an effective and important means of reducing tobacco consumption." Accordingly, the FCTC obliges parties to implement a range of different types of tobacco-control policies including tax measures, advertising bans, health warnings, and measures to combat illicit trade. In this context, it is fairly clear that FCTC parties view each of these measures as necessary to control tobacco and not as alternatives to one another.

However, the difficulty with using the FCTC in this manner lies in the fact that whether measures are complementary or alternative depends on the specific regulatory goal in question. This fact means that the relationship between particular measures cannot be defined in the abstract, such as by reference to the FCTC.

D. Conclusions on the necessity test, tobacco, alcohol, and diet

The decision in *Brazil – Retreaded Tyres* is likely to be an important point in the trajectory of the necessity test, particularly for measures to address tobacco, alcohol, and diet. In addition to the fact that these three areas all employ regulatory schemes composed of complementary measures, there is often a long chain of causation involved. At one end of the spectrum, high-fat food is a risk factor for obesity, which in turn is a risk factor for the development of various health problems. A measure that seeks to discourage the consumption of high-fat food

97 Available at http://www.basel.int/meetings/sbc/workdoc/old%20docs/tech-usedtyres.pdf (visited 16/01/08).

98 Basel Convention on the Control of Transboundary Movements of Hazardous Wastes and Their Disposal, 1673 UNTS 126; 28 ILM 657 (1989).

99 Panel Report, *Brazil – Retreaded Tyres*, paras 7.81 and 7.187.

is quite remote in terms of the chain of causation from the onset of disease. It is possible that consumption of high-fat food might be a part of a diet that is healthy overall or that physical activity may prevent obesity. The relationship between consumption of alcohol and harm to health is closer, but a great deal continues to turn on the way in which alcoholic beverages are consumed. At the other end of the spectrum, there is a much closer causative link between tobacco consumption and harm to health than there is for food and alcoholic beverages.

The length of the chain of causation, particularly in the context of diet, leaves some to argue that government intervention is unwarranted. For example, some argue that food advertising does not cause obesity in children. Of course, this argument is simplistic and is not a serious analysis of the causes of childhood obesity. It is quite obvious that the intake of advertising alone will not make a child obese. The questions for consideration concern the extent to which advertising shapes unhealthy dietary patterns among children and the relationship of such patterns to obesity. Nonetheless, a member might target its measures at various points in the chain of causation in order to minimize the possibility of an adverse health outcome.

This was also the case in *Brazil – Retreaded Tyres*, in the sense that there are any number of different interventions that can be made to address the potential health implications of waste tires. In this sense, the dispute suggests that the availability of other measures directed at the same overall objective does not necessarily undermine the necessity of a particular measure. Equally, the import ban in that dispute was not ultimately upheld as lawful under Article XX. The panel found that the requirements of the *chapeau* had not been met, and this final element of the Article XX(b) is now considered.

2.2. *The Requirements of the* Chapeau

If a party relying on Article XX establishes the necessity of the measure, a panel will consider the requirements of the *chapeau*. The *chapeau* denies access to the Article XX exception where a measure is "applied in a manner which would constitute a means of arbitrary or unjustifiable discrimination between countries where the same conditions prevail, or a disguised restriction on international trade." These requirements are designed to prevent abuse of the exception and relate to the manner in which a measure is applied, rather than to the measure itself.[100] At the most basic level, the *chapeau* is an expression of the principle of good faith.[101] Beyond this, application of the *chapeau*

[100] Appellate Body Report, *US – Gasoline*, p. 22.

[101] Appellate Body Report, *United States – Import Prohibition of Certain Shrimp and Shrimp Products*, WT/DS58/AB/R, adopted 6 November 1998, DSR 1998:VII, 2755, paras 158–159.

is animated by the idea that "a balance must be struck between the right of a member to invoke an exception under Article XX and the duty of that same member to respect the treaty rights of other members."[102] As was suggested in Chapter 1, it is this aspect of the balancing mechanism found in Article XX that is focused on identifying measures applied for protectionist purposes.

Because the *chapeau* reflects the final step in application of Article XX(b), interpretation of the *chapeau* may have a significant impact on the permissiveness of the provision as a whole. For example, in *Brazil – Retreaded Tyres* a fairly permissive view of the necessity test was taken, but the measure was ultimately held to be unlawful under the *chapeau*. In reaching its conclusion, the Appellate Body focused on two aspects of the application of the measure. First, the Appellate Body concluded that an exemption from the import ban for the Southern Common Market (MERCOSUR) countries constituted arbitrary and unjustifiable discrimination. Second, the Appellate Body concluded that court injunctions permitting the importation of used tires meant that the ban on the importation of retreaded tires constituted arbitrary and unjustifiable discrimination. In each instance, the Appellate Body also reversed findings made by the panel to the effect that the import ban was not applied as a disguised restriction on trade.

For present purposes, the most significant aspect of the analysis lies in the MERCOSUR exemption and the analyzing of injunctions not as a part of the measure itself, but as relevant to the application of the measure. Had these issues been considered to constitute part of the measure, they would have been examined under the necessity test and the import ban may have been rejected as being unnecessary without even the need to consider alternative measures. The approach taken by the panel is entirely consistent with the wording of Article XX given that the *chapeau* expressly concerns application of a measure. In addition, the broader structure of the GATT dictates this approach. For example, in *Brazil – Retreaded Tyres* the import ban was found to violate Article XI, and it was this quantitative restriction that Brazil then sought to defend under Article XX(b). The MERCOSUR exemption and the injunctions were not found to be prohibited by a provision of the GATT, and therefore it was arguably inappropriate to consider them as a part of the measure in question. If on the other hand, the measure had been found to violate Article I (MFN treatment) of the GATT by virtue of the MERCOSUR exemption, then this would have been a part of the measure to be analyzed under the necessity test and the *chapeau* would not have come into consideration.[103]

[102] Ibid., para. 156.

[103] Arwel Davies, "Interpreting the Chapeau of GATT Article XX in Light of the 'New' Approach in Brazil – Tyres," 43(3) *Journal of World Trade*, (2009), pp. 507–539, pp. 531–534.

It is clear then, that the *chapeau* can play an important role in determining the permissiveness of Article XX(b). The extent of this role will depend on the circumstances. For example, where a national-treatment violation relates to application of a measure, there may be significant overlap in the analysis under the necessity test and the *chapeau*[104] despite the fact that the *chapeau* relates to a higher standard of discrimination than that applied in a national-treatment provision.[105] This can be contrasted with a quantitative restriction, such as an import ban on retreaded tires, where exemptions substantially undermine the measure as a whole and there is a clear distinction between the measure and its application.

The potential for overlap between necessity analysis and the *chapeau* can be attributed to similarities in the tests applied. In *Brazil – Retreaded Tyres* the Appellate Body stated that "analysis of whether application of a measure results in arbitrary or unjustifiable discrimination should focus on the cause of the discrimination, or the rationale put forward to explain its existence."[106] The Appellate Body then went on to state that an abuse of Article XX, contrary to the *chapeau*, occurs where the reasons given for discrimination "bear no rational connection to the objective falling within the purview of a paragraph of Article XX, or would go against that objective."[107] Thus, a panel will look at the way in which a measure is applied and at the connection between application and the regulatory objective underlying the measure.

What then, can be said about application of the *chapeau* in the contexts of tobacco, alcohol, and diet? Because the *chapeau* concerns the manner in which a measure is applied, application of the *chapeau* is itself heavily dependent on the circumstances surrounding an individual measure and its implementation. In this context, it is difficult to say a great deal about the *chapeau* that will be of universal relevance. Case studies in which application of a measure may violate the *chapeau* can be identified. For example, if an advertising ban was unevenly enforced, discrimination of the kind contemplated in the *chapeau* might occur. However, this example does not suggest anything of systemic relevance to tobacco, alcohol, and diet. Rather, it could be viewed as one of a virtually limitless number of different ways in which a measure, poorly applied, might not survive analysis under the *chapeau*.

In this context, there are two brief comments worth making. First, international instruments relating to tobacco, alcohol, and diet might be relevant

[104] Ibid., pp. 522–528.
[105] See Appellate Body, *US – Gasoline*, p. 23.
[106] Appellate Body Report, *Brazil – Retreaded Tyres*, para. 226.
[107] Ibid., para. 227.

to the analysis. For example, the FCTC may serve as evidence of the good faith (of a WTO Member in implementing an FCTC measure) and thereby strengthen the chances of that measure being upheld. Equally, the limited value of this evidence is obvious in light of the outcome in *Brazil – Retreaded Tyres*.[108]

Second, the general uncertainty that pervades application of the necessity test is also present in analysis under the *chapeau*. This uncertainty stems partly from the fact that the regulatory objective of a member is central to the analysis, and partly from the vagueness of the standards laid out in the *chapeau*.

3. CONCLUSION

In the introduction to this chapter a number of concerns were expressed about application of Article XX(b) of the GATT and Article XIV(b) of the GATS. One of these concerns was the general uncertainty surrounding application of the provisions and the potential for this uncertainty to foment regulatory-chill. The analysis suggests that concerns about uncertainty have some justification. At the most basic level, a look at the Appellate Body's weighing and balancing test shows that there is significant confusion about how exactly it is to be applied. For example, the role that the importance of a regulatory goal plays has not been clarified by the case law, and panels appear understandably lost in the process of ascribing importance to particular goals. The uncertainty associated with the necessity test and the need for greater attention to be paid to defining the regulatory goals of WTO Members were also highlighted by the panel report in *Brazil – Retreaded Tyres*. This problem is far from being unique to this dispute. The characterization of regulatory goals (an admittedly difficult task) has received little attention in disputes to date despite the fact that this process forms a crucial backdrop to the necessity test.

Another concern expressed about provisions such as Article XX(b) of the GATT was that the strict scrutiny required by the necessity test may not be appropriate in the context of measures to address distal causes of disease. To some extent, this concern was alleviated by the decision in *Brazil – Retreaded Tyres*, in which a ban on importation of retreaded tires was upheld as necessary despite its apparent causative distance from the protection of human health. Equally, it remains to be seen how the case law will develop.

Similarly, concern was expressed about identification of reasonably available alternative measures and what impact this might have on regulatory approaches that rely on use of complementary measures. To some extent this

[108] A similar approach was adopted by the panel in *Brazil – Retreaded Tyres*, para. 7.272.

concern was alleviated by the panel and Appellate Body decisions in *Brazil – Retreaded Tyres*, in which a distinction between complementary and alternative measures was recognized. By the same token, this distinction was not defined, and it remains to be seen how the case law will elaborate the distinction.

Although *Brazil – Retreaded Tyres* is not beyond criticism, it is a far-reaching step forward in terms of the development of the necessity test. Although the approach set out in that dispute has been criticized as being too deferential, this criticism is misplaced. In essence, the necessity element of Article XX(b) relates to the regulatory legitimacy of a measure rather than to the narrower question of whether the measure is in place for some disguised protectionist purpose, which is addressed under the *chapeau*. Given that the GATT is not a mechanism for the positive regulatory integration of the WTO membership, this type of deference is appropriate.

5

Product Regulation and Labeling Measures under the SPS and TBT Agreements

Some form of product regulation is likely to play an important role in any comprehensive policy to address noncommunicable disease associated with tobacco, alcohol, or diet. The concept of product regulation encompasses a variety of measures. In some cases, product regulation may function as a means of prohibition, such as where a good is deemed by government to be too harmful to be sold lawfully. In a similar vein, product regulation may be a means of reducing the harmfulness associated with consumption of a product category, such as where the product is prohibited in its more harmful forms. Alternatively, product regulation might prohibit products from taking particular forms not because of a direct relationship between form and harmfulness, but because of the attractiveness of specific product forms to identifiable consumer groups such as children. In addition, the regulation of product packaging may play an important role in providing information to consumers or in attempts to dissuade consumption.

Examples of product regulation of the first two types can be found in the context of diet. Some Pacific Island states have banned the sale of mutton flaps and turkey tails, which are cuts of meat that are extremely high in fat and often discarded in developed countries.[1] Similarly, a number of WTO Members are working to eliminate artificial trans fat from their food supply and to replace it with cis-unsaturated acids.[2] One option is to prohibit the presence of artificial trans fat in foods altogether, and another is to prohibit it above certain levels. Efforts to address trans fats have followed the growth

[1] See generally Deborah Gewertz and Frederick Errington, *Cheap Meat: Flap Food Nations and the Pacific Islands*, London, University of California Press, (2010).

[2] See M R L'Abbé, S Stender, C M Skeaff et al., "Approaches to Removing Trans Fats from the Food Supply in Industrialised and Developing Countries," 63 *European Journal of Clinical Nutrition*, (2009), pp. 550–567.

of an evidence base that suggests that trans-fatty acids increase the risk of coronary heart disease.[3]

In the alcohol context, similar regulatory measures are also used. Measures prohibiting the presence of toxins such as methanol are quite common and have proven to be uncontroversial in terms of trade law. This can be contrasted with the tobacco context, in which restrictions on constituents or emissions that are intended to reduce (rather than eliminate) the harmfulness of tobacco products is not well advanced for scientific reasons. The first session of the Conference of the Parties to the FCTC established a working group to develop guidelines to supplement Article 9, which governs regulation of the contents of tobacco products.[4] The working group reported back to the second session of the Conference of the Parties in 2007 that the development and validation of guidelines for measuring and testing cigarette contents and emissions is a number of years away.[5] The working group also reported back to the third session of the Conference of the Parties in November 2008, and indicated that the first step to be taken in elaborating guidelines on product regulation would be to validate a number of methods for measuring and testing the contents and emissions of cigarettes. This process is estimated to take five and a half years.[6]

The need to validate testing methods stems from the fact that existing International Organization for Standardization (ISO) testing standards have been criticized as flawed, particularly for the failure of smoking machines to replicate human behavior. One consequence of this is that smoking machines indicate that some cigarettes have lower quantities of tar and nicotine when, in fact, smokers ordinarily compensate by taking larger puffs, inhaling deeper, and smoking more of such cigarettes in order to receive similar levels of nicotine as emitted from other cigarettes. Smoking machines used in ISO testing

3 For this evidence base, see R Uauy, A Aro, R Clarke et al., "WHO Scientific Update on Trans Fatty Acids: Summary and Conclusions," 63 *European Journal of Clinical Nutrition*, (2009), pp. 568–575.

4 Third Report of Committee A, Conference of the Parties to the WHO Framework Convention on Tobacco Control, First Session, (Draft) A/FCTC/COP1/11, 17 February 2006, available at http://www.who.int/gb/fctc/PDF/cop1/FCTC_COP1_11-en.pdf, (visited 13/12/07).

5 Elaboration of Guidelines for Implementation of the Convention, Conference of the Parties to the Framework Convention on Tobacco Control, Second Session, Provisional Agenda Item 5.3.2, A/FCTC/COP/2/8, 26 April 2007, available at http://www.who.int/gb/fctc/PDF/cop2/FCTC_COP2_8-en.pdf, (visited 13/12/07), p. 2.

6 Elaboration of guidelines for implementation of Articles 9 and 10 of the WHO Framework Convention on Tobacco Control: Progress report of the working group, Conference of the Parties to the WHO Framework Convention on Tobacco Control, Third Session, Durban, South Africa, 17–22 November 2008, FCTC/COP/3/6, 21 August 2008, para. 14.

have also been misled by small holes in cigarette filters that are ordinarily covered by a smoker's fingers or lips at the time of inhalation.[7]

Although there is relatively little regulation of the contents of tobacco products for reasons relating to harmfulness, there are examples of regulation to make tobacco products less attractive. As mentioned in Chapter 1, the United States recently introduced a ban on flavored cigarettes (excluding menthol) with the aim of reducing the attractiveness of cigarettes to children.[8] Canada has also introduced a ban on flavorings that includes additives designed to make burley taste better.[9] Similarly, public health advocates have argued that "alcopops" should be banned. Alcopops include premixed alcoholic beverages that are attractive to underage drinkers, partly because of their flavor (one that generally lacks the taste of alcohol) and often because of their color. At the time of writing, a number of WTO Members are also considering bans on high-caffeine content in alcoholic beverages as a means of curbing alcohol-related violence.[10]

In the tobacco context, there are also at least three types of labeling measures that have a direct connection to the protection of human health.[11] Health warning labels are the most prominent of the three types of measures. Many states maintain measures requiring the attachment of health warnings to tobacco products.[12] The form of health warnings varies from simple textual warnings to graphic images, or a combination of both. As a general rule, health warnings make (negative) information about tobacco products available to consumers[13] and have a dissuasive impact on the purchase of tobacco products, thereby lowering the prevalence of tobacco consumption or individual consumption levels.[14]

7 See generally Lynne Kozlowski and Richard O'Connor, "Cigarette Filter Ventilation is a Defective Design because of Misleading Taste, Bigger Puffs, and Blocked Vents," 11(Suppl I), *Tobacco Control*, (2002), i40–i50.

8 Family Smoking Prevention and Tobacco Control Act, HR 1256, section 907.

9 Cracking Down on Tobacco Marketing Aimed at Youth Act, Bill C 32.

10 "Labour: Ban High-Caffeine Alcohol," *The Sunday Times*, February 7, 2010.

11 In the tobacco context, questions about labeling measures for tax enforcement purposes have also arisen. See Benn McGrady, "Illicit Trade: Tracking and Tracing of Tobacco Products and the World Trade Organization," *Asian Journal of WTO and International Health Law and Policy*, (March 2009), pp. 129–159.

12 See Omar Shafey, Suzanne Dolwick, and G. Emmanuel Guindon (eds), *Tobacco Control Country Profiles*, 2nd ed, American Cancer Society, Atlanta, GA, USA, (2003).

13 See generally Donald Kenkel and Likwang Chen, "Consumer Information and Tobacco Use," in Prabhat Jha and Frank Chaloupka (eds), *Tobacco Control in Developing Countries*, World Bank and World Health Organization, Oxford University Press, (2000), pp. 177–214 [hereinafter Kenkel and Chen, "Consumer Information"].

14 Ibid., pp. 207–209.

Many states also have specific laws banning the use of misleading descriptors when used in association with tobacco products. These laws are intended to address the use of descriptors such as "light" and "mild" in association with specific tobacco products. Such descriptors represent that the products with which they are associated are healthier than other tobacco products; however, the manner in which such cigarettes are ordinarily smoked means that there is little reason to expect that smokers of "light" or "mild" type cigarettes will have a lower risk of disease.[15]

A third type of labeling measure used in the tobacco context requires the disclosure of product constituents on packaging. Requirements of this type often relate only to tar and nicotine levels and are controversial because the reporting of this information can create a misleading perception that tobacco products with lower levels of tar and nicotine are less harmful to human health than products with higher levels.[16]

A range of similar measures are used in the context of food, where labeling requirements for packaged foods are typically used to provide information to consumers, to assist consumers in making healthy choices, and to encourage manufacturers to sell relatively healthy foods.[17] It is becoming increasingly common for states to require the disclosure of nutrition information on packaging, such as the amount of fat (including saturated fat), cholesterol, sodium, carbohydrate (including fiber and sugars), and protein. A number of states also require quantitative ingredient labeling, whereby packaged foods must include a list of ingredients.

The types of measures imposed in the tobacco and food contexts can be contrasted with those used in the context of alcoholic beverages. In the latter context, mandatory labeling relevant to health is rarely as onerous as in the tobacco and food contexts. Some WTO Members require the attachment of

[15] See Michael Guerin, "Sensitivity of the Federal Trade Commission Test Method to Analytical Parameters," in "The FTC Cigarette Test Method for Determining Tar, Nicotine and Carbon Monoxide Yields of US Cigarettes," report of the NIC expert committee, Bethesda, Maryland: National Institutes of Health (NIH publication No. 96–4028) (1996), pp. 135–150; Nadine-Rae Leavell, "The Low Tar Lie," 8 *Tobacco Control*, (1999), pp. 433–439; National Institutes of Health, National Cancer Institute, Smoking and Tobacco Control: Risks Associated with Smoking Cigarettes with Low Machine-Measured Yields of Tar and Nicotine, (2001), p. 60; Lynne Kozlowski, Marvin Goldberg, Christine Sweeney et al., "Smoker Reactions to a Radio Message that Light Cigarettes are as Dangerous as Regular Cigarettes," 1 *Nicotine and Tobacco Control*, (1999), pp. 67–76; Saul Shiffman, Janine Pillitteri, Steven Burton et al., "Smokers' Beliefs About 'Light' and 'Ultra-Light' Cigarettes," 10 (Suppl 1) *Tobacco Control*, (2001), pp. i24–i32 at i17.

[16] Ibid.

[17] See generally Corinna Hawkes, *Nutrition Labels and Health Claims: The Global Regulatory Environment*, Geneva, World Health Organization, (2004), p. v.

one or more warning labels to alcoholic beverages,[18] and it is common for states to require a declaration of alcohol by volume and/or a statement setting out the number of standard units of alcohol in a beverage.[19] Although neither warning labels nor consumer-information measures are the norm, this may change over time, particularly given adoption of the Global Strategy Alcohol.

It also appears that alcohol labeling may be more controversial than tobacco labeling. As was mentioned in Chapter 1, a number of WTO Members recently expressed concern at a meeting of the TBT Committee about alcohol-labeling measures notified by Thailand. One argument is not particularly credible: that public information campaigns are less-restrictive means of achieving the regulatory goal. This argument ignores the concept of complementary measures discussed in Chapter 4 and ignores the fact that information campaigns may not reach consumers in the way that labeling will. On the other hand, the second concern – that labels should not suggest that all forms of alcohol consumption is harmful – may be more likely to raise questions in the context of necessity analysis.

In addition to falling within the scope of the GATT, these types of measures are governed by more specific rules in the SPS and TBT Agreements. This chapter addresses the extent to which these specific rules affect domestic regulatory autonomy to implement the aforementioned types of measures. The chapter is divided into four parts. Part 1 examines the scope of the SPS Agreement in order to determine which of the these measures is governed by the agreement.

Part 2 examines application of the SPS Agreement to measures such as bans on mutton flaps and turkey tails in order to illustrate how the agreement applies in the absence of relevant international standards, guidelines, or recommendations. The analysis also considers how the SPS Agreement might apply in the context of questions that relate to the nutritional qualities of foods.

Part 3 addresses application of the SPS Agreement in the context of food-labeling measures. Because relevant international recommendations and guidelines exist in this context, part 3 highlights the potential implications of the value afforded to harmonization in Article 3 of the SPS Agreement. This may be significant in a context in which regulatory diversity is important

[18] For example, in the United States, the Alcoholic Beverage Labeling Act of 1988, 27 USC 201–211 requires the attachment of a government warning.

[19] See, for example, the Australia New Zealand Food Standards Code, Standard 2.7.1, Labeling of Alcoholic Beverages and Food Containing Alcohol.

due to factors such as the differing nutritional profiles of different WTO Members.

Finally, part 4 examines application of the TBT Agreement to tobacco-labeling measures and measures banning alcopops and flavorings in tobacco products. Recent U.S. and Canadian measures banning certain flavorings in tobacco products have been the subject of discussion in the TBT Committee,[20] giving rise to concerns about application of the TBT Agreement to these types of measures. These concerns also arise in light of the fact that packaging and labeling measures have been the subject of a significant body of academic commentary in the contexts of biotechnology and measures designed to protect the environment.[21]

1. WHICH TYPES OF MEASURES IS THE SPS AGREEMENT APPLICABLE TO?

The popular perception of the SPS Agreement is that it applies to food-safety measures and measures intended to prevent the spread of pests or diseases. Certainly, at the time of its negotiation it was not contemplated widely that the agreement might be used in the context of measures governing the nutritional qualities of foods or the regulation of tobacco products. Nonetheless, the scope of the agreement suggests that it may apply at least to the former category of measures. Article 1, paragraph 1 of the SPS Agreement provides that it applies "to all sanitary and phytosanitary measures which may, directly or

[20] Minutes of the Meeting of 5–6 November 2009, Committee on Technical Barriers to Trade, World Trade Organization, 22 December 2009, G/TBT/M/49, paras 6–18.

[21] See for example, Elliot Staffin, "Trade Barrier or Trade Boon? A Critical Evaluation of Environmental Labeling and its Role in the 'Greening' of World Trade," 21 *Columbia Journal of Environmental Law*, (1996), pp. 205–286; Atsuko Okubu, "Environmental Labeling Programs and the GATT/WTO Regime," 11 *Georgetown International Environmental Law Review*, (1998–1999), pp. 599–646; Surya Subedi, "Balancing International Trade with Environmental Protection: International Aspects of Eco-Labels," 25 *Brooklyn Journal of International Law*, (1999), pp. 373–405; C. Ford Runge and Lee Ann Jackson, "Labeling, Trade and Genetically Modified Organisms," 34(1) *Journal of World Trade*, (2000), pp. 111–222; Teresa Hock, "The Role of Eco-Labels in International Trade: Can Timber Certification be Implemented as a Means of Slowing Deforestation," 12 *Colorado Journal of International Environmental Law and Policy*, (2002), pp. 347–365; Carlos Lopez-Hurtado, "Social Labeling and WTO Law," 5 *Journal of International Economic Law*, (September 2002), pp. 719–746; Manoj Joshi, "Are Eco-Labels Consistent with World Trade Organization Agreements," 38(1) *Journal of World Trade*, (2004), pp. 69–92; John Emslie, "Labeling Programs as a Reasonably Available Least Restrictive Trade Measure Under Article XX's Nexus Requirement," 30 *Brooklyn Journal of International Law*, (2005), pp. 485–545.

indirectly, affect international trade." The phrase "sanitary and phytosanitary measures" is defined in Annex A, which states:

> 1. Sanitary or phytosanitary measure – Any measure applied:
>   (a) to protect animal or plant life or health within the territory of the Member from risks arising from the entry, establishment or spread of pests, diseases, disease-carrying organisms or disease-causing organisms;
>   (b) to protect human or animal life or health within the territory of the Member from risks arising from additives, contaminants, toxins or disease-causing organisms in foods, beverages or feedstuffs;
>   (c) to protect human life or health within the territory of the Member from risks arising from diseases carried by animals, plants or products thereof, or from the entry, establishment or spread of pests; or
>   (d) to prevent or limit other damage within the territory of the Member from the entry, establishment or spread of pests.
>
> Sanitary or phytosanitary measures include all relevant laws, decrees, regulations, requirements, and procedures including, inter alia, end-product criteria; processes and production methods; testing, inspection, certification, and approval procedures; quarantine treatments including relevant requirements associated with the transport of animals or plants, or with the materials necessary for their survival during transport; provisions on relevant statistical methods, sampling procedures, and methods of risk assessment; and packaging and labelling requirements directly related to food safety.

The application of the SPS Agreement differs depending on whether the context of tobacco, alcohol, or diet is at issue.

1.1. *Tobacco-Control Measures*

Indonesia, in its Request for Consultations with the United States concerning U.S. bans on flavored cigarettes, asserted that the ban is a violation of various provisions of the SPS Agreement.[22] However, the measure in question and the other tobacco-control measures addressed in this study do not constitute "sanitary or phytosanitary" measures. Therefore, the SPS Agreement does not apply to them. It is clear that none of paragraphs (a), (c), or (d) applies to tobacco-control measures. Paragraph (a) relates to measures applied to protect "animal or plant life or health" and is not applicable to tobacco-control measures

[22] United States – Measures Affecting the Production and Sale of Clove Cigarettes, Request for Consultations by Indonesia, World Trade Organization, WT/DS406/1, G/L/917, G/SPS/GEN/1015, G/TBT/D/38, 14 April 2010, p. 2.

that are applied to protect human health. Paragraph (c) concerns diseases that are "carried" by animals, plants, or products thereof and is not applicable to tobacco-control measures, which seek to prevent disease caused by tobacco products rather than carried by them. Similarly, paragraph (d) concerns entry, establishment, or spread of pests, another issue not relevant to tobacco control. Accordingly, paragraph (b) is the only paragraph that could conceivably encompass tobacco-control measures. That provision addresses goods that cause disease (including to humans) through their use and would apply to tobacco-control measures if tobacco is a "food, beverage or feedstuff."

Article 3.2 of the DSU provides that the WTO-covered agreements should be interpreted in accordance with "the customary rules of interpretation of public international law." Such rules are set out in the Vienna Convention on the Law of Treaties (Vienna Convention),[23] Article 31(1) of which provides that a treaty's terms should be interpreted in accordance with their ordinary meaning, in context and in light of their object and purpose. The panel on measures affecting the approval and marketing of biotech products(hereafter *EC – Biotech Products*) addressed the definition of the term "food" and stated:

> [T]he common definition of a "food" is a substance taken into the body to maintain life and growth.[24] Thus, we consider that a substance which a human being or an animal consumes for nutritional reasons may be classified as a "food."[25]

In accordance with this approach, the ordinary meaning of the term would not encompass cigarettes.

Although the dictionary definition used by the panel is valuable, there are a range of tobacco products that are taken orally. Chewing tobacco is placed in the mouth and chewed, and other forms of tobacco such as snuff can be placed between a consumer's lip and gum. Although these forms of tobacco are conceptually closer to the category of food than cigarettes or tobacco taken nasally, they still fall outside the ordinary definition of the term. These products are not edible in that they are not intended to be swallowed and do not provide genuine nourishment to the body.

The ordinary meaning of the term food also accords with how WTO Members have implemented their notification obligations under the SPS and

[23] Vienna Convention on the Law of Treaties, May 23, 1969, 1155 U.N.T.S. 331; 8 I.L.M. 679 (1969).

[24] L. Brown (ed.), *The Shorter Oxford English Dictionary*, Oxford University Press, (2002), Vol. 1, p. 1001.

[25] Panel Report, *EC – Measures Affecting the Approval and Marketing of Biotech Products*, (February 7, 2006), WT/DS291–293, [hereinafter EC – Biotech Products], para. 7.291.

TBT Agreements. The vast majority of notifications with respect to tobacco-control measures have been made under the TBT Agreement. Those notifications made under the SPS Agreement generally relate to the spread of pests or to traces of pesticides on tobacco products.[26] In addition, the Codex Alimentarius Code of Ethics for International Trade in Food, a standard that might be used in application of the SPS Agreement, excludes tobacco and other substances used only as drugs from its definition of the term food.[27] In summary, the SPS Agreement does not apply to the tobacco-control measures considered in this study as they do not constitute SPS measures.

1.2. *Alcohol*

Measures to regulate the constituents of alcoholic beverages would appear to fall within the scope of paragraph (b). For example, bans on the presence of methanol or other toxins would fall within the scope of paragraph (b). Equally, these types of measures are well established and have not proven over time to be controversial. Consequently, this type of measure will not be addressed in further detail in discussion of the substance of the SPS Agreement.

Like tobacco-control measures, product bans on alcopops would not fall within the scope of the SPS Agreement. Although the aim of such a measure may be to protect health, the measure would not be concerned with additives, contaminants, toxins, or disease-causing organisms. Accordingly, the measure would fall beyond the scope of the SPS Agreement and is discussed later in the context of the TBT Agreement.

1.3. *Diet*

The two types of product-regulation measures identified earlier were restrictions or prohibitions on the inclusion of trans fat in processed foods and the outright prohibition of certain foods such as mutton flaps and turkey tails. Although measures focused on the nutritional qualities of foods were not contemplated at the time the SPS Agreement was concluded, some have argued that this type of measure does not differ in a significant way from a food-safety measure. For example, Philip James and others have suggested:

> [I]t could be argued that saturated fats, sugars or salt have many features analogous to classic toxicants, in that repeated exposure of the population to

[26] See, for example, Notification, Committee on Sanitary and Phytosanitary Measures, World Trade Organization, Argentina, G/SPS/N/ARG/14, 23 February 1998.

[27] Code of Ethics for International Trade in Food, CAC/RCP 20–1979 (Rev. 1–1985), para. 3.1.

appreciable amounts of these foods would induce the population risk factors to rise (e.g. raised blood cholesterol, weight gain and increases in hypertension). In that sense, saturated fats are just as damaging, if not more harmful on a population basis, as the steady consumption of modest amounts of heavy metal.[28]

This suggests that there is nothing inherently distinct about measures addressing the nutritional qualities of foods that would be particularly influential in examining the scope of the SPS Agreement. This can be illustrated through examples relating to added trans-fatty acids in processed foods and product restrictions relating to total fat content in unprocessed foods such as meat.

In each case, the applicability of the SPS Agreement will depend on whether the measure is a measure to protect human life or health from risks arising from additives, contaminants, toxins, or disease-causing organisms in food.

It is arguable that trans-fatty acids constitute an additive. The panel in *EC – Biotech Products* considered the definition of the term additive. In doing so, the panel cited a number of definitions, including a dictionary definition to the effect that an additive is "a substance added to another so as to give it specific qualities." The panel also cited a Codex definition, which states:

> Food additive means any substance not normally consumed as a food by itself and not normally used as a typical ingredient of the food, whether or not it has nutritive value, the intentional addition of which to food for a technological (including organoleptic) purpose in the manufacture, processing, preparation, treatment, packing, packaging, transport or holding of such food results, or may be reasonably expected to result, (directly or indirectly) in it or its by-products becoming a component of or otherwise affecting the characteristics of such foods. The term does not include "contaminants" or substances added to food for maintaining or improving nutritional qualities.[29]

Although neither of these definitions is dispositive of the meaning of the term in the SPS context,[30] they suggest that artificial trans fat would fall within the definition of an additive under Annex A(1) of the SPS Agreement. More particularly, artificial trans fat is often used in cooking, either as a component of a hydrogenated oil used in frying or as a form of shortening used in baked goods. Trans fat can increase the shelf life of goods, and the use of hydrogenated oils affects the solidity of products. For example, the presence of

[28] Philip James, Nipa Rojoongwaskinkul, Tashmai Rikshasuta et al., "Food Imports and Dietary Change: A Perspective from Thailand," in Hawkes et al., *Trade, Food, Diet and Health: Perspectives and Policy Options*, Wiley Blackwell, (2010), pp. 169–191, p. 184.

[29] Panel Report, *EC – Biotech Products*, para. 7.292.

[30] Ibid., para. 7.300.

hydrogenated oils in margarine affects the ability of the consumer to spread the product immediately after refrigeration.

Because a measure restricting or prohibiting artificial trans fat in foods would (in the present example) be a measure having the purpose of protecting human health, it is likely that the measure would constitute an SPS measure.

In the case of a ban on the import and sale of mutton flaps or turkey tails, the question is whether naturally occurring fat content constitutes a disease-causing organism. At first glance, it appears that this is unlikely to be the case. Although an animal may be an organism when it is alive, a cut of meat would not appear to fall within this definition. Similarly, given that the meat is from an organic source, the high-fat content of the meat could not be construed as an additive. An ordinary reading of the terms "contaminant" and "toxin" would also not appear to encompass the issue.

On the other hand, this conclusion might have merit as a black-letter interpretation of paragraph (b) but could lead to absurdity. The idea that measures governing the importation of an animal could address a disease-causing organism but measures addressing cuts of meat from that animal would not appears to undermine the agreement. The idea that such a ban falls outside the scope of the SPS Agreement also cannot be reconciled with the conclusion that measures addressing the quantity of certain additives such as fat would fall within the scope of the agreement. Finding a ban on mutton flaps to be beyond the scope of the agreement would mean that product regulation in the context of processed foods could fall within the scope of the SPS Agreement, whereas regulation of cuts of meat would not.

This analysis highlights the fact that the SPS Agreement was not concluded with questions concerning the nutritional value of foods in mind. It is difficult to identify the scope of the agreement, particularly in the case of foods that are not processed. Nonetheless, for purposes of discussion it will be assumed that a measure banning mutton flaps and turkey tails would be an SPS measure.

2. APPLYING THE REQUIREMENTS OF THE SPS AGREEMENT TO FOOD REGULATION

Assuming that the SPS Agreement applies to the measures in question, it is worthwhile to explore the differences between the SPS Agreement and the GATT, as well as the specific implications this might have for the measures. This is best explored through a case study on bans on mutton flaps and turkey tails because these types of measures are used to address obesity. Although examining application of the SPS Agreement to restrictions on trans-fatty acids would enhance understanding of how the agreement applies to processed foods, such restrictions appear to be motivated by food-safety concerns with respect to coronary heart disease. In this context, analyzing application of the SPS Agreement to such measures is not as conducive to identifying how the SPS Agreement applies in the context of nutrition.

In examining the case study relating to mutton flaps and turkey tails, some brief comments are made about necessity and harmonization before the requirements of risk assessment are considered.

2.1. A *Positive Requirement of Necessity*

Article 2 of the SPS Agreement establishes the basic rights and obligations of WTO Members. Article 2.2 provides:

> Members shall ensure that any sanitary or phytosanitary measure is applied only to the extent necessary to protect human, animal or plant life or health, is based on scientific principles and is not maintained without sufficient scientific evidence, except as provided for in paragraph 7 of Article 5.

The necessity requirement is adapted from Article XX(b) of the GATT. The *chapeau* of Article XX of the GATT is also reflected in Article 2.3 of the SPS Agreement, which states:

> Members shall ensure that their sanitary and phytosanitary measures do not arbitrarily or unjustifiably discriminate between Members where identical or similar conditions prevail, including between their own territory and that of other Members. Sanitary and phytosanitary measures shall not be applied in a manner which would constitute a disguised restriction on international trade.

Because these rules mirror the more general rules laid out in Article XX(b) of the GATT, there is nothing novel in the concept of necessity being applied to measures relating to the nutritional value of foods. Equally, under Article XX, the necessity test is one part of an exception that may excuse violation of a prohibition. It is not clear that a ban of the type contemplated would result in a violation of the GATT. A complete ban on the sale of a particular food, such as mutton flaps, might not favor domestic goods leading to violation of Article III:4. In addition, the analysis of Article XI set out in Chapter 3 suggests that the ban on quantitative restrictions in GATT Article XI:1 would not apply to the measure if it were a ban in place throughout the domestic economy as a whole, but enforced at the border through a ban on importation.[31]

In contrast to the GATT Article XX(b) exception, the necessity test in Article 2 of the SPS Agreement takes the form of a positive obligation. A consequence of this is that the necessity requirement is always applicable to SPS measures. As such, the measure in question is arguably an example of a situation in which a member might not need to invoke Article XX(b) of the GATT, but where the measure might be subjected to a necessity analysis under the SPS Agreement.

In some ways the necessity requirement in Article 2 is also more demanding than the necessity test in Article XX(b) of the GATT. For example, the necessity requirement in Article 2 requires that WTO Members base measures on scientific evidence and a risk assessment in accordance with Article 5.[32] As discussed later, this may be difficult to comply with in a context in which the extent of risk at the population level is dependent on consumer behavior.

The necessity requirement in Article 2 also attaches significance to regulatory harmonization in a way that the GATT does not. Article 3 of the SPS Agreement governs harmonization and three aspects of this provision are of particular relevance. Article 3.1 imposes an obligation on members to base measures on international standards, guidelines, or recommendations (hereinafter collectively referred to as "standards"). Article 3.2 deems measures conforming to such standards, guidelines, or recommendations as necessary to protect health and creates a presumption that such measures are consistent with the SPS Agreement and the GATT. Finally, Article 3.3 restricts the circumstances in which members are free to maintain a higher level of protection than is present in international standards.

Annex A of the SPS Agreement limits the range of standards that might be used under the SPS Agreement. Annex A defines the phrase "international standards, guidelines and recommendations" as follows:

(a) for food safety, the standards, guidelines and recommendations established by the Codex Alimentarius Commission relating to food additives, veterinary drug and pesticide residues, contaminants, methods of analysis and sampling, and codes and guidelines of hygienic practice;

[31] One possible exception to this is where there is no domestic production of a good, as is said to be the case in Fiji with respect to mutton flaps. With respect to Fiji, see Anne Marie Thow and Wendy Snowdon, "The Effect of Trade and Trade Policy on Diet and Health in the Pacific Islands," in Hawkes et al., *Trade, Food, Diet and Health*, pp. 147–168, p. 147.

[32] In addition to guiding interpretation of Article 5 of the SPS Agreement (see Appellate Body Report, *EC – Hormones*, para. 180), Article 2 also has application as a standalone provision that is broader than Article 5 (see Appellate Body Report, *Australia – Salmon*, paras 138 and 252; see also Panel Report, *Australia – Salmon*, para. 8.52).

(b) for animal health and zoonoses, the standards, guidelines and recommendations developed under the auspices of the International Office of Epizootics;
(c) for plant health, the international standards, guidelines and recommendations developed under the auspices of the Secretariat of the International Plant Protection Convention in cooperation with regional organizations operating within the framework of the International Plant Protection Convention; and
(d) for matters not covered by the above organizations, appropriate standards, guidelines and recommendations promulgated by other relevant international organizations open for membership to all Members, as identified by the Committee.

In the context of a case study on measures banning mutton flaps and turkey tails, there are no Codex standards that are of obvious application. Although commodity standards exist, they have not been tailored for purposes of addressing issues such as obesity. The SPS Committee has also not identified any other relevant standards under paragraph (d). Accordingly, the potential implications of Article 3 are discussed in further detail later in the context of labeling measures, for which relevant Codex standards do exist. For present purposes, it is sufficient to note that the focus on harmonization may minimize regulatory flexibility and experimentation.

The purposes underlying the GATT and the SPS Agreement also differ. It will be recalled from Chapters 1 and 3 that the GATT seeks to balance regulatory autonomy with the goal of enforcing tariff commitments by ensuring that illegitimate nontariff barriers to trade are not used to circumvent those commitments. This balancing act is ultimately one aimed at permitting legitimate regulation while preventing illegitimate protectionism. The affirmative necessity requirement in Article 2 of the SPS Agreement means that preventing the circumvention of tariff commitments is not the only apparent goal of the policy balancing provisions in the SPS Agreement. Rather, other goals such as protecting market access through regulatory harmonization are pursued.

It should also be noted that it is not clear that the general approach to the necessity test in Article XX(b) of the GATT will be imported into the SPS context. The Appellate Body has made this much clear in the context of Article 5.5 of the SPS Agreement, which resembles the *chapeau* of Article XX of the GATT. In *EC – Hormones* the Appellate Body warned against the 'casual importation' of reasoning used in the GATT context into the SPS context.[33] With this in

[33] Appellate Body Report, *EC – Hormones*, para. 239.

mind, the more specific provisions of Article 5 of the SPS Agreement are now considered below in light of the GATT case law on Article XX(b).

2.2. *Risk Assessment, Scientific Principles, and Necessity*

The requirement that WTO Members base SPS measures on risk assessments was introduced in Article 5 of the SPS Agreement. Because the SPS Agreement was not concluded with measures to address the nutritional qualities of foods in mind, one question that arises is whether it is appropriate to require that measures be based on risk assessments in this context. One concern is that an obligation to base measures on risk assessments could stand in the way of experimental regulation aimed at addressing harm caused by well-established risks.

Article 5 of the SPS Agreement states:

Article 5
Assessment of Risk and Determination of the Appropriate Level of Sanitary or Phytosanitary Protection

1. Members shall ensure that their sanitary or phytosanitary measures are based on an assessment, as appropriate to the circumstances, of the risks to human, animal or plant life or health, taking into account risk assessment techniques developed by the relevant international organizations.
2. In the assessment of risks, Members shall take into account available scientific evidence; relevant processes and production methods; relevant inspection, sampling and testing methods; prevalence of specific diseases or pests; existence of pest- or disease-free areas; relevant ecological and environmental conditions; and quarantine or other treatment.
3. In assessing the risk to animal or plant life or health and determining the measure to be applied for achieving the appropriate level of sanitary or phytosanitary protection from such risk, Members shall take into account as relevant economic factors: the potential damage in terms of loss of production or sales in the event of the entry, establishment or spread of a pest or disease; the costs of control or eradication in the territory of the importing Member; and the relative cost-effectiveness of alternative approaches to limiting risks.
4. Members should, when determining the appropriate level of sanitary or phytosanitary protection, take into account the objective of minimizing negative trade effects.
5. With the objective of achieving consistency in the application of the concept of appropriate level of sanitary or phytosanitary protection against risks to human life or health, or to animal and plant life or health, each Member shall avoid arbitrary or unjustifiable distinctions in the levels it considers to

be appropriate in different situations, if such distinctions result in discrimination or a disguised restriction on international trade. Members shall cooperate in the Committee, in accordance with paragraphs 1, 2 and 3 of Article 12, to develop guidelines to further the practical implementation of this provision. In developing the guidelines, the Committee shall take into account all relevant factors, including the exceptional character of human health risks to which people voluntarily expose themselves.

6. Without prejudice to paragraph 2 of Article 3, when establishing or maintaining sanitary or phytosanitary measures to achieve the appropriate level of sanitary or phytosanitary protection, Members shall ensure that such measures are not more trade-restrictive than required to achieve their appropriate level of sanitary or phytosanitary protection, taking into account technical and economic feasibility.
7. In cases where relevant scientific evidence is insufficient, a Member may provisionally adopt sanitary or phytosanitary measures on the basis of available pertinent information, including that from the relevant international organizations as well as from sanitary or phytosanitary measures applied by other Members. In such circumstances, Members shall seek to obtain the additional information necessary for a more objective assessment of risk and review the sanitary or phytosanitary measure accordingly within a reasonable period of time.
8. When a Member has reason to believe that a specific sanitary or phytosanitary measure introduced or maintained by another Member is constraining, or has the potential to constrain, its exports and the measure is not based on the relevant international standards, guidelines or recommendations, or such standards, guidelines or recommendations do not exist, an explanation of the reasons for such sanitary or phytosanitary measure may be requested and shall be provided by the Member maintaining the measure.

At first glance, the obligation to base measures on a risk assessment would appear to create a significant procedural hurdle for members seeking to prohibit the sale of a good such as mutton flaps This impression is neither entirely dispelled nor confirmed by the case law.

A. Basing a measure on a risk assessment

In order for a measure to be based on a risk assessment under Article 5.1, there must be an objective relationship between the risk assessment and the measure[34] in the sense that "the results of the risk assessment must sufficiently warrant – that is to say, reasonably support – the SPS measure at stake."[35] Thus,

[34] Ibid., para. 189.
[35] Ibid., para. 193.

the requirement to base measures on a risk assessment concerns whether the measure is rationally related to a risk identified in that assessment.[36] Leaving aside the requirement that a risk assessment exist, a rational-relationship test of this type is not particularly onerous. The more pressing concern is likely to be how a risk assessment is carried out.

Paragraph 4 of Annex A of the SPS Agreement defines the phrase "risk assessment" in the following terms:

> The evaluation of the likelihood of entry, establishment or spread of a pest or disease within the territory of an importing Member according to the sanitary or phytosanitary measures which might be applied, and of the associated potential biological and economic consequences; or the evaluation of the potential for adverse effects on human or animal health arising from the presence of additives, contaminants, toxins or disease-causing organisms in food, beverages or feedstuffs.

It is the second part of this definition of a risk assessment that is at issue in the context of measures to address the nutritional qualities of foods. A member would be required to evaluate the potential adverse effects on human health caused by consuming the food in question. If it is assumed that the food in question is particularly high in fat, it is reasonable to expect that the potential adverse effects would be obvious and that such a requirement might be met easily. This conclusion finds support in the Appellate Body report in *EC – Hormones*, a case concerning restrictions on beef treated with growth hormones, where it was concluded that Article 5 does not create an independent procedural requirement that individual members carry out a risk assessment every time an SPS measure is implemented. Rather, a measure might find justification in a risk assessment carried out by another member or by an international organization.[37] In addition, the applicable definition of risk assessment in Annex A only calls for assessment of the *potential* occurrence of adverse effects. As the Appellate Body has concluded, the concept of potential relates to possibility and not to the higher threshold of probability.[38] Furthermore, such a possibility need not be evaluated in quantitative terms.[39]

On the other hand, the process of risk assessment requires both identification of potential adverse effects on human health and an evaluation of the potential for those adverse health effects to occur.[40] The first step of identifying

[36] See discussion in Scott, *WTO Sanitary and Phytosanitary Measures*, p. 105

[37] Appellate Body Report, *EC – Hormones*, para. 190.

[38] Ibid., para. 184.

[39] Ibid., para. 184.

[40] Panel Report, *EC – Hormones*, para. 8.98 (US), 8.101 (Canada).

potential adverse effects on health might not be as easy as it appears because the process would have to be done with specificity.[41] As the Appellate Body held in *EC – Hormones*, it is not sufficient to rely on studies of such generality that adverse effects and their potential for occurrence is not identified.[42] The case law suggests that risk assessment must focus on a particular risk and its cause,[43] and that risk of disease must be evaluated on a disease-specific basis.[44] As Joanne Scott has put it, "the obligation to conduct an assessment of 'risk' is not satisfied merely by a general discussion of the disease sought to be avoided by the imposition of a phytosanitary measure."[45]

The second step, involving an evaluation of the potential for the adverse effects to occur, may be more difficult. For example, even if obesity were considered a disease, it is multicausal in character, and there is a long chain of causation between the consumption of a specific food and the onset of obesity. If obesity were not itself considered a disease, but merely a risk factor for other diseases, the chain of causation would be longer and the difficulty of assessing the potential for adverse effects to occur would be heightened. In this respect, the potential for adverse effects turns largely on the behavior of consumers. Accordingly, a WTO Member would have to take account of a variety of unpredictable factors, such as the way in which a particular food is consumed, the groups in society likely to consume the food, and whether those groups are likely to achieve energy balance in terms of their overall dietary intake and physical activity. The difficulty in predicting outcomes is one reason why regulation is somewhat experimental. These factors may make it difficult to base a measure on a risk assessment notwithstanding the flexibility of the phrase "based on."

B. Provisional measures under Article 5.7

Where scientific evidence is insufficient to permit a member to comply with the requirements of Article 5.1 (to base a measure on a risk assessment), Article 5.7 permits a member to adopt provisional measures.[46] The relevant scientific evidence will be considered insufficient where the available evidence does not allow the performance of an adequate assessment of the risks required by

[41] See Appellate Body Report, *EC – Hormones*, para. 200.
[42] Ibid., para. 199.
[43] Appellate Body Report, *Japan – Apples*, para. 202, fn 372.
[44] Panel Report, *Australia – Salmon*, para. 8.74.
[45] Scott, *WTO Sanitary and Phytosanitary Measures*, p. 94.
[46] For a discussion of the relationship between Articles 5.1 and 5.7, see Panel Report, *EC – Biotech Products*, paras 7.2984–7.3000; See also Scott, WTO Sanitary and Phytosanitary Measures, pp. 113–155.

Article 5.1.[47] In the context of the type of risk assessment at issue, this would be the case where the evidence does not allow a member to evaluate the possibility of adverse effects on human health arising from the presence of an additive or disease-causing organism in a food.

The terms of Article 5.7 take account of new or novel risks and have been compared to the precautionary principle. The difficulty associated with carrying out a risk assessment suggests that evidence may often be insufficient in the context of measures, such as a ban on mutton flaps and turkey tails. Where this is the case, and Article 5.7 is triggered, three other requirements must be met. These are as follows:

- the measure is adopted on the basis of available pertinent information;
- the member adopting the measure seeks to obtain the additional information necessary for a more objective assessment of risk; and
- the member adopting the measure reviews the measure accordingly within a reasonable period of time.[48]

Where evidence is insufficient, a member may rely on "available pertinent information" in adopting a measure. Article 5.7 mentions information provided by international organizations, meaning that information provided by the WHO that suggests the existence of a risk may meet this standard. Evidence linking a nutrition transition with increased rates of obesity might also constitute available pertinent information. For example, population-level evidence of a change in diet that correlates with increased rates of obesity might be pertinent information forming the basis for adoption of a measure. If this were the case, Article 5.7 would permit the kind of regulatory experimentation that may be necessary to decrease the prevalence of obesity. Of course, it remains to be seen whether changes in diet could be attributed to isolated products, such as mutton flaps or turkey tails.

Where pertinent evidence does exist, a member banning mutton flaps and turkey tails would have to seek further information for a more objective assessment of the risk and would have to review the measure. This could be done by examining the effectiveness of the measure. Populationwide trends showing changes in dietary habits or in the prevalence of noncommunicable diseases may constitute objective evidence of the risk in question. Although Article 5.7 comes with the procedural burdens associated with seeking further information and reviewing a measure, these requirements are not unreasonable. It ought to be expected that review and further evidence gathering are

47 Appellate Body Report, *Japan – Apples*, para. 179.

48 Appellate Body Report, *Japan – Agricultural Products II*, para. 89.

essential aspects of regulatory experimentation. A requirement of this character is also significantly less onerous than the obligation to base a measure on a risk assessment under Article 5.1, which does not apply where Article 5.7 can be invoked. Thus, to the extent that scope for experimentation is at issue, Article 5.7 might provide some relief where pertinent information is available. Equally, this conclusion is questionable in light of the fact that long time periods are required to assess the effectiveness of these types of measures.

C. Inconsistent approaches to risk where risk turns largely on consumer behavior

Article 5.5 of the SPS Agreement obliges each WTO Member to avoid arbitrary or unjustifiable distinctions in the levels of health protection that it considers appropriate in different situations, if such distinctions result in discrimination or a disguised restriction on international trade. This provision mirrors the *chapeau* of Article XX of the GATT and may be problematic in the context of product-regulation measures.

In the context of a ban on mutton flaps and turkey tails, a question may arise as to why a member has prohibited these high-fat foods without also prohibiting other foods with similar nutritional qualities. This poses some difficulty in the sense that two foods with similar nutritional profiles do not necessarily pose the same risks in terms of their capacity to cause a condition such as obesity. Rather, consumption patterns affect the degree of risk. The level of protection that a member seeks may vary wildly from product to product depending on factors other than the objective characteristics of those products. A food that is high in fat may pose an unacceptable level of risk where that food is consumed widely. On the other hand, a food with substantially the same nutritional profile might be considered to fall within an acceptable level of risk on the basis that it is not consumed widely. Put simply, the acceptable level of risk could vary from food to food based on consumption patterns.

Another problem may be posed by the technical difficulty associated with imposing measures that are applied equally to comparable goods. For example, artificial trans-fatty acids are restricted in some countries whereas trans fats naturally occurring in meats are not. This is reflective of a general trend to regulate processed foods without regulating comparable fresh foods in the same manner. For example, under Canadian law, different labeling requirements apply to different meats. Cured meats, seasoned meats, and ground meats must be labeled, but raw, single-ingredient unground meat, meat byproducts, poultry meats, poultry-meat byproducts, and other products are exempted. The rationale for the exemption lies in the lack of representative data on these types of meat.[49]

Equally, distinctions on the latter grounds might be considered justifiable. In *EC – Hormones* the Appellate Body considered whether the EC maintained unjustifiable distinctions between hormone-treated meat and meat containing naturally produced hormones. The Appellate Body concluded that such distinctions were justifiable, citing the fact that addressing hormones naturally occurring in food would require "such a massive governmental intervention in nature and in the ordinary lives of people as to reduce the comparison itself to an absurdity."[50]

Whether distinctions based on consumer behavior would be considered justifiable is open to question. The Appellate Body has also stated that arbitrary or unjustifiable differences in levels of protection might operate as a warning signal that the measure in question, as applied, might result in discrimination or a disguised restriction on trade.[51] This may be the case in the context of measures such as prohibitions on mutton flaps. Equally, if a population consumes foods with similar nutritional qualities in different ways, there may be a reasonable justification for an inconsistent approach to foods with similar nutritional profiles.

In *EC – Hormones* the Appellate Body also considered how the question of where the effect of a measure falls might indicate discrimination or a disguised restriction. The fact that there was a higher percentage of beef treated with growth-promoting hormones from Canada and the United States was considered simply to be a reflection of the fact that those countries had allowed the practice for a long time whereas the EC had not.[52] Thus, the extent to which the effect of a measure falls on imported as compared to domestic goods was considered, but was not dispositive on the facts. Rather, in reaching its decision, the Appellate Body relied heavily on an historical analysis concerning the bona fides of the EC.

The language of Article 5.5 and the manner of its interpretation in *EC – Hormones* suggests that the provision will be interpreted in much the same manner as the *chapeau* of Article XX of the GATT. As is the case in that context, a further source of concern is likely to be the imperfect forms of regulation that are created by domestic regulatory politics. In determining

49 Mary L'Abbé, Janine Lewis, and Christina Zehaluk, "The Potential of the Codex Alimentarius to Promote Healthy Diets Worldwide – The Canadian Experience of Implementation," in Hawkes et al., *Trade, Food, Diet and Health*, pp. 238–226, pp. 255–256.

50 Appellate Body Report, *EC – Hormones*, para. 221.

51 Ibid., para. 215.

52 Ibid., para. 245.

how to address risk, regulators (and politicians) take account of a range of issues, including social preferences and a wish to avoid unnecessary paternalism. The lawfulness of tobacco products provides an example of this. Tobacco products cause the premature deaths of approximately half of those who are regular users, yet the sale of tobacco products is rarely prohibited. One reason for this lies in problems of enforcement. Another explanation is simply that consumption is too widespread and bound up in concepts of individual liberty for democratically elected governments to ban the sale of tobacco products. This type of internal regulatory politics makes it difficult for a WTO Member to present a consistent response to risk in different contexts.

By the same token, the Appellate Body has shown some sensitivity to problems of regulatory politics. In *EC – Hormones* the Appellate Body recognized that Article 5.5 does not, strictly speaking, impose an obligation to ensure consistency in risk tolerance. Rather, the provision is modeled on the *chapeau* of GATT Article XX(b) and seeks to prevent arbitrary and unjustifiable discrimination and disguised restrictions on trade. The Appellate Body further noted that "the goal set is not absolute or perfect consistency, since governments establish their appropriate levels of protection frequently on an *ad hoc* basis and over time, as different risks present themselves at different times."[53]

In summary, there are a number of different factors that may make it difficult for a WTO Member to comply with Article 5.5 while taking the types of product-regulation measures under consideration. Whether inconsistent approaches to risk will be considered justified is likely to depend very much on the circumstances and is difficult to predict. Most notably, the rule in Article 5.5 weighs against small-scale measures, such as a ban on mutton flaps, which may be important for public health purposes and important in terms of understanding the potential impact of different measures on the onset of disease. Article 5.5 suggests that systemwide rules governing all foods with similar nutritional characteristics are a preferable approach despite the fact that they may be more trade restrictive in their effect. This might be viewed as a recipe for regulatory paralysis in many states due to the size of the regulatory undertaking and the potential imposition on individual and economic liberty.

D. Least trade-restrictive means

A further elaboration of the necessity test is found in Article 5.6 of the SPS Agreement, which requires members to ensure that measures are not more trade restrictive than required to achieve their appropriate level of protection.

[53] Ibid., para. 213.

A footnote to this provision states that "a measure is not more trade-restrictive than required unless there is another measure, reasonably available taking into account technical and economic feasibility, that achieves the appropriate level of sanitary or phytosanitary protection and is significantly less restrictive to trade."

The most obvious distinction between this test and the necessity test under Article XX(b) of the GATT is that a purported alternative under the SPS Agreement needs to be significantly less trade restrictive in order to impugn the measure in dispute. It seems safe to assume that this requirement can only soften the necessity requirement in the SPS Agreement as compared to that of Article XX(b) of the GATT.

Another apparent difference between the two tests is that the technical and economic feasibility of a measure must be taken into account in determining whether an alternative measure is reasonably available. Whereas Article XX does not provide for this approach expressly, the case law suggests that these are two of any number of factors that might be considered in the context of reasonable availability under Article XX(b). Scott has also argued that it is not clear under the SPS Agreement whether mere administrative difficulties, which do not affect the reasonable availability of a measure under Article XX, would be relevant under Article 5.6.[54] Despite this argument, the wording of the SPS Agreement appears merely to entrench the consideration of factors in a way that may affirm regulatory autonomy.

Scott has also argued that the differences between the contexts and in the wording of Article 5.6 as compared to Article XX(b) suggest that some of the factors used in the weighing and balancing test would not be relevant under Article 5.6. In particular, Scott has suggested that the degree to which a measure contributes to its regulatory objective should not be considered under Article 5.6.[55] This conclusion might find support in Article 5 of the SPS Agreement, because basing a measure on a risk assessment could ensure that the measure makes a contribution to elimination of the risk in question. The same might be said where a measure is based on pertinent information under Article 5.7.

A further difference between the SPS Agreement and Article XX of the GATT lies in the way in which a member's chosen level of protection is evaluated. In *Australia – Salmon* the Appellate Body held that it was not sufficient to simply imply the appropriate level of protection chosen by a member from the measure in question, because this would assume that the measure

[54] Scott, *The WTO Agreement on Sanitary and Pytosanitary Measures*, p. 161.

[55] Ibid., p. 161.

always achieves the appropriate level of protection.[56] With this in mind, the Appellate Body concluded that "[w]hat is required under Article 5.6 is an examination of whether possible alternative SPS measures meet the appropriate level of protection *as determined by the Member concerned*."[57] This can be contrasted with the manner in which a member's regulatory goal is determined under the GATT, which was discussed in Chapter 4. By the same token, the Appellate Body also recognized that giving a member the discretion to determine the level of protection is open to abuse. The Appellate Body stated:

> This does not mean, however, that an importing Member is free to determine its level of protection with such vagueness or equivocation that the application of the relevant provisions of the SPS Agreement, such as Article 5.6, becomes impossible. It would obviously be wrong to interpret the SPS Agreement in a way that would render nugatory entire articles or paragraphs of articles of this Agreement and allow Members to escape from their obligations under this Agreement.[58]

Following this, the Appellate Body identified the circumstances in which it is necessary for a panel to depart from the level of protection identified by a member. The Appellate Body stated that "where a Member does not determine its appropriate level of protection, or does so with insufficient precision, the appropriate level of protection may be established by panels on the basis of the level of protection reflected in the SPS measure actually applied."[59]

This is a clear departure from the approach taken under the GATT, where a member's regulatory goal is assessed in an objective fashion. Although a member's statement of intent is one factor for consideration, it is not afforded the deference that is apparent in *Australia – Salmon*. One inference that might be drawn from this is that a WTO Member has far greater control over the direction of the necessity analysis under the SPS Agreement than under the GATT (provided that the member does not put forward a vague regulatory purpose or risk tolerance). Because necessity analysis is built around a given regulatory purpose, analysis of necessity under the SPS Agreement may be more deferential than it is under the GATT. This view also accords with the different standard of trade restrictiveness under the SPS Agreement, in the sense that an alternative must be significantly less trade restrictive in order to impugn a measure.

[56] Appellate Body Report, *Australia – Salmon*, para. 203.
[57] Ibid., para. 204 (italics in original).
[58] Ibid., para. 206.
[59] Ibid., para. 207.

2.3. *Concluding Observations on Product Regulation under the SPS Agreement*

The previous analysis leaves open the question of whether a product ban of the type contemplated would survive analysis under the SPS Agreement. This will depend very much on local circumstances and the effect of measures. Nonetheless, the necessity requirement in the SPS Agreement appears more permissive in some ways than Article XX(b) of the GATT. This should not be a surprise given that the requirement is a positive obligation rather than an exception. This conclusion must, therefore, be tempered by the fact that some measures that would not violate GATT prohibitions may be subjected to necessity analysis under the SPS Agreement. This conclusion must also be tempered by the need to base a measure on a risk assessment under Article 5.1 and by the potential impact of Article 5.5.

It is also worth noting that, in theory, a measure might comply with this more permissive necessity requirement but be indefensible under Article XX(b) of the GATT. However, the presumption in Article 2.4 would shift the burden onto a complainant under Article XX(b), making it more difficult for a complainant to succeed because it would bear the burden of demonstrating a measure to be unnecessary. A panel may also be loathe to find that a measure is necessary under the SPS Agreement but indefensible under Article XX(b).

3. FOOD-LABELING MEASURES UNDER THE SPS AGREEMENT

The two types of food-labeling measures that were identified at the beginning of the chapter are measures requiring the disclosure of nutritional information and quantitative ingredient labeling (where packaged foods must include a list of ingredients). The terms of the SPS Agreement discussed previously are also relevant to these measures. In addition, two Codex instruments are particularly relevant to labeling measures of this type. The Guidelines on Nutrition Labeling have the following stated purposes:

To ensure that nutrition labeling is effective:

- In providing the consumer with information about food so that a wise choice of food can be made;
- In providing means for conveying information of the nutrient content of a food on the label;
- In encouraging the use of sound nutrition principles in the formulation of foods which would benefit public health;

- In providing the opportunity to include supplementary nutrition information on the label;

To ensure that nutrition labeling does not describe a product or present information about it which is in any way false, misleading, deceptive or insignificant in any manner.

To ensure that no nutrition claim is made without nutrition labeling.[60]

The guidelines provide that a nutrient declaration should be voluntary for all foods other than those for which nutrition claims are made.[61] By the same token, the guidelines recognize that nutrient declarations may be mandatory and recognize the legitimacy of declarations that are required by national legislation or national dietary guidelines.[62] The General Standard for the Labeling of Prepackaged Foods[63] also applies in the context of prepackaged foods. The standard provides that with the exception of single-ingredient foods, a list of ingredients shall be declared on product labeling.[64] Each of these instruments also includes provisions to the effect that product labeling should not be false, misleading, or deceptive. For example, Section 3 of the General Standard for Labeling of Prepackaged Food states: "Packaged food shall not be described or presented on any label or in any labeling in a manner that is false, misleading or deceptive or likely to create an erroneous impression regarding its character in any respect."

The difficulty that consumers may have in understanding labels has also led some to argue for more interventionist labeling systems. For example, a state might use a signpost strategy for foods, whereby green and red symbols (replicating traffic lights) are used to indicate the level of calories, fat, sugar, and sodium contained in a packaged food.[65]

3.1. *Application of the SPS Agreement to Labeling Measures*

The first question for consideration is whether the SPS Agreement applies to measures of the type under consideration. The analysis in part 1 of this chapter suggests that this will not be the case in the tobacco context, but that

60 Guidelines on Nutrition Labeling, CAC/GL 2–1985.

61 Ibid., para. 3.1.2.

62 Ibid., para. 3.2.1.4.

63 General Standard for the Labeling of Prepackaged Foods, CODEX STAN 1–1985.

64 Ibid., para. 4.2.1.

65 The U.K. Food Standards Agency has developed a labeling system of this type for use on a voluntary basis. See www.eatwell.gov.uk/foodlabels (visited 02/03/10). See also Notification, World Trade Organization, Committee on Sanitary and Phytosanitary Measures, World Trade Organization, Republic of Korea, G/SPS/N/KOR/307, 17 December 2008.

it may be the case in the contexts of food and alcoholic beverages. Because international standards exist in the context of food, it is worthwhile to examine the issue in that context. Assuming that the labeling measures would be implemented either through law or another requirement, the issue for examination would be whether the measures in question are measures to protect human life or health from risks arising from additives, contaminants, toxins, or disease-causing organisms in food.

The panel report in *EC – Approval and Marketing of Biotech Products* offers considerable guidance on this question. The panel had to consider whether a number of purposes associated with rules governing marketing approval fell within the scope of Annex A(1). One of the stated purposes of the measure was to ensure that consumers were not misled. Marketing approval was, therefore, conditional on compliance with labeling requirements, including an obligation to disclose the presence of genetically modified organisms. In considering whether the measure fell within the scope of Annex A(1), the panel stated that "to the extent that Regulation 258/97 is applied to ensure that novel foods not mislead the consumer, it does not constitute a measure applied to protect the life or health of consumers from risks arising from, e.g., additives or contaminants in foods."[66] On this basis, the panel found the measure to fall outside the scope of the SPS Agreement.

Under this approach, where the purpose of a labeling measure is to provide consumers with information or to prevent them from being misled, the SPS Agreement would not apply. Depending on a WTO Member's purpose (as judged objectively), labeling measures that compel the disclosure of nutritional information or the disclosure of ingredients might, therefore, fall beyond the scope of the SPS Agreement. Of course, the merits of this approach are questionable in the present context. Even where measures are framed as mere consumer-information measures, health protection is an implicit purpose because the information in question allows consumers to make decisions that affect their health.

In any case, some labeling measures will have a more obvious health purpose than others. For example, a traffic light labeling scheme is likely to have the purpose of encouraging consumption of healthful foods and discouraging consumption of relatively unhealthy foods. Where this is the case, and the unhealthy foods in question constitute additives, as salt and added sugar may, the measure would most likely fall within the scope of the SPS Agreement.

How then, might the SPS Agreement govern a labeling scheme of such a character? The requirement to carry out a risk assessment under Article 5 of the SPS Agreement was discussed earlier and need not be examined here again. It is sufficient to note that various risks can be identified as being

[66] Panel Report, *EC –Biotech Products*, para. 7.412.

associated with consumption of particular constituents, such as fat, sugar, and sodium. The requirement of necessity under Article 2 of the SPS Agreement was also examined. This requirement is also relevant in the context of labeling measures. However, given that Codex standards exist for food labeling, the starting point is Article 3.1 of the SPS Agreement, which states:

> To harmonize sanitary and phytosanitary measures on as wide a basis as possible, Members shall base their sanitary or phytosanitary measures on international standards, guidelines or recommendations, where they exist, except as otherwise provided for in this Agreement, and in particular in paragraph 3.

At first glance, this requirement is worrying given that the Global Strategy Diet expresses concerns about regulatory harmonization. For example, in referring to the formulation of national strategies, the Global Strategy Diet recognizes that national circumstances will determine priorities.[67] The need for flexibility lies in differing nutritional profiles in different states and partly in the behavioral causes of poor diet, which differ from community to community. In addition, culture, culinary traditions, and geography are a few of the other factors that dictate a need for regulatory diversity. Hence, there is a concern that provisions promoting harmonization through the use of international standards may be unduly restrictive.

However, the reasons for regulatory diversity touched on in the Global Strategy Diet suggest that WHO member-states were concerned about universal approaches that set the bar too high. In the trade-law context, there is a tendency to think of the rationale behind harmonization in terms of market access. In line with this tendency, WTO Members show concern where other members exceed standards, because this may have the effect of interfering with market access. This suggests that disputes would be more likely to arise if a Codex standard sets the bar too low and members wish to exceed it. If this were the case, measures might not be "based on" standards under Article 3.1.

On the other hand, in *EC – Hormones* the Appellate Body stressed that the purpose of Article 3.1 is not to vest international standards, which are recommendatory in nature, with legal force.[68] A measure can be based on a standard without conforming to it, although the dividing line between the two is somewhat uncertain. In *EC – Hormones* the Appellate Body gave the example of a measure that incorporates only some but not all of the elements of a standard as being based on that standard.[69]

[67] Global Strategy Diet, para. 35.
[68] Appellate Body Report, *EC – Hormones*, para. 165.
[69] Ibid., para. 163.

In the present context, concerns might be raised about the ability of members to implement mandatory labeling requirements, mandatory ingredient disclosure measures and other measures such as traffic light labeling schemes. However, the relevant Codex instruments contemplate different types of labeling in a fashion that anticipates traffic light labeling schemes. The General Standard for Labeling of Prepackaged Food states that "[a]ny information or pictorial device written, printed, or graphic matter may be displayed in labeling provided that it is not in conflict with the mandatory requirements of this standard and those relating to claims and deception given in Section 3 – General Principles."[70] The Guidelines on Nutrition Labeling also contemplate labels that are supplementary to the disclosure of nutritional information. In this respect, the guidelines suggest that labels containing such information should be "accompanied by consumer education programs to increase consumer understanding and use of the information."[71] This suggestion relates to a basic principle of nutrition labeling that is set out in the guidelines, where it is stated:

> The information should not lead consumers to believe that there is exact quantitative knowledge of what individuals should eat in order to maintain health, but rather to convey an understanding of the quantity of nutrients contained in the product. A more exact quantitative delineation for individuals is not valid because there is no meaningful way in which knowledge about individual requirements can be used in labelling.[72]

Thus, from a public health perspective, it is important that labeling measures do not promote the consumption of foods in a way that may have adverse consequences for health. There is a risk, for example, that describing a food as healthful (or giving it a green light) will encourage consumption of that food in a way that undermines a balanced diet. It is with considerations such as this in mind that states regulate the use of health claims on foods. In this respect, the Codex Guidelines for Use of Nutrition and Health Claims stress that "[h]ealth claims should be supported by a sound and sufficient body of scientific evidence to substantiate the claim, provide truthful and non-misleading information to aid consumers in choosing healthful diets and be supported by specific consumer education."[73]

[70] General Standard for the Labeling of Prepackaged Foods, CODEX STAN 1–1985, para. 7.1.
[71] Guidelines on Nutrition Labeling, CAC/GL 2–1985, para. 5.3.
[72] Guidelines on Nutrition Labeling, CAC/GL 2–1985, principles for nutrition labeling.
[73] Codex Alimentarius Commission, Guidelines for Use of Nutrition and Health Claims, CAC/GL 23–1997.

Assuming that any health claims associated with a labeling scheme are substantiated, the question at issue concerns whether a traffic light labeling scheme conforms to the international standards or seeks a higher level of protection. In this respect, Articles 3.2 and 3.3 of the SPS Agreement are relevant. Article 3.2 creates a presumption of lawfulness for measures conforming to international standards, whereas Article 3.3 limits the circumstances in which a member may seek a higher level of protection than is provided for in a relevant international standard. The provisions state:

> 3.2 Sanitary or phytosanitary measures which conform to international standards, guidelines or recommendations shall be deemed to be necessary to protect human, animal or plant life or health, and presumed to be consistent with the relevant provisions of this Agreement and of GATT 1994.
>
> 3.3 Members may introduce or maintain sanitary or phytosanitary measures which result in a higher level of sanitary or phytosanitary protection than would be achieved by measures based on the relevant international standards, guidelines or recommendations, if there is a scientific justification, or as a consequence of the level of sanitary or phytosanitary protection a Member determines to be appropriate in accordance with the relevant provisions of paragraphs 1 through 8 of Article 5.

A footnote to Article 3.3 states:

> For the purposes of paragraph 3 of Article 3, there is a scientific justification if, on the basis of an examination and evaluation of available scientific information in conformity with the relevant provisions of this Agreement, a Member determines that the relevant international standards, guidelines or recommendations are not sufficient to achieve its appropriate level of sanitary or phytosanitary protection.

On the one hand, the wording of the General Standard for Labeling of Prepackaged Food contemplates measures beyond its terms and offers conditional support for such measures. This suggests that where the relevant conditions in the standard are complied with, a measure could be considered to conform to international standards despite going beyond their content.

On the other hand, the General Standard for Labeling of Prepackaged Food does not contemplate specifically the use of a traffic light labeling scheme. The language in question is general, and it is clear that the measure is a step beyond those suggested expressly in the standard. In addition, as was noted, the requirement that measures "conform to" a standard in order for the presumption to have effect differs from a requirement that measures be based on international standards. The requirement of conformity is the more demanding of the two, and requires that a measure "embody the international standard completely and, for practical purposes, [convert] it into a municipal standard."[74]

On the face of it, it is difficult to predict which of Articles 3.2 or 3.3 would apply. Although this appears problematic, it may not have as great a practical difference as the text of Article 3 suggests. The Appellate Body has held that the fact that a measure does not conform to an international standard does not shift the burden of proof onto the respondent. Rather, the complainant continues to bear the burden of demonstrating that measures not conforming to a standard violate the SPS Agreement.[75] Equally, as Oliver Landwehr has argued, the effect of this is minimal given that a burden of presenting evidence still shifts to the respondent.[76] Accordingly, a member may have to bring evidence of the need for a traffic light labeling scheme of the type in question in order to justify the measure under Article 3.3. Any such evidence may have to suggest that the standard labeling measures are an inadequate means of informing consumers of the risks associated with different foods. A member may also have to bring evidence justifying the application of a red signal to a particular food. This may be more difficult in a context where national dietary guidelines are diverse by reason of a state's nutritional profile or cultural and culinary traditions.

The example also highlights how unpredictable an analysis under Article 3 of the SPS Agreement may be. It is assumed that a measure cannot both conform to an international standard and result in a higher level of protection. This requires that the term "conform" be interpreted in quite a strict manner. Even so, it may still be difficult to identify whether the presumption of lawfulness should apply or whether a member should have to justify the adoption of a higher level of protection.

4. APPLICATION OF THE TBT AGREEMENT TO LABELING MEASURES, BANS ON FLAVORED CIGARETTES, AND ALCOPOPS

In addressing application of the TBT Agreement to product regulation, including labeling measures, the first question for consideration concerns

74 Appellate Body Report, *EC – Hormones*, para. 170.

75 Ibid., para. 102.

76 Oliver Landwehr, "Article 3 of the SPS Agreement," in Rüdiger Wolfrum, Peter-Tobias Stoll, and Anja Seibert-Fohr, *WTO: Technical Barriers and SPS Measures*, Leiden, Martinus Nijhoff Publishers, (2007), p. 425.

which types of measures fall within the scope of the agreement. Article 1.5 of the TBT Agreement specifies that the agreement does not apply to sanitary or phytosanitary measures as defined in Annex A of the SPS Agreement. Therefore, if it is assumed that the SPS Agreement applies to the measures discussed previously, the TBT Agreement would not apply to those measures.

Conversely, if it is assumed that tobacco-control measures fall outside the scope of the SPS Agreement, the TBT Agreement would apply where those measures constitute technical regulations. The phrase "technical regulation" is defined in Annex 1.1 of the agreement as a "[d]ocument which lays down product characteristics or their related processes and production methods, including the applicable administrative provisions, with which compliance is mandatory. It may also include or deal exclusively with terminology, symbols, packaging, marking or labeling requirements as they apply to a product, process or production method."

In *EC – Asbestos*, the Appellate Body examined Annex 1.1 and stated that "[t]he heart of the definition of a 'technical regulation' is that a document must 'lay down' – that is, set forth, stipulate or provide – 'product characteristics.'"[77] Such characteristics include "any objectively definable 'features,' 'qualities,' 'attributes,' or other 'distinguishing mark' of a product.... product characteristics include, not only features and qualities intrinsic to the product itself, but also related 'characteristics,' such as the means of identification, the presentation and the appearance of a product."[78]

It seems quite clear that tobacco- and alcohol-labeling measures fall within the scope of this definition. It is also likely that bans on flavored cigarettes and bans on alcopops would fall within the scope of the TBT Agreement. Although at first glance the latter measures may not appear to lay down product standards, they would prohibit certain products based on their characteristics. Such a measure would indirectly lay down product standards in the sense that products taking a particular form would be prohibited.

The provision of the TBT Agreement that is most likely to be relevant to these measures is Article 2. Paragraphs 1–5 of that provision state:

> Preparation, Adoption and Application of Technical Regulations by Central Government Bodies
>
> With respect to their central government bodies:
>
> 2.1 Members shall ensure that in respect of technical regulations, products imported from the territory of any Member shall be accorded treatment no

[77] Appellate Body Report, *European Communities – Measures Affecting Asbestos and Asbestos-Containing Products*, [hereinafter *EC – Asbestos*] WT/DS135/AB/R, adopted 5 April 2001, DSR 2001:VII, 3243, para. 67.

[78] Ibid.

less favourable than that accorded to like products of national origin and to like products originating in any other country.

2.2 Members shall ensure that technical regulations are not prepared, adopted or applied with a view to or with the effect of creating unnecessary obstacles to international trade. For this purpose, technical regulations shall not be more trade-restrictive than necessary to fulfil a legitimate objective, taking account of the risks non-fulfilment would create. Such legitimate objectives are, inter alia: national security requirements; the prevention of deceptive practices; protection of human health or safety, animal or plant life or health, or the environment. In assessing such risks, relevant elements of consideration are, inter alia: available scientific and technical information, related processing technology or intended end-uses of products.

2.3 Technical regulations shall not be maintained if the circumstances or objectives giving rise to their adoption no longer exist or if the changed circumstances or objectives can be addressed in a less trade-restrictive manner.

2.4 Where technical regulations are required and relevant international standards exist or their completion is imminent, Members shall use them, or the relevant parts of them, as a basis for their technical regulations except when such international standards or relevant parts would be an ineffective or inappropriate means for the fulfilment of the legitimate objectives pursued, for instance because of fundamental climatic or geographical factors or fundamental technological problems.

2.5 A Member preparing, adopting or applying a technical regulation which may have a significant effect on trade of other Members shall, upon the request of another Member, explain the justification for that technical regulation in terms of the provisions of paragraphs 2 to 4. Whenever a technical regulation is prepared, adopted or applied for one of the legitimate objectives explicitly mentioned in paragraph 2, and is in accordance with relevant international standards, it shall be rebuttably presumed not to create an unnecessary obstacle to international trade.

Of those provisions, it is Article 2.2 that is most relevant. Like Article 2 of the SPS Agreement, Article 2.2 of the TBT Agreement creates an affirmative necessity requirement. The purpose of Article 2.2 and its relationship to provisions such as Article III:4 of the GATT remains somewhat unclear.[79] Although

[79] On the telos of the agreement, see Michael Ming Du, "Domestic Regulatory Autonomy under the TBT Agreement: From Non-Discrimination to Harmonization" 6(2) *Chinese Journal of International Law*, (2007), pp. 269–306; for discussion, see also Robert Howse and Elisabeth Türk, "The WTO Impact Upon Internal Regulations: A Case Study of the Canada – EC Asbestos Dispute," in George Bermann and Petros Mavroidis (eds), *Trade and Human Health and Safety*, New York, Cambridge University Press, (2006), pp. 77–117, p. 99 [hereinafter Howse and Türk, "The WTO Impact Upon Internal Regulations"].

it appears that the GATT and the TBT Agreement act concurrently (in the sense that a claim can be brought under either), it remains difficult to identify the breadth of Article 2.2.

The wording of Article 2.2 of the TBT Agreement also highlights other distinctions between the necessity requirement here and the test under Article XX(b) of the GATT. The first sentence of Article 2.2 refers to the way in which technical regulations are "prepared, adopted or applied." Similarly, the final sentence of Article 2.2 provides that inter alia "available scientific and technical information, related processing technology or intended end-uses of products" are relevant to assessment of the risks in question. Robert Howse and Elisabeth Türk have argued that these references distinguish Article 2.2 from the GATT by establishing the regulatory process as the focus of the provision.[80] However, the first sentence of Article 2.2 creates an obligation to ensure that technical regulations are not prepared, adopted, or applied *with the effect of* creating unnecessary obstacles to international trade. Thus, as Howse and Türk themselves acknowledge,[81] the nature of the necessity test in Article 2.2 is such that there is some focus on the effects of technical regulations on trade.

These observations prompt two questions. The first question concerns when a technical regulation will be considered "trade restrictive." The second question concerns whether the necessity requirement in Article 2.2 is to be interpreted in much the same manner as that of Article XX. Each of these issues is somewhat uncertain.

4.1. *When Is a Technical Regulation Trade Restrictive?*

The question of when a technical regulation is trade restrictive could be answered in one of two ways. On the one hand, it might be that every technical regulation is "trade restrictive" in nature, and that there is no need to demonstrate separately that a technical regulation also possesses some specific element of trade restrictiveness. In this respect, the TBT Agreement addresses the proliferation and use of technical regulations as barriers to trade. The TBT Agreement takes a different standpoint from other WTO-covered agreements in that its purpose is not merely to prevent protectionist measures. The existing provisions of the GATT are sufficiently broad so as to serve this purpose. Like the SPS Agreement, one purpose of the TBT Agreement is to minimize impediments to trade by encouraging the harmonization of technical regulations. This is particularly evident in Article 2.4, which requires the use

80 Howse and Türk, "The WTO Impact Upon Internal Regulations," p. 101.

81 Ibid.

of relevant international standards except where they would be ineffective or inappropriate means of pursuing a legitimate objective. Similarly, the preamble to the TBT Agreement emphasizes that international conformity in technical regulations can improve the efficiency of production and facilitate international trade.[82] Given this focus, each measure constituting a technical regulation could be considered trade restrictive.

On the other hand, it is arguable that trade restrictiveness is a separate element of Article 2.2 and that there must be a separate examination of the issue. In *EC – Sardines* the panel exercised judicial economy in not examining the lawfulness of an EC measure under Article 2.2 but nonetheless commented that it was trade restrictive.[83] In evaluating the legal status of this comment, the Appellate Body stated that it "could have been relevant to a legal analysis under Article 2.2."[84] This passage could be interpreted as suggesting that not all technical regulations are trade restrictive. An alternative interpretation is that the Appellate Body was referring to the fact that technical regulations may be trade restrictive to different degrees. This view appears to be correct, and is consistent with the fact that Article 2.2 requires that technical regulations shall not be more trade restrictive than necessary.

If it is assumed that all technical regulations are in some way trade restrictive, it still remains to be seen how trade restrictiveness will be construed. This can be illustrated by reference to the Thai alcohol-labeling measures recently notified to the TBT Committee and mentioned in Chapter 1. One of the comments made by WTO Members in the TBT Committee was that the proposed labels could mislead consumers by suggesting that drinking any level of alcohol could lead to health problems.[85] The Thai notification to the TBT Committee suggests that six different types of labels will be applied:

Type 1. "Drinking alcohol causes the [sic] hypertension liver cirrhosis";
Type 2. "Alcohol intoxication leads to the accidents";
Type 3. "Drinking alcohol leads to unconsciousness and even death";
Type 4. "Drinking alcohol leads to inferior sexual performance";

[82] See paragraph 3 of the preamble.

[83] Panel Report, *European Communities – Trade Description of Sardines*, WT/DS231/R and Corr.1, adopted 23 October 2002, modified by Appellate Body Report, WT/DS231/AB/R, DSR 2002:VIII, 3451, para. 6.11 see also fn 35.

[84] Appellate Body Report, *European Communities – Trade Description of Sardines*, WT/DS231/AB/R, adopted 23 October 2002, DSR 2002:VIII, 3359, para. 311.

[85] WTO: 2010 News Items, 24 and 25 March 2010 Technical Barriers To Trade, Tobacco and alcohol technical barriers among members' trade concerns available at http://www.wto.org/english/news_e/news10_e/tbt_24mar10_e.htm (visited 18/04/10).

Type 5. "Drinking alcohol leads to adverse health effect [sic] and family problems";

Type 6. "Drinking alcohol is a bad influence on children and young people"[86]

The pictorial warnings associated with these labels depict six different scenes in photographic form. The first picture captures cirrhosis of the liver. Another picture captures a naked man whose genitals are covered by a hand giving a "thumbs-down," as if to depict impotence. Another picture captures a traffic accident in which a motorbike and its rider are strewn across the road. Another picture captures a father clenching his fist as if to strike his wife while his son pulls at his leg. Another picture depicts a suicide, showing a stool kicked out from under a man's feet that appear to be hanging. The final picture depicts a father drinking in the presence of a young child.

The comments made in the TBT Committee appear to suggest that the warnings go too far in the sense that many of the scenarios depicted may only arise in the context of excessive consumption of alcohol. This might suggest that the measures are more trade restrictive than is necessary to protect health. However, the earlier analysis suggests that the trade restrictiveness of the measure lies in the imposition of a marking requirement that differs from that adopted in other countries, and not from any disproportionate message in the markings. In accordance with this view, the TBT Agreement would justify inquiry into whether warnings are necessary to protect health but not into the content of the warnings themselves. On the other hand, if the content of the warnings were considered to restrict trade by impeding market access, then the content of the warnings would be open to question. It remains to be seen which approach would be taken. It is worth stating, however, that the focus of analysis should be on the manner in which a measure affects trade rather than commercial activity per se. That is, the focus should be on questions of market access.

4.2. *Legitimate Objectives*

The objectives listed in Article 2.2 of relevance to the measures in question are the protection of human health or safety and the prevention of deceptive practices. In line with the analysis in Chapter 4, the measures in question appear likely to fall within the scope of these categories given the risks to health that

[86] Notification, Committee on Technical Barriers to Trade, World Trade Organization, Thailand, G/TBT/N/THA/332, 21 January 2010.

exist (and the risk of deception through marketing or advertising) and the role of labeling in addressing those risks.

It is also worth noting that the inclusive character of the provision creates additional flexibility where more than one regulatory objective can be identified, such as where a labeling measure might have the dual purpose of protecting health and of providing consumers with information. The opportunity to argue that the provision of information to consumers is itself a legitimate objective may be important, because demonstrating that the measure protects health would require a member to show a connection between the provision of information and the protection of health. Accordingly, the inclusive character of Article 2.2 could increase the likelihood that a labeling measure will be compliant in the event of a dispute.

4.3. *Measures That Are More Trade Restrictive Than Necessary*

The first question to consider in applying the necessity requirement of Article 2.2 is whether it functions in much the same manner as the necessity test found in Article XX of the GATT. It was argued earlier in the context of the SPS Agreement that the positive character of the necessity requirement in that agreement, as distinct from the exceptional character of the necessity test under Article XX(b) of the GATT, suggests that the SPS necessity requirement is not stricter than that of the GATT. If anything, the terms of the SPS Agreement suggest that the SPS necessity requirement may be more deferential.

The fact that the necessity requirement of Article 2.2 is also a positive requirement suggests that the requirement should not be stricter than the necessity test in Article XX(b) of the GATT. Three other aspects of the wording of Article 2.2 also merit attention.

First, the rebuttable presumption of lawfulness created by Article 2.5, which must be read alongside Article 2.4, suggests that a measure departing from relevant international standards will be unlawful under Article 2.2 unless it can be justified as necessary. This could suggest that the sole focus of the provision is the unnecessary departure of a measure from relevant international standards. That is, the presumption could suggest that the TBT Agreement does not invite an inquiry into the general necessity of a measure, but only invites an inquiry into the necessity of a departure from international standards. However, this is not the case under the SPS Agreement, where a similar presumption applies. On the contrary, conformity to standards merely functions as one factor to be taken into account in decision making.

Second, consideration of the risks nonfulfillment of the objective would create raises the question of whether the TBT Agreement requires a different approach to weighing and balancing than is used under Article XX of the GATT. Panagiotis Delimatsis has argued that this aspect of the test implies a variety of cost-benefit analysis.[87] Others such as Marceau and Trachtman have argued that this can be viewed as a part of the weighing and balancing test first set out in *Korea – Various Measure on Beef*.[88] However, in 2002 Marceau and Trachtman also viewed the weighing and balancing test as requiring a cost-benefit analysis, a conclusion that cannot be correct in light of the fact that members may choose the level of health protection that is appropriate to their needs.[89] Marceau and Trachtman also point to an earlier incarnation of Article 2.2, which specifically included a reference to proportionality.[90] The subsequent deletion of this reference could suggest that the concept of proportionality (an approach interfering with regulatory autonomy to a lesser degree than cost-benefit analysis) was not something that the drafters could agree on. The meaning of this phrase, therefore, is open to question.

One way of interpreting Article 2.2 would be to say that consideration of the risks of nonfulfillment is akin to the notion under GATT Article XX(b) that a purported alternative measure is not reasonably available if it would not appear to achieve the level of health protection that a WTO Member is seeking. That is, in considering whether a measure would achieve the regulatory objective, a panel must give consideration to the risks that a purported alternative would or would not address. However, the ordinary wording of Article 2.2 appears to refer to risks that nonfulfillment of the regulatory objective would create. Thus, the wording does in fact suggest that the extent of a risk to health needs to be considered as a part of a weighing and balancing process.

Another way of interpreting Article 2.2 is to say that the risks should be taken into account not in determining the necessity of a measure, but in identifying the existence of a legitimate regulatory objective. Put another way, the risks that nonfulfillment of a regulatory objective entail should be used to guide

87 Panagiotis Delimatsis, "Determining the Necessity of Domestic Regulations in Services, The Best is Yet to Come," 19(2) *European Journal of International Law*, (2008), pp. 365–408, p. 378.

88 Gabrielle Marceau and Joel Trachtman, "The Technical Barriers to Trade Agreement, the Sanitary and Phytosanitary Measures Agreement, and the General Agreement on Tariffs and Trade: A Map of the World Trade Organization Law of Domestic Regulation of Goods," 36(5) *Journal of World Trade*, (2002), pp. 811–881, p. 831, [hereinafter Marceau and Trachtman, "A Map of the World Trade Organization"].

89 See Donald Regan, "The Meaning of 'Necessary' in GATT Article XX and GATS Article XIV: The Myth of Cost-Benefit Balancing," 6(3) *World Trade Review*, (2007), pp. 347–369.

90 Marceau and Trachtman, "A Map of the World Trade Organization," p. 831.

determination of whether an objective is legitimate where it does not fall within one of the enumerated categories. Where a measure does not fall within one of the enumerated categories, the smaller the risk involved, the less likely that a legitimate regulatory objective falling within the scope of the provision exists.

The merits of this interpretation are reinforced by the absence of any other criteria to be used in determining what constitutes a legitimate objective. In fact, if the risk were to be weighed as a part of the necessity analysis, a panel would have almost unfettered discretion to determine the subject-matter scope of Article 2.2. Combined with the fact that weighing the risk in necessity analysis is such a significant departure from the approach under GATT Article XX (in which members can choose their own level of risk tolerance), the latter interpretation of Article 2.2 appears to be appropriate.

Third, it is worth noting that Article 2.2 lacks a requirement equivalent to the *chapeau* of Article XX of the GATT. It will be recalled from Chapter 4 that under Article XX of the GATT, the *chapeau* is the final hurdle and minimizes the permissiveness of Article XX. The *chapeau* relates to the bona fides concerning the way in which a measure is applied. The absence of an equivalent requirement can only suggest that no such requirement exists in the context of Article 2.2.

In summary, it remains to be seen how the apparent differences between the necessity requirement in Article 2.2 of the TBT Agreement and the necessity test in Article XX(b) of the GATT will be interpreted. In this context, it is difficult to assess the extent to which WTO Members enjoy regulatory autonomy under the TBT Agreement. Nonetheless, it is possible to make a few comments on tobacco-labeling measures and bans on flavored cigarettes and alcopops.

In the context of tobacco-labeling measures, guidelines to Article 11 of the FCTC are likely to constitute international standards that will often establish a presumption of lawfulness. Partial guidelines for implementation of Articles 9 and 10 of the FCTC may also share this status.[91] Annex 1 to the TBT Agreement defines the term "standard" as a

> [d]ocument approved by a recognised body, that provides, for common and repeated use, rules, guidelines or characteristics for products or related processes and production methods, with which compliance is not mandatory. It may also include or deal exclusively with terminology, symbols, packaging, marking or labelling requirements as they apply to a product, process or production method.

[91] Report of Committee A (Draft), Conference of the Parties to the WHO Framework Convention on Tobacco Control, Fourth Session, Punta del Este, Uruguay 15 – 20 November 2010, (Draft) FCTC/COP/4/28, 20 November 2010.

This definition excludes those aspects of the FCTC that are mandatory. As such, the obligatory requirements of Article 11 of the FCTC would not constitute standards. In any case, the nonmandatory FCTC Guidelines on Packaging and Labeling of Tobacco Products set out what is arguably best practice in the field of tobacco control. The guidelines address design elements of health warnings such as the location, size, form, use of pictorials, colors, rotation of warnings, and message content. The guidelines also address a range of other issues, such as information on constituents and emissions and product-category considerations. Similarly, partial guidelines to Article 9 and 10 go further than the FCTC and recommend that FCTC parties "should regulate, by prohibiting or restricting, ingredients that may be used to increase palatability in tobacco products."[92]

It is not entirely clear how closely a measure would have to be related to a standard in order for it to be in accordance with it. The language in Article 2.5 differs from the language in the SPS Agreement, which refers either to measures being based on or conforming to international standards and from the language of Article 2.4, which refers to measures using standards as their basis. In that context, the panel in *EC – Sardines* held that an international standard will be considered to be the basis for a measure where the standard is used as the principal constituent or fundamental principle for the measure.[93] This concept is not easy to define in the abstract, but it is clear that where a measure is contradictory to a standard, it cannot be said that the measure uses the standard as its basis.[94] Similarly, at the very least, a measure contradictory to a standard could not be considered to be in accordance with it under Article 2.5.

However this test is applied, guidelines to Articles 9, 10 and 11 of the FCTC are likely to provide comfort to WTO Members. The guidelines are framed in permissive terms (as compared to guidelines that suggest certain types of measures should not be implemented) that may offer guidance in interpretation of the necessity requirement. The same might be said for the Global Strategy Alcohol,[95] although it is questionable whether the instrument is sufficiently specific to be considered an international standard. With respect to labeling, the instrument merely states that policy interventions include "providing consumer information about, and labeling alcoholic beverages

92 Ibid., para. 3.1.2.2(i).

93 Appellate Body Report, *EC – Sardines*, paras 243–245.

94 Ibid., para. 248.

95 The same might be said for the Global Strategy Diet, although for reasons discussed earlier, measures relating to food will ordinarily fall exclusively within the scope of the SPS Agreement, which has a closed definition of international standards, guidelines, or recommendations.

to indicate, the harm related to alcohol."[96] Equally, even general terms that encourage labeling measures or regulation of palatability might be sufficient to establish a presumption of lawfulness. Such terms may legitimize the use of labeling measures in the same way that the terms of the General Standard for Labeling of Prepackaged Food contemplate measures above and beyond those listed in that standard.

The other point of principle worth mentioning here is that the TBT Agreement grants a presumptive value to international standards, including private standards, but grants no value to mandatory requirements. In effect, this favors the use of private standards over public binding instruments (such as the FCTC) in application of the TBT Agreement. Although the FCTC has developed guidelines that alleviate this concern in the context of labeling, the preference attached to nonbinding standards under the TBT Agreement is worrying. The fact that industry-led private standards can be afforded such a status while extraneous treaty rules may not, suggests that the TBT Agreement is skewed in favor of private over public interests. This conclusion is only reinforced by the treatment of Article 31(3)(c) of the Vienna Convention by the panel in *EC – Approval and Marketing of Biotech Products*. The balance between instruments such as standards and extraneous treaties is discussed in further detail in Chapter 6.

Nonetheless, it seems likely that a clause encouraging FCTC parties to regulate ingredients used to increase the palatability of tobacco products, for example, would establish a presumption of necessity under Article 2 of the TBT Agreement in the case of measures restricting flavors. This may enhance policy space if measures are to be subjected to the type of necessity analysis undertaken pursuant to Article XX(b) of the GATT. The presence of FCTC guidelines would suggest that the regulatory objective is important and could lend credibility to arguments concerning the contribution of the measure to health protection. Equally, Article 2.2 provides that a panel should consider the risks that nonfulfillment of the objective would create, and that available scientific information should be considered in this context. If it is assumed that this factor is to be considered in determining necessity (as compared to determining whether a legitimate objective exists), this raises a question of what degree of evidence is required.

It will be recalled that under the GATT Article XX(b) test, it is only necessary to show that a measure makes a material contribution to the regulatory objective. By this, it is meant that there must be a genuine relationship of ends and means between the objective pursued and the measure at issue.

96 Global Strategy Alcohol, para. 36(f).

In contrast, Article 2.2 of the SPS Agreement requires that SPS measures be based on scientific principles and not maintained without sufficient scientific evidence, except where Article 5.7 applies. Thus, the requirement in the TBT Agreement is less demanding than the SPS Agreement, which requires a risk assessment; but the TBT Agreement still appears to invite a scientific approach to the presentation of a defense. Although there is a clear relationship of ends and means between restrictions on flavors (and prohibitions on alcopops) and preventing youth consumption or take-up, WTO Members would be wise to base their measures on other evidence. This might include ex ante studies or surveys, or an ex post analysis of the effects of a measure.

Much will also depend on the form of the measure and national health priorities. Differing consumer preferences in the territory of different WTO Members and the makeup of a tobacco market may be influential. This is particularly so where regulation is aimed at prohibiting products such as alcopops or flavored cigarettes, which initiate young people into tobacco consumption or drinking.

Much may also depend on the disparate impact of measures. For example, U.S. bans restrict clove cigarettes but exempt menthol. Canadian restrictions also exempt menthol, but prohibit flavorings that are used in blended-style cigarettes. Equally, these concerns relate more to questions of national treatment and could be argued under Article III:4 of the GATT or Article 2.1 of the TBT Agreement, rather than Article 2.2. In this respect, as Marceau and Trachtman have noted, there is no necessity exception to Article 2.1 in the TBT Agreement. It is therefore conceivable that a measure could violate Article III:4 of the GATT, be defensible under Article XX(b), but be prohibited by Article 2.1. This suggests that the requirements of Article 2.1 might be interpreted differently to the national-treatment standard in Article III:4 of the GATT. More specifically, the absence of an exception to Article 2.1 suggests that regulatory purpose may play a greater role in interpretation of that provision. This might be compared to the interpretation of the concept of national treatment in international investment law, where an exception is also absent.[97] An alternative view is that lawfulness would turn on whether Article XX of the GATT could cure a violation of Article 2.1, an issue discussed in Chapter 4.

The range of possible approaches also highlights how difficult it may be to predict whether a measure will be upheld. For example, the U.S. ban on flavored cigarettes might not withstand scrutiny under the *chapeau* of GATT Article XX(b) by virtue of the exemption for menthol cigarettes. On the other

[97] See generally Nicholas Di Mascio and Joost Pauwelyn, "Nondiscrimination in Trade and Investment Treaties: Worlds Apart or Two Sides of the Same Coin?" 102 *American Journal of International Law*, (2008), pp. 48–89.

hand, Article 2.2 lacks a provision comparable to the *chapeau*, and if regulatory purpose were to play a greater role under Article 2.1 than under GATT Article III, a violation may not arise.

Another source of unpredictability might lie in Article 2.8 of the TBT Agreement, which provides that "[w]herever appropriate, Members shall specify technical regulations based on product requirements in terms of performance rather than design or descriptive characteristics." The goal of this provision is to prevent government interventions that impose unnecessary adjustment costs. One commentary illustrates how the provision is intended to work in practice:

> enacting a regulation which states that *fire-proof doors* must be made from X or Y material does not meet the test of Art. 2.8 TBT (assuming it is feasible to enact such a regulation in terms of *performance requirements*); conversely, a regulation which states that *fire-proof doors* should be able to resist for 15 minutes when exposed to fire (assuming a certain measurement of temperature), *irrespective* of their production process, would meet this test.[98]

As this illustration suggests, Article 2.8 does not prevent WTO Members from regulating the palatability of tobacco products or alcoholic beverages. Rather, the provision merely governs the way that WTO Members go about such regulation. This can be illustrated through the tobacco case study. One way of framing restrictions on flavors is to restrict the presence of specific ingredients in tobacco products that give those products a particular flavor. For example, the presence of ingredients producing a strawberry flavor could be prohibited. This approach would specify a technical regulation based on the design or descriptive characteristics of a product, rather than based on the performance of the product. The question would, therefore, be whether it is appropriate to specify the technical regulation in terms of performance characteristics. For example, a WTO Member might prohibit tobacco products that produce the flavor or odor of strawberry. This would restrict flavored-tobacco products without necessarily restricting the use of specific ingredients or additives.

It remains to be seen whether the latter approach would be considered appropriate. From a regulatory standpoint, there are good reasons to specify the ingredients in question. The most obvious of these reasons is that the prohibition on specific ingredients is easier to administer than a prohibition that requires an individual determination of whether a product produces a prohibited flavor or odor. This may also be true in the case of fire doors, in the

[98] Petros Mavroidis, George Berman, and Mark Wu, *The Law of the World Trade Organization (WTO): Documents, Cases & Analysis*, West, (2010), p. 271.

sense that it is easier to require certain materials than to test compliance with a technical regulation. The key distinction between the two, however, is that determining whether a particular flavor is produced involves a degree of subjectivity that is not present in the context of fire doors. Whereas a fire door will either withstand a given temperature for a specified time or it will not, different decision makers may adopt different views on whether a particular flavor is produced by a tobacco product. For this reason, restricting the ingredients directly may be the only suitable means of restricting flavors.

The other circumstance in which it may not be appropriate to cast measures in the form of performance standards is where the flavor is not a characterizing flavor, but nonetheless contributes to the palatability of a tobacco product. In theory, it would be possible to elaborate a law prohibiting attempts to increase palatability, but such a law would prove very difficult to apply as a consequence of vagueness. For this type of measure, it is likely that a law restricting the presence of particular ingredients would comply with Article 2.8.

5. CONCLUSION

This chapter began by analyzing the scope of the SPS and TBT Agreements. It was concluded that some forms of dietary regulation aimed at reducing noncommunicable disease, such as food-labeling measures and bans on the sale of mutton flaps and turkey tails, may fall within the scope of the SPS Agreement. It was also concluded that tobacco-control measures of the type considered in this study and most alcohol-control measures fall outside the scope of the SPS Agreement. Equally, tobacco- and alcohol-control measures, such as labeling measures and product regulation falling outside the scope of the SPS Agreement, will be governed by the TBT Agreement.

This chapter then illustrated some differences between the necessity requirements in the SPS and TBT Agreements and the necessity test in Article XX(b) of the GATT, as well as how those differences affect measures to protect health. The most prominent of these differences lies in the positive character of the necessity requirements in the SPS and TBT Agreements as compared to the exceptional character of Article XX of the GATT. This positive (or obligatory) character is a shift from the GATT, where regulatory autonomy is shaped both by the reach of the prohibitions in provisions such as Articles III and XI as well as by the scope of the general exceptions in Article XX(b).

The obligatory character of the necessity requirement in the SPS and TBT Agreements reduces regulatory autonomy in the sense that every SPS measure and technical regulation may have to be justified as necessary. Equally, this conclusion is qualified in a number of ways. First, the analysis in Chapter 3 suggests that a wide array of facially nondiscriminatory health measures may inadvertently violate GATT prohibitions, meaning that justification under Article XX(b) may often be required. Second, the analysis of Article XX(b) of the GATT in Chapter 4 suggests that although a degree of unpredictability surrounds application of that provision, it offers a high degree of deference to domestic regulatory decisions. Third, the wording of each of the SPS and TBT Agreements suggests that the necessity requirements in those agreements are not stricter than those of the GATT and, in some respects, may be more deferential.

As is the case with the necessity test in Article XX(b) of the GATT, uncertainty is a significant source of concern. The meaning and effect of different provisions in the SPS and TBT Agreements is far from clear in many respects, and this undermines the ability of a national regulator to determine the lawfulness of a measure in advance of implementation. In addition to concerns about uncertainty, particular provisions may be problematic in the contexts of measures to address tobacco and diet.

Much has been written about the difficulty of complying with the requirement in Article 5.1 that SPS measures be based on a risk assessment. This literature need not be repeated here, other than to say that compliance may also be difficult in the present context. There is a particular risk that the requirements of Article 5.5 of the SPS Agreement could entrench regulatory paralysis in the context of food regulation. Although Article 5.5 is modeled on the *chapeau* of GATT Article XX and is not strictly speaking a requirement to maintain consistent approaches to risk, it is possible that regulatory experimentation and targeted interventions will fall afoul of Article 5.5. This provision ought to be interpreted in a manner sensitive to the difficulty that governments face in maintaining a consistent approach to dietary risks.

In the context of food labeling, questions also arise about the preference afforded to harmonization under Article 3 of the SPS Agreement. Leaving aside concerns about harmonization in a context in which states have differing nutritional profiles, it remains to be seen when a presumption of consistency with the SPS Agreement will be made.

The TBT Agreement is also a source of uncertainty. The case studies examined were restrictions on flavored-tobacco products and restrictions on the sale of alcopops. The existence of a national-treatment requirement in Article 2.1 of the TBT Agreement in the apparent absence of a health exception could be problematic given the discussion of national treatment in Chapter 3. Similarly, it remains to be seen how the preference afforded to performance standards in Article 2.8 will be interpreted in the context of the measures in question.

6

Reallocating Authority at the International Level: Delegation, Legalization, and Harmonization

Chapters 2–5 of this study focused on the substantive rules governing the balancing of trade and health under WTO law. However, prior to this study, a number of law reform proposals have been made with the intention of addressing the implications of WTO law for public health in the tobacco, alcohol, and dietary contexts. These proposals either explicitly or implicitly concern questions of institutional choice and the allocation of authority. This chapter examines the merits of these proposals in three parts by reference to the concepts of delegation, legalization, and harmonization.

Part 1 examines the issue of delegation, which encompasses the questions of who should make decisions about the lawfulness of public health measures, as well as whether balancing mechanisms should be further theorized so as to minimize the discretion held by delegated authorities such as the WTO Dispute Settlement Body (DSB). In this respect, tobacco-control advocates have argued for the so-called exclusion of tobacco and tobacco products from the scope of trade agreements. This proposal suggests that a specific set of rules should be created in order to theorize the relationship between trade and tobacco control in a more complete manner than the balancing mechanisms found in the WTO-covered agreements.

Part 2 examines the issue of international legalization. Legalization concerns whether international public health instruments should take on binding forms, as in the case of the FCTC, in order to balance out the effects of the trade regime. Public health groups have advocated this approach. For example, during public consultations concerning the Global Strategy Diet, civil society groups argued for the conclusion of a treaty modeled on the FCTC.[1] Public health advocates have also argued for the conclusion of a framework

[1] Global Strategy on Diet, Physical Activity and Health, Meeting with Civil Society and Non-Governmental Organisations, Geneva, 17 May 2003, World Health Organization.

convention on alcohol control.[2] These proposals envisage a shift from nonbinding instruments to instruments that are legally binding under international law. These proposals also contemplate use of legal instruments as a means of counterbalancing the WTO Agreement. In this respect, the foreword to the FCTC suggests that the treaty was created to act as a counterweight to processes of trade liberalization, such as those associated with the WTO Agreement. The foreword states:

> The WHO FCTC was developed in response to the globalization of the tobacco epidemic. The spread of the tobacco epidemic is facilitated through a variety of complex factors with cross-border effects, including trade liberalization and direct foreign investment.

In examining legalization, this chapter surveys the literature on the advantages and disadvantages of nonbinding as compared to binding norms. The analysis then draws on Chapter 2 in examining the differences that nonbinding and binding instruments may have in terms of balancing the need for regulatory autonomy with the values underlying the WTO Agreement. Finally, part 2 examines whether the FCTC can truly be construed as a response to trade processes, or whether conclusion of the FCTC might be a response to other collective-action problems.

Part 3 then addresses the merits of further international harmonization as a means of balancing regulatory autonomy with the interests underlying the trade regime. Some commentators have argued for further harmonization, particularly in the dietary context.[3] This approach has been viewed both as a means of cementing the lawfulness of various measures under the SPS and TBT Agreements as well as an alternative to binding international agreements. The presumptions of lawfulness in Article 2.5 of the TBT Agreement and Article 3.2 of the SPS Agreement suggest that harmonization might enhance regulatory autonomy while also easing barriers to trade.

In addressing further harmonization, part 3 returns to the question of how WTO law relates to other treaty regimes. This issue, which was addressed

[2] See Donald Zeigler, "International Trade Agreements Challenge Tobacco and Alcohol Control Policies," 25 *Drug and Alcohol Review*, (November 2006), pp. 567–579, p. 577; Robin Room, "International Control of Alcohol: Alternative Paths Forward," 25 *Drug and Alcohol Review*, (November 2006), pp. 581–595; Sally Casswell and Thaksaphon Thamarangsi, "Reducing Harm From Alcohol: Call to Action," 373 *Lancet*, (2009), pp. 2247–2257.

[3] Roger Magnusson, "Non-Communicable Diseases and Global Health Governance: Enhancing Global Processes to Improve Health Development," 3(2) *Globalization and Health*, (2007), p. 12 [hereinafter Magnusson, "Non-Communicable Diseases and Global Health Governance"].

in Chapter 2, is revisited in light of the presumptive value afforded to international standards under the SPS and TBT Agreements. It is argued that, barring amendment of the WTO Agreement to alter the status of extraneous treaties, in certain circumstances, extraneous treaties should also be afforded presumptive value in application of the covered agreements. This argument flows from the presumption against conflict, which serves as the starting point in analysis of how different treaties relate to one another.

In weighing the issues associated with delegation, legalization, and harmonization, it is argued in this chapter that the preferable approach is to pursue changes that do not upset the structure of the WTO Agreement. It is better to pursue legalization and harmonization than to attempt to make significant changes to well-established rules relating to delegation within the WTO. Although legalization and harmonization are not without their own difficulties, they offer avenues through which the interests underlying both trade and health can be balanced as public health regulation develops.

The approaches discussed in this chapter are also guided by political reality. In Chapters 2–5, various suggestions have been made concerning how the covered agreements should be interpreted. Although some of these suggestions are likely to be controversial, they each seek to work within the existing legal framework and to minimize challenges to the authority and legitimacy of the WTO. The suggestions made in his chapter also seek to work within the existing legal framework while guiding application of WTO law in a way that promotes outcomes that reflect a reasonable balance between the interests undergirding trade and health.

Ultimately, this approach views the roles of legalization and harmonization as means of filling out the open-textured character of WTO balancing mechanisms. In terms of public international law, this approach is intended to minimize fragmentation by enhancing normative integration. This is also consistent with the need to address public health's own fragmentation dilemma, known as global health governance. Put another way, the fragmentation of roles and responsibilities within the field of global health, without proper coordination and integration, is seen as a challenge to public health itself.[4]

4 See, for example, Obijiofor Aginam, *Global Health Governance: International Law and Public Health in a Divided World*, Toronto, University of Toronto Press, (2005); Lawrence O. Gostin, "Meeting Basic Survival Needs of the World's Least Healthy People toward a Framework Convention on Global Health," 96 *Georgetown Law Journal*, (2008), pp. 331–392.

1. DELEGATION

As demonstrated in Chapters 2–5, the status quo is such that the WTO DSB is delegated power to determine the lawfulness and, therefore, legitimacy of public health measures in a trade context. WTO panels and the Appellate Body also have a high degree of discretion in terms of their decision making. There is significant uncertainty with respect to how each of the provisions discussed in Chapters 2–5 may be interpreted. The phrases "less favourable treatment" and "so as to afford protection" remain elusive in the context of hard cases despite their centrality to the GATT. The distinction between behind-the-border internal regulations and border measures restricting market access is also not entirely clear under the GATT or GATS. Similarly, application of the necessity test in Article XX(b) of the GATT is heavily dependent on the discretion of a panel. Much also remains unknown about application of the SPS and TBT Agreements. Although recent case law suggests a highly deferential approach on questions of necessity, this uncertainty, in the hands of the WTO DSB, raises two questions about delegation. The first question concerns who should be delegated the power to make decisions about the lawfulness and legitimacy of domestic health measures. The second question is whether the uncertainty associated with the WTO-covered agreements could be remedied by a more complete theorization of the relevant rules.

1.1. *Who Should Make the Decisions?*

The delegation of decision-making power concerning the pursuit of a range of social objectives to the WTO DSB is at the heart of what is often referred to as the WTO's legitimacy crisis.[5] Critics of the WTO have argued that it is inappropriate for a panel of trade policy experts to be delegated the task of evaluating the relative merits of measures designed to achieve domestic public health goals.[6] These critics would view procedural mechanisms available to a panel, such as the ability to seek expert advice, as inadequate to remedy the lack of expertise and legitimacy of panels. Critics might even argue that the WTO's legitimacy crisis is exacerbated by the application of the same procedural mechanisms in a way that largely excludes civil society participation in dispute resolution, such as through the submission of *amicus curiae* briefs.

5 See generally, Daniel Esty, "The World Trade Organization's Legitimacy Crisis," 1(1) *World Trade Review*, (2002), pp. 7–22.

6 Similar arguments have been made with respect to trade and the environment. For a summary, see Carlos Correa, "Implementing National Public Health Policies in the Framework of WTO Agreements," 34(5) *Journal of World Trade*, (2000), pp. 89–121, p. 110.

Underlying this position is the principle of subsidiarity, a principle of institutional choice that suggests that decisions should be made at the lowest level of government capable of addressing a problem.

However, it is important to view the allocation of authority to the WTO DSB within a broader context. In their study on genetically modified organisms, Mark Pollack and Greg Shaffer identified a variety of different approaches to the allocation of authority in the context of dispute resolution. Pollack and Shaffer argued that a panel might

(a) interpret agreements so as to show a great deal of deference to domestic decision makers;
(b) perform a stringent review under a relatively clear rule (such as a presumptive rule that product bans are unlawful), in effect, allocating decision making to the market;
(c) interpret agreements so as to allocate decision making to an international political process, such as the Codex Alimentarius Commission;
(d) make substantive decisions itself by engaging in the type of weighing and balancing undertaken in the necessity test; or
(e) attempt to focus on the procedural legitimacy of a measure rather than its substantive legitimacy.[7]

Although Pollack and Shaffer were analyzing the way in which the panel's decision in *EC – Biotech Products* would allocate authority at the international level, the analysis is indicative of alternative approaches to delegation. The analysis in Chapters 1–5 suggests that a variety of these approaches to allocating authority may be used, depending on the circumstances. The decision in *Brazil – Retreaded Tyres* suggests that panels may engage in some substantive weighing and balancing but show a great deal of deference to domestic decision makers. The analysis of the SPS Agreement in Chapter 4 suggests that standard-setting bodies may also be allocated significant authority. Finally, analysis of the *chapeau* of Article XX of the GATT suggests that the procedural legitimacy associated with a measure also plays a role in decision making but is not the sole focus. Depending on which of these approaches is adopted and how it is applied, the delegation of authority to a panel may interfere with domestic regulatory autonomy to differing degrees. Put another way, the analysis offered by Pollack and Shaffer shows that the extent to which domestic regulatory autonomy is interfered with depends partly on how allocated power is exercised and not simply on the type of body that wields power.

7 Mark Pollack and Greg Shaffer, *When Cooperation Fails: The International Law and Politics of Genetically Modified Foods*, New York, Oxford University Press, (2009), pp. 205–206.

There is some merit to criticisms leveled at the role of the WTO DSB as an arbiter of the regulatory legitimacy of public health measures. However, when the analysis in Chapters 1–5 is viewed in light of the framework developed by Pollack and Shaffer, it is apparent that the DSB has often exercised its power in a restrained manner. The DSB does make substantive decisions through weighing and balancing, but it has shown significant deference in its interpretation of the necessity test. If anything, the weighing and balancing approach appears to have increased judicial deference to domestic policy choices. In some contexts, the rules also allocate decision-making authority to political bodies such as standard-setting bodies, and it is arguable that the deference shown in necessity analysis makes procedural issues the new focus of dispute settlement. For example, it might be said that the *chapeau* of Article XX of the GATT now plays a more important role than prior to the elaboration of the weighing and balancing test. Similarly, SPS disputes have tended to focus on the relationship between a measure and a risk assessment rather than on the substantive necessity requirement (although this may be contrary to the urgings of the Appellate Body).

On the other hand, the way in which the panel in *EC – Biotech Products* interpreted Article 31(3)(c) of the Vienna Convention shows a reluctance to cede authority in the context of other treaties. The way in which the WTO DSB has allocated authority back to WTO Members also does not remedy concerns about expertise and the capacity of a trade-law panel to make decisions about health measures. Critics of the WTO might also be more concerned with national sovereignty than they are with the actual identity of an international decision maker.[8] Thus, there are two concerns: one about the allocation of authority to trade experts rather than health experts, and another about allocation of authority to international bodies. It seems unlikely, however, that WTO Members would accept a shift away from decision making at the international level. Given the potential for states to backslide on the commitments they make under the WTO Agreement, some form of compulsory dispute resolution is necessary to ensure the credibility of those commitments.[9] Similarly, it seems unlikely that WTO Members would accept some formal shift of authority (that is not contemplated in existing WTO rules) away from the DSB to an international health authority. Although small changes can be made, such as the use of expert groups as consultants to a

8 See Wenhua Shan, Penelope Simmons, and Dalvinder Singh, *Redefining Sovereignty in International Economic Law*, Oxford, Hart Publishing, (2008).

9 For a more detailed argument, see Pierre Sauvé and Americo Beviglia Zampetti, "Subsidiarity Perspectives on the New Agenda," 3(1) *Journal of International Economic Law*, (2000), 83–114.

WTO panel,[10] exploration of whether the WTO DSB should be stripped of its decision-making powers is not likely to be a particularly fruitful exercise in terms of the development of international law.

This leaves one approach to delegation that is worth exploring, which is whether the substantive rules can be theorized in a more complete way so as to reflect the specific circumstances of tobacco, alcohol, and diet.

1.2. *Can the Relevant Rules Be Theorized in a More Complete Manner?*

One objection to the type of balancing tests discussed in Chapters 4 and 5 is that domestic regulators require clear answers and a reasonable degree of certainty before a measure will be implemented. Deferential practice by panels and the Appellate Body is subject to change and is inherently unpredictable, suggesting a need to create new mechanisms to replace the incompletely theorized balancing mechanisms found in provisions such as Article XX(b) of the GATT.

From the outset, the international political value of a rather vague balancing mechanism such as Article XX(b) must be recognized. Cass Sunstein has argued that incompletely theorized agreements are an important means by which lawmakers reach consensus that might not otherwise be achieved.[11] In this vein, it is often possible to reach agreement on general principles, but not possible to agree on how those general principles apply to individual circumstances. This is arguably the case in the context of the WTO-covered agreements. Some general principles govern the lawfulness of individual health measures, but rules governing specific types of health measures have not been negotiated. One possible exception to this is in the context of access to medicines and the TRIPS Agreement, in which specific rules have been negotiated.[12] Another partial exception to this conclusion might be found in the role of international standards, guidelines, and recommendations concluded under the auspices of bodies such as the Codex Alimentarius Commission. Although these instruments are not definitive of the lawfulness of specific

[10] Alberto Alemanno, "The Dialogue Between Judges and Experts in the EU and WTO," in Filippo Fontanelli, Giuseppe Martinico, and Paolo Carrozza, (eds), *Shaping Rule of Law Through Dialogue: International and Supranational Experiences*, Groningen, Europa Law Publishing, (2010), 345–373.

[11] See generally, Cass Sunstein, *Legal Reasoning and Political Conflict*, New York, Oxford University Press, (1996).

[12] See, for example, World Trade Organization, "Doha Ministerial 2001, Declaration on the TRIPS Agreement and Public Health" (adopted on November 14, 2001); Decision of the General Council of 30 August 2003 (Implementation of paragraph 6 of the Doha Declaration on the TRIPS Agreement and public health).

health measures, they do offer guidance and, arguably, some comfort to WTO Members.

Leaving these partial exceptions aside, regulatory diversity and differing market-access interests offer explanations for why WTO Members would take this approach. In writing about determinacy in law (as an aspect of legitimacy) Thomas Franck took a similar position to Sunstein. Franck argued that "[s]ome degree of indeterminacy is inevitable in any body of rules and, as noted, it may even have its uses in promoting agreement and achieving flexibility."[13] Franck referred to the issue as being the difference between an "idiot rule" and a "sophist rule." In Franck's terms, an idiot rule is a simple and utterly clear rule, whereas a sophist rule is less obvious in its operation and might, for example, set out general standards that then need to be applied to individual cases. In Franck's view, a sophist rule, "in the absence of a legitimate, impartial interpreter, is likely to be perceived as illegitimate because it can be made to appear to permit anything."[14] On the other hand, an idiot rule risks being so strict in its application that it causes "irrationality, unfairness or perceived incoherence at the fringes of its application."[15]

The difficulty associated with striking a balance between rules that are sufficiently certain in their outcome while also being coherent (both internally and in their relations with external rules) is an issue underlying discussion of the relationship between trade and health. On the one hand, reliance on Article XX(b)–type balancing provisions does not guarantee specific outcomes and, as noted, the legitimacy of WTO panels is open to question. On the other hand, creating rules that do guarantee specific outcomes could pose problems in terms of policy coherence. This tension can be illustrated by reference to two options that have been proposed in the context of tobacco control. Tobacco-control advocates have argued for the so-called exclusion of tobacco from trade agreements, and the possibility of a waiver for tobacco-control measures has also been discussed. These options serve as useful case studies to highlight the difficulties associated with completely theorizing the relationship between WTO law and measures to address tobacco, alcohol, and diet.

A. Case study: the "exclusion" of tobacco from trade agreements

The position most commonly articulated within the tobacco-control community is that tobacco and tobacco products should be excluded from bilateral

[13] Thomas Franck, *The Power of Legitimacy Among Nations*, New York, Oxford University Press, (1990), p. 53 [hereinafter Franck, *The Power of Legitimacy Among Nations*].

[14] Ibid., p. 83.

[15] Ibid.

and multilateral trade agreements.[16] For example, Callard, Chitanondh, and Weissman have argued that "[i]n the international trade agreement frameworks, tobacco and tobacco products should be specifically excluded" and that "[c]ountries should not have to subject their tobacco control regulations to the WTO or other trade agreement screens."[17]

In a conceptual sense, the benefits of exclusion might be twofold. First, exclusion ought to protect tobacco-control measures from exposure to the provisions of trade agreements that restrict the use of nontariff barriers to trade. Second, because trade agreements may prompt liberalization of tobacco markets, the exclusion of tobacco from trade agreements may minimize the possibility of liberalization stimulating tobacco consumption.[18]

However, it is fairly clear that the policy of exclusion prioritizes tobacco control over international trade without seeking to preserve the benefits of trade or trade agreements. This not only undermines the development of coherence between the two regimes but could also lead to unwanted consequences. For example, the exclusion of "tobacco products" from nontariff commitments would permit trade-distorting laws irrespective of whether they have a public health rationale. Although it may not always be possible to preserve the rationales underlying international trade and tobacco control completely, a policy of exclusion fails to recognize any potential benefit from further liberalization of the tobacco sector and also fails to recognize potential losses or costs associated with protectionism. Complete theorization of this type would, therefore, cause incoherence, a conclusion consistent with Franck's analysis.

Further support for this conclusion is found in the way in which the concept of exclusion has been defined by its proponents. Callard, Chitanondh, and Weissman, for example, express the proposal as being "to exclude and

[16] See, for example, C. Callard, H. Chitanondh, and R Weissman, "Why Trade and Investment Liberalisation May Threaten Effective Tobacco Control Efforts," 10 *Tobacco Control*, (2001), pp. 68–70 [hereinafter Callard, Chitanondh, and Weissman, "Trade and Investment Liberalisation"]; William Onzivu, "The Public Health Implications of the Association of South East Asian Nations (ASEAN) Legal Regime on Tobacco Control," 4(2) *Australian Journal of Asian Law*, (2002), pp. 160–187, p. 168; Robert Weissman, International trade agreements and tobacco control: threats to public health and the case for excluding tobacco from trade agreements, November 2003, v 2.0 available at http://www.fctc.org/x/cd/documents/EA_trade_backgrd.pdf (visited 26/11/07) [hereinafter Weissman, The Case for Excluding Tobacco].

[17] Callard, Chitanondh, and Weissman, "Trade and Investment Liberalisation," p. 69; This proposal has found support in at least one trade agreement, albeit temporarily. The Pacific Island Countries Trade Agreement (Done at Nauru August 18, 2001) excluded tobacco and alcohol from its terms, albeit not on a permanent basis.

[18] It should be noted that not all acts of trade liberalisation will occur as a result of trade agreements.

remove tobacco and tobacco products from bilateral and multilateral trade agreements that would have negative public health consequences."[19] By the same token, they appear to view all trade agreements as having such negative public health consequences. Writing separately, Weissman has proposed a more specific formulation of exclusion. He argues that "[t]here is no technical difficulty in exempting tobacco from trade agreements – a simple declaration that the agreement does not apply to tobacco products, in words no more complicated than those, would be sufficient."[20] Based on this conclusion, he proposes that trade agreements should contain a carve-out to the effect that "[n]othing in this Agreement shall be construed to apply in any way to tobacco products."[21]

There are, however, two problems with these broad formulations. First, the proposal is not necessarily in the interests of public health, because the exclusion of tobacco in such a broad fashion would also prevent the use of trade agreements to the benefit of public health. For example, such a broad definition would prevent the use of trade agreements to address domestic support in the tobacco sector wherever it has the effect of suppressing the price of tobacco products and thereby stimulating consumption.[22]

Second, to apply the proposal of exclusion only to tobacco and tobacco products does not completely protect tobacco-control measures from challenges based on provisions governing the use of nontariff barriers to trade. Disputes could arise in relation to associated goods or services. For example, in the case of an advertising ban, claims could be brought under the GATT in relation to advertising as a good where it is a physical product or combines to constitute a physical product,[23] or under the GATS in relation to the supply of services. To be effective, the exclusion of tobacco products would also have to encompass "associated goods and services." This approach would further undermine coherence by permitting trade-distorting laws in relation to such goods and services, again, where there is not necessarily a health rationale supporting the measure.

19 Callard, Chitanondh, and Weissman, "Trade and Investment Liberalisation," p. 68.

20 Weissman, "The Case for Excluding Tobacco," p. 28.

21 Ibid.

22 On domestic support see P. Zhang and C. Husten, "Impact of the Tobacco Price Support Program on tobacco control in the United States," 7 *Tobacco Control*, (1998), pp. 176–182; K. Warner, "The Economics of Tobacco: Myths and Realities," 9 *Tobacco Control*, (2000), pp. 78–89; "Projections of Tobacco Production Consumption and Trade to the year 2010," Food and Agriculture Organisation of the United Nations, Rome 2003, p. 1, available at http://www.fao.org/DOCREP/006/Y4956E/Y4956E00.HTM (visited 26/11/07).

23 Appellate Body Report, *Canada – Certain Measures Concerning Periodicals*, WT/DS31/AB/R, adopted 30 July 1997, DSR 1997:I, 449, pp. 17–19.

Equally, there are exceptions in the GATT that grant WTO Members greater discretion than the general exceptions in Article XX. As Weissman has pointed out, the security exceptions in Article XXI give WTO Members a discretion that is not present in Article XX. The relevant part of Article XXI provides that nothing in the GATT shall be construed "to prevent any contracting party from taking any action which it considers necessary for the protection of its essential security interests." The scope of this exception is then limited by reference to specific classes of goods, such as fissionable materials and traffic in arms.

Although the form of Article XXI differs from Weissman's call for "exclusion," the provision does suggest an alternate model of delegation whereby each WTO Member is allocated the authority to restrict trade in goods where the member itself considers it necessary for a given purpose. Under Franck's analysis, this type of rule would be an idiot rule because it could cause irrationality, unfairness, and incoherence. By placing the decision-making power in the hands of the WTO Member implementing the measure, this approach would support the use of measures that are not necessary for the protection of human health. In fact, an exception of this type would give almost unquestioned precedence to public health over the policies underlying trade agreements.

B. Case study: the grant of a waiver

Werner Meng has argued that the grant of a waiver may be one means of coordinating the FCTC and WTO Agreement.[24] This argument appears to be prompted by the fact that in 2003 the WTO Ministerial Conference granted a waiver with respect to so-called conflict diamonds.[25] That decision waived Articles I:1, XI:1, and XIII:1 of the GATT with respect to measures set out in the Kimberly Process Certification Scheme, which include restrictions on the importation of diamonds from nonparticipating states.[26]

[24] Werner Meng, "Conflicting Rules in the WHO FCTC and Their Impact," in Thomas Cottier, Joost Pauwelyn, and Elisabeth Burgi Bonanomi (eds), *Human Rights and International Trade*, New York, Oxford University Press, (2005), pp. 334–339, [hereinafter Meng, "Conflicting Rules in the WHO FCTC"], p. 337; see also Allyn Taylor, "Trade, Human Rights and the WHO Framework Convention on Tobacco Control: Just What the Doctor Ordered?" in Thomas Cottier, Joost Pauwelyn, and Elisabeth Burgi Bonanomi (eds), *Human Rights and International Trade*, New York, Oxford University Press, (2005), pp. 322–344.

[25] Referring to Waiver Concerning Kimberly Process Certification Scheme for Rough Diamonds, Council for Trade in Goods, 24 February 2003, World Trade Organization, G/C/W/432/Rev.1 (03–1136); see also Joost Pauwelyn, "WTO Compassion or Superiority Complex?: What to make of the WTO Waiver for 'Conflict Diamonds,'" 24 *Michigan Journal of International Law*, (2003), pp. 1177–1207.

[26] See http://www.kimberleyprocess.com/ (visited 26/11/07).

In the WTO context, waivers are governed by Article IX:3 of the WTO Agreement, Article XXV of the GATT, and the Guiding Principles to Article XXV.[27] Article IX:3 provides that the Ministerial Conference may decide to waive a WTO obligation in "exceptional circumstances," and sets out the rules governing decision making with respect to waivers. Article XXV sets out similar requirements in respect of the GATT system, and the Guiding Principles further elaborate on that provision. Paragraph (c) of the Guiding Principles provides that, in general, the contracting parties "should not grant an application in cases where they are not satisfied that the legitimate interests of other contracting parties are adequately safeguarded." It is also noteworthy that waivers granted by the Ministerial Conference under Article IX of the WTO Agreement are intended to be temporary in nature.[28] This is reflected in Article IX:4 of the WTO Agreement, which provides that waivers should be the subject of annual review in order to determine whether the exceptional circumstances justifying their grant continue to exist. Although a waiver might be used on an ongoing basis, this approach is not contemplated in the text of the WTO Agreement.

The grant of a waiver is also a procedural mechanism that says nothing of the substantive obligations to be waived. Meng himself recognizes this in concluding that the difficulty in determining the merits of a waiver lie in determining its potential content. Meng dismisses the grant of a waiver that would exempt or exclude tobacco trade entirely from the WTO Agreement on the basis that it would "remove the subject of concealed protectionism that the Thailand cigarettes panel was confronted with from the control of WTO law."[29] However, rather than formulating an alternative approach, Meng proposes the consideration of two options.

Meng argues that the rules "about the standard of risk assessment should be coordinated,"[30] and that in this respect, rules "for the protection of health should be balanced with property concerns in order to coordinate the regulations with human rights concerns."[31] This suggestion says little, however,

[27] Article XXV – Guiding Principles to be Followed by the Contracting Parties in Considering Applications for Waivers from Part I or Other Important Obligations of the Agreement, Adopted on 1 November 1956 (BISD 5S/25) available at http://www.worldtradelaw.net/misc/waiverprinciples.pdf (visited 02/10/2007).

[28] Hunter Nottage and Thomas Sebastian, "Giving Legal Effect to the Results of WTO Trade Negotiations: An Analysis of the Methods of Changing WTO Law," 9(4) *Journal of International Economic Law*, (2006), pp. 989–1016, [hereinafter Nottage and Sebastian, "Giving Legal Effect"], p. 1002.

[29] Meng, "Conflicting Rules in the WHO FCTC," p. 337.

[30] Ibid., p. 338.

[31] Ibid., p. 338.

concerning the substance of a waiver, and is little more than a suggestion that a waiver should balance the benefits of trade with the protection of health.

Meng has also argued that any waiver may have to be augmented by equivalent rules in the FCTC.[32] In particular, Meng has argued that the possibility of protectionist-type abuse of the right to protect health should be addressed, possibly by the use of a rule equivalent to the *chapeau* of Article XX of the GATT.[33] However, during the negotiation of the FCTC the parties considered the inclusion of wording to the effect that "trade policy measures for tobacco control purposes should not constitute a means of arbitrary or unjustifiable discrimination or a disguised restriction on international trade."[34] This wording was ultimately not acceptable to a number of FCTC parties and was deleted.

Although there is theoretical merit to the positive coordination of the two regimes, there are a number of problems with seeking to build an obligation into the FCTC to replace any obligation that might be waived. The most obvious problem is that the substantive law governing the relationship between trade and tobacco control would not be altered by shifting WTO obligations into the domain of the FCTC. Rather, the same obligations would merely apply to a different set of parties and would be subject to different rules governing dispute settlement.

C. Conclusion on "completely theorizing" the relationship

In recognizing that the ultimate question in considering the merits of a waiver lies in its substance, Meng alludes to the difficulty associated with completely theorizing the relationship between trade and health. On the one hand, policies such as the "exclusion" of tobacco from trade agreements disregard the potential benefits of trade. This reflects the difficulty associated with maintaining policy coherence while theorizing the legal relationship completely.

Notwithstanding the pervasive uncertainty associated with provisions such as Article XX(b) of the GATT, it does not appear possible to completely theorize the relationship between trade and health while maintaining policy coherence. Rather, it appears that the law is ultimately best served by

32 Ibid., p. 337.

33 Ibid., p. 338.

34 World Health Organization, Proposed Draft Elements for a WHO Framework Convention on Tobacco Control: Provisional Texts with Comments of the Working Group, Intergovernmental Negotiating body of the WHO Framework Convention on Tobacco Control, First Session, Provisional Agenda 8, A/FCTC/INB1/2, 26 July 2000, p. 9, available at www.who.int/gb/fctc/ (visited 6/2/04).

incremental development through dispute settlement, rather than through an all-encompassing attempt to theorize the relationship between trade and health. In this way, some delegation to the WTO DSB can be viewed as the best means of addressing the difficulty of theorizing the relationship in a complete manner. This approach also reflects the fact that it is not possible to take account of all future possibilities. It is not possible to envisage all of the different public health challenges that WTO Members may face, all of the different ways in which WTO Members might implement a measure to address those challenges, or the possible implications of all measures for the trade regime.

The difficulty associated with "completely theorizing" the relationship between trade and tobacco control is equally applicable in other health contexts. This difficulty is also one explanation for the reliance placed on harmonization in the SPS and TBT Agreements. In those contexts, harmonization acts as something of a mid-point between the decision-making authority of the DSB and complete theorization. Although international standards, guidelines, and recommendations theorize the action that WTO Members might take on a certain issue, they do so without the consequences associated with using blunt rules that seek to define the exact scope of regulatory autonomy. Hence, although the conclusions drawn previously concerning complete theorization may be obvious, they highlight the role and importance of extraneous instruments in filling out the balancing tests found in WTO law. With this in mind, the discussion now turns to international legalization and harmonization.

2. INTERNATIONAL LEGALIZATION

In calling for the conclusion of treaties to address diet and harmful alcohol use, public health advocates have assumed that the binding form of the FCTC is preferable to the nonbinding form of instruments, such as the global strategies. This can be examined from a number of different perspectives. First, there is a body of commentary on the relative benefits of nonbinding instruments as compared to binding instruments, including with respect to questions of compliance and effectiveness. Second, the analysis in Chapter 2 suggests that there are some distinctions under the law of treaties between how the binding norms of the FCTC might interact with WTO law as compared to the nonbinding content of an instrument like the global strategies. Third, it is worth examining the reasons underlying the conclusion of the FCTC in greater detail to determine whether it truly was concluded as a response to processes of trade liberalization.

2.1. *Binding and Nonbinding Instruments*

Perhaps the primary attraction to the conclusion of binding instruments in the contexts of diet and alcohol is the prospect of embedding public health interventionism in the international system. Restraints on intervention are embedded in WTO law partly through provisions governing nontariff barriers to trade. Public health interventions must be justified against the backdrop of rules that favor noninterventionism (even if preventing government intervention is not the stated purpose of those rules). In addition, others such as David Fidler have argued that the political objectives associated with trade agreements, such as national security, economic power, and international order, dwarf public health concerns such as those relating to obesity.[35] In this context, further international legalization in the public health context might be viewed as a means to embed public health interventionism in international law.

In public health circles, there is also an impression that the FCTC legitimized tobacco control in a way that has ended debates about the efficacy and legitimacy of the basic measures included in the treaty. This impression is consistent with constructivist theories of international relations that suggest the international system can shape the interests of states, and that interests may be ideational or identity based, rather than founded on rational self-interest. Accepting this impression for the sake of argument, legalization might give similar prominence, legitimacy, and momentum to regulation in the contexts of diet and alcohol. Although this may be the case, Chapters 2–5 focused on questions of regulatory autonomy and not on the separate question of how international law might be best used to protect public health. The latter question involves a far broader project than that encompassed by this study. Accordingly, legalization is examined here in terms of whether and how the conclusion of binding legal norms might affect regulatory autonomy.

By the same token, there is a rich body of literature, from both law and political science, examining the merits of legalization and the circumstances in which states agree to formalize their relations through international law. Much of the legal literature addresses the concept of so-called soft law as distinct from hard law. The distinction between these concepts will not be taken up in detail here. Nor will the phrases "soft law" or "hard law" be adopted. As Christine Chinkin has argued, "[t]here is a wide diversity in the instruments of

35 David Fidler, "The Impact of International Trade and Investment Rules on the Ability of Governments to Implement Interventions to Address Obesity: A Case Study on the European Charter on Counteracting Obesity," in Hawkes et al., *Trade, Food, Diet and Health: Perspectives and Policy Options*, Wiley Blackwell, (2010), pp. 279–297, p. 280.

so-called soft law which makes the generic term a misleading simplification."[36] In the present context, the question at hand simply concerns the merits of using nonbinding international instruments as compared to binding international instruments in the form of treaties. This is not to suggest that binding treaties are the only form of international legalization,[37] or that nonbinding instruments might not be incorporated into law either domestically or by reference.[38] Rather, this approach is adopted largely because of the binding model provided by the FCTC and its potential application in the contexts of diet and alcohol.

There are a number of factors that might be taken into account in determining the merits of a nonbinding instrument as compared to a binding treaty. Without doubt, binding treaties have some advantages, such as through the application of the law of treaties, including the presumption against conflict. Binding treaties may also have some less formal advantages, such as dissuading WTO Members from initiating disputes. Similarly, it has been argued that a framework convention on alcohol control would create an "institutionalised forum for cooperation and negotiation" that might not exist in the context of a nonbinding instrument.[39]

Equally, it should not be assumed that binding instruments necessarily lead states to make deeper commitments in terms of substance. Some commentators even describe treaty obligations that take the form of very general obligations as a type of soft law.[40] Kenneth Abbott and Duncan Snidal have examined instruments in terms of their "bindingness" by reference to the extent of obligation, precision, and delegation (such as delegation to a judicial body through a dispute resolution mechanism).[41] Similarly, Kal Raustiala has examined the relationship between the form and substance of international treaties, concluding that treaties often reflect a balance between the depth of substantive commitments and the extent of oversight by monitoring or judicial bodies.[42] George Downs and others have also argued that compliance

[36] Christine Chinkin, "The Challenge of Soft Law: Development and Change in International Law," 38 *International and Comparative Law Quarterly*, (1989), pp. 850–866, p. 850.

[37] See discussion in Martha Finnemore and Stephen Toope, "Alternatives to 'Legalization': Richer Views of Law and Politics," 55(3) *International Organization*, (Summer 2001), pp. 743–758.

[38] Chinkin, "The Challenge of Soft Law," p. 859.

[39] Casswell and Thamarangsi, "Reducing Harm From Alcohol," p. 2254.

[40] R. Baxter, "International Law in her Infinite Variety," 29 *International and Comparative Law Quarterly*, (1980), pp. 549–566.

[41] Kenneth Abbot and Duncan Snidal, "Hard and Soft Law in International Governance," 54(3) *International Organization*, (Summer 2000), pp. 421–456.

[42] Kal Raustiala, "Form and Substance in International Agreements," 99 *American Journal of International Law*, (2005), pp. 581–615.

with treaty commitments does not necessarily say anything about the extent to which a treaty has improved cooperation between states parties. For example, where states merely commit to do things that they are already doing, the commitment may not be particularly meaningful in terms of policy change.[43]

The FCTC contains many shallow commitments that for the most part are not particularly precise, and the treaty contains a weak mechanism for dispute resolution. Article 6 of the FCTC (price and tax measures to reduce demand for tobacco) provides an example of a shallow commitment. Parties are not obliged to harmonize taxes (which may minimize incentives for illicit trade) or to ensure that taxes internalize external costs associated with tobacco consumption. Rather, the most relevant part of the provision is highly discretionary in character. Article 6.2 states:

> 2. Without prejudice to the sovereign right of the Parties to determine and establish their taxation policies, each Party should take account of its national health objectives concerning tobacco control and adopt or maintain, as appropriate, measures which may include:
> (a) implementing tax policies and, where appropriate, price policies, on tobacco products so as to contribute to the health objectives aimed at reducing tobacco consumption; and
> (b) prohibiting or restricting, as appropriate, sales to and/or importations by international travellers of tax- and duty-free tobacco products.

Similarly, Article 13 of the FCTC (tobacco advertising promotion and sponsorship) provides an example of a central obligation that is not particularly precise. Article 13.2 requires that "[e]ach Party shall, in accordance with its constitution or constitutional principles, undertake a comprehensive ban of all tobacco advertising, promotion and sponsorship." What constitutes a comprehensive ban is not apparent from the text of the FCTC itself.

Article 27 of the FCTC also reflects a rather shallow commitment to dispute resolution. Article 27.2 permits parties to accept as compulsory, "ad hoc arbitration in accordance with procedures to be adopted by consensus by the Conference of the Parties."

This brief analysis is not to suggest that the FCTC is a weak instrument. On the contrary, the nature of a framework convention is such that the treaty text is composed of general terms that are supplemented by further guidelines and optional protocols. For example, the Conference of the Parties to the

[43] George Downs, David Rocke, and Peter Barsoom, "Is the Good News about Compliance Good News about Cooperation?" 50(3) *International Organization*, (Summer 1996), pp. 379–406.

FCTC has elaborated guidelines to the implementation of Article 13 (tobacco advertising promotion and sponsorship), which guide interpretation of that provision. These guidelines are intended to reflect best practice, consistent with the idea that states may be more likely to make a deep statement about regulatory best practice in a nonbinding instrument.[44]

Whether such a relationship between the depth of a commitment and bindingness exists is a matter for empirical study that is beyond the scope of this chapter. Nonetheless, it has been possible to observe the existence of such a relationship in the negotiation of FCTC guidelines. The nonbinding character of guidelines has been invoked by FCTC parties as a reason not to open discussion of the content of draft guidelines presented to the Conference of the Parties for adoption. This is also consistent with the fairly common argument that nonbinding instruments are easier to achieve than binding ones.[45]

Where such a relationship exists between the depth of a possible obligation and the bindingness of an instrument, this will have implications for the role that an instrument might play in interpretation of WTO law. For example, if states are only prepared to agree to very general terms in a binding commitment but are prepared to set out best-practice regulation in a nonbinding guideline, it may be that the nonbinding guideline offers more hope that public health practice will be taken into account in WTO dispute resolution. This is also consistent with Broude's theory that nonbinding approaches to interpretation are less threatening to the adjudicative authority of WTO panels.

Nonbinding instruments may also be less threatening where there is a significant divergence among the views of states.[46] This issue was discussed in Chapter 5 in the context of diet, in which it was noted that for nutritional, cultural, and other reasons, WHO member-states stressed the need for flexibility in the Global Strategy Diet.

A related justification for the use of nonbinding instruments is that they may constitute a stepping stone to further legalization. For example, a nonbinding instrument might raise domestic regulatory standards and propel a subsequent process of treaty making by making the need for closer cooperation between states more apparent.[47] In this sense, a nonbinding agreement, such as a global strategy, should not necessarily be viewed as an alternative

44 Although it is argued in Chapter 2 that FCTC guidelines may be a subsequent agreement of the parties, in concluding the guidelines the Conference of the Parties to the FCTC addressed the issue strictly as a question of whether the guidelines were binding or not.

45 Abbott and Snidal, "Hard and Soft Law," p. 423.

46 Ibid., p. 445.

47 Ibid., pp. 446–447.

to a binding instrument.[48] In addition to these processes, as the discussion in Chapter 2 illustrated, nonbinding instruments enter into the body of law through their use in treaty interpretation.

Another factor that may weigh in favor of the use of nonbinding instruments is the need to engage nonstate actors.[49] For example, the Global Strategy Diet directs recommendations toward the private sector as well as toward states. Equally, this point should not be overstated. There is no reason that nonbinding instruments directed at nonstate actors cannot be associated with a binding treaty, such as a framework convention. Similarly, it is often argued that nonbinding instruments are easier to amend than treaties,[50] and it has been argued that this supports experimental responses as new situations arise.[51] In light of the need for regulatory experimentation in areas such as diet, this type of flexibility may be important. As in the case of nonstate actors, however, there is no reason why binding and nonbinding instruments cannot be combined in an effective manner, as is arguably the case in the context of the FCTC.

In summary, it should not simply be assumed that binding international instruments are superior to nonbinding instruments. In particular, where the form of the chosen instrument affects its content, this may have implications for the use of an instrument in interpretation of WTO law. It may well be the case that nonbinding instruments offer a superior means of normative integration where the terms of such instruments are quite precise and reflect best practice in relation to public health. Although it was argued in Chapter 2 that Article 31(3)(c) imposes a broad and special obligation on decision makers in the context of treaty rules, the panel in *EC – Approval and Marketing of Biotech Products* did not interpret Article 31(3)(c) in this way. By the same token, the FCTC is also illustrative of an approach that combines binding norms in the treaty text with guidelines that, on their own, do not bind parties.

48 Wolfgang Reinicke and Jan Martin Witte, "Challenges to the International Legal System: Interdependence, Globalization, and Sovereignty: The Role of Non-Binding International Legal Accords," in Dinah Shelton (ed), *Commitment and Compliance: The Role of Non-Binding Norms in the International Legal System*, New York, Oxford University Press, (2000), p. 76.

49 Christine Chinkin, "Normative Development in the International Legal System," in Shelton, *Commitment and Compliance*, pp. 21–42, p. 30; in the specific context of diet, see Derek Yach, Corinna Hawkes, Joanne Epping Jordan et al., "The World Health Organization's Framework Convention on Tobacco Control: Implications for Global Epidemics of Food-Related Deaths and Disease," 24 *Journal of Public Health Policy*, (2003), pp. 274–290, p. 274.

50 See, for example, Charles Lipson, "Why are some Agreements Informal?" 45(4) *International Organization*, (Autumn 1991), pp. 495–538, p. 501.

51 Mary Ellen O'Connell, "The Role of Soft Law in a Global Order," in Shelton, *Commitment and Compliance*, pp. 100–114, p.110.

2.2. *Conflicts between Treaties*

The law of treaties does not apply to nonbinding international instruments such as the global strategies. Accordingly, one of the apparent advantages of legalization through binding treaties is the prospect of using a conflicts clause to establish the legal relationship between different instruments. Although this type of clause applies in the event that two treaty provisions cannot be reconciled, it is worthwhile to examine conflicts clauses for two reasons. First, examination of the prospect of conflicts between the FCTC and WTO Agreement completes the analysis of regulatory autonomy in the tobacco-control context. Second, and more important for present purposes, the potential role of conflicts clauses weighs on the merits of legalization. In particular, the fact that the law of treaties does not apply to nonbinding instruments arguably creates a legal hierarchy of interests in favor of the interests underlying the trade regime at the expense of those underlying public health. This may also send signals to policy makers about the relative importance of different policies. With this in mind, it is worth examining application of the law of treaties to conflicts clauses.

There are a number of principles reflected in Article 30 of the Vienna Convention that are widely accepted as reflecting customary international law.[52] Such principles include *lex prior* (the principle that where an express statement concerning the relationship with another treaty is included, that statement will be given effect), *lex posterior* (the treaty later in time prevails to the extent of any inconsistency), and the principle of seeking the legislative intent of the parties.[53] It is also widely accepted that the three requirements that must be fulfilled in order for a conflict to exist under customary international law are the overlap of subject matter, overlap of parties, and overlap of both of these elements at the relevant point in time. In this respect, Article 30 states:

Article 30

Application of successive treaties relating to the same subject-matter

1. Subject to Article 103 of the Charter of the United Nations, the rights and obligations of States parties to successive treaties relating to the same subject-matter shall be determined in accordance with the following paragraphs.

[52] On Article 30 generally see Fragmentation of International Law: Difficulties Arising from the Diversification and Expansion of International Law, Report of the Study Group of the International Law Commission, Finalized by Martii Koskenniemi, International Law Commission, Fifty-eighth Session, Geneva, 1 May–9 June and 3 July–11 August 2006, A/CN.4/L.682, 13 April 2006 [hereinafter Koskenniemi, Fragmentation of International Law], paras 251–266.

[53] Ian Sinclair, *The Vienna Convention on the Law of Treaties*, Manchester, Manchester University Press, 2nd ed., (1984), p. 96.

2. When a treaty specifies that it is subject to, or that it is not to be considered as incompatible with, an earlier or later treaty, the provisions of that other treaty prevail.
3. When all the parties to the earlier treaty are parties also to the later treaty but the earlier treaty is not terminated or suspended in operation under article 59, the earlier treaty applies only to the extent that its provisions are compatible with those of the latter treaty.
4. When the parties to the later treaty do not include all the parties to the earlier one:
   (a) as between States parties to both treaties the same rule applies as in paragraph 3;
   (b) as between a State party to both treaties and a State party to only one of the treaties, the treaty to which both States are parties governs their mutual rights and obligations.
5. Paragraph 4 is without prejudice to article 41, or to any question of the termination or suspension of the operation of a treaty under article 60 or to any question of responsibility which may arise for a State from the conclusion or application of a treaty the provisions of which are incompatible with its obligations towards another State under another treaty.

Article 30 does not necessarily set out all customary international law governing the resolution of conflicts. As Ian Sinclair argued, "Article 30 of the Vienna Convention is in many respects not entirely satisfactory," and "this is an area where State practice is continually developing, and where it may possibly have been premature to seek to establish fixed guidelines (through the codification of custom as the Vienna Convention)."[54] This conclusion is discussed in further detail by reference to the maxim of *lex specialis*.

A. The express language of the FCTC and WTO Agreement

As is apparent from Article 30(2) of the Vienna Convention, the first issue for consideration is whether the treaties themselves govern the issue through express language. Article 2 of the FCTC governs its relations with other treaties. It states:

Article 2
Relationship between this Convention and other agreements and legal Instruments

1. In order to better protect human health, Parties are encouraged to implement measures beyond those required by this Convention and its protocols, and nothing in these instruments shall prevent a Party from imposing stricter requirements that are consistent with their provisions and are in accordance with international law.

[54] Ibid., p. 98.

2. The provisions of the Convention and its protocols shall in no way affect the right of Parties to enter into bilateral or multilateral agreements, including regional or subregional agreements, on issues relevant or additional to the Convention and its protocols, provided that such agreements are compatible with their obligations under the Convention and its protocols. The Parties concerned shall communicate such agreements to the Conference of the Parties through the Secretariat.

There are two notable aspects of this provision. First, it is silent on the question of the relationship between the FCTC and other instruments or agreements concluded prior to it (such as the WTO Agreement). The consequence of this is that the matter is governed by rules of customary international law.

Second, in respect of agreements or instruments concluded after the FCTC, Article 2.2 provides that the FCTC does not affect the rights of parties to conclude such agreements provided that they are compatible with the obligations of those parties under the Convention and its protocols. This type of provision seeks to "guarantee the normative power of the earlier treaty"[55] and acts as an exception to the *lex posterior* rule. This provision serves "to resolve a possible conflict between an earlier treaty and a later treaty in favour of the earlier treaty."[56] Thus, the express language of the FCTC means that the FCTC should prevail in the event of a conflict with a treaty concluded later in time than it.

In contrast to the FCTC, the WTO Agreement contains provisions governing conflicts between WTO-covered agreements, but does not include any express language governing relations between the WTO Agreement and other treaties such as the FCTC. In light of this, relations between the WTO Agreement and the FCTC are governed by the terms of the FCTC and customary rules, such as those in Article 30.[57]

B. Overlapping subject matter

Of the three elements, the question of when treaties relate to the same subject matter is most often contentious. As Pauwelyn has argued, treaties will necessarily relate to the same subject matter when they conflict.[58] For this reason

55 Koskenniemi, Fragmentation of International Law, p. 135, para. 268.

56 Hans Aufrict, "Supersession of Treaties in International Law," 37 *Cornell Law Quarterly*, (1951–1952), pp. 655–700, pp. 666–667.

57 See generally Joost Pauwelyn, "The Role of Public International Law in the WTO: How Far Can We Go?" 95 *American Journal of International Law*, (2001), pp. 535–578; in respect of arguments relating to the impact of this on MFN principles, see the discussion in Chapter 2 with respect to Article 31(3)(c).

58 Joost Pauwelyn, *Conflict of Norms in Public International Law: How WTO Law Relates to Other Rules of International Law*, New York, Cambridge University Press, (2003), p. 365 [hereinafter Pauwelyn, *Conflict of Norms*].

(and to avoid confusion) the notion of treaties relating to the same subject matter is used here interchangeably with the term "conflict."[59]

There exist both narrow and broad views on the question of when treaties conflict. Wilfred Jenks first expressed the narrow view, stating that "a conflict in the strict sense of incompatibility arises only where a party to the two treaties cannot simultaneously comply with its obligations under both treaties."[60] However, there are at least three problems with the narrow view. First, this view resolves conflicts between rights and obligations by automatically preferring obligations over rights.[61] That is, under the narrow view, a right cannot conflict with an obligation because the party entitled to the right may comply with its obligations by not exercising the right.

Second, the narrow view does not recognize a conflict in circumstances in which it is possible to comply with the two norms in question. Pauwelyn gives the example of two divergent obligations with respect to copyright protection in which one obligation obliges protection for a period of forty years whereas the other obliges protection for fifty years.[62] In this situation, a conflict cannot arise under the narrow view because it is possible to comply with both of these norms by protecting copyright for fifty years. It is perhaps these problems with the narrow view that Jenks was referring to when he recognized that a divergence between treaties falling short of a conflict may nonetheless defeat the object of one or both of the treaties in question and "may from a practical point of view be as serious as a conflict."[63]

In response to these problems, a number of commentators have argued in favor of broader formulations of the concept of conflicts.[64] Pauwelyn has identified four situations in which a conflict or overlap of subject matter may occur between treaties.[65] These include:

1. a command in a given situation that state A "shall do" X conflicts with a command in the same situation that state A "shall do Y" (Y being either different from or mutually exclusive with X);
2. a command in a given situation that state A "shall do" X conflicts with a prohibition in the same situation that state A "shall not do X";

[59] See also Koskenniemi, Fragmentation of International Law, p. 17 where Article 30 is treated within the broader concept of "conflicts."

[60] Wilfred Jenks, "Conflict of Law-Making Treaties," 30 *British Year Book of International Law*, (1953), pp. 401–453, p. 426 [hereinafter Jenks, "Conflict of Law-Making Treaties"].

[61] Pauwelyn, *Conflict of Norms*, 188.

[62] Ibid., pp 180 – 181.

[63] Jenks, "Conflict of Law-Making Treaties," p. 426

[64] For a summary of the literature, see Pauwelyn, *Conflict of Norms*, pp. 166–169.

[65] Ibid., p. 179.

3. a command in a given situation that state A "shall do" X conflicts with a right (exemption) in the same situation that state A "need not do" X (it may for example, do Y); and
4. a prohibition in a given situation that state A "shall not do" X conflicts with a right (permission) that in the same situation that state A "may do" X.

More recently, Koskenniemi has advocated a "wide notion of conflict as a situation where two rules or principles suggest different ways of dealing with a problem."[66] In addition, Erich Vranes, in his study on the application of legal theory to the question of conflicts under international law, has argued that the definition of norm conflict should read: "There is a conflict between two norms, *one of which may be permissive*, if in obeying or applying one norm, the other one is necessarily or possibly prohibited."[67]

Whereas case law tends to support the narrow view, whether rights and obligations may conflict has not received significant attention. Within the context of the WTO-covered agreements, conflicts between these agreements are governed by the General Interpretive note to Annex 1A, which states:

> In the event of conflict between a provision of the [GATT] and a provision of another agreement in Annex 1A to the Agreement establishing the World Trade Organisation (referred to in the agreements in Annex 1A as the "WTO Agreement"), the provision of the other agreement shall prevail to the extent of the conflict.

In applying this provision, the panel in *EC – Bananas III* defined conflict as encompassing

> (i) clashes between obligations contained in GATT 1994 and obligations contained in agreements listed in Annex 1A, where those obligations are mutually exclusive in the sense that a Member cannot comply with both obligations at the same time, and (ii) the situation where a rule in one agreement prohibits what a rule in another agreement explicitly permits.[68]

This decision has been criticized on the basis that the panel did not need to consider the interpretive note in order to resolve the dispute in

[66] Koskenniemi, Fragmentation of International Law, para. 25.

[67] Erich Vranes, "The Definition of 'Norm Conflict' in International Law and Legal Theory," 17(2) *European Journal of International Law*, (2006), pp. 395–418, p. 415 (emphasis in original).

[68] Panel Report, *European Communities – Regime for the Importation, Sale and Distribution of Bananas, Complaint by the United States*, WT/DS27/R/USA, adopted 25 September 1997, modified by Appellate Body Report, WT/DS27/AB/R, DSR 1997:II, 943, para. 7.159.

question.[69] Nonetheless, the decision supports a broader view of the concept of conflict concerning the relations between different WTO-covered agreements. However, in *Guatemala – Cement* the Appellate Body adopted what appears to be a narrow formulation of conflict. The Appellate Body stated that provisions must be "mutually inconsistent" in order for a conflict to arise, and that this will only be the case where "adherence to one provision will lead to violation of the other."[70]

The panel reports in *Indonesia – Autos*[71] and *Turkey – Textiles*[72] also favored the narrow approach. In *Indonesia – Autos* the panel considered the report in *EC – Bananas III*, and in particular the proposition that an express permission could conflict with a right. The panel stated:

> [N]either the Bananas III panel nor Indonesia cites any support for the proposition that a "conflict," within the meaning of public international law, can exist in a situation where a rule in one agreement explicitly permits what a rule in another agreement prohibits. The absence of any citation is due to the fact that the rule under public international law is clear: a conflict exists only in situations where obligations are mutually exclusive; i.e., "when two (or more) treaty instruments contain obligations which cannot be complied with simultaneously."[footnote omitted][73]

In drawing this conclusion, the panel quoted the work of Karl.[74] This is problematic for at least two reasons. First, Vranes argues that Karl, in his main work on the subject, adopted the broader definition of conflict advocated by Engisch,[75] which is translated by Vranes as existing

> 1) if conduct of a given type is at the same time prohibited and permitted, or prohibited and prescribed, or prescribed and not prescribed in a given legal

[69] Gabrielle Marceau, "Conflicts of Norms and Conflicts of Jurisdictions: The Relationship between the WTO Agreement and MEAs and other Treaties," 35(6) *Journal of World Trade* (2001), pp. 1081–1132 p. 1085.

[70] Appellate Body Report, *Guatemala – Anti-Dumping Investigation Regarding Portland Cement from Mexico*, WT/DS60/AB/R, adopted 25 November 1998, DSR 1998:IX, 3767, paras 65–66; in respect of norms of competence, see also Vranes, "The Definition of 'Norm Conflict' in International Law and Theory," pp. 415 – 418.

[71] Panel Report, *Indonesia – Certain Measures Affecting the Automobile Industry*, WT/DS54/R, WT/DS55/R, WT/DS59/R, WT/DS64/R and Corr.1, 2, 3, and 4, adopted 23 July 1998, DSR 1998:VI, 2201.

[72] Panel Report, *Turkey – Restrictions on Imports of Textile and Clothing Products*, WT/DS34/R, adopted 19 November 1999, modified by Appellate Body Report, WT/DS34/AB/R, DSR 1999:VI, 2363 [hereinafter *Turkey – Textiles*].

[73] Panel Report, *Indonesia – Autos*, para. 5.344.

[74] The panel quoted Karl, "Conflicts between Treaties," in R. Bernhardt (ed.), *Encyclopaedia of Public International Law*, Amsterdam, North-Holland Pub Co, (1984), p. 468.

[75] Erich Vranes, "The Definition of 'Norm Conflict' in International Law and Legal Theory," p. 402.

> order. Or if incompatible ways of conduct are prescribed at the same time … 2) if a concrete conduct appears at the same time to be prohibited and permitted etc in a given legal order.[76]

Second, it is problematic to attach so much weight to any one particular commentary on a topic of public international law where an issue is contentious. More particularly, in attaching significance to commentary it must be emphasized that the international law commission took the broad view in the formulation of Article 30 of the Vienna Convention. That is, Article 30(1) and 30(4)(b) of the Vienna Convention refer to the "rights and obligations" of parties.[77]

Subsequent to *Indonesia – Autos*, the panel in *Turkey – Textiles* considered the definition of conflict under public international law. That panel placed express reliance on the definition given by Jenks, stating:

> [A] conflict of law-making treaties arises only where simultaneous compliance with the obligations of different instruments is impossible.… There is no conflict if the obligations of one instrument are stricter than, but not incompatible with, those of another, or if it is possible to comply with the obligations of one instrument by refraining from exercising a privilege or discretion accorded by another.[78]

Of course, the express reliance by the panel on Jenks in the absence of further reasoning means that *Turkey – Textiles* does not add to the issue other than by expressing support for this position.

In a break from this limited concept of conflict, the panel in *US – Upland Cotton* endorsed a broader view. The panel had to consider the effect of Article 21.1 of the Agreement on Agriculture, which states, "[t]he provisions of GATT 1994 and of other Multilateral Trade Agreements in Annex 1A to the WTO Agreement shall apply subject to the provisions of this Agreement." The panel identified a number of different circumstances in which this clause might have effect, including in the case of "an explicit authorisation in the text of the *Agreement on Agriculture* that would authorise a measure that, in the absence of such an express authorisation, would be prohibited by Article 3.1(b) of the *SCM Agreement*."[79] This contemplates the possibility that a permissive provision or a right may conflict with an obligation.

[76] See ibid., p. 406, fn 67.

[77] Pauwelyn, *Conflict of Norms*, pp. 171–172.

[78] Panel Report, *Turkey – Textiles*, para. 9.92 quoting Jenks, "Conflict of Law-Making Treaties," pp. 426–427.

[79] Panel Report, *United States – Subsidies on Upland Cotton*, WT/DS267/R, and Corr.1, adopted 21 March 2005, modified by Appellate Body Report, WT/DS267/AB/R, para. 7.1038.

As the previous discussion outlines, significant uncertainty with respect to the definition of conflict exists under international law. To some extent, this uncertainty is not problematic for the purposes of this case study because there are only two types of conflicts that are likely to arise between the FCTC and trade agreements. First, conflicts within "Category 2" of Pauwelyn's framework may arise. The FCTC sets out a number of obligations to regulate tobacco. These obligations are command-type obligations in the mould of "state A shall do X." In contrast, the WTO-covered agreements and other trade agreements contain negative commands that prohibit parties from engaging in specified conduct. These negative commands are in the mould of "state A shall not do X." As such, it ought to be expected that potential conflicts between FCTC obligations and trade obligations may arise in the form of "Category 2" conflicts. Because a conflict under "Category 2" falls within both the narrow and broad approaches to defining conflict, it is not necessary to adopt a position on which of these approaches is correct in order to resolve a conflict of this type.

Second, it is possible that "Category 4" conflicts may arise between the FCTC and trade agreements. It was stated that WTO obligations fall within the mould of "state A shall not do X" type of obligations. FCTC obligations may also fall within the category of rights or permissive statements such as "state A may do X." An example of such a statement is found in Article 13.7 of the FCTC, where it is stated:

> 7. Parties which have a ban on certain forms of tobacco advertising, promotion and sponsorship have the sovereign right to ban those forms of cross-border tobacco advertising, promotion and sponsorship entering their territory and to impose equal penalties as those applicable to domestic advertising, promotion and sponsorship originating from their territory in accordance with their national law. This paragraph does not endorse or approve of any particular penalty.

The extent to which Article 13.7 of the FCTC will conflict with trade agreements may be dependent on whether advertising bans of the type described are protected by provisions such as Article XX(b) of the GATT and Article XIV(b) of the GATS. For present purposes, however, it is sufficient to note that the potential for conflicts between FCTC rights (or permissive statements) and the prohibitive content of trade agreements does exist. It is also notable that Article 13.7 appears to anticipate uncertainty about whether FCTC parties can ban the entry of advertising to their territory, a concern that might have arisen by virtue of the WTO Agreement.

The better view under the law of treaties appears to be that it is possible for rights of this type to conflict with obligations under international law. This approach is adopted in the language of Article 30 of the Vienna Convention. Similarly, despite a perception that the narrow approach is the prevailing view,[80] the majority of commentary supports a broader definition of conflict.[81] Most important, as Vranes has argued, any rule governing conflicts has a purpose that is not fulfilled adequately if the utility of rights and permissive statements is undermined by the manner in which conflict is itself defined.[82]

Notwithstanding this conclusion, it appears possible that WTO panels are likely to adopt a narrower view of conflict. Although panels have only considered conflicts between WTO-covered agreements, they have relied on public international law concepts in order to resolve the issues and have shown a clear preference toward the narrow view. Whether the Appellate Body will adopt the same approach remains to be seen. In this respect, it is arguable that decision makers are naturally inclined to prefer the full application of the system of law granting their authority.[83]

C. Overlapping parties

The combined effect of Article 30(3) and Article 30(4) is that where two states are engaged in a dispute, they must both have been parties to the relevant treaties at the time of the alleged breach in order for the rules governing the resolution of conflicts to apply. For example, where one disputant is a party to the FCTC and another is not, it is not possible for the rules governing conflicts to apply to the legal relations between those members in a WTO dispute.

D. Timing

At first glance, the question of which treaty is first in time appears not to be important in the context of the FCTC and WTO Agreement. That is, if the FCTC is later in time, it appears to be protected by the rule of *lex posterior* as set out in Article 30 of the Vienna Convention. In addition, if the WTO Agreement is later in time, the effect of Article 2 of the FCTC is that the FCTC prevails in the event of conflict. This conclusion is, however, complicated by limitations on the use of the *lex posterior* rule that stem from the difficulty associated with putting a "time label" on a treaty.

The test to be applied in determining which of two treaties is the first in time is not settled. The dominant view is that the date of the adoption of the

80 See, for example, Vranes, "The Definition of 'Norm Conflict' in International Law and Legal Theory," p. 395.

81 In this respect, see the summary in Pauwelyn, *Conflict of Norms*, pp. 166–169.

82 On the telos of defining conflicts, see generally Vranes, "The Definition of 'Norm Conflict' in International Law and Legal Theory."

83 See generally Marceau, "Conflicts of Norms and Conflicts of Jurisdictions."

treaty is the relevant point in time for the purposes of Article 30.[84] However, this principle is qualified. As Sinclair states, "the rules laid down in Article 30 have effect for each individual party to a treaty only as from the date of entry into force of the treaty for that party."[85] As such, the date of ratification is the more appropriate date to apply where both states were not party to a treaty from its entry into force.

This is problematic where states have ratified treaties in a different order than the order in which the treaties were concluded. For example, if disputants ratified the FCTC prior to the WTO Agreement, the WTO Agreement would be later in time despite being concluded prior to the FCTC. Similarly, the issue becomes more complicated where disputants have ratified treaties in a different order to one another. For example, the application of Article 30 is problematic if one party were to have ratified the FCTC prior to the WTO Agreement and the other had ratified the WTO Agreement prior to the FCTC.[86]

As a result of the difficulties associated with putting a time label on a treaty, it will not always be possible to apply the *lex posterior* rule. Rather, the circumstances may be such that the rule does not reflect the legislative intent of the parties. This is one reason underlying the need to consider other rules such as *lex specialis* in order to resolve a conflict.

E. How will any conflict be resolved?

The previous analysis addressed the question of when a conflict will arise. This question is separate from the question of how any such conflict will be resolved, which concerns the question of which treaty prevails in the event of conflict.

(a) THE APPROACH

Although the use of the principle of *lex posterior* is no longer controversial, the notion that it should be applied in a strict fashion, as suggested by the text of Article 30, is questionable.[87] The rule of *lex posterior* is an application of the broader principle that requires a treaty interpreter to seek to determine the legislative intent of the parties. As an application of this broader principle, Article 30 is subject to limitations that are not apparent from the text of the provision. For

84 For a summary of this commentary see Koskenniemi, Fragmentation of International Law, p. 120, para. 232.

85 Ibid.

86 See E.W. Vierdag, "The Time of the 'Conclusion' of a Multilateral Treaty," 59 *British Year Book of International Law*, (1988), pp. 75–112, p. 102.

87 See generally Pauwelyn, *Conflict of Norms*, pp. 367–409; Koskenniemi, Fragmentation of International Law, paras 223–266.

example, in addition to complications with respect to time labels, difficulties arise with respect to the question of legislative intent where the treaty contexts and parties involved are not the same,[88] as is the case with the WTO and the FCTC.

Two consequences stem from these problems. First, in terms of Article 30, one treaty cannot be considered to be "successive" to another under Article 30 simply because it is concluded later in time.[89] Where circumstances suggest that the legislative intent of the parties cannot be derived from the mere fact that one treaty was concluded later than another, the rule in Article 30 may not apply. Second, the fact that the rule of *lex posterior* cannot solve all conflicts means that other methods of conflict resolution must be applied. The rule of *lex specialis derogat legi generali* (specific law derogates from general law) is the most prominent of these interpretive methods. This rule has long had a place in international law[90] and is also used to identify the legislative intention of the parties.[91] As Pauwelyn argues, a "WTO obligation not to restrict trade, *irrespective of the product involved*, must be seen as *less specific* than an obligation (or permission) to restrict trade *in the specific products* A *and* B (which are, for example, labeled harmful)."[92] That is, it is most likely that any elements of the FCTC that compel a violation of a WTO-covered agreement will be considered more specific than the WTO obligations in question.

(b) DISCERNING THE LEGISLATIVE INTENT IN LIGHT OF SUPPLEMENTARY MATERIALS

The question of the relationship between the FCTC and the WTO Agreement was the subject of significant debate during FCTC negotiations, and three distinct proposals were made.

At the first session of negotiations it was proposed that the following provision be included in the convention: "[T]rade policy measures for tobacco control purposes should not constitute a means of arbitrary or unjustifiable discrimination or a disguised restriction on international trade."[93]

88 See generally Pauwelyn, *Conflict of Norms*, p. 368.
89 See ibid., pp. 385–409.
90 See generally, Koskenniemi, Fragmentation of International Law, paras 46–87.
91 Pauwelyn, *Conflict of Norms*, p. 388; see also Koskenniemi, Fragmentation of International Law, for discussion of the legitimacy of the rule from a nonvoluntary perspective.
92 Pauwelyn, *Conflict of Norms*, p. 389 (emphasis in original).
93 World Health Organization, Proposed Draft Elements for a WHO Framework Convention on Tobacco Control: Provisional Texts with Comments of the Working Group, Intergovernmental Negotiating Body of the WHO Framework Convention on Tobacco Control, First session, Provisional Agenda 8, A/FCTC/INB1/2, 26 July 2000, p. 9 available at www.who.int/gb/fctc/ (visited 6/2/04).

During the fourth session of negotiations it was proposed that the following guiding principle should constitute part of the text of the FCTC:

> Priority should be given to measures taken to protect public health when tobacco control measures contained in this Convention and its protocols are examined for compatibility with other international agreements.[94]

During the fifth session a provision governing the relationship between the FCTC and other agreements and legal instruments was inserted into the Chair's text of the draft. That provision provided that "[n]othing in this convention and in its related protocols shall be interpreted as implying in any way a change in rights and obligations of a Party under any existing treaty."[95]

The three proposals and the eventual silence of the FCTC on the issue all reflected different approaches. The position proposed at the first session represented an attempt to balance the interests of trade and public health by obliging parties to the FCTC not to use tobacco-control measures in a discriminatory fashion. The position considered at the fourth session was intended to ensure that the terms of the FCTC prevail over existing trade agreements in the event of conflict. In contrast, the position considered at the fifth session represented the view that preexisting trade obligations should not be altered by the conclusion of the FCTC.

The extent to which a decision maker might rely on this drafting history in determining the outcome of a conflict is unclear. The drafting history of the FCTC suggests that the law of treaties, as reflected in Article 30 of the Vienna Convention, is not a predictable or reliable route by which to resolve differences between the FCTC and the WTO Agreement.

(c) CONCLUSION ON THE CURRENT RELATIONSHIP

The operation of the law of treaties is such that the FCTC has a high degree of protection from the WTO Agreement in the event of conflict between the two treaties. Article 2 of the FCTC, the rule of *lex posterior* and the rule of *lex specialis*, appear likely to resolve conflicts in favor of the FCTC.

94 World Health Organization, Co-Chairs' Working Papers: final revisions, Working Group 2, Intergovernmental Negotiating Body of the WHO Framework Convention on Tobacco Control, Fourth Session, Provisional Agenda item 4, A/FCTC/INB4/2(a), 24 January 2002, p. 3 available at www.who.int/gb/fctc/ (visited 6/2/04).

95 World Health Organization, New Chair's Text of a Framework Convention on Tobacco Control, Intergovernmental Negotiating Body of the WHO Framework Convention on Tobacco Control, Fifth Session, A/FCTC/INB5/2, 25 June 2002, Article 2(3), p.4, available at www.who.int/gb/fctc/ (visited 6/2/04).

The limitations on this conclusion, such as the rule that the FCTC cannot bind nonparties, and uncertainty with respect to how the rules might be applied are inherent to the law of treaties itself.

The manner in which a conflict will be resolved is not, however, the end of the matter. Rather, the question of how a conflict is defined (and, therefore, when a conflict will arise) is also central to the relationship between the WTO Agreement and the FCTC. In this respect, there are limitations on when conflicts between FCTC obligations and WTO prohibitions will occur. Similarly, it is not entirely clear that FCTC rights or permissions will be held to be capable of conflicting with WTO prohibitions. These limitations restrict application of Article 2 of the FCTC and the *lex posterior* and *lex specialis* rules.

With respect to conflicts between obligations and prohibitions, it appears that the FCTC will only offer protection to tobacco-control measures where the aspect of those measures in violation of the WTO-covered agreements is either compelled or permitted by the FCTC. As such, the FCTC would only appear to offer protection in circumstances where the WTO Agreement necessarily prohibits the possibility of a WTO Member from implementing a particular measure.

In terms of the FCTC and the WTO Agreement, the analysis points to a complex relationship that can be guided by some fundamental principles but that defies simplification. The nature of the law of treaties means that there is no one universally applicable answer to the question of how conflicts will be resolved. These conclusions also suggest that conflicts clauses may not be a particularly compelling reason to seek legalization in the contexts of diet and alcohol. Not only do these clauses not seek to reconcile different interests, but there are some significant limitations on the role that the law of treaties could play in resolving legal conflicts between the WTO Agreement and future treaties. In theory, conflicts clauses could be drafted to overcome many of these problems. All but the requirement that there be an overlap of parties could be addressed through the manner in which a clause is drafted. However, it is this requirement that is most likely to be problematic, because a dispute appears more likely to arise between two WTO Members where the complainant is a nonparty to the relevant public health instrument. In addition, the FCTC experience shows the political difficulties of negotiating a clause that would favor treaties other than the WTO Agreement. There is also likely to be an underlying institutional reluctance on the part of WTO panels to conclude that an extraneous treaty prevails over the WTO Agreement.

2.3. *Treaties as a Response to Trade Processes*

The foreword to the FCTC describes the treaty as a response to the globalization of the tobacco epidemic, including trade liberalization. In Chapter 1, the potential impacts of trade liberalization on consumption patterns and the flow-on effects for health were outlined. This description of how trade relates to public health suggested that the indirect impacts of trade policy on consumer preferences is as much an issue in the contexts of alcohol and diet as it is in the context of tobacco. Similarly, in Chapters 3, 4, and 5, questions of regulatory autonomy were examined, and it was concluded that concerns about regulatory autonomy are just as applicable in the alcohol and dietary contexts as in the tobacco context. Accordingly, it might be argued that treaties are also necessary in these contexts in order to respond to trade processes.

Such an argument would take the foreword to the FCTC at face value and assume that other factors were not at work. Contrary to this assumption, however, disagreement concerning inclusion of a conflicts clause suggests that different parties had different views about the purpose and functions of the FCTC. Consequently, the extent to which the FCTC was intended to be a response to trade processes is questionable.

The question of why states concluded the FCTC is ultimately an empirical question to be examined using methods developed in the field of political science. Although finding an answer to this question is beyond the scope of this study, it is possible to draw on international relations theory in order to explain the structure and functions of the Convention. It is also possible to give a functional account of the FCTC, which seeks to identify the incentives facing WHO member-states at the time the Convention was concluded. These approaches suggest that the FCTC serves a variety of functions unrelated to the relationship between trade and tobacco control described in Chapters 1–5.

This account, which is based on an assumption that parties were rational and self-interested, suggests that there are a number of possible explanations for conclusion of the FCTC. Whereas some WHO member-states may have viewed the FCTC as a response to the "globalization of the tobacco epidemic," others most likely viewed the FCTC as a means to solve collective-action problems. In addition, a liberal account of the FCTC suggests that the Convention may function as a means of government hand-tying and of shifting power from industry to public health groups.

A. Responding to the "globalization of the tobacco epidemic"

The foreword to the FCTC indicates that it was developed in response to the globalization of the tobacco epidemic. However, it is not clear that this description of the rationale for the treaty explains the incentives facing all parties. The "explosive increase" in tobacco use described in the foreword to the FCTC was not occurring everywhere at the time the treaty was under negotiation. Rather, per-capita consumption of tobacco was declining in many developed countries and increasing in many developing countries. One oft-quoted statistic suggested that of the 5.4 million deaths attributed to tobacco consumption in the year 2000, only half were in the developing world, but that approximately 70 percent of deaths by the year 2030 would occur in developing countries.[96] This statistic suggested that the health issues associated with tobacco consumption also constituted an issue of global equity, with the developed world profiting from the export of chronic disease to developing countries.

In this context, tobacco control touched on two important issues for developing countries. First, the rise of tobacco consumption in developing countries reflected the vulnerability associated with their place in the international economic order. As described in Chapter 1, a number of developing countries had witnessed stimulation of the demand for tobacco products after opening their markets at the behest of the United States.

Second, the economic implications of tobacco consumption for development became clearer. It had long been apparent that tobacco, as an addictive and harmful product, diverted household income from items such as food, education, and health care. Work commissioned by the World Bank also highlighted the broader economic consequences of tobacco consumption and suggested that the high cost of health care and lost productivity caused by tobacco consumption resulted in economic losses to many countries.[97] The failure of these countries to use (or to enforce) tax measures to internalize the external costs of tobacco consumption meant that consumption was undermining economic development as well as public health.

In considering the incentives facing WHO member-states, those states facing increasing rates of tobacco consumption (primarily developing countries) had a strong incentive to implement tobacco-control measures at the domestic level. These same states also had an incentive to seek assistance

96 See Majid Ezzati and Alan Lopez, "Estimates of Global Mortality Attributable to Smoking in 2000," 362(9387) *Lancet*, (2003), pp. 847–852; Judith MacKay and Michael Eriksen, The Tobacco Atlas, World Health Organization, 2002 available at http://www.who.int/tobacco/en/atlas11.pdf (visited 28/02/09).

97 James Lightwood, David Collins, Helen Lapsley, et al., "Estimating the Costs of Tobacco Use, in Tobacco Control in Developing Countries," pp. 63–103.

from developed countries.[98] The assistance needs of developing countries are reflected in the preamble to the FCTC. Article 4.3 also states:

> International cooperation, particularly transfer of technology, knowledge and financial assistance and provision of related expertise, to establish and implement effective tobacco control programmes, taking into consideration local culture, as well as social, economic, political and legal factors, is an important part of the Convention.

In light of this provision and the history of negotiations, a functional analysis would suggest that the globalization of the tobacco epidemic raised awareness about the problems facing developing countries and increased the incentives for them to pursue tobacco control domestically and to seek assistance at the international level. However, this conclusion does not offer an account of the incentives for developed countries to participate in the FCTC. Accordingly, this analysis of incentives does not alone explain conclusion of the FCTC.

B. International cooperation to solve collective-action problems

Under the framework convention approach to treaty making, a general commitment in the treaty text is supplemented by more detailed terms in optional protocols and guidelines. The FCTC borrowed this approach from international environmental law. In that context, Abram Chayes and Antonia Handler Chayes argued that states cooperate in the pursuit of mutual regulatory gains, a view that was prominent at the time the FCTC was concluded.[99] Assuming a widely held state preference to protect public health from risks associated with tobacco, the text of the FCTC and the work of the Conference of the Parties both suggest that the possibility of mutual regulatory gains constituted an incentive for concluding the treaty. In particular, there is a strong argument that illicit trade in tobacco products and cross-border tobacco advertising are regulatory problems requiring international collective action.

Article 15 of the FCTC governs illicit trade in tobacco products, examples of which include smuggling, illicit manufacturing, and counterfeiting. The provision implicitly recognizes that illicit trade can be cross-border in character. Article 15.2 obliges parties (within whose territory a product is manufactured) to require product markings that assist other states in determining

98 See Allyn Taylor, "An International Regulatory Strategy for Global Tobacco Control," 21 *Yale Journal of International Law*, (1996), pp. 257–304, pp. 300–301, where it was argued that the FCTC should include an international tobacco control fund to support developing countries.

99 Abram Chayes and Antonia Handler Chayes, *The New Sovereignty: Compliance with International Regulatory Regimes*, Harvard University Press, (1996).

whether a product is legally for sale within their territories. Similarly, Article 15.4 refers to the exchange of information among customs, tax, and other authorities, and Article 15.6 obliges parties to promote cooperation between national, regional, and intergovernmental organizations relating to investigations, prosecutions, and proceedings. As these measures suggest, addressing the cross-border aspects of illicit trade requires coordination and cooperation at the international level.

For this reason, parties to the FCTC are negotiating an optional protocol to govern illicit trade in tobacco products. The latest draft of the text under negotiation suggests that domestically and internationally focused obligations are likely to be undertaken.[100] That is, parties will be obliged to implement inwardly focused measures to strengthen their domestic laws and law enforcement, as well as outwardly focused measures aimed at facilitating coordination.

Article 13 of the FCTC governs tobacco advertising, promotion, and sponsorship. In essence, the provision requires parties to impose a "comprehensive" ban on tobacco advertising, promotion, and sponsorship. Paragraphs 7 and 8 of Article 13 recognize that advertising, promotion, and sponsorship may be transferred across borders. In this respect, Article 13.7 affirms the sovereign right of each party to ban the entry of advertising, promotion, and sponsorship into its territory. Article 13.8 obliges parties to "consider the elaboration of a protocol setting out appropriate measures that require international collaboration for a comprehensive ban on cross-border advertising, promotion, and sponsorship."

The first session of the Conference of the Parties to the FCTC delegated the task of considering elaboration of a protocol to a group of experts.[101] The expert group reported back to the second session of the Conference of the Parties and recommended not addressing cross-border advertising through a protocol until the central obligation of Article 13 – to implement a "comprehensive" ban on advertising, promotion, and sponsorship – is properly understood.[102] As a consequence, the parties elected to prepare guidelines for the implementation of Article 13 and to consider the need for a binding legal approach to cross-border advertising at a later date.[103]

[100] WHO Framework Convention on Tobacco Control, Conference of the Parties, Intergovernmental Negotiating Body on a Protocol on Illicit Trade in Tobacco Products Second session, Geneva, 20–25 October 2008, FCTC/COP/INB-IT/2/3, 18 August 2008.

[101] WHO Framework Convention on Tobacco Control, Conference of the Parties, First Session, Second Report of Committee A, (Draft) A/FCTC/COP/1/10, 17 February 2006.

[102] WHO Framework Convention on Tobacco Control, Conference of the Parties, Second Session, Elaboration of a Template for a Protocol on Cross-Border Tobacco Advertising, Promotion and Sponsorship, A/FCTC/COP/2/10, 19 April 2007, see para. 12.

[103] First Report of Committee A (Draft), WHO Framework Convention on Tobacco Control, Conference of the Parties, Third Session, (Draft) FCTC/COP/3/22, 22 November 2008.

As is the case with respect to illicit trade, the issues concern collective-action problems of relevance to all parties. This conclusion is reflected in recommendations adopted by the Conference of the Parties concerning a possible future protocol. These recommendations suggest that the key elements of a protocol would be notification and response procedures in relation to cross-border advertising, cooperation between enforcement agencies, rules governing the exercise of jurisdiction, and rules governing the enforcement of foreign judgments.[104]

In summary, the FCTC functions as a mechanism to address collective-action problems associated with the preference for tobacco control. This conclusion is consistent both with the managerial theory offered by Chayes and Chayes and with other theories of state behavior. For example, rational institutionalism suggests that international regimes are established by states in order to address problems of coordination and collaboration under conditions of interdependence.[105] Although a detailed discussion of the application of these theories to formation of the FCTC is beyond the scope of this study, it is useful to note that characterization of the treaty as a mechanism to address collective-action problems is consistent with rational institutionalism. The use of a binding instrument might also be explained by problems of cooperation arising from differing tolerances for tobacco advertising and illicit trade.

C. Liberal accounts of government hand-tying

An alternative explanation for the conclusion of the treaty consistent with liberal international relations theory is that other actors sought to ensure that states were committed to tobacco control. These actors include health advocates within government and civil society. This is consistent with a liberal theory of international relations, which suggests that the fundamental actors in international politics are individuals and private groups, and that state preferences reflect the views of groups within domestic society. The theory also suggests that states are the sum of their different parts, including government officials and civil society groups such as industry, nongovernmental organizations, and academics. Liberal theory also assumes that interdependence among state preferences influences state behavior. Along these lines, state preferences can create a perceived stake in a matter that may explain policies or strategies in the realm of foreign affairs, such as cooperative strategies in

[104] Ibid., p. 7.

[105] See generally, David Baldwin, (ed), *Neorealism and Neoliberalism: The Contemporary Debate*, New York, Columbia University Press, (1993).

the context of treaties. [106]Along these lines, Judith Goldstein and others have argued:

> Governments and domestic groups may also deliberately employ international legalization as a means to bind themselves or their successors in the future. In other words, international legalization may have the aim of imposing constraints on domestic political behavior.[107]

With respect to government officials, Anne-Marie Slaughter has argued that the development of transgovernmental networks of officials who work in specific interest areas has led to the disaggregation of states and has undermined their capacity to speak with a single coherent voice in different international fora.[108] When applied in the context of the FCTC, if a preference for tobacco control is assumed, this theory suggests that domestic health officials may have used the FCTC as a means of tying the hands of their own governments in a context where action on tobacco may otherwise be contested politically. Observation of FCTC meetings suggests that this analysis has some merit. Governmental delegates can often be heard referring to the need for stronger obligations in order to prompt their domestic government to act.

The influence of public health groups is also evident in the text of the treaty. Article 4.7 of the FCTC states that "[t]he participation of civil society is essential in achieving the objective of the Convention and its protocols." Additionally, the preamble to the FCTC emphasizes

> the special contribution of nongovernmental organizations and other members of civil society not affiliated with the tobacco industry, including health professional bodies, women's, youth, environmental and consumer groups, and academic and health care institutions, to tobacco control efforts nationally and internationally and the vital importance of their participation in national and international tobacco control efforts.

The conclusion that the FCTC reinforces the influence of government health officials and civil society groups with a public health focus is also evident in Article 5.3 of the FCTC, which provides that, "[i]n setting and implementing their public health policies with respect to tobacco control, Parties shall act to protect these policies from commercial and other vested interests of the tobacco industry in accordance with national law." Guidelines for the

[106] For this formulation of liberal theory, see Andrew Moravcsik, "Taking Preferences Seriously: A Liberal Theory of International Politics," 51 *International Organization*, (1997), pp. 513–553.

[107] Judith Golstein, Miles Kahler, Robert Keohane, et al., "Introduction: Legalisation and World Politics," 54(3) *International Organization*, (Summer 2000), pp. 385–399, p. 393.

[108] Anne-Marie Slaughter, A *New World Order*, Princeton University Press, (2004).

implementation of this provision seek to undermine the influence of the tobacco industry by imposing a range of transparency requirements that affect contact with government. These guidelines also encourage FCTC parties to limit the influence of domestic government agencies that may oppose tobacco control. Paragraphs 4.8 and 4.9 state:

> 4.8 Parties should not allow any person employed by the tobacco industry or any entity working to further its interests to be a member of any government body, committee or advisory group that sets or implements tobacco control or public health policy.
>
> 4.9 Parties should not nominate any person employed by the tobacco industry or any entity working to further its interests to serve on delegations to meetings of the Conference of the Parties, its subsidiary bodies or any other bodies established pursuant to decisions of the Conference of the Parties.

The power shift inherent in the FCTC can also be observed in practical terms. For example, at the third and fourth sessions of an Intergovernmental Negotiating Body on a Protocol on Illicit Trade in Tobacco Products, the body voted to close the public gallery while permitting the presence of accredited observers. The effect of this decision was to exclude tobacco industry representatives from the public gallery while permitting civil society groups with a health focus to participate in the meeting.

Provisions such as Articles 4.7 and 5.3 of the FCTC provide strong textual support for a liberal account of legalization in the tobacco-control context. This textual support is reinforced by the conduct of meetings. In summary, liberal accounts of legalization applied to the FCTC suggest that the treaty functions as a means of binding the hands of government and of shifting political power from industry to health groups within government and civil society.

D. Conclusions on why legalization occurred in the tobacco-control context

The previous analysis of the FCTC suggests that there were three primary incentives underlying conclusion of the treaty. Addressing illicit trade in tobacco products and cross-border tobacco advertising provided incentives for collective action in the form of the FCTC. This conclusion is also supported by the ongoing work agenda of the Conference of the Parties. The possibility of gaining transfers of technical and financial assistance also constituted an incentive for developing countries, particularly in a context where they stood to lose the most from tobacco consumption. This conclusion is also supported by the ongoing calls from developing countries for assistance. In addition to these circumstances, domestic actors such as health officials and civil society had incentives to bind the hands of their governments in support of tobacco control.

Each of these reasons also offers an explanation of the fact that many provisions of the treaty are inwardly focused, in the sense that they compel action at the domestic level. Each party's commitment to address illicit trade or cross-border advertising would not be credible without domestic action. Thus, a commitment to implement a number of domestic measures also played a role in signaling commitment to the issues of collective concern. Similarly, requests for assistance from developing countries would not be credible in the absence of a commitment to implement measures that are viewed as basic tobacco-control measures. Therefore, commitment to implement these basic measures by developing countries signaled that requests for assistance were bona fide. Finally, the need for inwardly focused obligations is consistent with an intent to tie the hands of government so as to solidify domestic commitment to the issues. When viewed together, these three arguments offer hypotheses about the conclusion of the FCTC that are alternatives to the idea that it was concluded as a response to trade processes.

Of course, these hypotheses have not been tested in a rigorous manner. There are also other hypotheses that appear credible. For example, it might be argued that the international system itself induced ideational change that has affected states' perceived interests in tobacco control. This could be reflected in the preamble to the FCTC, which recalls a number of human rights instruments. The instruments recalled include Article 12 of the International Covenant on Economic Social and Cultural Rights (ICESCR) and General Comment 14 issued by the Committee on Economic, Cultural and Social Rights, which was issued only a few months before FCTC negotiations began. Equally, this argument is not developed further here, and other hypotheses are not tested because the task at hand is not to explain the FCTC. Rather, the point is that the FCTC cannot be viewed simply as a response to trade liberalization or to the impact of trade agreements on regulatory autonomy. The binding character of the FCTC is most likely attributable to other factors.

E. Implications for legalization in the contexts of diet and alcohol

To the extent that arguments for treaties modeled on the FCTC are based on the premise that the FCTC was a response to trade processes, the previous analysis undermines these arguments. This does not in itself suggest that health treaties should not be used as counterweights to trade agreements, but it does suggest that the FCTC is not, strictly speaking, a precedent for this approach. The fact that the FCTC provides guidance in the interpretation of open-textured WTO rules relating to necessity and compels parties to implement public health measures is a byproduct of other functions served by the treaty. Nonetheless, if the preconditions underlying conclusion of the FCTC were also present in the contexts of alcohol and diet, the outcome might be similar.

It is worthwhile then, to touch upon whether these preconditions are met in the contexts of alcohol and diet. If not, one possible conclusion is that states would be unlikely to adopt binding instruments in these contexts unless some other incentives are present. Another possible conclusion is that if the incentives underlying adoption of the FCTC are not replicated in the contexts of alcohol and diet, states may be unlikely to adopt a binding instrument of significant depth unless other incentives are present. Yet another possible conclusion is that if states were to adopt a binding instrument in such circumstances, ratification and compliance may not be high in the absence of other incentives. The latter two of these conclusions are in line with the previous discussion about binding and nonbinding norms. By the same token, the predictive value of the previously developed theories is quite limited. This is particularly so for liberal international relations theory, because industry is considered to be a legitimate part of solutions to problems such as obesity.[109]

In addition, the earlier discussion is not a detailed analysis of state behavior in the tobacco context. Accordingly, what follows is intended to be a brief discussion of some of the factors that might be taken into account in future decision making and is not a detailed prediction of state behavior.

(a) THE GLOBALIZATION OF NONCOMMUNICABLE DISEASE

There are a number of obvious similarities between the globalization of the tobacco epidemic and the spread of noncommunicable diseases relating to diet and alcohol. The total health burden of noncommunicable disease is currently greater in developing countries.[110] Factors that facilitate increases in this burden will also have greater relative effects in developing countries for reasons relating to the weakness of their health systems and because health constitutes a driver of economic growth. As described in Chapter 1, the spread of dietary- and alcohol-related noncommunicable disease to the developing world is also partly associated with trade liberalization.

[109] For discussion of the role of industry, see Mickey Chopra, Sarah Galbraith, and Ian Darnton-Hill, "A Global Response to a Global Problem: The Epidemic of Overnutrition," 80(12) *Bulletin of the World Health Organization*, (2002), pp. 952–958.

[110] Global Strategy Diet, para. 6.

These factors suggest that developing countries have an incentive to conclude a treaty as a means of accessing assistance in the dietary and alcohol contexts. However, there are at least two reasons why developing countries might not deem this incentive sufficient to merit a push for conclusion of a treaty. First, in the FCTC context, a significant flow of technical and financial assistance from developed countries to developing countries is yet to be realized. At the second session of the Conference of the Parties, developing countries raised this issue and were met with an almost uniform response from developed countries to the effect that developing countries must first identify their needs before assistance can be given.

Rather than states, it is private donors such as Michael Bloomberg and the Bill & Melinda Gates Foundation that have contributed new resources to the field. The $500 million contributed between these two sources has been channeled to developing countries partly through the WHO Tobacco Free Initiative, which is a separate entity to the FCTC secretariat, and partly through nongovernmental organizations.[111] Although conclusion of the FCTC may have encouraged these donations, the example of the FCTC suggests that conclusion of a treaty may not necessarily be the best means of accessing financial assistance.

Second, the economic incentives may differ in the contexts of diet and alcohol as compared to tobacco. Although a handful of developing countries were concerned about the impact of the FCTC on their tobacco growers and industries, the World Bank made an economic case for tobacco control based on the costs of morbidity and mortality.[112] In contrast, the G77 and a number of developing countries raised last-minute concerns about the text of the Global Strategy Diet. One explanation for this is that developing countries with strong sugar industries view global regulatory action as a threat to their economic development. This perceived threat is heightened by the fact that the outcomes associated with international cooperation are uncertain. Whereas only a handful of developing countries had tobacco industries that might be seriously affected by the FCTC, action on dietary-related disease may affect a range of industries and, therefore, have more significant implications for the economic development of a larger number of developing countries. Similar conclusions might be drawn with respect to the alcohol context, because the wine sector of a number of middle-income countries is growing.

111 See http://www.tobaccocontrolgrants.org/ (visited 24/04/09).

112 Curbing the Epidemic: Governments and the Economics of Tobacco Control, The World Bank, 1999, Washington, DC.

Equally, the conclusion that the economic incentives facing developing countries may differ in the dietary and alcohol contexts is not a static one. The argument that developing countries may see a treaty as a means of seeking assistance is also valid in these contexts. However, at present, questions persist about whether state-to-state assistance would be forthcoming. In addition, this account of why developing countries might wish to conclude a treaty does not provide an account of why developed countries with relatively open markets would view the issue as requiring collective action or participation on their part.

(b) COLLECTIVE-ACTION PROBLEMS

In theory, there is no reason why cross-border advertising or illicit trade (such as smuggling) couldn't also cause collective-action problems in the context of food. For example, limitations on food or beverage advertising directed at children could be undermined by enforcement problems associated with banning Internet-based advertising. In this respect, a regional consultation meeting conducted as part of the development of the Global Strategy Diet noted that "[t]here are few restrictions on cross-border advertising, and messages are received unscreened from the host country."[113] Cross-border advertising by food companies is also quite common. It is possible to find games and animations directed at children on the Internet and companies such as McDonald's and Coca-Cola sponsor international sporting events.[114] Similarly, cross-border food smuggling could undermine fiscal or other measures.

It is worth noting, however, that in the context of tobacco control, a significant number of states maintained advertising bans and taxation policies prior to negotiation of the FCTC.[115] With these measures in place, it was possible to identify how cross-border processes were undermining tobacco control at the domestic level. This can be distinguished from the dietary context because regulation of the type contemplated in that context is still in its nascent stage. Although this fact does not mean that the prospect of measures being undermined by cross-border processes is not real, it could suggest that there is not sufficient incentive for collective action to address the issue.

The current state of regulation could also mean that there is not sufficient consensus among states concerning the best means of approaching obesity

[113] WHO Global Strategy on Diet, Physical Activity and Health: South-East Asia Regional Consultation Meeting Report, New Delhi, India, 10 – 12 March 2003.

[114] For a discussion, see Lobstein, "Tackling Childhood Obesity in an Era of Trade Liberalisation," p. 200.

[115] See, for example, Ruth Roemer, *Legislative Action to Combat the World Tobacco Epidemic*, (2nd ed), World Health Organization, Geneva, 1993.

and dietary-related diseases. In contrast, in the tobacco context, the extent of existing domestic regulation meant that there was a significant evidence base to draw on in identifying the most effective regulatory interventions to protect population health. The World Bank and WHO presented this evidence base to states in 1999, around the time negotiations began.[116]

Putting diet to one side, there is a long history of illicit trade in alcohol products. Both tobacco and alcohol products are the subject of heavy taxation, creating an incentive for tax evasion through smuggling, bootlegging, and unlawful production such as home brewing or distillation. With the possible exception of some types of unlawful production, there is nothing to suggest that illicit trade in alcoholic beverages would be strictly of a domestic character. On the contrary, global distribution chains suggest that problems such as smuggling are as likely to be cross-border problems as they are domestic problems. In this respect, the Global Strategy Alcohol recognizes the need to reduce the public health impact of illicit alcohol and informally produced alcohol as a specific area for policy interventions.[117] This may suggest that there is some merit to the conclusion of a framework convention on alcohol control.

Equally, attempts to address illicit trade in tobacco products have proven difficult within the framework of the FCTC. One difficulty has been the fact that the UN Convention on Transnational Organized Crime (UNTOC) already provides a legal framework within which protocols have been negotiated to address illicit activity. This treaty, which was negotiated under the auspices of the UN Office on Drugs and Crime (UNODC), establishes a multilateral system to govern cooperation in matters of transnational organized crime and is supplemented by protocols on trafficking in persons, the smuggling of migrants, and illicit manufacturing and trafficking in firearms.[118]

The legal framework established by UNTOC includes general rules relating to issues such as jurisdiction, mutual legal assistance, and extradition. In the FCTC protocol negotiations, these issues have proven particularly difficult. Unlike UNTOC, the FCTC does not include general rules governing these issues, meaning that they might be addressed in a protocol itself. However, this is problematic given that there is already a multilateral legal regime in place to govern these issues. Consequently, the parties must either rely by cross-reference on rules set out in the UNTOC or create a new regime.

[116] See Curbing the Epidemic: Governments and the Economics of Tobacco Control, Washington DC, World Bank, 1999.

[117] The Draft Global Strategy to Reduce the Harmful Use of Alcohol, paras 37–39.

[118] United Nations Convention against Transnational Organized Crime, 40 ILM 335 (2001); UN Doc. A/55/383 at 25 (2000); UN Doc. A/RES/55/25 at 4 (2001).

Relying on a cross-reference is problematic because there is not a complete overlap of parties between the two treaties, resulting in objections from non-parties to UNTOC. Equally, creating a new regime that differs from that established in UNTOC is problematic for parties to UNTOC, who would prefer to administer only one multilateral system of cooperation with respect to transnational organized crime. In addition, it is not clear that the secretariat to the FCTC, which is housed within WHO, has the institutional capacity to support a protocol of the character in question.[119]

In the context of cross-border advertising, there is also little doubt that the issues are conceptually similar in the contexts of alcohol and tobacco. In each context, advertising via the Internet, cable television, and in periodicals may enter one jurisdiction from another, thereby undermining domestic measures. The Global Strategy Alcohol recognizes this, stating that "[t]he transmission of alcohol marketing messages across national borders and jurisdictions on channels such as satellite television and the Internet, and sponsorship of sports and cultural events is emerging as a serious concern in some countries."[120] However, as is the case in the dietary context, advertising restrictions relating to alcoholic beverages are not commonplace, and with the exception of some Islamic countries where sale of alcohol is prohibited, domestic alcohol advertising restrictions are rarely comprehensive.[121] This is distinct from the tobacco context because restrictions on tobacco advertising were widespread prior to negotiation of the FCTC.

In summary, it is conceivable that the preconditions for negotiation of the FCTC could exist in the contexts of alcohol or diet, either at present or in the future. However, the fact that domestic tobacco-control measures were widespread prior to the negotiation of the FCTC appears to have been important for conclusion of the treaty. Against this backdrop, there was a need for parties to signal a general commitment to tobacco control in order to appear credible in the context of attempts to address collective-action problems. It could have been this process of signaling that made it possible to conclude a treaty composed of obligations to implement what are on their face domestically focused measures to control tobacco. This creates something of a "catch-22" for those who advocate the use of treaties as a means of prompting domestic action. On the one hand, a certain level of domestic action is required for a treaty to be

[119] See generally Neil Boister, "Recent Progress in the Development of a Protocol on the Illicit Trade in Tobacco Products," 5(1) *Asian Journal of WTO & International Health Law and Policy*, (2010), pp. 53–86.

[120] Draft Global Strategy to Reduce the Harmful Use of Alcohol, para. 29.

[121] Jon Nelson, "Alcohol Advertising Bans, Consumptions and Control Policies in Seventeen OECD Countries, 1975–2000," *Applied Economics*, (2008), pp. 1–21, p. 7.

worthwhile. On the other hand, in the absence of a treaty, there is nothing compelling domestic action.

However, the earlier discussion about the relative merits of nonbinding and binding norms has highlighted that binding instruments may not always be the best means of generating the domestic action that health advocates seek. Although some would argue that states observe international law much of the time,[122] there is a body of commentary on commitment and compliance that suggests otherwise, or that attributes compliance to the fact that states often make binding commitments to carry out acts that they already undertake.

Put another way, there is little merit to pursuing an international treaty unless there is some reason to expect that states will alter their behavior as a consequence of the treaty. One reason might be rational self-interest. For instance, based on rational choice theory, Andrew Guzmán has argued that states comply with obligations out of concerns relating to reciprocity, retaliation, and reputation.[123] Alternatively, states might alter their behavior as they internalize norms, as suggested by Harold Koh,[124] or they might comply with treaties where they are considered legitimate, as suggested by Franck. Alternatively still, state capacity may have a significant influence on the impact of a treaty on state behavior, as Chayes and Chayes have argued.

This is not to suggest that it will be easy to predict how a legal obligation will alter state behavior. This is difficult enough to determine after a treaty has been concluded. As Jonathan Charney has also argued, the relative rates of compliance with binding and nonbinding norms "will remain unproven because the factors that influence compliance substantially overlap."[125] Nonetheless, before advocating binding legal instruments, some thought must be given to the question of compliance. In the present context, it seems unlikely that states will pressure one another to comply with obligations to implement domestic health measures.[126] Accordingly, in light of the aforementioned perceived incentives, it is questionable whether binding instruments in the alcohol or dietary contexts would induce sufficient action from states at this point in time.

[122] Louis Henkin, *How Nations Behave: Law and Foreign Policy*, New York, Columbia University Press, (1979), p. 26.

[123] Andrew Guzmán, *How International Law Works: A Rational Choice Theory*, New York, Oxford University Press, (2008), pp. 33–48.

[124] Harold Hongju Koh, "Why Do Nations Obey International Law?" 106(8) *Yale Law Journal*, (1997), pp. 2599–2659.

[125] Jonathan Charney, "Commentary: Compliance with International Soft Law," in Shelton, *Commitment and Compliance*, pp. 115–118, p.116.

[126] Allyn Taylor, "Making the World Health Organization Work: A Legal Framework for Universal Access to the Conditions for Health," 18(4) *American Journal of Law & Medicine*, (1992), pp. 301–346, p. 338.

As suggested, this is not intended to be a rigorous analysis of the prospects of compliance. There is also the underlying constructivist theory that suggests the international system shapes identities and interests of states. Constructivism conflicts with theories based on rational choice, and for some, an international treaty negotiation may be a vehicle for ideational change that leads to changes in state behavior.

3. INTERNATIONAL HARMONIZATION

As was discussed in Chapters 2 and 5, the SPS and TBT Agreements each contain presumptions of lawfulness in the context of international standards. Article 3.2 of the SPS Agreement states:

> Sanitary or phytosanitary measures which conform to international standards, guidelines or recommendations shall be deemed to be necessary to protect human, animal or plant life or health, and presumed to be consistent with the relevant provisions of this Agreement and of GATT 1994.

This provision creates a presumption that applies not only to the SPS Agreement, but also to the GATT. This can be contrasted with the relevant part of Article 2.5 of the TBT Agreement, which applies only to that agreement and states:

> Whenever a technical regulation is prepared, adopted or applied for one of the legitimate objectives explicitly mentioned in paragraph 2, and is in accordance with relevant international standards, it shall be rebuttably presumed not to create an unnecessary obstacle to international trade.

These provisions must be read in light of obligations in each of the agreements to use relevant international standards. Under Article 3.1 of the SPS Agreement there is a general obligation to base SPS measures on international standards, guidelines, or recommendations. Failure to base a measure on a relevant standard, guideline, or recommendation may be justified under Article 3.3 if the standards, guidelines, or recommendations in question are not sufficient to achieve that member's chosen level of sanitary or phytosanitary protection.

Under Article 2.4 of the TBT Agreement, where relevant international standards exist or their completion is imminent, members are obliged to use relevant parts of those standards as the basis for their technical regulations. The exception to this requirement arises where use of the standards would be "an ineffective or inappropriate means for the fulfillment of the legitimate objectives pursued, for instance because of fundamental climatic or geographical factors or fundamental technological problems."

In each instance, the rebuttable presumption of compliance that is created where a measure is based on a relevant international instrument offers a potential shield to a member defending a measure. This suggests that the conclusion of new instruments such as standards, guidelines, and recommendations may assuage some concerns relating to regulatory autonomy in the contexts of the SPS and TBT Agreements.

As Roger Magnusson has argued, the development of international standards may also help shape industry behavior in the absence of a binding obligation.[127] Compliance with nonbinding standards may be viewed by industry either as a means of avoiding or delaying regulatory intervention or as an expression of social responsibility. Nonbinding standards may also encourage states to implement regulatory measures where those states may not otherwise act. To the extent that standards are viewed as legitimate, they may exert a compliance pull despite the fact that they are not binding. This is particularly likely where a reason for regulatory inaction is uncertainty about the best approach to adopt.

From a trade policy perspective, further harmonization may lower the transaction costs associated with compliance, suggesting that harmonization may increase coherence between trade and public health. Similarly, standards may fill out the open-textured character of necessity and other tests in WTO law.

In the context of a legal study, such as this one, there are limits on what may be said about future international harmonization. The task of creating standards is a technical one. Nonetheless, it is possible to comment on the merits of harmonization generally and how harmonization might proceed in the contexts of tobacco, alcohol, and diet.

3.1. *Harmonization and Regulatory Autonomy*

Harmonization can have a mixed effect on regulatory autonomy. Poor standards may undermine regulatory autonomy under the SPS and TBT Agreements, particularly where a member seeks to exceed a given standard. This possibility stems from the obligation to base measures on international standards, guidelines, or recommendations under the SPS Agreement, and to use relevant standards as the basis for technical regulations under the TBT Agreement. This concern was discussed in Chapter 5 in the contexts of Articles 3.1 and 3.3 of the SPS Agreement and Article 2.4 of the TBT Agreement. It was recognized that these provisions provide some flexibility. For example, to base a measure on a standard does not require strict conformity to the standard. The failure to base

[127] Magnusson, "Non-Communicable Diseases and Global Health Governance," p. 1.

a measure on a standard also does not mean that the burden of proof shifts back to the member defending a measure under the SPS or TBT Agreements. In addition, each provision identifies circumstances in which failure to base a measure on standards will be justified. In the context of the SPS Agreement, this is the case where there is a scientific justification or where a member seeks a higher level of protection in accordance with a risk assessment carried out under Article 5. In the context of the TBT Agreement, this is the case where basing a measure on an international standard would be an ineffective or inappropriate means of pursuing the regulatory objective in question.

Nonetheless, international standards lack authority and legitimacy. Much has been written about this concern in the context of the Codex Alimentarius Commission. Various criticisms have been leveled against the commission, including that it lacks transparency, is dominated by the interests of a handful of developed countries who have the regulatory capacity to drive harmonization, and is subject to regulatory capture by industry groups.[128] These concerns undermine both the argument for using Codex standards in WTO dispute settlement and the usefulness of Codex standards as a means to promote regulatory change at the domestic level. In the latter respect, if Franck's theory of the power of legitimacy among nations is to be accepted, standards are more likely to exert a compliance pull where they are concluded through a process that is viewed as legitimate and where they receive some form of symbolic validation by states. [129]

Concerns about the legitimacy of international standards are perhaps greatest in the context of private standard setting bodies like the International Standards Organization (ISO). It will be recalled from Chapter 5 that ISO standards used for testing the contents and emissions of cigarettes have been criticized widely as flawed testing methods. Because these types of standards may be taken into account in the context of the TBT Agreement, there is a legitimate concern that low or flawed international standards may impede domestic regulation.

The great deal that has been written on the pitfalls of international harmonization need not be repeated here. Rather, it is sufficient to note that the

[128] For a sample of the literature see Steven Bernstein & Erin Hannah, "Non-State Global Standard Setting and the WTO: Legitimacy and the Need for Regulatory Space," 11(3) *Journal of International Economic Law*, pp. 575–608; Yoshiko Naiki, "Accountability and Legitimacy in Global Health and Safety Governance: The World Trade Organization, the SPS Committee, and International Standard-Setting Organizations," 43(6) *Journal of World Trade*, (2009), pp. 1255–1279.

[129] On legitimacy and its compliance pull, see Thomas Franck, *The Power of Legitimacy Among Nations*.

benefits of harmonization are dependent on the content of the standards in question. In particular, standards that are set at a low level of protection or that provide for limited government intervention may not actually be a sound means of providing guidance on interpretation of the necessity test. Similarly, standards lacking legitimacy may not have a compliance pull that induces regulatory activity by domestic authorities. With these concerns in mind, it is worthwhile to comment on how further harmonization might be carried out in the contexts of tobacco, alcohol, and diet.

3.2. *Harmonization in Context*

The discussion of the SPS and TBT Agreements in Chapter 5 highlighted the fact that different agreements and standards apply in each of the contexts of tobacco, alcohol, and diet. Because product-regulation measures addressing diet fall within the scope of the SPS Agreement, it is worth discussing these measures first.

A. The dietary context

Commentators have argued for the use of standards as an alternative model to the conclusion of a treaty in the dietary context. For example, Magnusson has argued that a treaty-based approach that seeks to consolidate "the regulation of food composition, labeling, health claims, food advertising and children's health and nutrition into a single instrument would likely fail due to political divisions and industry opposition."[130] In place of a treaty, therefore, Magnusson argues that the WHO should use its constitutional power to make regulations by developing separate standards for salt, fats, sugar, labeling and marketing.[131]

However, shifting the responsibility for harmonization from the Codex Alimentarius Commission to the WHO has its own drawbacks. Most obviously, under Annex A of the SPS Agreement, Codex food safety standards, guidelines, and recommendations relating to food additives are recognized automatically under the SPS Agreement. Whereas the Annex also makes provision for "appropriate standards, guidelines and recommendations promulgated by other relevant international organisations open for membership to all Members," such organizations must be identified by the SPS Committee. Most important, this provision only applies in the case of matters not covered by the organizations listed in earlier paragraphs of the provision. Thus,

[130] Magnusson, "Non-Communicable Diseases and Global Health Governance," p. 12
[131] Ibid.

to argue that the WHO could be recognized under Annex A would require a conclusion that the matters in question do not fall within the ambit of the Codex Alimentarius Commission's work.

This conclusion seems unsustainable in light of Article 1 of the Statutes of the Codex Alimentarius Commission. The provision states:

> The Codex Alimentarius Commission shall, subject to Article 5 below, be responsible for making proposals to, and shall be consulted by, the Directors-General of the Food and Agriculture Organization (FAO) and the World Health Organization (WHO) on all matters pertaining to the implementation of the Joint FAO/WHO Food Standards Programme, the purpose of which is:
>
> (a) protecting the health of the consumers and ensuring fair practices in the food trade;
> (b) promoting coordination of all food standards work undertaken by international governmental and non governmental organizations;
> (c) determining priorities and initiating and guiding the preparation of draft standards through and with the aid of appropriate organizations;
> (d) finalizing standards elaborated under (c) above and publishing them in a Codex Alimentarius either as regional or worldwide standards, together with international standards already finalized by other bodies under (b) above, wherever this is practicable;
> (e) amending published standards, as appropriate, in the light of developments.

The phrase "protecting the health of the consumers" in paragraph (a) appears sufficiently broad as to place the issues within the ambit of Codex's work. Accordingly, WHO regulations would not be recognized under the SPS Agreement.

There is also a question of whether there is in fact any procedural or substantive difference between the adoption of WHO regulations as compared to conclusion of a treaty. Article 21 of the Constitution of the World Health Organization grants the WHA the power to adopt regulations governing a range of issues. Article 22 permits reservations to regulations and provides that regulations come into force for all WHO member-states unless they advise the Director-General of the WHO of their rejection of the regulations. As is to be expected, regulations are negotiated among the member-states of the WHO before being put to the WHA for adoption. Consequently, in terms of process at least, it is difficult to see how the adoption of WHO regulations differs from the negotiation of a treaty.

This may also be true in a formal sense. Article 2(1)(a) of the Vienna Convention defines a treaty as "an international agreement concluded between States in written form and governed by international law, whether embodied in a single instrument or in two or more related instruments and whatever its particular designation." In a formal sense, there is no difference between a WHO regulation and a treaty. Most important, either a treaty or WHO regulations are capable of constituting a binding instrument to which states may opt in or out of respectively.

In addition to the fact that WHO regulations are not likely to constitute standards under the SPS Agreement, there are other issues to consider. The character of WHO regulations as treaties calls into question the appropriateness of such instruments for purposes of harmonization. There is a distinction between a technical standard, such as one that proposes limits on the total percentage of fat in a food, and a rule that compels a state to set such limits. Whereas the standard creates a benchmark, the rule would be something of a universal regulatory straitjacket that may be inappropriate in many domestic contexts, depending on the nutritional profile of a population.

Use of WHO regulations in place of Codex standards would contradict the approach envisioned in the Global Strategy Diet. Although the Codex Alimentarius Commission has not traditionally been perceived as a forum for promoting healthy diets,[132] paragraph 59 of the Global Strategy Diet recognizes the potential benefits of standards drawn up by the commission. The relevant passage states:

> Public health efforts may be strengthened by the use of international norms and standards, particularly those drawn up by the Codex Alimentarius Commission. [footnote omitted] Areas for further development could include: labelling to allow consumers to be better informed about the benefits and content of foods; measures to minimize the impact of marketing on unhealthy dietary patterns; fuller information about healthy consumption patterns, including steps to increase the consumption of fruit and vegetables; and production and processing standards regarding the nutritional quality and safety of products. Involvement of governments and nongovernmental organizations as provided for in the Codex should be encouraged.[133]

Within the Codex Alimentarius Commission, work is underway on implementation of this passage. In 2006, the WHO and FAO prepared a draft action

[132] Mary L'Abbé, Janine Lewis, and Christina Zehaluk, "The Potential of the Codex Alimentarius to Promote Healthy Diets Worldwide – The Canadian Experience of Implementation," in Hawkes, et al., *Trade, Food, Diet and Health: Perspectives and Policy Options*, Wiley Blackwell, (2010), p. 238.

[133] Global Strategy Diet, para. 59.

plan for implementation of the Global Strategy Diet.[134] The draft action plan recommended a number of different steps that could be taken within the context of Codex. Since formulation of this plan, amendments have been made to relevant instruments, such as the Guidelines on Nutrition Labeling, Guidelines for Use of Nutrition and Health Claims, and the General Standard for the Labeling of Prepackaged Food.

At the time of writing, the work of the Codex Alimentarius Commission addresses a number of issues relating to the Global Strategy Diet. These issues include revision of the Guidelines on Nutrition Labeling concerning the list of nutrients that are always declared on a voluntary or mandatory basis and principles for legibility and readability of nutrition labels.[135]

The discussion of these issues indicates that the Codex Alimentarius Commission is engaged in an ongoing process of harmonization in the dietary context. This process does offer a route through which regulatory autonomy can be enhanced and the trade restrictiveness of regulatory interventions can be minimized. This is not to say that concerns about poor standards and the legitimacy of the Codex Alimentarius Commission have been overcome. Rather, the point to note is that further harmonization is already under way in the dietary context. This weighs against the merits of large-scale law reform at the present point in time. Equally, this does not suggest that there is anything inherently wrong in taking such approaches, although detailed legal obligations may sometimes be an inappropriate means of harmonization.

Accordingly, the question being debated at present concerns how the Codex Alimentarius Commission should go about the task of harmonization. Member-states of the commission have expressed varying views on this issue,[136] as have

[134] See Codex Alimentarius Commission, Request for Comments on Draft Action Plan for Implementation of the Global Strategy on Diet, Physical Activity and Health, September 2006, CL 2006/44-CAC.

[135] Codex Alimentarius Commission, Report of the Thirty-Seventh Session of the Committee on Food Labeling, Calgary, Canada, 4–8 May 2009. ALINORM 09/32/22; The work of the Codex Committee on Nutrition and Foods for Special Dietary Uses is also relevant to implementation of the Global Strategy Diet. The committee is developing nutrient reference values for nutrients associated with risk of noncommunicable diseases.

[136] See, for discussion, Codex Alimentarius Commission, Twenty-Ninth Session, Update: Implementation of the WHO Global Strategy on Diet, Physical Activity and Health: Action that Could be Taken by Codex, CAC/29 LIM/6; Codex Alimentarius Commission, Codex Committee on Food Labeling, Matters referred by FAO and WHO: Implementation of the Global Strategy on Diet, Physical Activity and Health (CL2006/44-CAC), Thirty-Fifth Session, Ottawa, Canada, April 30–May 4, 2007, CX/FL 07/35/3.

members of civil society.[137] It is clear from these views, however, that some aspects of the question of how Codex should go about its task are beyond the scope of this study because they do not relate to the question of how standards might address the impact of WTO law. The question for present purposes is how further harmonization might address the issues discussed in Chapter 5 of this study.

Obviously, new standards that enhance harmonization might be valuable. For example, standardization of the list of nutrients to be disclosed on product labels and guidelines encouraging mandatory labeling would reduce the (albeit low) risk that divergent approaches might lead to disputes. It is where measures draw regulatory distinctions between different goods that disputes appear more likely to arise. For example, this may occur in the context of product regulation where the constituents of a food are regulated in a way that has a greater impact on foods originating in the territory of a particular WTO Member. This may occur where a labeling measure is not neutral but seeks to dissuade consumption of certain types of foods, as a traffic light labeling system may.

At the heart of each of these measures is a question about the fitness of certain foods (whether a food alone or an ingredient in a processed food) for human consumption. This question concerns the extent to which particular foods may be consumed as a part of a balanced diet. Accordingly, it is standards that might be used for purposes of drawing regulatory distinctions between different goods that are most likely to be useful under the SPS Agreement.

Within the context of Codex, these types of standards may be found in at least two forms. First, as was discussed in Chapter 5, the Guidelines for use of Nutrition and Health Claims address claims that relate to dietary guidelines or healthy diets, and may be relevant for purposes of measures such as traffic light labeling schemes. This instrument offers guidance on when health claims should be permitted with respect to different constituents. For example, the guidelines establish conditions based on which it may be acceptable to make a claim that a food is low in, very low in, or free of sodium.[138]

In a domestic context, these guidelines could be used not only for purposes of restricting the circumstances in which health claims are made on packaging,

137 Center for Science in the Public Interest, Codex Alimentarius vis-à-vis The WHO Global Strategy on Diet, Physical Activity and Health Food Standardisation to Support the Reduction of Chronic Diseases (Food and Diet for a Healthy Long Life), available at http://cspinet.org/reports/WHOGlobalStrategyCODEX.pdf.

138 Codex Alimentarius Commission, Guidelines for Use of Nutrition and Health Claims, CAC/GL, p. 5.

but also for purposes of a mandatory traffic light labeling scheme. For example, a WTO Member might use the classification of a food as high in, low in, or free of sodium as a basis for giving the food a red or green light on its packaging.

At present, guidelines governing health claims are established with respect to energy, fat, saturated fat, cholesterol, sugars, sodium, protein, vitamins and minerals, and dietary fiber. Amending these guidelines to include trans fat would constitute an improvement that may be important in the event of a dispute arising under the SPS Agreement. Equally, at the time of writing, this issue remains controversial. The Codex Committee on Food Labeling considered adding trans-fatty acids to the list of ingredients to be declared on product labels. A number of delegations objected on the basis that trans fat is not an issue of concern in their countries.[139]

Second, nutrition reference values (which outline the levels of intake of nutrients considered adequate to meet nutritional needs) may be developed for nutrients associated with increased or decreased risk of noncommunicable disease. Were reference values to be framed in terms of upper limits on intake, these values might assist in justifying product-regulation measures or measures such as traffic light labeling. Equally, guidelines that are express in recognizing the autonomy of states to set their own dietary guidelines and upper limits on intake may also provide sufficient regulatory autonomy. At the time of writing, the Codex Committee on Nutrition and Foods for Special Dietary Uses is reviewing how nutrient reference values might be used in this context.[140] It is possible that member-states may favor an approach that supports flexibility at the national level. A recent discussion paper prepared by the United States and Thailand supported this approach and cited the preamble to WHA resolution 57.17, which endorses the Global Strategy Diet and states:

> [A]ppropriate intake levels for energy, nutrients and foods, including free sugars, salt, fats, fruits, vegetables, legumes, whole grains, and nuts shall be

[139] Codex Alimentarius Commission, Joint FAO/WHO Food Standards Programme, Report of the Thirty-Seventh Session of the Codex Committee on Food Labeling, ALINORM 09/32/22, paras 23–26; see also Codex Alimentarius Commission, Joint FAO/WHO Food Standards Programme, Report of the Thirty-Eighth Session of the Codex Committee on Food Labeling, ALINORM 10/33/22, paras 42–52.

[140] See, for example, Codex Alimentarius Commission, Joint FAO/WHO Food Standards Programme, Codex Committee on Nutrition and Foods for Special Dietary Uses, Thirty-First Session, Discussion Paper on the Nutrient Reference Values (NRVS) for Nutrients Associated with Risk of Noncommunicable Diseases, July 2009, CX/NFSDU 09/31/08; see also Codex Alimentarius Commission, Joint FAO/WHO Food Standards Programme, Codex Committee on Nutrition and Foods for Special Dietary Uses, Principles and Criteria for the Development of NRVs for Labeling Purposes for Nutrients Associated with risk of Diet-Related Noncommunicable Diseases at Step 4, CX/NFSDU 10/32/7.

> determined in accordance with national dietary and physical activity guidelines based on the best available scientific evidence and as part of Member States' policies and programmes taking into account cultural traditions and national dietary habits and practices.[141]

If Codex guidelines are to be express in recognizing the differing circumstances of states in this context, autonomy is likely to be enhanced. Although harmonization may be undermined by such an approach, different cultural and culinary influences and differing nutritional profiles in different states suggest that some flexibility is required.

Third, Codex Guidelines on Nutrition Labeling could be amended so as to include sodium or salt[142] and trans fat in the list of nutrients to be declared on packaging.[143] This might alleviate any concerns held by WTO Members that require these nutrients to be declared. Equally, WTO disputes relating to this type of measure appear unlikely.

In summary, there are limits on the extent to which Codex instruments might influence WTO disputes of the types contemplated in Chapter 5. Health claims and nutrition reference values appear to be most relevant, and broadening the list of nutrients in the Guidelines for use of Nutrition and Health Claims appears most likely to be influential. Each of these processes should be guided by the principle that there is some need for regulatory diversity. Standards, guidelines, and recommendations should not be framed in a way that places upper limits or restrictions on regulation, but rather in a way that anticipates future regulation.

B. The tobacco context

In the tobacco context, the character of the FCTC as a framework convention means that guidelines are used to supplement the terms of the treaty. As discussed in Chapter 5, guidelines supplementing Article 11 of the FCTC already govern packaging and labeling of tobacco products. In addition, at the time of writing, the development of guidelines to Articles 9 (regulation of the contents of tobacco products) and 10 (regulation of tobacco product disclosures) is under way. In the short term, this process is most likely to influence the lawfulness of measures restricting flavored tobacco products, such as those

[141] Fifty-Seventh World Health Assembly, Global Strategy on Diet, Physical Activity and Health, 22 May 2004, WHA 57.17.

[142] At the time of writing, states have been unable to agree on the use of terminology because sodium reflects the nutrient in question, but the term salt is more easily understood by consumers in some states.

[143] Mary L'Abbé, et al., "The Potential of the Codex Alimentarius," pp. 257–261.

discussed in Chapter 5. In this context, it seems appropriate for guidelines to recognize the regulatory purposes of reducing palatability and to use an inclusive list of the types of ingredients that might be restricted. This approach recognizes the different regulatory objectives of states and that the need for different measures may differ from state to state.

This approach would also not prejudge questions of national treatment. Guidelines recognizing that some restrictions on flavored tobacco products have a legitimate regulatory purpose would not suggest that all types of measures will be necessary. Nor would this approach lay out justifications for exemptions, such as for menthol cigarettes. Accordingly, inclusive standards, as are set out in partial guidelines to Article 9 and 10 seem appropriate.

Guidelines to Articles 9 and 10 could also be developed in a way that has implications for regulation to address the relative healthfulness of tobacco products. Equally, the future of ongoing work under Articles 9 and 10 of the FCTC is open to question. The fact that product regulation is at the periphery of tobacco control means that low priority is often given to activities under Articles 9 and 10 when the Conference of the Parties to the FCTC allocates its budget. This could be problematic as the open definition of international standards under the TBT Agreement means that a range of different instruments could be used in application of the agreement. For example, one possibility is that ISO standards might be used by a WTO panel and that a WTO Member engaged in product regulation would have to establish the inappropriateness of those standards. This possibility lends weight to the conclusion that FCTC parties should maintain a work agenda under Articles 9 and 10 of the FCTC, with a view to establishing international standards through FCTC processes. This approach is likely to create benefits in terms of the pooling of national expertise and should ensure that the process of harmonization is driven by states rather than industry.

C. The alcohol context

At present, harmonization is less of a concern in the alcohol context than it is in the dietary and tobacco contexts. As was discussed in Chapter 5, existing product standards in the alcohol context are aimed primarily at ensuring the safety of alcoholic beverages by eliminating toxins such as methanol. While a dispute could arise, these types of measures appear relatively uncontroversial under the SPS Agreement.

In addition to these types of product standards, the Codex Alimentarius Commission could develop standards for labeling measures that would fall within the scope of the TBT Agreement. As is the case with tobacco-labeling measures, the diversity of approaches that WTO Members might take to labeling suggests that standards would have to be inclusive and a guide to best practice. This suggests that guidelines or recommendations modeled on the guidelines to Article 11 of the FCTC may be an appropriate instrument to build on the language included in the Global Strategy Alcohol.

3.3. *The Presumptive Value of Treaty Rules*

In Chapter 5, it was recognized that the definition of international standards in the TBT Agreement gives presumptive value to private standards, but not to mandatory treaty rules. As was discussed earlier, this means that FCTC guidelines may constitute standards, but that the mandatory terms of the treaty may not. As such, the prevailing approach creates an incentive for states to pursue normative integration through nonbinding harmonization rather than through binding forms of legalization. Put another way, the prevailing approach creates a disincentive for the creation of binding international laws in the public health context. This disincentive suggests the need for law reform within the WTO to give health treaties, such as the FCTC, at least the same status as nonbinding standards, guidelines, and recommendations.

Barring law reform of this character, there are judicial approaches to enhancing the integration of health treaties and WTO law, other than those discussed in Chapter 2. The way that mandatory treaty rules may be used to guide analysis of WTO law was discussed in Chapter 2, where it was recognized that there are a number of different methods of normative integration. These methods include using mandatory treaty rules extraneous to WTO law as evidence of facts, in the interpretation of norms and pursuant to Article 31(3)(c) of the Vienna Convention on the Law of Treaties. It was also noted that the roots of normative integration lie in the presumption against conflict.

Having identified the presumption against conflict as one source of normative integration, full operation should be given to that presumption in WTO law. Measures implemented pursuant to an extraneous treaty should be presumed to comply with WTO law in certain circumstances. In the case of health measures, this means that measures implemented pursuant to a treaty such as the FCTC should be presumed to be necessary to protect human health. The effect of such a presumption would be much the same as the effect of the presumptions based on standards under the SPS and TBT Agreements, in that a complainant would bear the burden of establishing that a measure is unnecessary. Applying the presumption in this way would give further content to the relationship between trade and health, and would minimize the extent to which private standards are afforded a greater status than public treaty rules.

In evaluating the scope of any such presumption, there are two important questions to consider. The first concerns what it means for a measure to be implemented pursuant to a treaty such as the FCTC. In this respect, because the presumption has its roots in conflict avoidance, it is only where a conflict between treaties might arise that a presumption of lawfulness could operate. As such, the definition given to the concept of conflict is also determinative of the scope of any presumption. Assuming that a broad definition of conflict is to be applied for the reasons discussed, any presumption of lawfulness would also be broad. Under the case study of potential conflicts between the FCTC and the WTO Agreement offered earlier, this would mean that a presumption of lawfulness could operate where a respondent is compelled by the FCTC to implement the impugned aspect of the measure or where the impugned aspect of the measure reflects the exercise of a right under the FCTC.

The second question concerns when the presumption would apply, an issue that revolves around treaty membership in much the same way that interpretation of Article 31(3)(c) does. There are a number of different circumstances to distinguish. One circumstance is where all WTO Members are also parties to the extraneous treaty. In such a situation, objections based on treaty membership are not sustainable. The more difficult questions arise where not all WTO Members are parties to the extraneous treaty. Within this context, three scenarios can be distinguished. The first scenario is where both disputants are parties to the extraneous treaty. The second scenario is where one disputant is a party to the extraneous treaty, but the other is not. The third scenario is where neither disputant is a party to the extraneous treaty (but other WTO Members are).

Where both disputants are parties to the extraneous treaty, a conflict may arise between treaty obligations. As the analysis in Chapter 2 suggested, it is entirely consistent with the law of treaties for a treaty to be applied differently between some of the parties to that treaty only. This is implicit in Article 30 of the Vienna Convention. As such, where not all WTO Members are parties to an extraneous treaty, this should not prevent application of a presumption of lawfulness when both disputants are parties to the treaty in question.

The issue is more complex where only one disputant is a party to the extraneous treaty or where neither disputant is a party to that treaty. On the one hand, the roots of the presumption in rules governing conflicts suggest that a presumption should not apply, because a conflict is not possible without the disputants each being parties to the two treaties in question. On the other hand, where some WTO Members are parties to the extraneous treaty, the presumption might apply in disputes with similar factual scenarios but different disputants. In this sense, there is a broader question of normative integration in that the DSB should not interpret the WTO-covered agreements in isolation from public international law simply because the disputants may not be bound by the laws in question. In this respect, standards may have presumptive effect under the TBT Agreement even if a state has not consented to them and they are private in character. Nonetheless, the operation of the presumption in question is a procedural mechanism that does not compel a particular outcome. This weighs in favor of applying it only where both parties to a dispute are parties to the extraneous treaty.

The final question this analysis raises relates to the importance of Article 31(3)(c) of the Vienna Convention. Why is Article 31(3)(c) important even if the broadest view of the provision discussed in Chapter 2 might not translate into the context of the presumption against conflict? The reason lies in the fact that Article 31(3)(c) compels a treaty interpreter to take an extraneous treaty into account. This obligation, which is largely procedural, should be triggered more readily than simply where all WTO Members are parties to an extraneous treaty. In the context of the presumption against conflict, this obligation may also serve as a mechanism reinforcing full application of the presumption in WTO law. The analysis of Article 31(3)(c) set out in chapter 2 is also important because it demonstrates to full extent of the imbalance in WTO law, thereby suggesting the need for a new approach.

4. CONCLUSION

This chapter examined delegation, legalization, and harmonization as means to address the impact of WTO law on domestic regulatory autonomy. When viewed in its entirety, the discussion suggests that more is likely to be gained through the pursuit of legalization and harmonization than by attempting to change processes of WTO dispute settlement in any fundamental way.

The discussion of delegation suggested that little benefit in terms of coherence is likely to be gained by attempts to reallocate the task of dispute settlement to other international bodies or attempts to grant discretionary-type authority at the national level. In addition, the analysis suggested that it is not possible to theorize the relationship between trade and health completely while maintaining policy coherence. Rather, a more flexible incremental approach is desirable. Mechanisms such as Article XX(b) of the GATT can serve the purpose of facilitating coherence on a case-by-case basis.

The discussion of legalization suggested that conflicts clauses are of limited value as a justification for legalization. This is partly because complaints may be brought by states that are not parties to health treaties, and partly because of the limited circumstances in which conflicts may arise. There is significant doubt about whether a multilateral health treaty would compel conduct or grant a right to carry out conduct that would not be considered lawful after the policy-balancing provisions of the WTO-covered agreements are applied. How willing a WTO panel would be to apply a conflicts clause to the exclusion of a WTO-covered agreement also remains to be seen.

The discussion of legalization also suggested that the merits of concluding treaties in the contexts of diet and alcohol turn primarily on factors extraneous to the trade and health debate. In particular, whether there is a need for collective action by states was a significant issue of concern in conclusion of the FCTC. Despite the suggestion in the FCTC that it was concluded as a response to processes of trade liberalization, a closer analysis of the treaty and activities of the Conference of the Parties suggests that other reasons existed. To the extent that proposals for treaties relating to diet and alcohol are modeled on the FCTC, this suggests that there may be other preconditions for conclusion of treaties. In particular, the identification of collective-action problems that are of widespread concern would go some way to advancing calls for legalization modeled on the FCTC.

The third approach considered was further international harmonization in order to enhance the integration of health norms into WTO law through the SPS and TBT Agreements. The deference accorded to international standards in the SPS and TBT Agreements means that there is a clear role for international standards in this process. In the tobacco context, the conclusion of guidelines to the FCTC has generated standards for purposes of the TBT Agreement. A continued work agenda on product testing and regulation may be useful, but the benefits of such action remain to be seen. Similarly, in the dietary context, recent amendments to Codex standards in light of the Global Strategy Diet have taken greater account of noncommunicable diseases. By the same token, the prospects of meaningful harmonization for purposes of the SPS Agreement are limited by the differing nutritional profiles of different populations. These differing profiles mean that different WTO Members are likely to have differing dietary recommendations at the domestic level, making it difficult to conclude international standards of much depth on a variety of issues. The role of standards is also limited by the scope of the SPS and TBT Agreements, which do not encompass all measures to address tobacco, alcohol, or diet. This limitation may, however, be overcome to some extent if the presumption against conflict is given full effect under WTO law, and conformance to extraneous treaties is considered to create a presumption of necessity as standards may under the SPS and TBT Agreements.

7

Conclusion

This study set out to examine whether domestic regulatory autonomy preserved by the WTO-covered agreements reflects an appropriate balance between the protection of public health and the interests underlying the WTO Agreement. Chapters 1–5 examined this question by reference to interventions to prevent noncommunicable diseases associated with tobacco, alcohol, and diet. This question was also examined against the backdrop set out in Chapter 1, which suggests that the liberalization of trade in tobacco, alcohol, and food have played a role in increasing the prevalence of noncommunicable disease. Chapter 1 also highlighted how some developing countries are particularly vulnerable to noncommunicable disease as a consequence of weak health systems. Another source of vulnerability is the so-called double burden of disease associated with the need to address infectious diseases, such as malaria and HIV/AIDS, while also trying to address noncommunicable diseases.

Chapter 1 also set out a framework for analysis. It was suggested that the relationship between trade and health be examined by reference to two factors. The first factor was determinacy, meaning the ability of WTO Members to determine whether health measures are lawful. This concept was linked to the risk of regulatory chill, which encompasses the prospect that WTO Members may not implement lawful health measures for fear of violating the WTO Agreement. The second factor identified was the way in which WTO law balances the objectives underlying the WTO Agreement with the protection of public health. This concept was further refined by reference to concerns about market access, in the sense that rules governing nontariff barriers to trade need to balance market-access commitments made under the WTO Agreement with domestic regulatory autonomy. The relationship between prohibitions and exceptions was identified as important to this question, as was the interaction between WTO law and international health instruments.

Chapter 2 examined the way in which WTO law takes account of health instruments in dispute settlement. This analysis informed subsequent chapters that examined application of the covered agreements and whether binding health instruments are more appropriate than nonbinding instruments. In a more abstract sense, the way in which international health instruments are taken into account in WTO dispute settlement is an expression of how open WTO law is to interaction with extraneous international norms.

The analysis set out in Chapter 2 showed that, with the lead of the Appellate Body, WTO panels have been willing to take account of extraneous instruments (both binding and nonbinding) without reference to any rule enabling them to do so. Panels often rely on extraneous instruments as evidence of facts, and in some disputes extraneous instruments have been used in construing the scope of WTO norms. There is also nothing to suggest that panels are reluctant to draw on an extraneous norm where a covered agreement incorporates it by reference. For example, the role played by international standards, guidelines, and recommendations under the SPS Agreement, and international standards under the TBT Agreement, provides an avenue through which health interests may be integrated with WTO law.

On the other hand, the decision of the panel in *EC – Approval and Marketing of Biotech Products* shows considerable resistance to a mandatory rule compelling a panel to take account of an extraneous treaty rule, such as a provision of the FCTC. The narrow interpretation given to Article 31(3)(c) of the Vienna Convention suggests that there is only a very limited rule-based guarantee that relevant and applicable rules found in health treaties will be taken into account in WTO dispute settlement. It remains to be seen whether the approach of the panel will stand the test of time, and it was argued that the panel's approach is the only untenable interpretation of Article 31(3)(c). The effect that the decision will have on actual normative integration also remains to be seen. Nonetheless, the panel's decision suggests that WTO law is not as open to normative integration as it ought to be. The decision also suggests that nonbinding instruments may play a greater role in interpretation of WTO law than mandatory health norms such as treaty obligations. This could be taken to suggest a degree of normative imbalance between trade and health.

Chapter 3 examined application of the WTO-covered agreements to differential tax measures, subsidies, and restrictions on advertising and marketing. In the tax context, there is little doubt that a wide variety of effective tax and price measures may be implemented by WTO Members without violation of the GATT. For example, specific taxes that levy the same amount of tax on tobacco products or alcoholic beverages by volume are unlikely to result in violation of Article III:2 of the GATT in most circumstances. On the other hand, there is a greater chance that differential taxes will result in violation of the GATT. The very purpose of these types of taxes is to alter the conditions of competition between goods based on the relative health risks they pose. In altering the conditions of competition between goods in this way, there is always a chance that tax measures of this type will alter the conditions of competition between imported and domestic goods in a way that affords protection to domestic production.

The rejection of the aim and effects test suggests that the regulatory legitimacy of a measure drawing a distinction between products in this way is not likely to be determinative of whether a violation of GATT Article III is established. In Article III of the GATT, the focus of the like-products test is also on the extent to which goods are in competition with one another, and not on whether there is a legitimate reason for drawing a regulatory distinction between goods. The rejection of the aim and effects test also suggested that questions of regulatory legitimacy would not be particularly relevant to the question of when a measure acts to afford protection under Article III:2 of the GATT or constitutes less favorable treatment under Article III:4. However, the decision of the Appellate Body in *Dominican Republic – Importation and Sale of Cigarettes* could be read to suggest that a panel should evaluate explanations for a measure that do not relate to the fact that goods are imported. The panel report in *EC – Approval and Marketing of Biotech Products* took this one step further by concluding that it was not apparent that the EC measures were motivated by the imported status of biotech products as opposed to on safety grounds. As Howse and Horn argue, this appears to take the case law back to the aim and effects test, in the sense that the aim of a measure (and its regulatory legitimacy) is again relevant in contemporary case law.

Ultimately, the notion that the case law may have come full circle in this way only serves to highlight how unpredictable application of Article III of the GATT can be. As Hudec argued, panels often make a seat-of-the-pants judgment that resembles application of a "smell test." WTO Members are limited in their capacity to combat unpredictability stemming from tests of this type. It might be thought that members can, for the most part, avoid the possibility of violation by adopting a rigorously scientific approach to the way in which different goods are categorized for tax purposes. However, the process of drawing regulatory distinctions between goods is not an easy one, particularly in low-resource settings. Even in high-resource settings, different technical or methodological approaches are likely to generate different results. For example, in the dietary context there are various technical approaches to nutrition profiling that have differing consequences in terms of the categorization of goods. These different approaches might reflect the differing needs of countries with different nutritional profiles or different consumption patterns, or they may reflect deeper disagreement on how best to approach the categorization of goods. Either way, Article III of the GATT may, on occasion, be violated by a WTO Member acting in good faith for a legitimate regulatory purpose.

Leaving differential taxes to one side, the potential impact of Article III was also illustrated by reference to price floors, which have been advocated particularly in the alcohol context. Where imported goods would be cheaper than domestic goods but for a price floor, a violation of Article III:4 of the GATT is likely to occur. Of course, a WTO Member might argue that a price floor is defensible under Article XX(b) of the GATT, but it would appear that use of a specific tax and measures limiting discounting would be reasonably available alternative measures in most circumstances. Where these measures are reasonably available, it is difficult to see how this outcome would interfere unduly with domestic regulatory autonomy. On the contrary, price floors appear to be a rather crude means of dissuading consumption.

Chapter 3 also examined the use of tariffs as a form of tax aimed at dissuading consumption of a product or of certain product categories. As Fidler has argued, tariffs are unlikely to be a particularly effective means of protecting health where there is domestic production of relatively harmful goods at which tariffs are targeted. If anything, trade theory suggests that in the absence of some other government intervention, the imposition of high tariffs on relatively unhealthy goods will encourage domestic production of those goods. Equally, there may be circumstances in which tariff rates play a role in health policy, such as where domestic circumstances mean that local production of relatively less healthy goods does not occur. This may be the case, for example, in small island states that are not well endowed with factors of production. In such circumstances, a tariff may actually be a useful public health measure because other forms of taxation might be considered to act so as to afford protection to domestic production of other types of goods. Obviously, the extent to which a WTO Member might rely on tariffs in its health policy is not dependent on a body of legal rules that draws a line between legitimate and impermissible regulatory measures. Rather, this aspect of the relationship between trade and health is a question of power politics in the context of negotiations on market access.

Ultimately, this affirms the obvious conclusion that states with relatively closed markets for tobacco products, alcoholic beverages, and unhealthy foods should consider whether maintaining high tariffs might be an effective health policy on its own or possibly in combination with measures that restrict domestic production. By the same token, policy choices of this type may not reconcile the benefits of trade and health.

Chapter 3 then examined rules restricting the use of subsidies. It was concluded that differential taxes levied at the point of consumption may, in some circumstances, constitute actionable subsidies under the SCM Agreement. This could give rise to the authorization of countermeasures, including counter-subsidies. Given the potential for violation of Article III:2 of the GATT, the significance of this conclusion lies in the fact that the SCM Agreement does not include a health exception. Accordingly, regulatory autonomy may turn on the question of whether Article XX of the GATT extends to other covered agreements.

Chapter 3 also examined the use of agricultural subsidies as a means of promoting the availability of healthful foods such as fresh fruits and vegetables. It was concluded that the extent to which a member enjoys autonomy under the Agreement on Agriculture is directly related to the commitments made in that member's schedule. This is largely a function of the extent to which a member engaged in agricultural subsidization prior to the Uruguay Round. Consequently, the flexibility available to a member under the Agreement on Agriculture is determined partly by historical circumstances and partly by power relations as reflected in the commitments made by that member. This resembles the conclusion drawn in the context of tariff commitments under the GATT and suggests that some WTO Members have more autonomy than others.

Finally, Chapter 3 examined application of the GATS to restrictions on marketing, including both restrictions on advertising and restrictions on retailing. It was concluded that the decision of the Appellate Body in *US – Gambling* has blurred the lines between questions of internal regulation (traditionally governed by national treatment rules) and market access. The blurring of the distinction between the treatment of border measures and behind-the-border regulations in the GATS context has reduced the regulatory autonomy of members with specific market-access commitments in a significant way. Whereas measures banning advertising might be viewed as qualitative measures falling outside the realm of market-access commitments, other measures restricting retail sales may violate market-access commitments if those commitments are not limited in a member's schedule. Examples of this type include restrictions on the total number of liquor stores in designated areas and restrictions on the retail sale of products via remote means, such as over the Internet.

Although it is true that the largely voluntary character of the GATS means that members have a large degree of autonomy, the decision in *US – Gambling* moved the ground beneath policy makers in an unexpected way, meaning that prior commitments took on a new significance. To say that the GATS is largely voluntary also does not take the analysis very far. The WTO regime as a whole is voluntary. No state is required to become a member of the WTO, and any state could choose not to do so in order to preserve its regulatory autonomy. However, this denies the obvious fact that membership in the WTO and the commitments that come with membership are an important means of ensuring market access for domestic constituents. Again, it is only because of the merit associated with WTO membership that questions of domestic regulatory autonomy become important.

In summary, there are circumstances in which WTO Members may implement the types of measures discussed in good faith, but nonetheless violate prohibitions in a WTO-covered agreement. This is not to suggest that violation will be commonplace (or the subject of a dispute). Rather, the purpose of the analysis was to take some hard cases and examine how the prohibitions may apply. The analysis suggests two things of relevance to the balance between trade and health. First, the analysis suggests that there is significant uncertainty with respect to application of a number of prohibitions that are central to the WTO-covered agreements. Second, the analysis suggests that with a few limited exceptions, the prohibitions are not animated by the need to balance market-access commitments with other social goals. For this most part, this balancing exercise is left to application of exceptions.

Chapter 4 examined the extent to which exceptions, such as Article XX(b) of the GATT, preserve regulatory autonomy in the context of a violation of the covered agreements. In the first instance, it was concluded that Article XX(b) of the GATT has a limited application to violations of other covered agreements. The circumstance where Article XX might apply is where another covered agreement incorporates a GATT prohibition by reference, and the context suggests that Article XX(b) should apply. This suggests that Article XX(b) might apply in the context of a prohibited subsidy under the SCM Agreement, but will not apply in the context of a violation of the Agreement on Agriculture.

Chapter 4 then examined a number of concerns surrounding application of the necessity test to measures to address tobacco, alcohol, and diet. One of these concerns was that the search for the least trade-restrictive means of protecting health is not conducive to the adoption of regulatory strategies that rely on a range of complementary measures. The decisions of the panel and Appellate Body in *Brazil – Retreaded Tyres* suggest that this may no longer be a significant issue. Both the panel and Appellate Body recognized that complementary measures are not alternative measures for purposes of the necessity test. Although the concept of complementary measures remains to be elaborated in case law, this approach goes a long way to alleviating concern that measures such as tax measures and restrictions on advertising could be alternatives to one another.

Another concern examined in Chapter 4 was the possibility that measures to address distal causes of disease are unlikely to withstand scrutiny under the necessity test. More specifically, Chapter 4 examined how a long chain of causation between a risk factor and the onset of disease could suggest that a measure is not necessary. This concern is of particular significance in the dietary context where there are long chains of causation between a regulatory intervention and the prevention of disease. It was argued that the relatively relaxed threshold for determining when a measure makes a contribution to the protection of human health alleviates this concern to some extent. The fact that a panel can judge the contribution of a measure in qualitative terms, rather than merely in quantitative terms, also increases the scope for members to implement measures of this type.

Equally, application of the necessity test remains somewhat unpredictable, partly because a great deal depends on the way in which a panel characterizes a member's regulatory goal. The panel's decision in *Brazil – Retreaded Tyres* highlighted the way in which a narrowly construed regulatory goal can enhance the prospects of a measure being found to be lawful. Although the ultimate outcome of *Brazil – Retreaded Tyres* was arguably a good one, there is no guarantee that this will always be the case. On the contrary, where members make long-term quantitative goals to reduce the prevalence of smoking or obesity, this may lead to the characterization of regulatory goals in a broad and quantitative fashion for purposes of the necessity test. In such situations, it may become more difficult to justify the lawfulness of a measure. Ultimately, this suggests that members must be careful in the way in which they express their regulatory goals in national strategies to address noncommunicable diseases. Although broad quantitative goals have a place in guiding health policy, regulatory autonomy is likely to be better accommodated in the analysis in which qualitative goals are expressed in the context of specific measures.

Overall, this suggests that there is a high degree of judicial deference to domestic regulatory choices under the necessity test. This is not, however, the end of the analysis under provisions such as Article XX(b) of the GATT. Application of a measure remains to be examined under the *chapeau* of Article XX. The fact that the *chapeau* relates to application of a measure makes it difficult to draw meaningful conclusions about how the provision may impact measures addressing tobacco, alcohol, and diet. Nonetheless, there is potential for the *chapeau* to undermine domestic regulatory experimentation where differing approaches to like products are based on the consumption habits of a population. There is a risk that these types of approaches will be considered arbitrary or unjustifiable. This issue was discussed further in the context of Article 5.5 of the SPS Agreement.

In summary, the analysis in Chapter 4 suggests that the Article XX(b) exception leaves a wide margin for WTO Members to implement measures to address noncommunicable disease. This wide margin appears to be a reasonable balance between protecting market-access commitments and preserving domestic regulatory autonomy. By the same token, it can be difficult to predict application of the provision.

Chapter 5 drew on the conclusions in Chapter 4 and examined how the SPS and TBT Agreements govern product-regulation measures, including labeling measures. The SPS and TBT Agreements establish positive necessity requirements, as distinct from the exceptional character of the necessity test in Article XX(b) of the GATT. At face value, this positive necessity requirement is a greater incursion on domestic regulatory autonomy than is the case under the GATT, where a measure must violate a GATT prohibition before the necessity test comes into play.

However, this first impression is qualified by a number of factors. First, the discussion in Chapter 3 of provisions such as Articles III:4 and XI of the GATT suggests that WTO Members will be conscious of meeting the necessity test wherever health measures are implemented. Second, measures are deemed necessary and benefit from a presumption of lawfulness where SPS measures conform to relevant international standards, guidelines, or recommendations. In addition, even where this presumption does not apply, the burden of proof rests with the WTO Member bringing the claim. Third, the analysis in Chapter 5 suggests that the necessity requirement in the SPS Agreement may not be interpreted as strictly as that in Article XX(b) of the GATT. In particular, the way in which a member's regulatory goal (appropriate level of protection) is identified under the SPS Agreement suggests that members have greater control over the direction that necessity analysis will take. Put another way, a member has greater control over the characterization of the regulatory goal under the SPS Agreement, and this may increase the chances of a measure being considered necessary.

Equally, specific requirements in Article 5 of the SPS Agreement could be problematic in the dietary context. The example discussed in that context was a ban on the sale and importation of fatty cuts of meat, such as mutton flaps and turkey tails, that may fall within the scope of the SPS Agreement. This example highlighted how a member might treat products with comparable nutritional profiles differently because they pose different risks to a population depending on consumption habits. For cultural, economic, or other reasons, one food with a poor nutritional profile may be consumed in amounts that threaten health, whereas other foods with similar nutritional profiles may not. This creates a regulatory dilemma in the sense that regulating a popular food may alleviate a risk but also create a situation where regulation is based on a population's consumption habits as much as it is on the nutritional qualities of different foods. It remains to be seen how a WTO panel would apply Article 5.5 of the SPS Agreement in such a situation, and the outcome may differ depending on the circumstances. The same issue would arise under the GATT and would be relevant in interpretation of the *chapeau* of Article XX(b).

In the context of labeling measures, the existing international standards, guidelines, and recommendations appear to reinforce domestic regulatory autonomy rather than undermine it. In the SPS context, the Codex Alimentarius Commission has worked to update and reform relevant instruments in light of the Global Strategy Diet. These reforms have contemplated the prospect of WTO Members seeking a higher level of protection, such as through traffic light style labeling measures, and appear to contemplate the regulatory diversity that is foreshadowed in the Global Strategy Diet.

In the context of the TBT Agreement, guidelines to the FCTC appear likely to constitute international standards for purposes of Article 2. The content of guidelines to Article 11 of the FCTC, as an expression of best practice, appears to support the lawfulness of a wide range of evidence-based labeling measures. On the other hand, the lawfulness of measures banning the use of flavorings in tobacco products and alcopops remains to be seen in light of the manner in which such measures are implemented and impact market access. The TBT Agreement also contains provisions that are less predictable in their application than the necessity requirement in Article 2.2. For example, Article 2.1 includes a national treatment type obligation in the apparent absence of an exception, and Article 2.8 requires technical regulations to be cast in terms of performance standards rather than descriptive characteristics, wherever appropriate. It seems extremely difficult to predict how these provisions will be interpreted.

The novel provisions of the SPS and TBT Agreements, along with the relative lack of case law, create uncertainty as to how these provisions might be interpreted. This makes it difficult to judge how these agreements balance the preservation of market-access commitments with the protection of public health. In short, indeterminacy is a significant issue in the context of the SPS and TBT Agreements.

Chapter 6 examined a range of earlier proposals for law reform. The first proposal examined was the complete theorization of the relationship between the health measures addressed in Chapters 3–5 and WTO law. This proposal was examined by reference to a case study concerning the exclusion of tobacco from trade agreements. It was concluded that it is unlikely to be possible to completely theorize the relationship between WTO law and the measures in question while also maintaining reasonable balance between the protection of public health and the interests underlying trade agreements.

The second proposal examined was legalization, meaning the use of treaties in place of nonbinding instruments such as the global strategies. In this respect, the foreword to the FCTC suggests that the FCTC was a response to processes of trade liberalization, such as those associated with the WTO Agreement. However, a functional analysis of the FCTC suggests that the need to address collective-action problems in the form of cross-border illicit trade in tobacco products and cross-border tobacco advertising provides a stronger explanation for the treaty. These cross-border collective-action problems arguably created incentives for states to be bound to undertake basic regulatory measures at the domestic level in order to signal commitment to issues of collective concern. It remains to be seen whether any preconditions for new treaties modeled on the FCTC have been met, and this is an avenue for further research of an empirical character.

The analysis of the use of health instruments in application of WTO law set out in Chapter 2 is also relevant to the merits of health treaties. The analysis tended to suggest that nonbinding instruments are at no great disadvantage to binding treaties in terms of the way in which they may be used in WTO disputes to guide interpretation of WTO law. In fact, some nonbinding instruments, such as FCTC guidelines, may play a greater role by virtue of their use as international standards under the TBT Agreement. This is consistent with Broude's argument that stronger forms of normative integration are likely to challenge adjudicative authority and may, therefore, be less successful in the long run. Equally, this conclusion is not intended to suggest that nonbinding instruments are preferable to binding instruments in terms of enhancing cooperation between states or promoting action at the domestic level.

The inclusion of conflicts clauses in health treaties as a means of preserving the lawfulness of measures that violate a WTO-covered agreement was also examined. From the outset, it was noted that this approach is not one that seeks to balance the interests of public health with those underlying the trade regime. This approach seeks to assert public health over the trade regime. Leaving this aside, there are also a number of practical limitations inherent in conflicts clauses. Conflicts clauses only apply in the context of treaty law (and not in the context of nonbinding instruments), and both parties to a WTO dispute would have to be parties to a treaty that includes such a clause in order for it to have effect. The narrow definition traditionally accorded to the concept of a conflict under the law of treaties also means that conflicts would occur in only a very limited range of situations, such as where a health treaty compels the very aspect of a measure that is violative of WTO law.

The third issue considered was further harmonization. It was argued that the reliance on Codex standards under the SPS Agreement means that WHO regulations are not an appropriate means by which to embark on the development of further international standards, guidelines, or recommendations. Through its members, the Codex Alimentarius Commission is working to reform Codex instruments so as to support the goals set out in the Global Strategy Diet. This process may play an important role in balancing regulatory autonomy with trade goals under the SPS Agreement, although this depends on the shape of future standards, guidelines, and recommendations. In this respect, open standards, guidelines, or recommendations that contemplate government intervention beyond that expressly included in the instruments may be appropriate. This is particularly important in the dietary context, in which harmonization may be problematic for reasons relating to the different nutritional profiles of states. Further guideline development through the FCTC on product regulation and possibly further standardization in the alcohol context with respect to labeling measures may also reduce uncertainty while promoting regulatory harmonization.

Finally, it was argued that the presumption against conflict should be given its full effect in WTO law[, preferably through law-reform. Failing law-reform and assuming a judicial approach is necessary, s]ubject to the question of treaty membership, the presumption should operate in much the same way that the presumption of compliance operates under the SPS and TBT Agreements. This approach would enhance normative integration and go some way to remedying imbalance between the status accorded to private standards and treaty rules under the TBT Agreement.

So what does all this amount to? The one inescapable conclusion is that it is difficult to generalize about the relationship between trade and the new public health. The complexity of WTO law is apparent. So too is the fact that WTO Members may seek to protect human health in ways that are difficult to anticipate, partly because the new public health operates in a fast developing policy space in which regulatory experimentation is unavoidable. WTO Members also have different risk profiles. Some members are more risk averse than others, and some members face greater or different types of risks than others. Nonetheless, through case studies on taxation measures, restrictions on marketing, and product-regulation measures (including labeling measures) this study has sought to sketch the relationship between the two fields. Although the analysis has not sought to produce a comprehensive map of the relationship between trade and the new public health, the sketch provided has permitted some conclusions.

The first conclusion to be drawn is that there are problems of determinacy in the sense that it is difficult to anticipate how a number of issues will be resolved under WTO law. Although the analysis sought out hard cases, and there are many measures that are unlikely to be controversial, outcomes can be difficult to predict. The primary source of indeterminacy is the open-textured character of many provisions of WTO law. A wide margin of discretion is therefore afforded to WTO panels.

The second conclusion is that indeterminacy affects the analysis of balance between the interests of trade and health. Where the case law is well developed, as it is under GATT Article XX(b), it is possible to identify reasonable balance between the interests in question, as far as the substantive law is concerned. On the other hand, where the case law is not well developed and provisions could be interpreted in a number of ways, as is the case under the SPS and TBT Agreements, it is more difficult to comment. Nonetheless, some comfort can be taken from the fact that the Appellate Body of the WTO has shown considerable sensitivity to health objectives in recent decisions. The challenge for the DSB is whether this level of sensitivity can be shown as WTO Members build on their early efforts to address noncommunicable disease.

Glossary of Basic Trade Terms

The following glossary of terms constitutes a nontechnical explanation of some terms. It is intended to assist those lacking a background in international trade law.

Appellate Body refers to the standing body of seven persons established under Article 17 of the DSU. The Appellate Body hears appeals brought by WTO Members with respect to panel reports.

Applied tariff rate refers to the tariff rate that a WTO Member actually applies.

Bound tariff rate refers to the tariff rate that a WTO Member is bound not to exceed under the terms of its schedule of concessions to the GATT.

Common Agricultural Policy (CAP) refers to the EU system of subsidies and programs to support agriculture.

Comparative advantage refers to the theory that two or more countries generate economic gains from international trade where they have divergent opportunity costs in the production of goods or services.

Countermeasure refers to a measure authorized by the DSB and implemented by a WTO Member to counter the adverse effects of a subsidy.

Dispute Settlement Body (DSB) refers to the body established by Article 2 of the DSU. The DSB has responsibility for administering the DSU, and authority to establish panels, adopt panel and Appellate Body reports, maintain surveillance of implementation of rulings and recommendations, and authorize suspension of concessions and other obligations under the covered agreements.

Dispute Settlement Understanding (DSU) refers to the legal instrument setting out rules for the settlement of disputes within the WTO.

Harmonization refers to the adoption of international standards, guidelines, or recommendations that are taken into account in accordance with the terms of Article 3 of the SPS Agreement or Article 2 of the TBT Agreement.

Most-favored-nation (MFN) refers to the principle that WTO Members shall afford any advantage, favor, privilege, or immunity extended to goods or services of one WTO Member to like products of all WTO Members immediately and unconditionally. (See Article I of the GATT for an example in the context of trade in goods.)

National treatment refers to the principle that WTO Members shall not treat imported goods or services less favorably than like domestic goods or services. (See Article III of the GATT for an example in the context of trade in goods.)

Necessity test refers to the requirement that measures be necessary to protect human health or life in order for a WTO Member to invoke the exception in Article XX(b) of the GATT.

Nondiscrimination refers to the concept of less favorable treatment in the contexts of national treatment and MFN treatment.

Nontariff barrier to trade refers to barriers to trade other than tariffs, including regulatory measures.

Normative integration refers to a process whereby norms from different regimes are read together with a view to giving full effect to each norm.

Panel refers to a three-member body established by the DSB in order to hear a dispute between WTO Members concerning compliance with a WTO-covered agreement.

Quantitative restriction refers to a restriction on importation or exportation of goods, as prohibited by Article XI:1 of the GATT.

Risk assessment refers to "[t]he evaluation of the likelihood of entry, establishment or spread of a pest or disease within the territory of an importing Member according to the sanitary or phytosanitary measures which might be applied, and of the associated potential biological and economic consequences; or the evaluation of the potential for adverse effects on human or animal health arising from the presence of additives, contaminants, toxins or disease-causing organisms in food, beverages or feedstuffs" (as defined in paragraph 4 of Annex A of the SPS Agreement).

SPS measure refers to any measures applied:

(a) to protect animal or plant life or health within the territory of the Member from risks arising from the entry, establishment or spread of pests, diseases, disease-carrying organisms or disease-causing organisms;
(b) to protect human or animal life or health within the territory of the Member from risks arising from additives, contaminants, toxins or disease-causing organisms in foods, beverages or feedstuffs;
(c) to protect human life or health within the territory of the Member from risks arising from diseases carried by animals, plants or products thereof, or from the entry, establishment or spread of pests; or
(d) to prevent or limit other damage within the territory of the Member from the entry, establishment or spread of pests.

Sanitary or phytosanitary measures include all relevant laws, decrees, regulations, requirements and procedures including, inter alia, end product criteria; processes and production methods; testing, inspection, certification and approval procedures; quarantine treatments including relevant requirements associated with the transport of animals or plants, or with the materials necessary for their survival during transport; provisions on relevant statistical methods, sampling procedures and methods of risk assessment; and packaging and labeling requirements directly related to food safety.

(As defined in paragraph 1 of Annex A of the SPS Agreement.)

Schedule of concessions refers to a WTO Member's list of bound tariff rates annexed to the GATT in accordance with Article II.

Schedule of specific commitments refers to a WTO Member's list of specific commitments made under the GATS.

Subsidy refers to a measure falling within the definition set out in Article 1.1(a)(1) of the SCM Agreement, including financial contributions, direct transfers of funds or liabilities, forgoing of government revenue that is otherwise due, the provision of goods or services other than general infrastructure, payments to a funding mechanism, or income or price support, where a benefit is thereby conferred (such as to an industry or a firm). A subsidy may also be in the form of an export subsidy, where the benefit conferred is contingent upon export.

Tariff refers to a customs duty levied on the importation of a good.

Technical regulation refers to a "[d]ocument which lays down product characteristics or their related processes and production methods, including the applicable administrative provisions, with which compliance is mandatory. It may also include or deal exclusively with terminology, symbols, packaging, marking or labeling requirements as they apply to a product, process or production method" (as defined in paragraph 1 of Annex 1 to the TBT Agreement).

Trade liberalization refers to a process where barriers to trade, such as tariffs, are reduced or removed.

Treaty refers to "an international agreement concluded between States in written form and governed by international law, whether embodied in a single instrument or in two or more related instruments and whatever its particular designation" (as defined in Article 1(1)(a) of the Vienna Convention).

World Trade Organization (WTO) refers to the international organization established by the WTO Agreement as the successor to the GATT on January 1, 1995.

WTO-covered agreement refers to an agreement listed in Appendix 1 of the DSU.

Bibliography

Agreements and Treaties

Basel Convention on the Control of Transboundary Movements of Hazardous Wastes and Their Disposal, 1673 UNTS 126; 28 ILM 657 (1989).

Basel Convention Technical Guidelines on the Identification and Management of Used Tyres, available at http://www.basel.int/meetings/sbc/workdoc/old%20docs/tech-usedtyres.pdf.

Cartagena Protocol on Biosafety to the Convention on Biological Diversity, 39 ILM 1027 (2000).

Convention against Illicit Traffic in Narcotic Drugs and Psychotropic Substances, 28 I.L.M. 493 (1989).

Convention on Biological Diversity, Done at Rio de Janeiro, 5 June 1992, 31 ILM 818 (1992).

Convention on the Elimination of All Forms of Discrimination Against Women, GA res. 34/180, 34 UN GAOR Supp. (No. 46) at 193, UN Doc. A/34/46; 1249 UNTS 13; 19 ILM 33 (1980).

Convention on the Prevention and Punishment of the Crime of Genocide,78 UNTS 277.

Convention on the Rights of the Child, GA res. 44/25, annex, 44 UN GAOR Supp. (No. 49) at 167, U.N. Doc. A/44/49 (1989); 1577 UNTS 3; 28 ILM 1456 (1989).

International Covenant on Economic, Social and Cultural Rights, GA Res. 2200A (XXI), 21 UN GAOR Supp. (No. 16) at 49, UN Doc. A/6316 (1966); 993 UNTS 3; 6 ILM 368 (1967).

Marrakesh Agreement Establishing the World Trade Organization, Apr. 15, 1994, The Legal Texts: The Results of the Uruguay Round of Multilateral Trade Negotiations 4 (1999), 33 I.L.M. 1144 (1994).

North American Free Trade Agreement, 32 I.L.M. 289, 605 (1993).

Pacific Island Countries Trade Agreement, Done at Nauru August 18, 2001.

Protocol against the Illicit Manufacturing of and Trafficking in Firearms, Their Parts and Components and Ammunition, supplementing the United Nations Convention against Transnational Organised Crime, G.A. res. 255, Nov. 15, 2000, U.N. Doc. A/RES/55/255 (2001).

Protocol on Strategic Environmental Assessment to the Convention on Environmental Impact Assessment in a Transboundary Context, Done at Kiev (Ukraine), 21 May 2003.
Statute of the International Court of Justice, 3 Bevans 1179; 59 Stat. 1031; T.S. 993; 39 AJIL Supp. 215 (1945).
United Nations Convention against Transnational Organized Crime, 40 ILM 335 (2001); UN Doc. A/55/383 at 25 (2000); UN Doc. A/RES/55/25.
United Nations Convention on the Law of the Sea, Done at Montego Bay, 10 December 1982, 21 ILM 1261 (1982).
United Nations Economic Commission for Europe Convention on Access to Information, Public Participation in Decision-making and Access to Justice in Environmental Matters, done at Aarhus, Denmark, on 25 June 1998.
Vienna Convention on the Law of Treaties, May 23, 1969, 1155 U.N.T.S. 331; 8 I.L.M. 679 (1969).
World Health Organization: Framework Convention on Tobacco Control, May 21, 2003, 42 I.L.M. 518 (2003).

Articles

Abbot, Kenneth and Snidal, Duncan, "Hard and Soft Law in International Governance," 54(3) *International Organization*, (Summer 2000), 421–456.
Abi-Saab, Georges, "Fragmentation or Unification: Some Concluding Remarks," 31 *New York Journal of International Law and Politics*, (1998–1999), 919–933.
Alemson, M, "Advertising and the Nature of Competition in Oligopoly Over Time: A Case Study," 80 *The Economic Journal*, (1970), 282–306.
Anderson, Peter, Bruijn, Avalon de, Angus, Katherine, Gordon, Ross and Hastings, Gerard, "Impact of Alcohol Advertising and Media Exposure on Adolescent Alcohol Use: A Systematic Review of Longitudinal Studies," 44(3) *Alcohol & Alcoholism*, (2009), 229–343.
Appleberry, Robin, "It's a Woman Thing: Sex, Status, and Human Rights in the Tobacco Epidemic," 15 *Berkeley Women's Law Journal*, (2000), 312–326.
"Breaking the Camel's Back: Bringing Women's Human Rights to Bear on Tobacco Control," 13 *Yale Journal of Law and Feminism*, (2001), 71–96.
Atik, Jeffrey, "Science and International Trade – Third Generation Scholarship," 26 *Boston College International and Comparative Law Review*, (2003), 171–181.
Aufrict, Hans, "Supersession of Treaties in International Law," 37 *Cornell Law Quarterly*, (1951–1952), 655–700.
Bagwell, Kyle, Mavroidis, Petros and Staiger, Robert, "It's a Question of Market Access," 96 *American Journal of International Law*, (2002), 56–76.
Bartkowski, Alicia, "The World Health Organization's Framework Convention on Tobacco Control, Free Trade and the American Example," 2 *Journal of International Business and Law*, (Spring 2003), 146–173.
Bates, Clive, Fagerström, Karl, Jarvis, Martin, et al., "European Union Policy on Smokeless Tobacco: A Statement in Favour of Evidence Based Regulation for Public Health," 12 *Tobacco Control*, (2003), 360–367.
Baxter, R, "International Law in her Infinite Variety," 29 *International and Comparative Law Quarterly*, (1980), 549–566.

Bernstein, Steven and Hannah, Erin, "Non-State Global Standard Setting and the WTO: Legitimacy and the Need for Regulatory Space," 11(3) *Journal of International Economic Law*, (2008), 575–608.

Bloche, M. Gregg, "WTO Deference to National Health Policy: Toward an Interpretive Principle," 5(4) *Journal of International Economic Law*, (2002), 825–848.

Blouin, Chantal, Chopra, Mickey and van der Hoeven, Rolph, "Trade and Health 3: Trade and Social Determinants of Health," 373 (9662), *The Lancet*, London (Feb 7–Feb 13, 2009), 504–505.

Boister, Neil, "Recent Progress in the Development of a Protocol on the Illicit Trade in Tobacco Products," 5(1) (2010), *Asian Journal of WTO & International Health Law and Policy*, 53–86.

Bown, Chad and Trachtman, Joel, "Brazil – Measures Affecting Imports of Retreaded Tyres: A Balancing Act," 8(1) *World Trade Review*, (2009), 85–135.

Callard, Cynthia, Chitanondh, Hatai and Weissman, Robert, "Why Trade and Investment Liberalisation may Threaten Effective Tobacco Control Efforts," 10 *Tobacco Control*, (2001), 68–70.

Carmody, Chios, "WTO Obligations as Collective," 17(2) *European Journal of International Law*, (2006), 419–443.

Casswell, Sally and Thamarangsi, Thaksaphon, "Reducing Harm from Alcohol: Call to Action," 373 *Lancet*, (2009), 2247–2257.

Charney, Jonathan, "The Impact of the International Legal System of the Growth of International Courts and Tribunals," 31 *New York Journal of International Law and Politics*, (1998–1999), 697–708.

Charnovitz, Steve, "GATT and the Environment: Examining the Issues," 4 *International Environmental Affairs*, (1992), 203–233.

"An Analysis of Pascal Lamy's Proposal on Collective Preferences," 8(2) *Journal of International Economic Law*, (2005), 449–472.

"The WTO'S Environmental Progress," 10(3) *Journal of International Economic Law*, (2007), 685–706.

Chinkin, Christine, "The Challenge of Soft Law: Development and Change in International Law," 38 *International and Comparative Law Quarterly*, (1989), 850–866.

Chopra, Mickey, Galbraith, Sarah and Darnton-Hill, Ian, "A Global Response to a Global Problem: The Epidemic of Overnutrition," 80(12) *Bulletin of the World Health Organization*, (2002), 952–958.

Correa, Carlos, "Implementing National Public Health Policies in the Framework of WTO Agreements," 34(5) *Journal of World Trade*, (2000), 89–121.

Crow, Melissa, "Smokescreens and State Responsibility: Using Human Rights Strategies to Promote Global Tobacco Control," 29 *Yale Journal of International Law*, (2004), 209–250.

Davey, William and Sapir, André, "The Soft Drinks Case: The WTO and Regional Agreements," 8(1) *World Trade Review*, (2009), 5–23.

Davies, Arwel, "Interpreting the Chapeau of GATT Article XX in Light of the 'New' Approach in *Brazil – Tyres*," 43(3) *Journal of World Trade*, (2009), 507–539.

Delimatsis, Panagiotis, "Determining the Necessity of Domestic Regulations in Services, The Best is Yet to Come," 19(2) *European Journal of International Law*, (2008), 365–408.

Depken, Craig, "The Effects of Advertising Restrictions on Cigarette Prices: Evidence from OECD Countries," 6 *Applied Economics Letters*, (1999), 307–309.

Desmedt, Axel, "Proportionality in WTO Law," 4 *Journal of International Economic Law*, (2001), 441–480.

Dhooge, Lucien, "Smoke Across the Waters: Tobacco Production and Exportation as International Human Rights Violations," 22 *Fordham International Law Journal*, (1998), 355–456.

Di Mascio, Nicholas and Pauwelyn, Joost, "Nondiscrimination in Trade and Investment Treaties: Worlds Apart or Two Sides of the Same Coin?" 102 *American Journal of International Law*, (2008), 48–89.

Doll, R, Peto, R, Wheatley, K, et al., "Mortality in Relation to Smoking: 40 Years' Observation on Male British Doctors," 309 *British Medical Journal*, (8 Oct. 1994), 901–911.

Downs, George, Rocke, David and Barsoom, Peter, "Is the Good News about Compliance Good News about Cooperation?" 50(3) *International Organization*, (Summer 1996), 379–406.

Dresler, Carolyn and Marks, Stephen, "The Emerging Right to Tobacco Control," 28 *Human Rights Quarterly*, (2006), 599–651.

Duetsch, L, "Structure, Performance, and the Net Rate of Entry into Manufacturing Industries," 41 *Southern Economic Journal*, (1975), 450–456.

Eckhardt, Joseph, "Balancing the Interests in Free Trade and Health: How the WHO's Framework Convention on Tobacco Control Can Withstand WTO Scrutiny," 12 *Duke Journal of Comparative and International Law*, (Winter 2002), 197–230.

Ehlermann, Claus-Dieter and Ehring, Lothar, "The Authoritative Interpretation under Article IX:2 of the Agreement Establishing the World Trade Organization: Current Law, Practice and Possible Improvements," 8(4) *Journal of International Economic Law*, (2005), 803 – 824.

Ehring, Lothar, "De Facto Discrimination in World Trade Law National and Most-Favoured-Nation Treatment – or Equal Treatment?" 36(5) *Journal of World Trade*, (2002), 921–977.

Emslie, John, "Labeling Programs as a Reasonably Available Least Restrictive Trade Measure Under Article XX's Nexus Requirement," 30 *Brooklyn Journal of International Law*, (2005), 485–545.

Esty, Daniel, "The World Trade Organization's Legitimacy Crisis," 1(1) *World Trade Review*, (2002), 7–22.

"Good Governance at the World Trade Organization: Building a Foundation of Administrative Law," 10(3) *Journal of International Economic Law*, (2007), 509–527.

Ezzati, Majid and Lopez, Alan, "Estimates of Global Mortality Attributable to Smoking in 2000," 362(9387) *The Lancet*, (2003), 847–852.

Fauchald, Ole Kristian, "Flexibility and Predictability Under the World Trade Organization's Non-Discrimination Clauses," 37(3) *Journal of World Trade*, (2003) 443–482.

Ferguson, J, "Advertising and Liquor," 40 *Journal of Business*, (1967), 414–434.

Fidler, David, Drager, Nick and Lee, Kelley, "Managing the Pursuit of Health and Wealth: The Key Challenges," 373 *The Lancet*, London, (Jan 22–29, 2009), 325–331.

Finnemore, Martha and Toope, Stephen, "Alternatives to 'Legalization': Richer Views of Law and Politics," 55(3) *International Organization*, (Summer 2001), 743–758.

Fischer-Lescano, Andreas and Teubner, Cunther, "Regime Collisions: The Vain Search for Legal Unity in the Fragmentation of Global Law," 25 *Michigan Journal of International Law*, (2004), 999–1046.

Fitzmaurice, Gerald, "The Law and Procedure of the International Court of Justice 1951–4: Treaty Interpretation and Other Treaty Points," 33 *British Yearbook of International Law*, (1957), 203–293.

Foulds, J, Ramström, L, Burke, M, et al., "Effect of Smokeless Tobacco (Snus) on Smoking and Public Health in Sweden," 12 *Tobacco Control*, (2003), 349–359.

French, Duncan, "Treaty Interpretation and the Incorporation of Extraneous Legal Rules," 55(2) *International & Comparative Law Quarterly*, (2006), 281–314.

Furberg, H, Bulik, C, Lerman, C, et al., "Is Swedish Snus Associated with Smoking Initiation or Smoking Cessation?" 14 *Tobacco Control*, (2005), 422–424.

Gilmore, Anna and McKee, Martin, "Exploring the Impact of Foreign Direct Investment on Tobacco Consumption in the Former Soviet Union," 14 *Tobacco Control*, (2005), 13–21.

Golstein, Judith, Kahler, Miles, Keohane, Robert and Slaughter, Anne-Marie, "Introduction: Legalisation and World Politics," 54(3) *International Organization*, (Summer 2000), 385–399.

Gorecki, P, "The Determinants of Entry by Domestic and Foreign Enterprises in Canadian Manufacturing," 58 *The Review of Economics and Statistics*, (1976), 485–488.

Gostin, Lawrence, "Meeting Basic Survival Needs of the World's Least Healthy People toward a Framework Convention on Global Health," 96 *Georgetown Law Journal*, (2008), 331–392.

Gould, Ellen, "Trade Treaties and Alcohol Advertising Policy," 26(3) *Journal of Public Health Policy*, (2005), 359–376.

Grieshaber-Otto, Jim, Sinclair, Scott and Schacter, Noel, "Impacts of International Trade, Services and Investment Treaties on Alcohol Regulation," 95(Supplement 4) *Addiction*, (2000), S491–S504.

Hafner, Gerhard, "Pros and Cons Ensuing from Fragmentation of International Law," 25 *Michigan Journal of International Law*, (2004), 849–863.

Hagihara, A, and Takeshita, Y, "Impact of American Cigarette Advertising on Imported Cigarette Consumption in Osaka, Japan," 4 *Tobacco Control*, (1995), 239–244.

Hammond, D, Fong, G, McDonald, P, "Impact of the Graphic Canadian Warning Labels on Adult Smoking Behaviour," 12 *Tobacco Control*, (Dec. 2003).

Hammond, D, Fong, G, McNeill, A, et al., "Effectiveness of Cigarette Warning Labels in Informing Smokers about the Risks of Smoking: Findings from the International Tobacco Control (ITC) Four Country Survey," 15 *Tobacco Control*, (June 2006), iii19–iii25.

Hammond, D, Wiebel, F, Kozlowski, L, et al., "Revising the Machine Smoking Regime for Cigarette Emissions: Implications for Tobacco Control Policy," 16 *Tobacco Control*, (2007), 8–14.

Harris, M, "Entry and Long-term Trends in Industry Performance," 21 *Antitrust Bulletin*, (1976), 295–314.

Hirschey, M, "The Effect of Advertising on Industrial Mobility, 1947–72," 54 *Journal of Business*, (1981), 329–339.

Hock, Teresa, "The Role of Eco-Labels in International Trade: Can Timber Certification be Implemented as a Means of Slowing Deforestation," 12 *Colorado Journal of International Environmental Law and Policy*, (2001), 347–365.

Holak, S and Reddy, S, "Effects of a Television and Radio Advertising Ban: A Study of the Cigarette Industry," 50 *Journal of Marketing*, (October 1986), 219–227.

Horn, Henrik and Mavroidis, Petros, "Still Hazy after All These Years: The Interpretation of National Treatment in the GATT/WTO Case-law on Tax Discrimination," 15(1) *European Journal of International Law*, (2004), 39–69.

Howse, Robert, "From Politics to Technocracy-and Back Again: The Fate of the Multilateral Trading Regime," 96(1) *American Journal of International Law*, (January 2002), 94–117.

Howse, Robert and Horn, Henrik, "European Communities – Measures Affecting the Approval and Marketing of Biotech Products," 8(1) *World Trade Review*, 49–83.

Hsieh, Chee-Ruey, Hu, Teh Wei and Lin, Chien Fu Jeff, "The Demand for Cigarettes in Taiwan: Domestic Versus Imported Cigarettes," *Contemporary Economic Policy*, 17(2), (April 1999), 223 – 234.

Hudec, Robert, "The GATT Legal System: A Diplomat's Jurisprudence," 4 *Journal of World Trade Law*, (1970), 615–665.

Hughes, John, "Do 'Light' Cigarettes Undermine Cessation?" 10(Supp I) *Tobacco Control*, (2001), i41–42.

Kup, Meichum, Heeb, Jean-Luc, Gmel, Gerhard and Rehm, Jüngen, "Does Price Matter? The Effect of Decreased Price on Spirits Consumption in Switzerland," 27(4) *Alcoholism: Clinical and Experimental Research*, (2006), 720–725.

Jackson, John, "The Crumbling Institutions of the Liberal Trade System," 12 *Journal of World Trade Law*, (1978), 93–106.

"Governmental Disputes in International Trade Relations: A Proposal in the Context of GATT," 13 *Journal of World Trade Law*, (1979), 1–21.

"Fragmentation or Unification Among International Institutions: The World Trade Organization," 31 *New York University Journal of International Law and Politics*, (1998–1999), 823–831.

Jenks, Wilfred, "Conflict of Law-Making Treaties," 30 *British Year Book of International Law*, (1953), 401–453.

Joshi, Manoj, "Are Eco-Labels Consistent with World Trade Organization Agreements," 38(1) *Journal of World Trade*, (2004), 69–92.

Kingsbury, Benedict, Krisch, Nico and Stewart, Richard, "The Emergence of Global Administrative Law," 68 *Law and Contemporary Problems*, (Summer/Autumn 2005), 15–61.

Koskenniemi, Martii and Leino, Päivi, "Fragmentation of International Law? Postmodern Anxieties," 15 *Leiden Journal of International Law*, (2002), 553–579.

Kozlowski, Lynne, Goldberg, Marvin, Sweeney, Christine et al., "Smoker Reactions to a Radio Message that Light Cigarettes are as Dangerous as Regular Cigarettes," 1 *Nicotine and Tobacco Control*, (1999), 67–76.

Kozlowski, Lynne and Pillitteri, Janine, "Beliefs about 'Light' and 'Ultra-Light' Cigarettes and Efforts to Change those Beliefs: An Overview of Early Efforts and Published Research," 10(Supp I) *Tobacco Control*, (2001), i12–i16 at i15.

Kozlowski, Lynne and O'Connor, Richard, "Cigarette Filter Ventilation is a Defective Design because of Misleading Taste, Bigger Puffs, and Blocked Vents," 11(Suppl I), *Tobacco Control*, (2002), 140–150.

Kozlowski, Lynne, O'Connor, Richard and Quinio Edwards, Beth, "Some Practical Points on Harm Reduction: What to Tell Your Lawmaker and What to Tell Your Brother about Swedish Snus," 12 *Tobacco Control*, (2003), 372–373

Krieger, N, Northridge, M, Gruskin, S et al., "Assessing Health Impact Assessment: Multidisciplinary and International Perspectives," 57 *Journal of Epidemiology Community Health*, (2003) 659–662.

Krisch, Nico, "The Pluralism of Global Administrative Law," 17(1) *European Journal of International Law*, (2006), 247–278.

L'Abbé, M. R., Stender, S. Skeaff, C. M., Ghafoorunissa and Tavella, M., "Approaches to Removing Trans Fats from the Food Supply in Industrialised and Developing Countries," 63 *European Journal of Clinical Nutrition*, (2009), 550–567.

Lamy, Pascal, "The Place of the WTO and its Law in the International Legal Order," 17(5) *European Journal of International Law*, (2006), 969–984.

Lancet, The, "UK Alcohol Policy a Costly Decision for Public Health," 373 *The Lancet*, (2009), 1312.

Leavell, Nadine-Rae, "The Low Tar Lie," 8 *Tobacco Control*, (1999), 433–439.

Leebron, David, "Linkages'," 96 *American Journal of International Law*, (January 2002), 5–27.

Liberman, Jonathan and Mitchell, Andrew, "In Search of Coherence between Trade and Health: Inter-Institutional Opportunities," 25 *Maryland Journal of International Law*, (2010), 143–186.

Lin, Tsai-Yu, "Addressing the Issue of Trade in Services and Public Health in the Case of Tobacco: Are the FCTC Restrictions on Tobacco Advertising Inconsistent with the GATS?," 7(4) *The Journal of World Investment & Trade*, (August 2006), 545–561.

Lipson, Charles, "Why are some Agreements Informal?," 45(4) *International Organization*, (Autumn) 1991, 495–538.

Lopez-Hurtado, Carlos, "Social Labeling and WTO Law," 5 *Journal of International Economic Law*, (September 2002), 719–746.

MacDonald, J, "Entry and Exit on the Competitive Fringe," 52 *Southern Economic Journal*, (1986), 640–652.

MacDonald, Rhona and Horton, Richard, "Trade and Health: Time for the Health Sector to get Involved," 373 (9660), *The Lancet*, London, (Jan 24–Jan 30, 2009), 273–274.

Magnusson, Roger, "Non-Communicable Diseases and Global Health Governance: Enhancing Global Processes to Improve Health Development," 3(2) *Globalization and Health*, (2007).

Marceau, Gabrielle, "Conflicts of Norms and Conflicts of Jurisdictions: The Relationship Between the WTO Agreement and MEAs and Other Treaties," 35(6) *Journal of World Trade*, (December 2001), 1081–1131.

"WTO Dispute Settlement and Human Rights," 14(4) *European Journal of International Law*, (2002), 753–814.

Marceau, Gabrielle and Trachtman, Joel, "The Technical Barriers to Trade Agreement, the Sanitary and Phytosanitary Measures Agreement, and the General

Agreement on Tariffs and Trade: A Map of the World Trade Organization Law of Domestic Regulation of Goods," 36(5) *Journal of World Trade*, (2002), 811–881.

Mason Meier, Benjamin, "Breathing Life in the Framework Convention on Tobacco Control: Smoking Cessation and the Right to Health," 5 *Yale Journal of Health Policy, Law and Ethics*, (2005), 137–192.

Masson, R and Shaanan, J, "Stochastic-Dynamic Limit Pricing: An Empirical Test," 64 *The Review of Economics and Statistics*, (1984), 413–422.

Mattoo, Aaditya and Subramanian, Arvind, "Regulatory Autonomy and Multilateral Disciplines: The Dilemma and a Possible Resolution," 1 *Journal of International Economic Law*, (1998), 303–322.

McGrady, Benn, "TRIPS and Trademarks: The Case of Tobacco," 3(1) *World Trade Review*, (2004), 53–82.

"Trade Liberalisation and Tobacco Control: Moving from a Policy of Exclusion to a More Comprehensive Policy" 16 *Tobacco Control*, (2007), 280–283.

"Fragmentation of International Law or Systemic Integration of Treaty Regimes: EC – Biotech Products and the Proper Interpretation of Article 31(3)(c) of the Vienna Convention on the Law of Treaties," 42(4) *Journal of World Trade*, (2008), 589–618.

"Necessity Exceptions in WTO Law: Retreaded Tyres, Regulatory Purpose and Cumulative Regulatory Measures," 12 *Journal of International Economic Law*, (2009), 153–173.

"Illicit Trade: Tracking and Tracing of Tobacco Products and the World Trade. Organization," *Asian Journal of WTO and International Health Law and Policy*, (March 2009), 129–159.

McLachlan, Campbell, "The Principle of Systemic Integration and Article 31(3)(c) of the Vienna Convention," 54(2) *International & Comparative Law Quarterly*, (2005), 279–319.

Ming Du, Michael, "Domestic Regulatory Autonomy under the TBT Agreement: From Non-Discrimination to Harmonization," 6(2) *Chinese Journal of International Law*, (2007), 269–306.

Moravcsik, Andrew, "Taking Preferences Seriously: A Liberal Theory of International Politics," 51 *International Organization*, (1997), 513–553.

Naiki, Yoshiko, "Accountability and Legitimacy in Global Health and Safety Governance: The World Trade Organization, the SPS Committee, and International Standard-Setting Organizations," 43(6) *Journal of World Trade*, (2009), 1255–1279.

Nelson, Jon, "Alcohol Advertising Bans, Consumptions and Control Policies in Seventeen OECD Countries, 1975–2000," *Applied Economics*, (2008), 1–21.

Neumann, Jan and Türk, Elisabeth, "Necessity Revisited: Proportionality in World Trade Organization Law After Korea – Beef, EC – Asbestos and EC – Sardines," 37(1) *Journal of World Trade*, (2003), 199–233.

Nottage, Hunter and Sebastian, Thomas, "Giving Legal Effect to the Results of WTO Trade Negotiations: An Analysis of the Methods of Changing WTO Law," 9(4) *Journal of International Economic Law*, (2006), 989–1016.

Okubu, Atsuko, "Environmental Labeling Programs and the GATT/WTO Regime," 11 *Georgetown International Environmental Law Review*, (1998–1999), 599–646.

Onzivu, William, "The Public Health Implications of the Association of South East Asian Nations (ASEAN) Legal Regime on Tobacco Control," 4(2) *Australian Journal of Asian Law*, (2002),. 160–187.

Osiro, Deborah, "CATT/WTO Necessity Analysis: Evolutionary Interpretation and its Impact on the Autonomy of Domestic Regulation," 29(2) *Legal Issues in Economic Integration*, (2002), 123 – 141.

Palmeter, David and Mavroidis, Petros, "The WTO Legal System: Sources of Law," 92(3) *American Journal of International Law*, (1998), 398–413.

Pauwelyn, Joost, "The Role of Public International Law in the WTO: How Far Can We Go?" 95 *American Journal of International Law*, (2001), 535–578.

"A Typology of Multilateral Treaty Obligations: Are WTO Obligations Bilateral or Collective in Nature?"14(5) *European Journal of International Law*, (2003), 907–951.

"WTO Compassion or Superiority Complex?: What to make of the WTO Waiver for 'Conflict Diamonds,'" 24 *Michigan Journal of International Law*, (2003), 1177–1207.

"Recent Books on Trade and Environment: GATT Phantoms Still Haunt the WTO," 15(3) *European Journal of International Law*, (2004), 575–595.

"Rien ne Va Plus? Distinguishing Domestic Regulation from Market access in GATT and GATS," 4(2) *World Trade Review*, (2005), 131–170.

Peles, Y, "Rates of Amortization of Advertising Expenditures," 79 *Journal of Political Economy*, (1971), 1032–1058.

Prah Ruger, Jennifer, "Normative Foundations of Global Health Law," 96(2) *Georgetown Law Journal*, (2008), 423–443.

Ramström, L and Foulds, J, "Role of Snus in Initiation and Cessation of Tobacco Smoking in Sweden," 15 *Tobacco Control*, (2006), 210–214.

Raustiala, Kal, "Form and Substance in International Agreements," 99 *American Journal of International Law*, (2005), 581–614.

Regan, Donald, "Regulatory Purpose and 'Like Products' in Article III:4 of the GATT (With Additional Remarks on Article III:2)," 36(3) *Journal of World Trade*, (2002), 443–478.

"The Meaning of 'Necessary' in GATT Article XX and GATS Article XIV: The Myth of Cost-Benefit Balancing," 6(3) *World Trade Review*, (2007), 347–369.

Rehm, Jürgen, Mathers, Colin, Popova, Svetlana, Thavorncharoensap, Montarat, Teerawattanon, Yot and Patra, Joyadeep, "Global Burden of Disease and Injury and Economic Cost Attributable to Alcohol Use and Alcohol-Use Disorders," 373 *The Lancet*, (June 27, 2009), 2223–2233.

Rizzo, J and Zeckhauser, R, "Advertising and Entry: The Case of Physician Services," 98 *Journal of Political Economy*, (1990), 476–500.

Room, Robin, "International Control of Alcohol: Alternative Paths Forward," 25 *Drug and Alcohol Review*, (November 2006), 581–595.

Runge, C. Ford and Jackson, Lee Ann, "Labeling, Trade and Genetically Modified Organisms," 34(1) *Journal of World Trade*, (2000), 111–222.

Sands, Philippe, "Treaty, Custom and the Cross-Fertilisation of International Law," 1 *Yale Human Rights and Development Law Journal*, (1998), 85–105.

Sauvé, Pierre and Zampetti, America Beviglia, "Subsidiarity Perspectives on the New Agenda," 3(1) *Journal of International Economic Law*, (2000), 83–114.

Schwalbach, J, "Entry by Diversified Firms into German Industries," 5 *International Journal of Industrial Organization*, (1987), 43–49.

Schwartz, Brian, "WTO and GMOs: Analysing the European Communities Recent Regulations Covering the Labeling of Genetically Modified Organisms," 25(3) *Michigan Journal of International Law*, (2004), 771–811

Sebrié, E, Barnoya, J, Pérez-Stable, E, and Glantz SA. "Tobacco Industry Successfully Prevented Tobacco Control Legislation in Argentina," 14 *Tobacco Control*, (2005) e2.

Shaffer, E, Brenner, J and Houston, T, "International Trade Agreements: A Threat to Tobacco Control," 14 *Tobacco Control* (2005); (Suppl II);ii19-ii25.

Shapiro, D and Khemani, R, "The Determinants of Entry and Exit Reconsidered," 5 *International Journal of Industrial Organization*, (1987), 15–26.

Shapiro, Ira, "Treating Cigarettes as an Exception to the Trade Rules," XXII no. 1 SAIS Review (Winter–Spring 2002), 87–96.

Shaw, Sabrina and Schwartz, Riza, "Trade and Environment in the WTO: State of Play," 36(1) *Journal of World Trade*, (2002), 129–154, 134–137.

Shiffman, Saul, Pillitteri, Janine, and Burton, Steven et al., "Smokers' Beliefs About 'Light' and 'Ultra-Light' Cigarettes," 10 (Suppl 1) *Tobacco Control*, (2001), i24–i32 at i17.

Smith, Richard, Chanda, Rupa and Tangcharoensathien, Viroj, "Trade and Health 4: Trade in Health-Related Services," 373(9663) *The Lancet*, London, (Feb 14–Feb 20, 2009), 593–601.

Smith, Richard, Correa, Carlos and Oh, Cecilia, "Trade and Health 5: Trade, TRIPS, and Pharmaceuticals," 373(9664) *The Lancet*, London, (Feb 21–Feb 27, 2009), 684–691.

Smith, Richard, Lee, Kelley and Drager, Nick, "Trade and Health 6: Trade and Health: An Agenda for Action," 373(9665) *The Lancet*, London, (Feb 28–Mar 6, 2009), 768–773.

Staffin, Elliot, "Trade Barrier or Trade Boon? A Critical Evaluation of Environmental Labeling and its Role in the 'Greening' of World Trade," 21 *Columbia Journal of Environmental Law*, (1996), 205–286.

Subedi, Surya, "Balancing International Trade with Environmental Protection: International Aspects of Eco-Labels," 25 *Brooklyn Journal of International Law*, (1999), 373–405.

Sykes, Alan, "The Least Restrictive Means," 70(1) *The University of Chicago Law Review*, (2003), 403–419.

"Regulatory Protectionism and the Law of International Trade," 66(1) *The University of Chicago Law Review*, (1999), 1–46.

Symposium on the Boundaries of the WTO, 96(1) *American Journal of International Law* (January 2002).

Taylor, Allyn, "Making the World Health Organization Work: A Legal Framework for Universal Access to the Conditions for Health," 18(4) *American Journal of Law & Medicine*, (1992), 301–346.

"An International Regulatory Strategy for Global Tobacco Control," 21 *Yale Journal of International Law*, (1996), 257–304.

Telser, L, "Advertising and Cigarettes," 70 *Journal of Political Economy*, (1962), 471–499.

Thirlway, Hugh, "The Law and Procedure of the International Court of Justice 1960–1989 Part Three," 62 *British Year Book of International Law*, (1991), 1–76.

Trachtman, Joel, "Trade and … problems, Cost-Benefit Analysis and Subsidiarity," 9 *European Journal of International Law*, (1998), 32–85.

Uauy, R., Aro, A., Clarke, R., Ghafoorunissa, L'Abbé, M R., Mozaffarian, D., Skeaff, C M, Stender, S. and Tavella, M., "WHO Scientific Update on Trans Fatty Acids: Summary and Conclusions," 63 *European Journal of Clinical Nutrition*, (2009), 568–575.

Vierdag, E, "The Time of the 'Conclusion' of a Multilateral Treaty" 59 *British Year Book of International Law*, (1988), 75–112.

Vranes, Erich, "The Definition of 'Norms Conflict' in International Law and Legal Theory," 17(2) *European Journal of International Law*, (2006), 395–418.

Wagenaar, Alexander, Salois, Matthew and Komro, Kelli, "Effects of Beverage Alcohol Price and Tax Levels on Drinking: A Meta-Analysis of 1003 Estimates from 112 Studies," 104 *Addiction*, (2009), 179–190.

Waincymer, Jeffrey, "Reformulated Gasoline Under Reformulated WTO Dispute Settlement Procedures: Pulling Pandora out of the Chapeau?" 18(1) *Michigan Journal of International Law*, (1996), 141–181.

Wakefield, M and Letcher, T, "My Pack is Cuter than Yours," 11(2) *Tobacco Control*, (2002), 154–156.

Wakefield, M, Morley, C, Horan, J and Cummings KM. "The Cigarette Pack as Image: New Evidence from Tobacco Industry Documents," 11(Suppl 1) *Tobacco Control*, (2002), i73.

Warner, K, "The Economics of Tobacco: Myths and Realities," 9(1) *Tobacco Control*, (2000), 78–89.

Weiler, Joseph, "Comment, Brazil – Measures Affecting Imports of Retreaded Tyres (DS322)," 8(1) *World Trade Review*, (2009), 137–144.

Wen, C, Peterson, R, Cheng, T et al., "Paradoxical Increase in Cigarette Smuggling after the Market Opening in Taiwan," 15(3) *Tobacco Control*, (2006), 160–165.

Wike, Jonathan, "The Marlboro Man in Asia: U.S. Tobacco and Human Rights," 29 *Vanderbilt Journal of Transnational Law*, (1996), 329–361.

Woo, Alyssa, "Health Versus Trade: The Future of the WHO's Framework Convention on Tobacco Control," 35 *Vanderbilt Journal of Transnational Law*, (2002), 1731–1768.

Wu, Chuan-Feng, "State Responsibility for Tobacco Control: The Right to Health Perspective," 3(2) *Asian Journal of WTO & International Health Law and Policy*, (2008), 379–422.

Yach, Derek, Hawkes, Corinna, Joanne E., Epping, Jordan and Galbraith, Sarah, "The World Health Organization's Framework Convention on Tobacco Control: Implications for Global Epidemics of Food- Related Deaths and Disease," 24 *Journal of Public Health Policy*, (2003), 274–290.

Young, Margaret, "The WTO's Use of Relevant Rules of International Law: An Analysis of the Biotech Case," 56 *International & Comparative Law Quarterly*, (October 2007), 907–930.

Zedalis, Rex, "Labeling of Genetically Modified Foods: The Limits of GATT Rules," 35(2), *Journal of World Trade*, (2001), 301–347.

Zeigler, Donald, "International Trade Agreements Challenge Tobacco and Alcohol Control Policies," 25 *Drug and Alcohol Review*, (November 2006), 567 – 579.

Zhang, P and Husten, C, "Impact of the Tobacco Price Support Program on tobacco control in the United States," 7(2) *Tobacco Control*, (1998), 176–182.

Papers

Bernabe, Riza (2008). Treatment of special products: Implications of the Chair's May 2008 draft modalities text, ICTSD Project on Special Products and a Special Safeguard Mechanism, Issue Paper No.14, International Centre for Trade and Sustainable Development, Geneva, Switzerland.

Bloom, John, "Public Health, International Trade and the Framework Convention on Tobacco Control," Campaign for Tobacco-Free Kids, March 2001, available at http://tobaccofreekids.org/campaign/global/framework/docs/Policy.pdf (visited 12/12/07).

Broude, Tomer, "Principles of Normative Integration and the Allocation of International Authority: The WTO, The Vienna Convention on the Law of Treaties, and the Rio Declaration," Hebrew University of Jerusalem, Faculty of Law, Research Paper No. 07–08, August 2008.

Callard, Cynthia, Collishaw, Neil and Swenarchuk, Michele, "An Introduction to International Trade Agreements and their Impact on Public Measures to Reduce Tobacco Use," Physicians for a Smoke Free Canada, 2001, available at http://www.smoke-free.ca/pdf_1/Trade&Tobacco-April%202000.pdf (visited 10/01/08).

Center for Science in the Public Interest, Codex Alimentarius vis-à-vis The WHO Global Strategy on Diet, Physical Activity and Health Food Standardisation to Support the Reduction of Chronic Diseases (Food and Diet for a Healthy Long Life), available at http://cspinet.org/reports/WHOGlobalStrategyCODEX.pdf.

Chaloupka, Frank and Laixuthai, Adit, "US Trade Policy and Cigarette Smoking in Asia," NBER Working Paper Series, Working Paper 5543, April 1996.

Howse, Robert, "The Use and Abuse of Other 'Relevant Rules of International Law' in Treaty Interpretation: Insights from WTO Trade / Environment Litigation," ILJ Working Paper 2007/1, Institute for International Law and Justice, New York University School of Law, available at http://www.iilj.org/publications/documents/2007-1.Howse.web.pdf (visited 12/01/08).

Weissman, Robert, "International Trade Agreements and Tobacco Control: Threats to Public Health and the Case for Excluding Tobacco from Trade Agreements," November 2003, v 2.0 available at http://www.fctc.org/x/cd/documents/EA_trade_backgrd.pdf, (visited 26/11/07).

World Trade Institute, "Agricultural Exports as Engine of Growth for Developing Countries? A Case Study on International Trade in Tobacco," 2004, available at www.wti.org/conf/documents/TobaccoBookFinalBFJan2005printable.pdf (accessed 01/09/06).

Book Chapters

Alemanno, Alberto, "The Dialogue Between Judges & Experts in the EU and WTO," in Filippo Fontanelli, Giuseppe Martinico and Paolo Carrozza, (eds), *Shaping Rule of Law Through Dialogue. International and Supranational Experiences*, Groningen, Europa Law Publishing, (2010), 345–373.

Atik, Jeffrey, "Trade and Health," in Bethlehem, Daniel, McRae, Donald, Neufeld, Rodney and Van Damme, Isabelle, *The Oxford Handbook of International Trade Law*, New York, Oxford University Press, (2009), 597–618.

Atkins, Vincent, "Agricultural Trade Policy Instruments to Promote Healthy Diets in Developing Countries: An Assessment of the Opportunities within the Framework of the WTO Agreement and the Doha Development Agenda," in Hawkes, Corinna, et al., *Trade, Food, Diet and Health: Perspectives and Policy Options*, Wiley Blackwell, (2010), 264–278.

Kyle Bagwell, "The Economic Analysis of Advertising," in M Armstrong and R Porter, (eds), *Handbook of Industrial Organization*, Vol. 3, Elsevier, (2007).

Chaloupka, Frank, Hu, Teh-Wei, Warner, Kenneth, et al., "The Taxation of Tobacco Products" in Jha, Prabhat and Chaloupka, Frank, (eds), *Tobacco Control in Developing Countries*, World Bank and World Health Organization, Oxford University Press, (2000), 237–272.

Jonathan Charney, "Commentary: Compliance with International Soft Law," in Shelton, Dinah (ed) *Commitment and Compliance: The Role of Non-Binding Norms in the International Legal System*, Oxford University Press, New York, (2000).

Chinkin, Christine, "Normative Development in the International Legal System," in Shelton, Dinah (ed), *Commitment and Compliance: The Role of Non-Binding Norms in the International Legal System*, Oxford University Press, New York, (2000), 21–42.

Davey, William and Pauwelyn, Joost, "MFN Unconditionality: A Legal Analysis of the Concept in View of its Evolution in the GATT/WTO Jurisprudence with Particular Reference to the Issue of 'Like Product,'" in Cottier, Thomas and Mavroidis, Petros, (eds), *Regulatory Barriers and the Principle of Non-Discrimination in World Trade Law*, Ann Arbor, University of Michigan Press, (2000), 13–50.

Drewnowski, Adam, Hanks, Andrew and Smith, Trenton, "International Trade, Food and Diet Costs, and the Global Obesity Epidemic," in Hawkes, Corrina, et al., *Trade, Food, Diet and Health: Perspectives and Policy Options*, Wiley Blackwell, (2010), 77–90.

Farber, Daniel and Hudec, Robert, "GATT Legal Constraints on Domestic Environmental Regulations" in Bhagwati, Jagdish and Hudec, Robert, (eds), *Fair Trade and Harmonization: Prerequisites for Free Trade?* Volume 2, Cambridge MA, MIT Press, (1996), 59–94.

Fidler, David, "The Impact of International Trade and Investment Rules on the Ability of Governments to Implement Interventions to Address Obesity: A Case Study on the European Charter on Counteracting Obesity," in Hawkes, Corinna, et al., *Trade, Food, Diet and Health: Perspectives and Policy Options*, Wiley Blackwell, (2010), 279–297.

Gajalakshmi, C, Jha, Prabhat, Ranson, Kent et al., "Global Patterns of Smoking and Smoking Attributable Mortality," in Jha, Prabhat and Chaloupka, Frank, (eds), *Tobacco Control in Developing Countries*, World Bank and World Health Organization, Oxford University Press, (2000), 11–39.

Hawkes, Corinna, "The Influence of Trade Liberalisation and Global Dietary Change: The Case of Vegetable Oils, Meat and Highly Processed Foods," in Hawkes, Corrina, et al., *Trade, Food, Diet and Health: Perspectives and Policy Options*, Wiley Blackwell, (2010), 35–59.

Howse, Robert, "The Legitimacy of the World Trade Organization," in Coicaud, Jean-Marc and Heiskanen, Viejo, (eds), *The Legitimacy of International Organizations*, Tokyo, New York, United Nations University Press, (2001), 355–407.

Howse, Robert and Türk, Elisabeth, "The WTO Impact Upon Internal Regulations: A Case Study of the Canada – EC Asbestos Dispute," in Bermann, George and Mavroidis, Petros: (eds) *Trade and Human Health and Safety*, New York, Cambridge University Press, (2006), 77–117.

Hudec, Robert, "GATT/WTO Constraints on National Regulation: Requiem for an 'Aim and Effects' Test," in Hudec, Robert *Essays on the Nature of International Trade Law*, London, Cameron May, (2000), 359–395.

Huang, Sophia, "Global Trade of Fruits and Vegetables and the Role of Consumer Demand," in Hawkes, Corrina, et al., *Trade, Food, Diet and Health: Perspectives and Policy Options*, Wiley Blackwell, (2010), 60–76.

James, Philip, Rojoongwaskinkul, Nipa, Rikshasuta, Tashmai and Wasantwisut, Emorn, "Food Imports and Dietary Change: A Perspective from Thailand," in Hawkes, Corinna et al., *Trade, Food, Diet and Health: Perspectives and Policy Options*, Wiley Blackwell, (2010), 169–191.

Jamison, Dean, "Investing in Health," in Dean T. Jamison et al., *Disease Control Priorities in Developing Countries* (2nd ed), Oxford University Press, The World Bank, (2006), New York, 3–34.

Jha, Prabat, Musgrove, Philip, Chaloupka, Frank et al., "The Economic Rationale for Intervention in the Tobacco Market," in Jha, Prabhat and Chaloupka, Frank, (eds), *Tobacco Control in Developing Countries*, World Bank and World Health Organization, Oxford University Press, (2000), 153–174.

Joossens, Luk, Chaloupka, Frank, Merriman, David et al., "Issues in the Smuggling of Tobacco Products," in Jha, Prabhat and Chaloupka, Frank, (eds), *Tobacco Control in Developing Countries*, World Bank and World Health Organization, Oxford University Press, (2000), 393–406.

Josling, Tim, Orden, David and Roberts, Donna, "National Food Regulations and the WTO Agreement on Sanitary and Phytosanitary Measures: Implications for Trade-Related Measures to Promote Healthy Diets," in Hawkes, Corinna, et al., *Trade, Food, Diet and Health: Perspectives and Policy Options*, Wiley Blackwell, (2010), 219–237.

Kenkel, Donald and Chen, Likwang, "Consumer Information and Tobacco Use," in Jha, Prabhat and Chaloupka, Frank, (eds), *Tobacco Control in Developing Countries*, World Bank and World Health Organization, Oxford University Press, (2000), 177–214.

Koh, Harold Hongju, "Why Do Nations Obey International Law?" 106(8) *Yale Law Journal*, (1997), 2599–2659.

L'Abbé, Mary, Lewis, Janine and Zehaluk, Christina, "The Potential of the Codex Alimentarius to Promote Healthy Diets Worldwide – The Canadian Experience of Implementation," in Hawkes, Corinna et al., *Trade, Food, Diet and Health: Perspectives and Policy Options*, Wiley Blackwell, (2010), 238–256.

Lobstein, Tim, "Tackling Childhood Obesity in an Era of Trade Liberalisation," in Hawkes, Corrina, et al., *Trade, Food, Diet and Health: Perspectives and Policy Options*, Wiley Blackwell, (2010), 195–218.

Marceau, Gabrielle and Trachtman, Joel, "A Map of the World Trade Organization Law of Domestic Regulation of Goods," in Bermann, George and Mavroidis, Petros, (eds), *Trade and Human Health and Safety*, Cambridge University Press, New York, (2006), 9–77.

Meng, Werner, "Conflicting Rules in the WHO FCTC and Their Impact," in Cottier, Thomas, Pauwelyn, Joost and Burgi Bonanomi, Elisabeth, (eds), *Human Rights and International Trade*, New York, Oxford University Press, (2005), 334–339.

Noeth, Kristyn, "Taxation to control tobacco in developing states," in Brown Weiss, Edith and Jackson, John, (eds), *Reconciling Environment and Trade*, Ardsley, N.Y., Transnational Publishers, (2001), 101–132.

O'Connell, Mary Ellen, "The Role of Soft Law in a Global Order," Shelton, Dinah (ed), *Commitment and Compliance: The Role of Non-Binding Norms in the International Legal System*, Oxford University Press, New York, (2000) 100–114.

Popkin, Barry, "The Implications of the Nutrition Transition for Obesity in the Developing World," in David Crawford and Robert W. Jeffery, *Obesity Prevention and Public Health*, Oxford University Press, (2005), 75–100.

Prabhu, Maya and Atapattu, Sumudu, "The WHO Framework Convention on Tobacco Control: When the WHO Meets the WTO," in Cordonier Segger, Marie-Claire and Weeramantry, Christie, (eds), *Sustainable Justice: Reconciling Economic, Social and Environmental Law*, The Netherlands, Koninklijke Brill, (2005), 365–380.

Reinicke, Wolfgang and Witte, Jan Martin, "Challenges to the International Legal System: Interdependence, Globalization, and Sovereignty: The Role of Non-Binding International Legal Accords," in Shelton, Dinah (ed), *Commitment and Compliance: The Role of Non-Binding Norms in the International Legal System*, Oxford University Press, New York, (2000).

Saffer, Henry, "Tobacco Advertising and Promotion," in Jha, Prabhat and Chaloupka, Frank, (eds), *Tobacco Control in Developing Countries*, World Bank and World Health Organization, Oxford University Press, (2000), 215–236.

Schidhuber, Josef and Shetty, Prakash, "The European Union's Common Agricultural Policy and the European Diet: Is there a Link?" in Hawkes, Corrina, et al., *Trade, Food, Diet and Health: Perspectives and Policy Options*, Wiley Blackwell, (2010), 131–147.

Taylor, Allyn, Chaloupka, Frank, Guindon, Emmanuel, et al., "The Impact of Trade Liberalization on Tobacco Consumption," in Jha, Prabhat and Chaloupka, Frank, (eds), *Tobacco Control in Developing Countries*, World Bank and World Health Organization, Oxford University Press, (2000), 343–364.

Taylor, Allyn, "Trade, Human Rights and the WHO Framework Convention on Tobacco Control: Just What the Doctor Ordered?" in Thomas Cottier, Joost Pauwelyn and Elisabeth Burgi Bonanomi (eds), *Human Rights and International Trade*, New York, Oxford University Press, (2005), 322–344.

Terra, Ben, "Excises," in Thuronyi, Victor, (ed), *Tax Law Design and Drafting, International Monetary Fund*, (1996), Volume 1.

Thow, Anne Marie, and Snowdon, Wendy, "The Effect of Trade and Trade Policy on Diet and Health in the Pacific Islands," in Hawkes, Corrina, et al., *Trade, Food, Diet and Health: Perspectives and Policy Options*, Wiley Blackwell, (2010), 147–168.

Books

Aginam, Obijiofor, *Global Health Governance: International Law and Public Health in a Divided World*, Toronto, University of Toronto Press, (2005).

Alemanno, Alberto, *Trade in Food: Regulatory and Judicial Approaches in the EC and WTO*, London, Cameron May, (2007).

Baldwin, David (ed), *Neorealism and Neoliberalism: The Contemporary Debate*, New York, Columbia University Press, (1993).

Bermann, George and Mavroidis, Petros, (eds) *Trade and Human Health and Safety*, New York, Cambridge University Press, (2006).

Bernhardt, R, (ed.), *Encyclopedia of Public International Law*, Amsterdam, North-Holland Pub Co, (1984).

Bethlehem, Daniel, McRae, Donald, Neufeld, Rodney and Van Damme, Isabelle, *The Oxford Handbook of International Trade Law*, New York, Oxford University Press, (2009).

Bhagwati, Jagdish, *Termites in the Trading System: How Preferential Agreements Undermine Free Trade*, New York, Oxford University Press, (2008).

Bhagwati, Jagdish and Hudec, Robert, (eds), *Fair Trade and Harmonization: Prerequisites for Free Trade?* Volume 2, Cambridge MA, MIT Press, (1996).

Bhagwati, Jagdish and Srinivasan, T, *Lectures on International Trade*, Cambridge MA, MIT Press, (1983).

Bhala, Raj, *International Trade Law: Interdisciplinary Theory and Practice*, 3rd edition, LexisNexis, (2008).

Brown, L, (ed), *The Shorter Oxford English Dictionary*, Oxford, Oxford University Press, (2002), Vol. 1.

Brown Weiss, Edith and Jackson, John, (eds), *Reconciling Environment and Trade*, Ardsley, NY, Transnational Publishers, (2001).

Button, Catherine, *The Power to Protect: Trade, Health and Uncertainty in the WTO*, Portland, Hart Publishing, (2004).

Chayes, Abram and Chayes, Antonia Handler, *The New Sovereignty: Compliance with International Regulatory Regimes*, Harvard University Press, (1996).

Choi, Won-Mog, *"Like Products" in International Trade Law: Towards a Consistent GATT / WTO Jurisprudence*, New York, Oxford University Press, (2003).

Coicaud, Jean-Marc and Heiskanen, Viejo, (eds), *The Legitimacy of International Organizations*, Tokyo, New York, United Nations University Press, (2001).

Cordonier Segger, Marie-Claire and Weeramantry, Christie, (eds), *Sustainable Justice: Reconciling Economic, Social and Environmental Law*, The Netherlands, Koninklijke Brill, (2005).

Cottier, Thomas and Mavroidis, Petros, (eds), *Regulatory Barriers and the Principle of Non-Discrimination in World Trade Law*, Ann Arbor, University of Michigan Press, (2000).

Cottier, Thomas, Pauwelyn, Joost and Burgi Bonanomi, Elisabeth, (eds), *Human Rights and International Trade*, New York, Oxford University Press, (2005).

David Crawford and Robert W. Jeffery, *Obesity Prevention and Public Health*, Oxford University Press, (2005).

Dalal-Clayton, Barry and Sadler, Barry, *Strategic Environmental Assessment: A Sourcebook and Reference Guide to International Experience*, Earthscan, OECD, UNEP, IIED, (2005).

Epps, Tracey, *International Trade and Health Protection: A Critical Assessment of the WTO's SPS Agreement*, Cheltenham, Edward Elgar, (2008).

Fontanelli, Filippo, Martinico, Giuseppe and Carrozza, Paolo (eds), *Shaping Rule of Law Through Dialogue: International and Supranational Experiences*, Groningen, Europa Law Publishing, (2010).

Franck, Thomas, *The Power of Legitimacy Among Nations*, New York, Oxford University Press, 1990.

Garcia, Frank, *Trade, Inequality, and Justice: Toward a Liberal Theory of Just Trade*, Ardsley NY, Transnational Publishers, (2003).

Gewertz, Deborah, and Errington, Frederick, *Cheap Meat: Flap Food Nations and the Pacific Islands*, London, University of California Press, 2010.

Gostin, Lawrence, *Public Health Law: Power, Duty Restraint*, (2nd ed.) University of California Press Berkeley and Los Angeles, (2008).

Guzmán, Andrew, *How International Law Works: A Rational Choice Theory*, New York, Oxford University Press, (2008).

Hawkes, Corinna, Blouin, Chantal, Hensen, Spencer, Drager, Nick and Dubé, Laurette, *Trade, Food, Diet and Health: Perspectives and Policy Options*, Wiley Blackwell, 2010

Henkin, Louis, *How Nations Behave: Law and Foreign Policy*, New York, Columbia University Press, (1979).

Hudec, Robert, *Essays on the Nature of International Trade Law*, London, Cameron May, (2000).

Jackson, John, *World Trade and the Law of GATT*, Charlottesville, VA, The Michie Company, (1969).

Jackson, John, Davey, William and Sykes, William, *Legal Problems of International Economic Relations: Cases Materials and Text*, (5th ed), Thomson West, St. Paul MN, 2008.

Jamison, Dean, Breman, Joel, Measham, Anthony, Alleyne, George, Claeson, Mariam, Evans, David, Jha, Prabhat, Mills, Anne, Musgrove, Philip, (eds), *Disease Control Priorities in Developing Countries* (2nd ed), Oxford University Press, The World Bank, (2006).

Jha, Prabhat and Chaloupka, Frank, (eds), *Tobacco Control in Developing Countries*, World Bank and World Health Organization, Oxford University Press, (2000).

Mavroidis, Petros, *The General Agreement on Tariffs and Trade: A Commentary*, Oxford, Oxford University Press, (2005).

Pauwelyn, Joost, *Conflict of Norms in Public International Law: How WTO Law Relates to Other Rules of International Law*, New York, Cambridge University Press, (2003).

Pollack, Mark and Shaffer, Greg, *When Cooperation Fails: The International Law and Politics of Genetically Modified Foods*, New York, Oxford University Press, (2009).

Ruth Roemer, *Legislative Action to Combat the World Tobacco Epidemic*, (2nd ed), Geneva, World Health Organization, (1993).

Scott, Joanne, *The WTO Agreement on Sanitary and Phytosanitary Measures*, Oxford University Press, Oxford, 2007.

Shadikhodjaev, Sherzod, *Retaliation in the WTO Dispute Settlement System*, The Netherlands, Kluwer Law International, (2009).

Shafey, Omar, Dolwick, Suzanne and Guindon, G. Emmanuel, (eds), *Tobacco Control Country Profiles*, 2nd ed, American Cancer Society, Atlanta, GA, USA, (2003).

Shan, Wenhua, Simmons, Penelope and Singh, Dalvinder, *Redefining Sovereignty in International Economic Law*, Oxford, Hart Publishing, (2008).

Shelton, Dinah (ed), *Commitment and Compliance: The Role of Non-Binding Norms in the International Legal System*, New York, Oxford University Press, (2000).

Sinclair, Ian, *The Vienna Convention on the Law of Treaties*, Manchester, Manchester University Press, 2nd ed., (1984).

Slaughter, Anne-Marie, *A New World Order*, Princeton University Press, (2004).

Sunstein, Cass, *Legal Reasoning and Political Conflict*, New York, Oxford University Press, (1996).

Thuronyi, Victor, (ed), *Tax Law Design and Drafting, International Monetary Fund*, (1996), Volume 1.

Trebilcock, Michael and Howse, Robert, *The Regulation of International Trade*, London, Routledge, (2005).

Voon, Tania, *Cultural Products and the World Trade Organization*, Cambridge, Cambridge University Press, (2007).

Waincymer, Jeff, *WTO Litigation: Procedural Aspects of Formal Dispute Settlement*, London, Cameron May, (2002).

Wolfrum, Rüdiger Stoll, Peter-Tobias, Seibert-Fohr, Anja, *WTO: Technical Barriers and SPS Measures*, Leiden, Martinus Nijhoff Publishers, (2007).

WTO Analytical Index: Guide to WTO Law and Practice, Cambridge, Cambridge University Press, (2007).

Wunsch-Vincent, Sacha, *The WTO, the Internet and Trade in Digital Products: EC – US Perspectives*, Portland Or., Hart Publishing, (2006).

Newspaper Articles

AFP, "Taiwan Plans Junk Food Tax," December 22, 2009.

Alison Mutler, "Romanians Move to Tax the Once Beloved Fast Food," *AP*, February 17, 2009.

Bangkok Post, "Alcohol Consumption Bill Reaction, Boon Rawd: Law May Breach WTO Rules," Friday, March 16, 2007.

Fiji Times Online, "Nations in a Flap over Nothing," Thursday, January 7, 2010.

The Nation, "Council of State 'Set to Oppose Ban' on Drink Ads," Friday November 24 2006.

The Sunday Times, "Labour: Ban High-Caffeine Alcohol," February 7, 2010.

Websites

Australian Productivity Commission. See www.pc.gov.au.

Health Canada http://www.hc-sc.gc.ca/hc-ps/tobac-tabac/legislation/federal/amend_faq-modif-eng.php.

National Health Accounts http://www.who.int/nha/country/en/index.html.

World Health Organization Global Database on Body Mass Index, available at http://www.who.int/bmi/index.jsp.

Domestic Law

Australia
Australia New Zealand Food Standards Code.
Trade Practices (Consumer Product Information Standards) (Tobacco) Regulations 1994 (Cth).
Canada
Cracking Down on Tobacco Marketing Aimed at Youth Act.
Tobacco Act, 1997, c.13, s22(2)(b).
United State[s] of America.
Alcoholic Beverage Labeling Act of 1988, 27 USC 201 – 211.
Family Smoking Prevention and Tobacco Control Act, HR 1256, section 907.

Speeches

Lamy, Pascal, "The Emergence of Collective Preferences in International Trade: Implications in Regulating Globalisation," Conference on "Collective Preferences and Global Governance: What Future for the Multilateral Trading System," Brussels, September 15, 2004.

Official Documents and Reports

Australia
Australia: The Healthiest Country by 2020, National Preventative Health Strategy – The Roadmap for Action, 30 June 2009.
Canadian Standing Committee on Health
Carla Hills, "Legal Opinion with Regard to Plain Packaging of Tobacco Products Requirement under International Agreements," 3 May 1994 presented to the Canadian Standing Committee on Health.
Codex Alimentarius Commission
Codex Alimentarius Commission, Code of Ethics for International Trade in Food, CAC/RCP 20–1979 (Rev. 1–1985).
Codex Alimentarius Commission, General Standard for the Labeling of Prepackaged Foods, CODEX STAN 1–1985.
Codex Alimentarius Commission, Guidelines for Use of Nutrition and Health Claims, CAC/GL 23–1997.
Codex Alimentarius Commission Guidelines on Nutrition Labeling, CAC/GL 2–1985.
Codex Alimentarius Commission, Joint FAO / WHO Food Standards Programme, Codex Committee on Nutrition and Foods for Special Dietary Uses, Thirty-First Session, Discussion Paper on the Nutrient Reference Values (NRVS) for Nutrients Associated with Risk of Noncommunicable Diseases, July 2009, CX/NFSDU 09/31/08.
Codex Alimentarius Commission, Joint FAO / WHO Food Standards Programme, Codex Committee on Nutrition and Foods for Special Dietary Uses, Principles and Criteria for the Development of NRVs for Labeling Purposes for Nutrients Associated with risk of Diet-Related Noncommunicable Diseases at Step 4, CX/NFSDU 10/32/7.

Codex Alimentarius Commission, Report of the Thirty-Seventh Session of the Committee on Food Labeling, Calgary, Canada, 4 – 8 May 2009. ALINORM 09/32/22.

Codex Alimentarius Commission, Joint FAO / WHO Food Standards Programme, Report of the Thirty-Eighth Session of the Codex Committee on Food Labeling, ALINORM 10/33/22.

Codex Alimentarius Commission, Request for Comments on Draft Action Plan for Implementation of the Global Strategy on Diet, Physical Activity and Health, September 2006, CL 2006/44-CAC.

Codex Alimentarius Commission, Twenty-Ninth Session, Update: Implementation of the WHO Global Strategy on Diet, Physical Activity and Health: Action that Could be Taken by Codex, CAC/29 LIM/6; Codex Alimentarius Commission, Codex Committee on Food Labeling, Matters referred by FAO and WHO: Implementation of the Global Strategy on Diet, Physical Activity and Health (CL2006/44-CAC), Thirty-Fifth Session, Ottawa, Canada, April 30 – May 4, 2007, CX/FL 07/35/3.

Committee on Economic, Social and Cultural Rights

The Right to the Highest Attainable Standard of Health, General Comment 14, Committee on Economic, Social and Cultural Rights, Twenty-second session, E/C.12/2000/4, 11 August 2000.

Conference of the Parties to the WHO Framework Convention on Tobacco Control.

Draft Guidelines for the Implementation of Articles 9 and 10 of the WHO Framework Convention on Tobacco Control, WHO Framework Convention on Tobacco Control, Conference of the Parties to the Framework Convention on Tobacco Control, Fourth Session, Punta del Este, Uruguay, FCTC/COP/4/6, 15 August 2010.

Elaboration of Guidelines for Implementation of the Convention, Conference of the Parties to the Framework Convention on Tobacco Control, Second Session, Provisional Agenda Item 5.3.2, A/FCTC/COP/2/8, 26 April 2007, available at http://www.who.int/gb/fctc/PDF/cop2/FCTC_COP2_8-en.pdf, (visited 13/12/07).

Elaboration of Guidelines for Implementation of Articles 9 and 10 of the WHO Framework Convention on Tobacco Control: Progress report of the working group, Conference of the Parties to the WHO Framework Convention on Tobacco Control, Third Session, Durban, South Africa, 17–22 November 2008, FCTC/COP/3/6, 21 August 2008.

Elaboration of a Template for a Protocol on Illicit Trade in Tobacco Products, World Health Organization, Conference of the Parties to the WHO Framework Convention on Tobacco Control, second session, provisional agenda item 5.4.1, A/FCTC/COP/2/9, 19 April 2007 available at http://www.who.int/gb/fctc/PDF/cop2/FCTC_COP2_9-en.pdf, (visited 12/12/07).

Elaboration of a Template for a Protocol on Cross-Border Tobacco Advertising and Sponsorship, World Health Organization, Conference of the Parties to the WHO Framework Convention on Tobacco Control, Second Session, A/FCTC/COP/2/10, 19 April 2007 available at http://www.who.int/gb/fctc/PDF/cop2/FCTC_COP2_10-en.pdf, (visited 13/12/07).

First Report of Committee A (Draft), Conference of the Parties to the WHO Framework Convention on Tobacco Control, Second Session, (Draft)

A/FCTC/COP/2/17, 4 July 2007, available at http://www.who.int/gb/fctc/PDF/cop2/FCTC_COP2_17P-en.pdf (visited 10/10/2007).

First Report of Committee A (Draft), WHO Framework Convention on Tobacco Control, Conference of the Parties, Third Session, (Draft) FCTC/COP/3/22, 22 November 2008.

First Report of Committee B, Conference of the Parties to the WHO Framework Convention on Tobacco Control, Second Session, A/FCTC/COP/2/19, 6 July 2007 available at http://ftp.who.int/gb/fctc/PDF/cop2/FCTC_COP2_19-en.pdf, (visited 12/12/07).

Intergovernmental Negotiating Body on a Protocol on Illicit Trade in Tobacco Products, First Session, Geneva, 11–16 February 2008, Conference of the Parties to the WHO Framework Convention on Tobacco Control, FCTC/COP/INB-IT/1/INF.DOC./1, 12 December 2007 available at http://www.who.int/gb/fctc/PDF/it1/FCTC_COP_INB_IT1_ID1-en.pdf (visited 19/01/08).

Matters Identified in Decisions Taken by the Conference of the Parties that Call for Action in the Period Between its First and Second Sessions, Reporting and Exchange of Information, (decision FCTC/COP1(14)), Conference of the Parties to the WHO Framework Convention on Tobacco Control, Second Session, A/FCTC/COP/2/6, 9 May 2007, available at http://ftp.who.int/gb/fctc/PDF/cop2/FCTC_COP2_6-en.pdf, (visited 12/12/07).

Report of Committee A (Draft), Conference of the Parties to the WHO Framework Convention on Tobacco Control, Fourth Session, Punta del Este, Uruguay 15 – 20 November 2010, (Draft) FCTC/COP/4/28, 20 November 2010.

Second Report of Committee A, (Draft), WHO Framework Convention on Tobacco Control, Conference of the Parties, First Session, A/FCTC/COP/1/10, 17 February 2006.

Second Report of Committee A, Elaboration of Guidelines for Implementation of Article 13, Conference of the Parties to the WHO Framework Convention on Tobacco Control, Second Session, (Draft) A/FCTC/COP/2/18, 5 July 2007 available at http://www.who.int/gb/fctc/PDF/cop2/FCTC_COP2_18P-en.pdf, (visited 13/12/07).

Second Report of Committee B, Conference of the Parties to the WHO Framework Convention on Tobacco Control, Second Session, A/FCTC/COP/2/20, 6 July 2007, available at http://www.who.int/gb/fctc/PDF/cop2/FCTC_COP2_20-en.pdf (visited 20/11/2007).

Third Report of Committee A, Conference of the Parties to the WHO Framework Convention on Tobacco Control, First Session, (Draft) A/FCTC/COP1/11, 17 February 2006, available at http://www.who.int/gb/fctc/PDF/cop1/FCTC_COP1_11-en.pdf, (v visited 13/12/07).

Third Report of Committee A, Conference of the Parties to the WHO Framework Convention on Tobacco Control, Second Session, A/FCTC/COP/2/22, 6 July 2007 available at http://www.who.int/gb/fctc/PDF/cop2/FCTC_COP2_22-en.pdf (visited 12/12/07).

WHO Framework Convention on Tobacco Control, Conference of the Parties to the Framework Convention on Tobacco Control, Third Session, Durban, South Africa, FCTC/COP/3/5, 21 August 2008.

WHO Framework Convention on Tobacco Control, Guidelines for Implementation: Article 5.3, Article 8, Article 11, Article 13, World Health Organization, Geneva 2009.

European Commission

Anti-Contraband and Anti-Counterfeit Agreement and General Release, dated as of July 9, 2004 among Philip Morris International Inc., Philip Morris Products Inc., Philip Morris Duty Free Inc., and Philip Morris World Trade Sarl, the European Community represented by the European Commission and each Member State list on the signature pages, available at http://ec.europa.eu/anti_fraud/budget/agreement.pdf, (visited 12/12/07).

Handbook for Trade Sustainability Impact Assessment, European Commission, External Trade, March 2006, available at http://trade.ec.europa.eu/doclib/docs/2006/march/tradoc_127974.pdf (visited 23/11/07).

Food and Agricultural Organization of the United Nations.

Projections of Tobacco Production Consumption and Trade to the year 2010, Food and Agriculture Organization of the United Nations, Rome 2003, available at http://www.fao.org/DOCREP/006/Y4956E/Y4956E00.HTM (visited 26/11/07).

Gatt

Article XXV – Guiding Principles to be Followed by the Contracting Parties in Considering Applications for Waivers from Part I or Other Important Obligations of the Agreement, Adopted on 1 November 1956 (BISD 5S/25).

GATT Ministerial Decision of 14 April 1994, 33 I.L.M. 1267 (1994).

Marks of Origin, Report of the Working Party as adopted by the Contracting Parties at their meeting of 21 November 1958, L/912/Rev.1, 22 November 1958.

Report of the Working Party on Trade and Customs Regulations, Certificates of Origin, Marks of Origin and Consular Formalities, L/595, 15 November 1956.

Report of the Working Party on Border Tax Adjustments, adopted 2 December 1970, (L/3464).

Working Party Report, The Australian Subsidy on Ammonium Sulphate, GATT/CP.4/39, adopted 3 April 1950, BISD II/188.

Intergovernmental Negotiating Body on a Protocol on Illicit Trade in Tobacco Products.

Revised Chairperson's Text on a Protocol on Illicit Trade in Tobacco Products, and General Debate, Expert Review on a Possible Ban on Internet sales of Tobacco Products, WHO Framework Convention on Tobacco Control, Intergovernmental Negotiating Body on a Protocol on Illicit Trade in Tobacco Products, Third Session, Geneva, Switzerland, 28 June – 5 July 2009, FCTC/COP/INB-IT/3/INF.DOC./4, 7 May 2009.

WHO Framework Convention on Tobacco Control, Conference of the Parties, Intergovernmental Negotiating Body on a Protocol on Illicit Trade in Tobacco Products Second session, Geneva, 20–25 October 2008, FCTC/COP/INB-IT/2/3, 18 August 2008

International Law Commission

Draft Articles on the Law of Treaties with commentaries 1966, Reports of the Commission to the General Assembly, Yearbook of the International Law Commission, 1966, vol. II.

Fragmentation of International Law: Difficulties Arising from the Diversification and Expansion of International Law, Report of the Study Group of the International Law Commission, Finalised by Martii Koskenniemi, International Law Commission, Fifty-eighth Session, Geneva, 1 May–9 June and 3 July–11 August 2006, A/CN.4/L.682, 13 April 2006.

Second Report on the Law of Treaties by Mr. G.G. Fitzmaurice, Special Rapporteur, A/CN.4/107, Yearbook of the International Law Commission,1957, vol. II,.

Sixth Report on the Law of Treaties by Sir Humphrey Waldock, Special Rapporteur, Extract from the Yearbook of the International Law Commission:-1966, vol. II, A/CN.4/186 and Add.1, 2/Rev.1, 3–7.

Third Report on the Law of Treaties by Mr. G.G. Fitzmaurice, Special Rapporteur, A/CN.4/115 and Corr.1, Yearbook of the International Law Commission, 1958, Vol. II.

Third Report on the Law of Treaties, by Sir Humphrey Waldock, Special Rapporteur, Extract from the Yearbook of the International Law Commission:-1964, vol. II, Document:-A/CN.4/167 and Add.1–3,.

Miscellaneous

International Conference on Illicit Tobacco Trade, United Nations, New York City, July 30 – August 1, 2002, Co-Chairpersons' Report available at http://www.atf.treas.gov/tobacco/icitt/whatsnew.htm, (visited 12/12/07).

Michael Guerin, "Sensitivity of the Federal Trade Commission Test Method to Analytical Parameters," in "The FTC Cigarette Test Method for Determining Tar, Nicotine and Carbon Monoxide Yields of US Cigarettes," report of the NIC expert committee, Bethesda, Maryland: National Institutes of Health (NIH publication No. 96–4028) (1996).

Oslo Ministerial Declaration – Global Health: A Pressing Foreign Policy Issues of Our Time, *The Lancet*, London, 2007; 369, 1371 – 1378.

National Institutes of Health

National Institutes of Health, National Cancer Institute, Smoking and Tobacco Control: Risks Associated with Smoking Cigarettes with Low Machine-Measured Yields of Tar and Nicotine (2001).

United Nations

United Nations Ad Hoc Interagency Task Force on Tobacco Control, Conference of the Parties to the WHO Framework Convention on Tobacco Control, Second Session, A/FCTC/COP/2/4, 26 April 2007 available at http://www.who.int/gb/fctc/PDF/cop2/FCTC_COP2_4-en.pdf, (visited 12/12/07).

United Nations Environment Programme

UNEP Reference Manual for the Integrated Assessment of Trade-Related Policies, 2001, available at http://www.unep.ch/etb/publications/intAssessment/refmania-Final.pdf (visited 23/11/07).

United States General Accounting Office

United States General Accounting Office, Terrorist Financing: U.S. Agencies Should Systematically Asses Terrorists Use of Alternative Financing Mechanisms, GAO-04–163, November 2003.

World Bank

Sunley, Emil, Yurekli, Adya and Chaloupka, Frank, The Design, Administration and Potential Revenue of Tobacco Excises in Curbing the Epidemic: Governments and the Economics of Tobacco Control, Washington D.C., World Bank, (1999) available at http://web.worldbank.org/WBSITE/EXTERNAL/TOPICS/EXTHEALTHNUTRITIONANDPOPULATION/EXTETC/0,,contentMDK:20361460~menuPK:376607~pagePK:148956~piPK:216618~theSitePK:376601,00.html, (visited 12/12/07).

Yurekli, Adya and De Beyer, Joy, Design and Administer Tobacco Taxes, World Bank Economics of Tobacco Toolkit available at http://web.worldbank.org/WBSITE/EXTERNAL/TOPICS/EXTHEALTHNUTRITIONANDPOPULATION/EXTETC/0,,contentMDK:20365047~menuPK:478898~pagePK:148956~piPK:216618~theSitePK:376601,00.html, (visited 10/01/08).

World Customs Organization

World Customs Organization, Harmonised Systems Nomenclature available at http://www.wcoomd.org/ie/En/en.html.

World Health Assembly

Global Strategy on Diet, Physical Activity and Health, World Health Assembly, WHA57.17, May 2004.

Health Promotion and Healthy Lifestyles, 57th World Health Assembly, WHA 57.16.

International Trade and Health, 59th World Health Assembly, 59/15.

Public Health Problems Caused by Harmful Use of Alcohol, 58th World Health Assembly, WHA 58.26.

Strategies to Reduce Harmful Use of Alcohol, Report by the Secretariat, World Health Organization, 61st World Health Assembly, A61/13, 20 March 2008.

Tobacco or Health, Thirty-Ninth World Health Assembly, Fourteenth Plenary Meeting, 15 May 1986, Committee A, second report.

WHO's Programme on Smoking and Health, Thirty-Third World Health Assembly, 17th Plenary Meeting, 23 May 1980, Committee B, seventh report.

World Health Organization

Bettcher, Douglas, Subramaniam, Chitra, Guindon, Emmanuel et al., "Confronting the Tobacco Epidemic in an era of Trade Liberalization," WHO Commission on Macroeconomics and Health, World Health Organization, 2001, CMH Working Paper Series, WG 4: 8.

Breeze, C and Lock, K, (eds), Health Impact Assessment as part of Strategic Environmental Assessment: A Review of Health Impact Assessment Concepts, Methods and Practice to Support the Development of a Protocol on Strategic Environmental Assessment to the Espoo Convention, which Adequately Covers Health Impacts, World Health Organization, Regional Office for Europe, November 2001, available at http://www.euro.who.int/document/e74634.pdf (visited 23/11/07).

Draft Global Strategy to Reduce the Harmful Use of Alcohol, Revised version based on the outcomes of WHO Executive Board 126th Session, Geneva, 18–23 January 2010, 5 February 2010.

Esson, Katharine and Leeder, Stephen, The Millennium Development Goals and Tobacco Control : An Opportunity for Global Partnership, World Health Organization, 2004, available at http://www.who.int/tobacco/publications/mdg_final_for_web.pdf (visited 12/12/07).

Global Strategy to Reduce the Harmful Use of Alcohol, World Health Assembly, WHA 63.13, 21 May 2010.

Hawkes, Corinna, Nutrition Labels and Health Claims: The Global Regulatory Environment, World Health Organization, Geneva, 2004

Marketing of Food and Non-Alcoholic Beverages to Children, Report of a WHO Technical Forum and Technical Meeting Oslo, Norway, 2–5 May 2006.

Strategies to reduce the Harmful Use of Alcohol, World Health Organization, Executive Board, 126th Session, 22 January 2010, EB126.R11.
The World Health Report 2002: Reducing Risks, Promoting Healthy Life, World Health Organization, Geneva, 2002.
Tobacco Free Initiative, World Health Organization, Facts and Figures about tobacco, June 2007, available at http://www.who.int/tobacco/framework/cop/facts_and_figures_about_tobacco.pdf, (visited 01/02/08).
World Health Organization, Executive Board, 116th session, 28 April 2005, EB116/4.
WHO Expert Committee on Problems Related to Alcohol Consumption, WHO Technical Reports Series, Second Report, World Health Organization, Geneva 2007.
World Health Organization, Proposed Draft Elements for a WHO Framework Convention on Tobacco Control: Provisional Texts with Comments of the Working Group, Intergovernmental Negotiating Body of the WHO Framework Convention on Tobacco Control, First session, Provisional Agenda 8, A/FCTC/INB1/2, 26 July 2000, available at www.who.int/gb/fctc/ (visited 6/2/04).
World Health Organization, Co-Chairs' Working Papers: final revisions, Working Group 2, Intergovernmental Negotiating Body of the WHO Framework Convention on Tobacco Control, Fourth Session, Provisional Agenda item 4, A/FCTC/INB4/2(a), 24 January 2002, available at www.who.int/gb/fctc/ (visited 6/2/04).
World Health Organization, New Chair's Text of a Framework Convention on Tobacco Control, Intergovernmental Negotiating Body of the WHO Framework Convention on Tobacco Control, Fifth Session, A/FCTC/INB5/2, 25 June 2002, Article 2(3), available at www.who.int/gb/fctc/ (visited 6/2/04).
World Health Organization, Regional Committee for South-East Asia, Alcohol Consumption Control – Policy Options, SEA/RC59/R8.
World Health Report 2002: Reducing Risks, Promoting Healthy Life, World Health Organization, Geneva, 2002.
World Trade Organization
Certain New Measures by the United States addressing the ban on Clove Cigarettes, World Trade Organization, Committee on Technical Barriers to Trade, Communication from Indonesia, G/TBT/W/323, 20 August 2009.
Council for Trade in Services, Advertising Services, S/C/W/47, 9 July 1998 (98–2748).
"Doha Ministerial 2001, Declaration on the TRIPS Agreement and Public Health" (adopted on November 14, 2001); Decision of the General Council of 30 August 2003 (Implementation of paragraph 6 of the Doha Declaration on the TRIPS Agreement and public health).
India – Certain taxes and Other Measures on Imported Wines and Spirits, Request for Consultations by the European Communities, World Trade Organization, WT/DS380/1, G/L/855, G/SCM/D79/1, 25 September 2008.
Minutes of the Meeting of 5 – 6 November 2009, Committee on Technical Barriers to Trade, World Trade Organization, 22 December 2009, G/TBT/M/49.
Notification, Committee on Sanitary and Phytosanitary Measures, World Trade Organization, Argentina, G/SPS/N/ARG/14, 23 February 1998.

Notification, Committee on Sanitary and Phytosanitary Measures, World Trade Organization, Republic of Korea, G/SPS/N/KOR/307, 17 December 2008.

Notification, Committee on Technical Barriers to Trade, World Trade Organization, Thailand, G/TBT/N/THA/332, 21 January 2010.

Notification, Committee on Technical Barriers to Trade, World Trade Organization, Brazil, G/TBT/N/BRA/362, 12 February 2010.

Philippines – Taxes on Distilled Spirits, Request for Consultations by the United States, World Trade Organization, WT/DS403/1, G/L/914, 18 January 2010.

Thailand – Customs and Fiscal Measures on Cigarettes from the Philippines, Request for the Establishment of a Panel by the Philippines, World Trade Organization, WT/DS371/3, 6 October 2008.

United States – Measures Affecting the Production and Sale of Clove Cigarettes, Request for Consultations by Indonesia, World Trade Organization, WT/DS406/1, G/L/917, G/SPS/GEN/1015, G/TBT/D/38, 14 April 2010.

Waiver Concerning Kimberly Process Certification Scheme for Rough Diamonds, Council for Trade in Goods, 24 February 2003, World Trade Organization, G/C/W/432/Rev.1 (03–1136).

WTO Agreements and Public Health: A Joint Study by the WHO and the WTO Secretariat, World Health Organization and World Trade Organization, 2002, available at http://www.wto.org/english/res_e/booksp_e/who_wto_e.pdf, (visited 12/12/07).

WTO: 2010 News Items, 24 and 25 March 2010 Technical Barriers To Trade, Tobacco and alcohol technical barriers among members' trade concerns available at http://www.wto.org/english/news_e/news10_e/tbt_24mar10_e.htm (visited 18/04/10).

Cases

Arbitral Tribunals

Dispute Concerning Access to Information Under Article 9 of the OSPAR Convention, Final Award (Ireland v. the United Kingdom) (2 July 2003) Permanent Court of Arbitration, 42 I.L.M. (2003), 1138.

Guinea-Bissau / Senegal Maritime Boundary Arbitration (Award of 31 July 1989 [1990]) 83 ILR 1, 85.

SS Lotus Case (France v Turkey) PCIJ Ser A (1927), No 9 Permanent Court of International Justice.

Trail Smelter Arbitration (US v Canada) 3 RIAA (1941).

European Court of Justice

Konsumentombudsmannen v Gourmet International Products AB, ECJ, C-405/98, 8 March 2001.

International Court of Justice

Case Concerning the Gabcikovo-Nagymaros Project (Hungary v Slovakia), (1997) ICJ Reports, 7.

Case Concerning Oil Platforms (Iran v United States of America) (Merits) ICJ Rep 2003; 42 ILM 1334 (2003).

Competence of the General Assembly for the Admission of a State to the United Nations (Second Admissions Case) (1950), ICJ Reports, 4.

Maritime Delimitation and Territorial Questions between Qatar and Bahrain, Jurisdiction and Admissibility, Judgment, (1995) ICJ Reports, 6.
North Sea Continental Shelf Cases (Federal Republic of Germany v Denmark; Federal Republic of Germany v The Netherlands) ICJ Reports 1969, 3.
Territorial Dispute (Libyan Arab Jamahiriya/Chad), Judgment, (1994) I.C.J. Reports, 6.
United States Nationals in Morocco (1951) ICJ Reports, 189.

Index

www.ingramcontent.com/pod-product-compliance
Lightning Source LLC
LaVergne TN
LVHW052245200926
848481LV00002B/283
9781107657564